US INTELLIGENCE AND AL QAEDA

US INTELLIGENCE AND AL QAEDA

Analysis by Contrasting Narratives

Peter de Werd

EDINBURGH
University Press

Edinburgh University Press is one of the leading university presses in the UK. We publish academic books and journals in our selected subject areas across the humanities and social sciences, combining cutting-edge scholarship with high editorial and production values to produce academic works of lasting importance. For more information visit our website: edinburghuniversitypress.com

Edinburgh University Press Ltd
The Tun – Holyrood Road, 12(2f) Jackson's Entry, Edinburgh EH8 8PJ

First published in hardback by Edinburgh University Press 2020

Typeset in 10/12.5 Adobe Sabon by
IDSUK (DataConnection) Ltd

A CIP record for this book is available from the British Library

ISBN 978 1 4744 7806 9 (hardback)
ISBN 978 1 4744 7807 6 (paperback)
ISBN 978 1 4744 7808 3 (webready PDF)
ISBN 978 1 4744 7809 0 (epub)

CONTENTS

FIGURES AND TABLE

ON INTELLIGENCE

New theoretical approaches are slowly emerging in intelligence studies. It is a sign of maturing that echoes trajectories of other fields in international relations (IR). Increasingly, scholars are drawing on an array of interpretative, reflexivist and critical theories, providing new perspectives to ongoing debates, linking the study 'of' and 'for' intelligence (as phenomenon and practice).[1] In that spirit, this book lays out how theoretical components from critical discourse analysis and securitization theory substantiate a reflexivist methodology and method for analysing complex intelligence problems: analysis by contrasting narratives (ACN).[2] Narratives associated with entities involved in complex intelligence problems are identified, their development over time is analysed, and the multi-consequentiality of discursive and non-discursive events within and beyond narratives is studied. This narrative net assessment[3] includes the strategic narrative associated with an intelligence consumer that situates an intelligence organisation. In practice, ACN should be accomplished cooperatively by intelligence analysts, working-level policymakers, and possibly trusted outside experts. The ACN approach methodically increases the diversity of perspectives on events and circumstances, and highlights the significance of narratives in grasping and shaping intelligence problems. In essence, rather than 'telling truth' to power, this book argues that intelligence should jointly strive to 'consider the most relevant truths' to truly contribute to understanding.

As will be explained in more detail further on in this introduction, this book adopts a reflexivist critical theoretical stance. The notion of 'critical' is distinct from other day-to-day use in intelligence. Often, the latter form of 'thinking about thinking' or 'key assumptions check' relates to reflections on methodological rigour and logical reasoning standards when practicing intelligence analysis.[4] Critical approaches in IR are of a different, meta-theoretical nature. However, these approaches constitute a spectrum, reflecting different theoretical origins such as Marxism, feminism or post-colonialism. But it is also possible to recognise the value of the reflexivism promoted by critical approaches, without adopting an explicit emancipatory agenda of normatively deconstructing particular 'social wrongs' and 'liberating oppressed minorities'. Rather than assuming misrecognition and systematic distortion in service of particular processes of domination or colonisation, research reflects a more neutral position. Some critical theorists in IR might thus object to characterising the ACN methodology as critical, because of the constructive aim of contributing to sense-making and improving intelligence.[5] The self-reflexive comparative nature of ACN holds an implicit emancipatory potential. Bringing together multiple viewpoints widens understanding and puts the dominant strategic narrative in perspective. It is the narrative net assessment, rather than a preconceived normative idea of a researcher on what is 'wrong' in society that informs the sense-making process. Perpetual critique of dominant hegemonic practices for the sake of deconstruction alone leads to apathy.

Adopting the reflexivist critical theoretical stance advanced in this book already has profound implications: it leads to a fundamentally different view of intelligence than the way it is traditionally perceived in the Western world. Intelligence,[6] and particularly espionage, has often been deemed 'the second oldest profession in the world'.[7] Central to its practice has always been the operational and analytic tradecraft aggregated and asserted by professionals. The necessary intuitive and associative thinking emphasised the value of experience. It was only after the Second World War that Western intelligence became more fully institutionalised in agencies that served as comprehensive 'libraries for national security'.[8] Parallel to the bureaucratisation of intelligence, technical developments such as the invention of radar or programmable crypto decoding machines had a significant impact on the field. The mathematicians and other academics that were hired to work with (signals) intelligence contributed to an academic professionalisation of the field.[9] Parallel to various social sciences, the scientific ideal of the natural sciences was pursued in intelligence; for example, by incorporating a numerical standard for intelligence assessments.[10] The ultimate aim was to find the objective ground truth. To this day, this positivist empiricist paradigm of discovering truth has remained dominant in the practice and study of intelligence.[11] However, intelligence is different from positivist science.

First, there exists a tension between the scientific positivist ideal as traditionally adopted, and the purpose of intelligence: to be of use for a specific consumer.

In contrast to research at universities, intelligence is processed information that is required to be relevant, timely and actionable. Rather than a search for the comprehensive ground truth, intelligence mostly concerns the production of practical wisdom. A prime intelligence example is the successful US civil war mapmaker Jedidiah Hotchkiss, who was able to speedily provide rough sketches with the most relevant information that enabled fast decision-making, instead of drawing detailed comprehensive maps.[12] Within the dominant positivist paradigm, it seems intelligence is thus concerned with delivering objective packages of knowledge to consumers who use the secret and often difficult to obtain intelligence to their advantage. Problems, then, arise when information becomes 'distorted' in anticipation of intelligence consumer preferences, or when consumers ignore 'accurate' knowledge based on their preferences.[13] This is generally referred to as forms of politicisation of intelligence, a phenomenon that requires a constant effort to 'minimise' its effects.[14]

Secondly, the standard analytic methods in intelligence rely on pseudoscience. The bureaucratisation of Western intelligence resulted in the demand for audit trails. A major effort has been made in intelligence education to externalise thinking. Since the 1990s, structured analytic techniques and methods to stimulate critical thinking have been documented in a number of US 'doctrines' or reference works.[15] Intelligence professionals have become trained in logical rational and empirical reasoning to rid themselves of psychological pitfalls such as biases and presumptions.[16] Despite the stance of an array of 'structured analytic techniques' in intelligence today as the gold standard in education, from an academic perspective they reflect a proto-scientific practice characterised by various deficiencies and limitations.[17] In part, this is the result of intelligence managers requesting simplified versions of social science methods with 'some invented shortcuts' to ease their use as analytic techniques by professionals to produce intelligence.[18] However, it is also related to the distinct nature of intelligence. Even more so than with regular social science, complex intelligence problems are atypical, making reproducing and revalidating research difficult. Deliberate deception and propaganda activities by adversaries form another complicating factor. In the traditional intelligence paradigm, these actions are perceived as attempts to 'poison' the truth.[19] By raising structured analytic techniques to standard in intelligence, the simplified scientific methods risk camouflaging 'under a veil of objectivity' what is partially a subjective practice.[20]

Whereas during the Cold War the Soviet threat was the dominant frame in which to situate Western intelligence problems, especially over the last three decades the intelligence environment has changed significantly. Security is increasingly defined in broader terms that surpass the military domain to include environmental, economic, social and other problems. Intelligence problems are increasingly linked to other wider themes, issues and topics. On the international stage, more non-state actors pursue their own agenda, and gathering intelligence is decreasingly reserved for states. Uncertainty and the complexity of the intelligence process have increased. More than during the Cold War, the frames adopted to make sense of intelligence problems and create perspectives for action shift over time. For example, domestic radicalisation of youth can be perceived as a terrorism problem that requires law enforcement and security organisations to act, but under a different political government it might equate to a problem of societal inequality that is best approached by organising an inclusive dialogue. Such shifting perspectives among intelligence consumers cannot be without consequences for the production of intelligence. The shifting, broadening and deepening of intelligence problems has profound consequences for the way intelligence organisations and their processes are to be structured.

A number of intelligence failures and scandals have also made this clear and led to reforms of Western intelligence agencies and organisation of their oversight. Some intelligence scholars have called for a 'radical revolution' or 'paradigm' shift in intelligence studies.[21] However, such calls often concern shifts in the organisational sphere, such as liaising beyond the secret intelligence community in trusted networks, improving analytic training, adopting more flexible planning processes, creating new coordination bodies or increasing oversight. The concern was not explicitly moving beyond the positivist meta-theoretical paradigm in intelligence studies. The approaches and direction of the various efforts in academia to theorise and improve intelligence vary greatly.[22] Some have tried to offer a definition of intelligence or new models of the intelligence process, while others have studied what the focus of intelligence should be as its environment changes. Another discussion on intelligence theorising has evolved around the type of methodology that best fits the practice of intelligence.[23] Most intelligence scholars refrain from explicitly articulating the theoretical roots of their revolutionary new thinking in philosophical terms. Such theorising is only covered in a small part of the intelligence literature.[24]

Theoretical debates and developments in IR since the 1980s have not been very influential in intelligence studies. In terms of IR, academics have commonly described intelligence as the missing dimension in the study of international politics, while being one of the primary locations of international relations practice.[25] Over the last century, international relations theorising has been dominated by a rational positivist debate between (neo) realism (self-gain maximising power politics) and (neo)liberalism (establishing peace and collective security as long-term goal).[26] Since the 1980s, this debate has been challenged by (critical) interpretivist approaches such as social constructivism and postmodernism.[27] More recently, critical realism has surfaced as a way around the entrenchment of positivist empiricists and poststructuralist interpretivists; an approach that will be explained further on in this introduction.

Some of the reasons for intelligence studies to have developed more or less separate from philosophical debates in IR and political science relate to its practical orientation and concerns. In part, the secrecy surrounding intelligence has limited the development of intelligence studies as an academic IR subfield. In the twentieth century, intelligence studies consisted of historians documenting the activities of intelligence organisations that were revealed in declassified archived documents, official government reports or (un)sanctioned memoires of former employees.[28] Increasingly, academics have started to study intelligence processes. This has also been spurred by the need for academic intelligence education. Predominantly, intelligence scholars providing such education in the West and particularly in the United States have been able to draw on their own experience as intelligence practitioners.[29] In general, intelligence scholars have refrained from linking to other debates in related fields, such as security, war and terrorism studies.[30]

The dominant paradigm in intelligence studies remains objectivist/positivist.[31] Most intelligence literature also has an Anglo-American focus. In IR, critical approaches have developed in (non-Anglo-American) continental schools. Some of the critical questions asked are also of fundamental importance for intelligence. Should intelligence be driven by empiricism and stick to the facts, or does its estimating nature imply that methodologies follow from normative theorising? Is intelligence about explaining, understanding or both? The research in this book is grounded on meta-theoretical middle ground that acknowledges both. Some radical poststructuralists might not deem the approach in this book fits with critical or interpretivist theory. However, in the light of the traditional positivist paradigm, it is a clear move beyond and an effort to learn from debates in IR. Hence, this book contributes to a slowly emerging subfield of constructivist, postmodern and interpretivist, or 'critical' reflexivist approaches that has grown in the margins of intelligence studies.[32] They constitute the few scarce attempts to confer contemporary theoretical debates in international relations and political science in terms of intelligence.[33]

Beyond their very different direction and foci, these contributions all constituted attempts to review and enrich intelligence studies by recognising interpretivism. Several of them have emphasised the study of language and discourse as a primary concern for intelligence.[34] It was noted how ambiguous discourses, rather than objective truth, formed the basis of intelligence. And intelligence itself should also be regarded as a form of rhetoric that demands studying in terms of politicisation. Attempts to operationalise a postmodern perspective on intelligence have also provided additional insights into the relevance of narratives in this regard.[35] Intelligence is not an objective eye, rather, it is socio-politically situated and, hence, partly selectively shaping international political reality. Critical ideas are not limited to self-reflection and critique of intelligence as a political practice. As others have shown, constructivism can inform and enrich military and intelligence doctrine through its conceptualisation of ideational social or cognitive aspects (norms, values, cultures, ideas) in addition to traditional characteristics of the physical domain (fighting capabilities, logistics).[36] The critical ACN approach in this book includes self-reflexivism regarding the idea of intelligence as a practice situated in a socio-political strategic context. And in addition, this idea is also projected on the subject of intelligence as a means to widen understanding of complex intelligence problems.

Beyond ACN, further stimulating critical reflexivist debate in intelligence could prove to be fruitful. Not only in strengthening the intelligence practice, but also to improve the study of intelligence and further the acceptance of intelligence studies as a legitimate academic field.[37] It is beneficial to reflect on and learn from the development of critical security studies and study how debates and approaches are relevant for intelligence studies. How to define 'critical' for example? While recognising the pluriformity of critical approaches to security, an adequate general idea of the term 'critical' is provided in the following. More of an ethos than a coherent theoretical enterprise, critical approaches question the objectivity of knowledge that positivists take for granted and seek to explore the political, social and historical situatedness of social reality.[38] In philosophical terms, critical approaches adopt interpretivism at either the ontological or epistemological level. As formulated by the C.A.S.E. collective:

> Being critical means adhering to a rigorous form of skeptical questioning, rather than being suspicious or distrustful in the vernacular sense of those terms. But, it is also to recognize oneself as being partially framed by those regimes of truth, concepts, theories and ways of thinking that enable the critique. To be critical is thus also to be reflexive, developing abilities to locate the self in a broader heterogeneous context through abstraction and thinking.[39]

For intelligence studies, a critical approach then problematises what is central to 'intelligence', what it is and how it works within a socio-political context. An integral part of a critical approach is reflecting on the role of intelligence professionals and consumers in the framing of intelligence problems and their underlying concept of truth. The concept of truth is thus not disbanded but made more relative. Developments in the political context of the intelligence producer and consumer become part of the question or 'problem', rather than unquestioned assumptions, when researching or analysing problems.[40] Not only defining the substance but also the contours of an intelligence problem, as well as the effects of our own actions on the problem, becomes part of an integrated form of intelligence policy analysis. A net assessment is made at the working level between the perception of the intelligence consumer and other (hostile, neutral or friendly) entities. This is something very unusual for most traditional intelligence organisations that strictly focus on (potential) adversaries. Even more unheard of is for intelligence professionals to participate in reflecting on the effects of the consumer's actions on the intelligence problem; effectively getting cooperatively involved with policy analysis, while also becoming more aware of the basic and analytic nature of the 'models' or 'creations of reality' that follow from intelligence analysis.

Does this critical theoretical stance imply anti-foundationalism: is there no ground truth, then? This book holds that there is. In essence, the philosophical supposition in this book is that there is a 'real world' out there, but interpretations of 'real' material and social conditions also provide a foundation for entities to act. There are deeper intransitive natural and social structures, but also more transitive social practices and events. Critical realism, a contemporary and critical form of realism rooted in the work of British philosopher Roy Bhaskar, serves as a theoretical 'middle ground' that transcends the causation–constitutive or explaining–understanding divide, and the structure versus agency debate.[41] For decades, these distinctions have entrenched positivist empiricists and poststructuralists, particularly in international relations. For positivists, causal relations have been limited to efficient ('pushing and pulling') regularity relations of observables.[42] Research has involved pattern-seeking as an additive approach to 'stack' isolated singular causes (causal mechanisms) in 'closed systems'. This has placed logical determinism (or discovering laws) as the central aspect of the scientific endeavour. In this respect, the works of British philosopher David Hume on causation have been highly influential in shaping the core principles of positivist empiricist positions on causality.[43] Poststructural approaches that critique Humeanism have focused on understanding how ideational aspects (ideas, norms, conventions and discourses) are constitutive of the social world. However, in the rejection of Humean causality and avoidance of the terminology, these approaches are also unnecessarily 'reductionist' as they exclude materialistic and deterministic analysis.

Critical realism acknowledges a form of interpretivism and thus moves explicitly away from the objectivist–empiricist paradigm. In contrast to poststructuralism, however, critical realism views observation and interpretation as a matter of epistemology, not ontology. In other words, there is a 'real' world out there. Reality is regarded as differentiated.

> [C]ritical realists distinguish the real from the actual and the empirical. The 'real' refers to objects, their structures or natures and their causal powers and liabilities. The 'actual' refers to what happens when these powers and liabilities are activated and produce change. The 'empirical' is the subset of the real and the actual that is experienced by actors. Although changes at the level of the actual (e.g. political debates) may change the nature of objects (e.g. political institutions), the latter are not

7

reducible to the former, any more than a car can be reduced to its movements. Moreover, while empirical experience can influence behaviour and hence what happens, much of the social and physical worlds can exist regardless of whether researchers, and in some cases other actors, are observing or experiencing them.[44]

Critical realists do not conceive of the world in terms of either/or. Instead of viewing structure and agency as antithetical, critical realists hold that they conflate in a dialectical relationship. This dialectical relationship, or the free action of entities in the limiting context of deeper structures such as institutions, best explains both the natural/physical and various social realities that exist and influence each other. Reality is an 'open system' in which causal powers interact, enforce or counter each other. Whether causal powers in the domain of 'real' become active at the 'actual' level and can be observed as a fact in the 'empirical' domain depends not only on the social conditions that enable the activation of causal forces, but also on whether other powers work against it.[45] Causal powers can be active, dormant or countered.

For example, certain physical and social conditions in a dictatorship (political institution, 'real') can become challenged by economic and cultural globalisation (structural social process, 'real'), stimulated by the development of new technologies and international trade (social practices, 'actual'). The population of that dictatorial society thereby potentially gains the ability to critique and resist (political debate, 'actual') those in power and to organise physical or virtual demonstrations (experience, 'empirical') beyond government control. These demonstrations represent and can result in an effect on political debate and the development of new technologies, and eventually even influence the deeper social structures. Yet no new political institution is formed in and through these demonstrations; the dictatorship is still present as a 'real' social condition and has its (limiting, controlling) effect, although it is possible for the 'real' to eventually change. For researchers, it is possible to study how and why it does so.

Rather than avoiding the term 'causality', it is possible from a critical realist philosophical position (ontological philosophical realism and epistemological interpretivism) to rethink and reconceptualise causality beyond the traditional positivist empiricist Humean account of observable constant conjunctions.[46] Empiricism is not the only way of gaining knowledge. Unobservable processes of social construction can be understood by interpreting motives, reasons and meanings, ideas, rules, norms, and discourses, and the way these are influenced by the social context. Causes interact with and reflect other causes. Instead of additive analysis of singular causal mechanisms, the complexity of the social world requires an integrative approach. It is necessary to consider the 'network of causality' or 'causal complex', rather than singling out an individual causal mechanism.[47] Causes cannot be considered mechanisms, although causal processes or interactions of causes could perhaps arguably be considered in such a way. Critical realists do not necessarily reject the term 'mechanism', but in this book it is best avoided to reduce confusion with Humean associations.

The question is how to trace and analyse social conditions and powers to explain social processes in a causally adequate manner. Following German international relations professor Alexander Wendt and others, Aberystwyth University International Politics scholar Milja Kurki has made a fruitful effort to explore the use of Aristotle's fourfold conceptualisation of causes from a critical realist perspective.[48] Without attempting to address all of Aristotle's theorising, Kurki demonstrates that the typology of material, formal, efficient and final cause is instrumental in specifying the concept of 'causal complex' and identifying how multiple types of causes interact.

First, 'material cause' relates to the nature and properties of matter that enable and constrain possibilities of social action (in what way and for what matter can it be used). Material cause is more than substance, as it also encompasses artefacts. At a secondary level, matter can hence be thought of as formed objects with a passive potentiality that shapes basic conditions of social reality.[49] Without (materials to make) weaponry and bombs, there is no capability to act with violence. For Aristotle, all is related to a material base. It has ontological primacy. But the causal power of matter is also intertwined with the physical and conceptual arrangement or social structure in which it is used. Weapons possessed by a friendly entity hold different meaning, or potential, than those owned by an adversary. Furthermore, nowadays the social effects of information streams in the cyber domain seem less determined by material aspects. 'Formal causes' relate to the relatively stable ideational context that generates functional shapes of appearance. Ideas, conventions, norms and discourses affect the ways in which meanings are defined, articulated, circulated and conceived. Material causes can influence formal causes, as property can increase social status in some contexts. Conversely, a national security discourse can result in the (defensive) organisation of infrastructure. Both types of causes can be thought of as constitutive conditions or structures that enable and constrain possibilities for action or agency. They form 'related wholes within which intentional actors act and thereby reproduce or transform the facilitating social conditions (material and formal) of their own activity'.[50]

'Efficient causes' are what is generally conceived as causality. It is the entity or actor that activates movement, interaction and change. It brings about actions that reflect, recreate, and transform matter and form. This does not relate only to physical action: while discourses can be viewed as constitutive in terms of formal causes, discursive action also has efficient causative effects. By making (provocative) statements in certain settings, specific articulated meanings can become actualised and influence social reality. Actions are related to a purpose, but also situated in an ideational and material context. 'Final causes' are teleological. What are the motivations, visions, intentions or reasons for action? The purpose of action is related to efficient causes, but is distinct. Of course, the intended effect of actions can differ from what they actually cause. In the case of discourses, the underlying motivation or purpose recipients read into statements may differ widely from what a producer of texts has intended.

These four categories or types represent both constitutive structures (material and formal causes) and causative agency (efficient and final causes), or facilitating conditions and drivers. The various types of causes interactively generate, counter, enable or constrain phenomena in a particular social domain. Besides considering this interactive nature of the causal complex, also the dialectical relations between these types of causes and the way they influence or shape each other needs to be recognised. Over time, actions performed in a particular way can gradually alter the ideational context or result in adaptation of material circumstances. New infrastructure or technical capabilities can generate new visions, ideals or actions. The interaction or interconnectedness of the various types of causes will be explained further in the next chapter with respect to narratives. Any scientific methodology that relates to critical realism must be able to account for and reflect upon the activation of potential powers (or 'potentialities') against the backdrop of the distinction between deeper intransitive social structures and more transitive social practices and events. They have to acknowledge causal pluralism and approach a complex of causes holistically to study social phenomena.

Ontologically, the real world 'out there' consists of objects with 'real properties and causal powers by virtue of their composition'.[51] Scientists can make plausible causative statements as they study the nature and role of a plurality of causal powers that create social reality.

> Causes, for philosophical realists, are not equated with regularities but can be seen to refer to real ontological features of the world. Scientific causal explanation, then, is not equated with analysis of observable regularities, but is seen to arise from the construction of conceptual models that try to grasp the nature of objects through making existential claims about their constituting structures and causal powers, thereby enabling explanations of various 'actual' or empirical processes and tendencies. Regularities are of interest to science because they allow us to test theories regarding causal powers in artificial closed system environments. Yet, observed regularities do not constitute causality: causality exists in the underlying causal powers and causal explanation in accounting for these underlying causal powers.[52]

Because not all can be observed, observable regularities are neither necessary nor adequate to explain causal relations. This has implications for the way knowledge is gained. As British intelligence scholars Peter Gill and Mark Phythian describe, the creative process of abduction or re-description offers a way to find new connections by adopting and testing hypotheses about socially produced realities. Abductive research entails the process of accepting causality between certain social structures, processes and events, and in addition reflecting upon this relation as the research progresses. By assuming the social conditioning of a society by dictatorship and globalisation, political debate through demonstrations and other utterances generates meaning about the essence and workings of this conditioning. However, although the theoretical framework to study these situated demonstrations and utterances in context provides insights that are valid knowledge, it does not encompass all there is to know about the causal forces at play.

> Neither deduction nor induction alone is adequate in social science: we do not 'discover' new events but we do discover new connections and relations that are not directly observable and by which we can analyse already known occurrences in a novel way ... By applying alternative theories and models in order to discern connections that were not evident, intelligence scholars ... [are not] merely describing reality as if through a clear pane of glass: they are seeking to make sense and thus actively 'create' the worlds of intelligence, government and IR.[53]

To investigate the workings of causal complexes, scientists must combine experience in research with imagination. Knowledge is ultimately generated by experience, but not limited to it. Abductive exploration of possible relationships and connections between social phenomena provides potential ways to increase knowledge – like a spider jumping into the unknown not only based on that what it has experienced, but also with a vision in mind: the aim of spinning a web.[54] In that effort, completely value-free social science (or intelligence) does not exist, but researchers and analysts can investigate and define workings, effects and limits of interpretation while recognising that research itself also carries a form of meaning-making that is constrained or influenced because of social and political conditions. Ultimately, our knowledge is imperfect and 'theory-laden'.[55] Problematising the situatedness of intelligence analysis itself also opens up possibilities of a deeper understanding of what contexts, settings and perceptions of security drive the actions and shape the motivations of intelligence subjects.

A sense of the added value of a critical realist scientific approach to the predominantly positivist practice of intelligence analysis is gained by examining the 'intention, capability, activity' (ICA) framework.[56] The multiplicative 'mathematical' threat assessment model is highly appreciated in intelligence analysis, for example, for analysing terrorist threats. When comparing the Aristotelian typology of causes with this framework (intention – final cause, capability – material cause, activity – efficient cause), the formal cause is evidently backgrounded as a distinct analytical category. One could argue that the category 'intention' indirectly refers to motivation and worldview, and hence includes the cultural or ideational context; but the point is that formal causes are fundamental facilitating conditions that colour the meaning of actions. In addition to the question 'are there terrorists out there that target us?' the question 'why?' deserves more attention. What actors and audiences are involved, at what level and how are they socio-politically situated?

In intelligence, the focus often lies with adversaries or potential adversaries. This is demonstrated by the intelligence analysis method of Red Teaming in which analysts try to assess situations from an adversary perspective, attempting to act like the opponent. However, the number of actors associated with contemporary complex intelligence issues problematises this binary concept. Even though analysing the social dynamics between two adversaries, 'red' is ultimately a characterisation attributed from a 'blue' perspective. It would be more neutral and accurate to think in terms of a variety of colours that describe multiple actors and shift shape and colour as one's position, perspective and policy preferences change. In theory, a multitude of perspectives must be considered that relate to and reflect on each other. Therefore, in addition to incorporating and analysing the intelligence consumer's perspective, as another unconventional step for intelligence organisations (and many researchers in academia) the ACN methodology involves analysis of at least three perspectives in parallel to making sense of and explaining developments for a complex intelligence problem.[57] In theory, the number of relevant perspectives could be thought of as extensive. They could be identified at different levels and associated with various actors, some able to influence the problem and some unable to do so, but capable of critique and highlighting tensions and inconsistencies in the viewpoints of others.

How to identify and understand these different perspectives, what could provide the scientific mode of entry? An essential part of social reality lies in language use and communication that manifests in discourses, or narratives. There are other aspects of social reality, but the assumptions expressed in communication, either by articulation or the intentional lack thereof, are a central gateway to understand the perceptions that form the basis for people to act. Thus, the question becomes how to identify different narratives (as perspectives) that can eventually be compared and contrasted by focusing on a series of events such as terrorist attacks. Because of the interconnectedness of texts (intertextuality) and the organic nature of overlapping narratives, defining contours is an analytic decision that requires explication by the researcher. Narratives are only 'basic analytic narratives' established through a process of re-description.[58] They themselves carry a form of meaning-making that remains open to critique. As discussed further in Chapter 1, British language professor Norman

Fairclough's three-dimensional discourse model provides the theoretical basis to distinguish between fundamentally different social domains.[59] However, the ACN methodology refrains from adopting his strict, detailed and, hence, limitative functional linguistic method for textual analysis, instead seeking to analyse key parts of key texts, selected from a more extensive aggregation of texts. Fairclough's theoretical approach to critical discourse analysis makes it possible to identify narratives from the dense web of interconnected and overlapping texts, and to situate them in wider social practices and structures.

Combining texts into distinct narratives also requires a thematic focus. Otherwise the detailed inductive treatment of texts would either rigidly limit the scope of analysis or require an unrealistic analytical effort. But what should we look for in narratives? The concept of sociological securitization as outlined by Belgian international relations professor Thierry Balzacq provides an adequate lens.[60] Central to securitization is identifying an existential threat by others against a self before various types of audiences within specific contexts. In this book securitization dynamics is mapped in parallel narratives and multi-consequentiality of securitization efforts across social domains is investigated, which is an uncommon approach to securitization.[61] Also untraditional is that the research did not focus on 'successful' threat articulation per se, but examined the moves or 'efforts' made in this regard. First of all, the debate is still ongoing in security studies with regard to what exactly constitutes 'success' and how to determine whether this has been the case in specific instances.[62] In deviating from this quest, the 'looser' approach to centralise securitization efforts provided an adequate starting point to study various types of interacting causes and effects of 'securitization dynamics'. As discussed in the final chapter of this book, it also opened possibilities to bring more types of audiences into view.

The ACN methodology does not imply an exclusionary stance towards other analytical approaches that, for example, parallel methodologies from the natural sciences. They are in fact complementary. This relates to a core aspect of critical realism: there is not one methodology that can explain all there is to know about reality, as reality is differentiated. For ACN, this is illustrated in that texts are to be selected based on their relation to a series of security-related events, such as attacks and military strikes. Security is not per se an objective truth, but a reality manifesting partly in and through the use of language and non-discursive actions.

The complex intelligence problem of *Al Qaeda* demonstrates the ACN methodology in this book. As detailed further in the first chapter, it was assumed that the term *Al Qaeda* represented an organisation, a network and an ideology, in various forms and in various periods in time, to various entities (individual people, groups, networks, organizations, institutions). The timeframe defined for the research spanned from 1994 to early 2001. This was distinct from other discourse studies on either terrorism and the United States or *Al*

Qaeda in that the adopted timeframe ended before the attacks on 11 September 2001.[63] Much 'post-2001' research has been done on *Al Qaeda*. In contrast, the present study focused on the emergence of *Al Qaeda* and related events in narratives, which was more of a terra incognita. Compared with other research on *Al Qaeda*, the value of this book lies in its comparative nature of three different narratives. A consequence of analysing multiple narratives was that a compromise had to be made in terms of quantity. Other discourse analyses with a more one-sided focus on either the United States or *Al Qaeda* were more extensive in the selection of data per narrative. For instance, Adam Hodges gathered data from a higher number of US media outlets (between 2001 and 2008) and Donald Holbrook extended his quantitative analysis of *Al Qaeda* discourse from 1991 to 2013.

The first chapter discusses the theoretical components of critical discourse analysis and securitization in more detail, and describes the ACN methodology. Its narrative analysis framework (NAF) serves to identify and analyse narratives while narrative tracing (NT) focuses on multi-consequentiality of statements and actions, also linking the development of different narratives. Chapters 2, 3 and 4 correspond to the three narratives identified at the end of Chapter 1. The last chapter then combines the findings of the case studies and deals with narrative tracing in more detail. It also further discusses the value of the ACN methodology for intelligence studies.

NOTES

1. As described in Hamilton Bean, 'Intelligence Theory from the Margins, Questions Ignored and Debates Not Had', *Intelligence and National Security* 33(4) (2018): 527–40; Peter de Werd, 'Critical Intelligence Studies? A Contribution', *Journal of European and American Intelligence Studies* 1(1) (2018): 109–48.

2. Analysis 'by' Contrasting Narratives is used to emphasise the centrality of comparing and contrasting the development of the various narratives that have been identified. However, the term 'Analysis of Contrasting Narratives' could also be used as both adequately refer to the ACN methodology of identifying and analysing relevant narratives.

3. Referring to the comparative logic of net assessment, as performed by the US Department of Defense, Office of Net Assessment. Although used for a different purpose (forecasting), the approach seeks to compare and contrast multiple competitors in relation to US military policies, strategy and capabilities. See, for example, Paul Bracken, 'Net Assessment: a Practical Guide', *Parameters* (Spring 2006): 90–100.

4. For example, Loch K. Johnson (ed.), *Intelligence, Critical Concepts in Military, Strategic and Security Studies* (New York: Routledge, 2010); David T. Moore, 'Critical Thinking and Intelligence Analysis', occasional paper No. 14, NDIC, Washington, DC, 2007, 8. The undergraduate minor at Rutgers titled 'critical intelligence studies', while not related to critical IR theory, demonstrates tellingly the need for clarification. See also Rutgers, the State University of New Jersey, 'critical intelligence studies'.

5. For example, Claudia Aradau, Jef Huysmans, Andrew Neal and Nadine Voelkner (eds), *Critical Security Methods: New Frameworks for Analysis*, 4th edn (New York: Routledge, 2015), 1–22; Ken Booth, *Theory of World Security* (Cambridge: Cambridge University Press, 2007).

6. Intelligence is understood here as 'the . . . activities – targeting, collection, analysis, dissemination and action – intended to enhance security and/or maintain power relative to competitors by the forewarning of threats and opportunities'. As derived from Peter Gill and Mark Phythian, *Intelligence in an Insecure World*, 2nd edn (Cambridge: Polity, 2012), 19.

7. Phillip Knightley, *The Second Oldest Profession: Spies and Spying in the Twentieth Century* (New York: W. W. Norton, 1986).

8. Richard K. Betts, *Enemies of Intelligence: Knowledge and Power in American National Security* (New York: Columbia University Press, 2007), 5.

9. For example, Sherman Kent, *Strategic Intelligence for American World Policy* (Princeton: Princeton University Press, 1949); Roger Hilsman, 'Intelligence and Policy-Making in Foreign Affairs', *World Politics* 5(1) (1952): 1–45; Washington Platt, *Strategic Intelligence Production: Basic Principles* (New York: Praeger, 1957); also described in Stephen Marrin, *Improving Intelligence Analysis* (London: Routledge, 2011), 25–8, and Wilhelm Agrell and Gregory Treverton, *National Intelligence and Science: Beyond the Great Divide in Analysis and Policy* (Oxford: Oxford University Press, 2015), 85–7.

10. Sherman Kent, 'Words of Estimative Probability', *Studies in Intelligence* (1964): 49–65.

11. Gill and Phythian, *Intelligence in an Insecure World* , 33–4; Mark Lowenthal, *Intelligence: From Secrets to Policy*, 5th edn (London: Sage, 2012), 158; Jennifer Sims, 'The Theory and Philosophy of Intelligence', in Robert Dover, Michael S. Goodman and Claudia Hillebrand (eds), *Routledge Companion to Intelligence Studies* (New York: Routledge, 2014), 42–9.

12. Sims, 'Theory and Philosophy of Intelligence', 43; Shawn B. Stith, 'Foundation for Victory, Operations and Intelligence Harmoniously Combine in Jackson's Shenandoah Valley Campaign (1862)', Naval Postgraduate School Thesis, June 1993.

13. See, for example, Stephen Marrin, 'Revisiting Intelligence and Policy: Problems with Politicization and Receptivity', *Intelligence and National Security* 28(1) (2013): 1–4; an introduction to a special edition on politicisation.

14. Stephen Marrin, 'Rethinking Analytic Politicization', *Intelligence and National Security* 28(1) (2013): 32–54.

15. US CIA, *A Compendium of Analytic Tradecraft Notes*, vol. I, February 1997, available at: http://www.oss.net/dynamaster/file_archive/040319/cb27cc09c84d056b 66616b4da5c02a4d/OSS2000-01-23.pdf, last accessed 12 February 2018; US CIA, *A Tradecraft Primer: Structured Analytic Techniques for Improving Intelligence Analysis*, March 2009, available at: https://www.cia.gov/library/publications/publications-rss-updates/tradecraft-primer-may-4-2009.html; University of Foreign and Military Studies (UFMS), *The Applied Critical Thinking Handbook 7.0*, January 2015; Richards J. Heuer and Randolph H. Pherson, *Structured Analytic Techniques for Intelligence Analysis* (Washington, DC: CQ Press, 2011);

Marrin, *Improving Intelligence Analysis*, 28–33; Agrell and Treverton, *National Intelligence and Science*, 86–7.

16. Richards J. Heuer, *Psychology of Intelligence Analysis* (Pittsburgh, PA: Government Printing Office 1999).

17. Welton Chang, Elissabeth Berdini, David R. Mandel and Philip E. Tetlock, 'Restructuring Structured Analytic Techniques in Intelligence', *Intelligence and National Security* 33(3) (2018): 337–56.

18. Marrin, *Improving Intelligence Analysis*, 31.

19. Chad W. Fitzgerald and Aaron F. Brantly, 'Subverting Reality: the Role of Propaganda in 21st Century Intelligence', *International Journal of Intelligence and Counterintelligence* 30(2) (2017): 215–40.

20. Chang et al., 'Restructuring Structured Analytic Techniques'.

21. William J. Lahneman, 'The Need for a New Intelligence Paradigm', *International Journal of Intelligence and Counterintelligence* 23(2) (2010): 201–25; William J. Lahneman, *Keeping U.S. Intelligence Effective: the Need for a Revolution in Intelligence Affairs* (Lanham, MD: Scarecrow Press, 2011); William J. Lahneman, 'Is a Revolution in Intelligence Affairs Occurring?' *International Journal of Intelligence and Counterintellingence* 20(1) (2007): 1–17; David T. Moore, *Sensemaking: a Structure for an Intelligence Revolution* (Washington, DC: National Defense Intelligence College, 2011); Gregory F. Treverton, *Reshaping National Intelligence for an Age of Information* (Cambridge: Cambridge University Press, 2001).

22. See, for example, Gill, Marrin and Pythian, Intelligence *Theory: Key Questions and Debates* (New York: Routledge, 2009); Gregory Treverton et al., *Toward a Theory of Intelligence: Workshop Report* (Santa Monica, CA: RAND, 2006).

23. Gill, Marrin and Pythian, Intelligence *Theory*.

24. Loch K. Johnson, 'The Development of Intelligence Studies', in Robert Dover, Michael S. Goodman and Claudia Hillebrand (eds), *Routledge Companion to Intelligence Studies* (New York: Routledge, 2014), 10.

25. For example, Christopher Andrew and David Dilks, *The Missing Dimension: Governments and Intelligence Communities in the Twentieth Century* (Campaign, IL: University of Illinois Press, 1984); James Der Derian, *Antidiplomacy: Spies, Terror, Speed, and War* (Cambridge, MA: Blackwell, 1992), 21; Bob G. J. de Graaff, *De ontbrekende dimensie, intelligence binnen de studie van internationale betrekkingen*, oration, 2 March, , Utrecht University, 2012; Michael Fry and Miles Hochstein, 'Epistemic Communities: Intelligence Studies in International Relations', *Intelligence and National Security* 8(3) (1993): 14–28; Christopher Andrew, 'Intelligence, International Relations and "Under-theorization"', *Intelligence and National Security* 19(2) (2004): 170–84; Bob G. J. de Graaff, *De ontbrekende dimensie*; Loch K. Johnson and Allison M. Shelton, 'Thoughts on the State of Intelligence Studies: A Survey Report', *Intelligence and National Security* 28(1) (2013): 116.

26. Hans J. Morgenthau and Kenneth W. Thompson, *Politics Among Nations: the Struggle for Power and Peace*, 6th edn (New York: Knopf, 1985); Kenneth N. Waltz, *Theory of International Politics* (Reading, MA: Addison-Wesley, 1979); Robert O. Keohane (ed.), *Neorealism and Its Critics* (New York: Columbia University Press, 1986); Joseph S. Nye Jr., 'Neorealism and Neoliberalism', *World*

Politics 40 (1988) 2; Immanuel Kant, *Perpetual Peace* [1795], ed. Lewis White Beck (Indianapolis: Bobbs-Merill, 1957); John Locke, *Two Treatises of Government* [1689], 3rd Student Edition (Cambridge: Cambridge University Press, 1988); Thomas Risse-Kappen, *Cooperation Among Democracies: the European Influence on U.S. Foreign Policy* (Princeton, NJ: Princeton University Press, 1995).

27. Nicholas Onuf, *World of Our Making: Rules and Rule in Social Theory and International Relations* (Columbia, SC: University of South Carolina Press, 1989); Alexander Wendt, 'Anarchy is What States Make of It: the Social Construction of Power Politics', *International Organisation* 46 (1992): 2; Alexander Wendt, *Social Theory of International Politics* (New York: Cambridge University Press, 1999); James Der Derian and Michael J. Shapiro (eds), *International/Intertextual Relations: Postmodern Readings of World Politics* (New York: Lexington Books, 1989); Claire T. Sjolander and Wayne S. Cox (eds), *Beyond Positivism: Critical Reflections on International Relations* (Boulder, CO: Lynne Rienner, 1994).

28. Stuart Farson, 'Schools of Thought: National Perceptions of Intelligence', *Journal of Conflict Studies* (1989): 52–104.

29. Reflected, for example, in the conferences and literature generated by the International Association for Intelligence Education or the US Association of Former Intelligence Officers.

30. Johnson, 'The Development of Intelligence Studies', 3–22.

31. Fry and Hochstein, 'Epistemic Communities', 17; Gill and Phythian, *Intelligence in an Insecure World*, 34; Gill, Marrin and Pythian, Intelligence *Theory*; Lowenthal, *Intelligence*, xii.

32. As described in Bean, 'Intelligence theory from the margins'; de Werd, 'Critical Intelligence Studies?'

33. Der Derian, *Antidiplomacy*; Hamilton Bean, 'Rhetorical and Critical/Cultural Intelligence Studies', Intelligence and National Security 28(4) (2013): 495–519; Ralph G. V. Lillbacka, 'Realism, Constructivism, and Intelligence Analysis', International Journal of Intelligence and Counterintelligence 26(2) (2013): 304–31; Mary Manjikian, 'Positivism, Post-Positivism, and Intelligence Analysis', International Journal of Intelligence and Counterintelligence 26(3((2013): 563–82; Lahneman, *Keeping U.S. Intelligence Effective*; Gill and Phythian, *Intelligence in an Insecure World*, 33–52; Gill, Marrin and Pythian, Intelligence *Theory*, 54–72; Andrew Rathmell, 'Towards Postmodern Intelligence', Intelligence and National Security 17(3) (2002): 87–104.

34. Der Derian, *Antidiplomacy*; Bean, 'Rhetorical and Critical/Cultural Intelligence Studies', 499–500; Hamilton Bean, *No More Secrets: Open Source Information and the Reshaping of U.S. Intelligence* (Santa Barbara, CA: Praeger, 2011); Nathan Woodard, 'Tasting the Forbidden Fruit: Unlocking the Potential of Positive Politicization', *Intelligence and National Security* 28(1) (2013): 91–108; Gunilla Eriksson, *Swedish Military Intelligence: Producing Knowledge* (Edinburgh: Edinburgh University Press, 2016).

35. Rathmell, 'Towards Postmodern Intelligence'; Myriam D. Cavelty and Victor Mauer, 'Postmodern Intelligence: Strategic Warning in an Age of Reflexive Intelligence', *Security Dialogue* 40(2) (2009): 123–44.

36. William Mitchell, 'Agile Sense-Making in the Battlespace', *International C2 Journal* 4(1) (2010): 1–33; William Mitchell and Robert M. Clark, *Target-Centric Network Modeling: Case Studies in Analyzing Complex Intelligence Issues* (Washington, DC: CQ Press, 2016); William Mitchell, 'Instrumental Friend or Foe? Constructivist Activism in Security Means Analysis', *Politica* (2004).

37. Johnson and Shelton, 'Thoughts on the State of Intelligence Studies', 116; Stephen Marrin, 'Improving Intelligence Studies as an Academic Practice', *Intelligence and National Security* 31(2) (2016): 266–79.

38. This view is adopted from critical security studies, as in C.A.S.E. Collective, 'Critical Approaches to Security: a Networked Manifesto', *Security Dialogue* 37(4) (2006): 443–87.

39. Ibid., 476.

40. Keith Krause and Michael Williams (eds), *Critical Security Studies: Concepts and Strategies* (London: UCL Press, 1997), xi.

41. Roy A. Bhaskar et al., *The Formation of Critical Realism: a Personal Perspective* (London: Routledge, 2008); Jonathan Joseph, *The Social in the Global* (Cambridge: Cambridge University Press, 2012); Milja Kurki, *Causation in International Relations: Reclaiming Causal Analysis*, Cambridge Studies in International Relations, Kindle edn (Cambridge: Cambridge University Press, 2008); Bob Jessop, *State Power* (Cambridge: Polity, 2007); Colin Wright, *Agents, Structures and International Relations: Politics as Ontology* (Cambridge: Cambridge University Press, 2006); Gill and Phythian, *Intelligence in an Insecure World*, 49; and Gill, 'Theories of intelligence', 2^{12}.

42. As described in Kurki, *Causation in International Relations*, location 169.

43. Don Garrett, *Hume*, The Routledge Philosophers (London: Routledge, 2015).

44. Norman Fairclough, Bob Jessop and Andrew Sayer, 'Critical Realism and Semiosis', in Norman Fairclough (ed.), *Critical Discourse Analysis*, 2nd edn (London: Routledge, 2010), 204.

45. Berth Danermark, Mats Ekstrom, Liselotte Jakobsen and Jan Ch. Karlsson, *Explaining Society: Critical Realism in the Social Sciences* (New York: Routledge, 2002), 199.

46. Kurki, *Causation in International Relations*.

47. Thierry Balzacq (ed.), *Securitization Theory: How Security Problems Emerge and Dissolve* (Abingdon: Routledge, 2011), 18, 22–3, 47; Heikki Patomäki, *After International Relations: Critical Realism and the (Re)Construction of World Politics* (London: Routledge, 2002), 78–9; Heikki Patomäki and Colin Wright, 'After Post-Positivism? The Promises of Critical Realism', *International Studies Quarterly* 44(2) (2002): 213–37; Kurki, *Causation in International Relations*, location 1935; Gilberto Carvalho Oliveira, 'The Causal Power of Securitization: An Inquiry into the Explanatory Status of Securitization Theory Illustrated by the Case of Somali Piracy', *Review of International Studies*, published online, 29 November 2017, 21.

48. Alexander Wendt, 'Why a World State is Inevitable', *European Journal of International Relations*, 9(4) (2003): 491–542; Ruth Groff, *Critical Realism, Post-positivism and the Possibility of Knowledge* (London: Routledge, 2004); Kurki, *Causation in International Relations*; Oliveira, 'The Causal Power of Securitization', 1–22.

49. Kurki, *Causation in International Relations*, location 2604.

50. Ibid., location 2693.
51. Ibid., location 2316.
52. Ibid., location 2322–6.
53. Gill and Phythian, *Intelligence in an Insecure World*, 40.
54. Bob G. J. de Graaff, *De wetenschapper en de spin. Over de (on)mogelijkheid van toekomstverkenningen ten aanzien van radicalisering en terrorisme*, oration 22, January, Leiden University, 2008.
55. Paul Furlong and David Marsh, 'A Skin Not a Sweater: Ontology and Epistemology in Political Science', in David Marsh and Gerry Stoker (eds), *Theory and Methods in Political Science*, 3rd edn (New York: Palgrave, 2010), 205.
56. David J. Singer, 'Threat-Perception and the Armament-Tension Dilemma', *Journal of Conflict* 2(1) (1958): 94.
57. Some studies on discourses or securitization have studied two distinct narratives in parallel, such as Nicolina Montessano Montessori, *A Discursive Analysis of a Struggle for Hegemony in Mexico: the Zapatista Movement versus President Salinas de Gotari* (Saarbrücken: VDM Verlag, 2009), or Holger Stritzel and Sean C. Chang, 'Securitization and Counter-securitization in Afghanistan', *Security Dialogue* 46(6) (2015): 548–67. But far more common is to focus research on a single narrative.
58. The terms *basic* and *analytic* are derived from Lene Hansen, *Security as Practice: Discourse Analysis and the Bosnian War* (New York: Routledge, 2006), 75.
59. Norman Fairclough, *Discourse and Social Change* (Cambridge: Polity Press, 1992), 73.
60. Balzacq, *Securitization Theory*.
61. One of the exceptions is Stritzel and Chang, 'Securitization and Counter-securitization in Afghanistan'.
62. Stéphane J. Baele and Catarina P. Thomson, 'An Experimental Agenda for Securitization Theory', *International Studies Review* 19 (2017): 650–51; Thierry Balzacq, Sarah Léonard and Jan Ruzicka, '"Securitization" Revisited, Theory and Cases', *International Relations* 30(4) (2016): 518.
63. For example, Adam Hodges, *The 'War on Terror' Narrative, Discourse and Intertextuality in the Construction and Contestation of Sociopolitical Reality* (Oxford: Oxford University Press, 2011); Richard Jackson, *Writing the War on Terrorism: Language, Politics and Counter-Terrorism* (Manchester: Manchester University Press, 2005); Donald Holbrook, *The Al-Qaeda Doctrine: the Framing and Evolution of the Leadership's Public Discourse* (New York: Bloomsbury, 2014).

I

ACN: THEORY, METHODOLOGY, METHOD AND OBJECT OF RESEARCH

The ACN methodology helps to increase understanding of complex intelligence problems and widen the perceptual spectrum at an initial stage of analysis. It does not provide the intelligence analyst or policymaker with an objective truth, nor does it deliver clear-cut predictions. This is inherently impossible for complexities and extremely complicated for mysteries.[1] The approach is labour-intensive, hence less suitable for current intelligence, yet able to contribute to strategic warning and prevention. It reduces mirror-imaging and confirmation bias, and in turn decreases the risk in intelligence of self-deterrence from dissent in the light of a dominant political/strategic narrative.

The primary semiotic mode of entry to accomplish analysis of the multiple co-existing meanings of social events is through discourses. This chapter explains how critical discourse analysis (CDA), the concept of narratives, and securitization theory correspond to and complement each other. CDA enables one to identify and situate narratives that highlight social difference in distinct ways. Securitization provides a focus that is relevant for intelligence to compare and contrast these narratives. The chapter discusses the ACN methodology, and provides an outline of the method to identify and analyse narratives: the narrative analysis framework (NAF). As an extension, narrative tracing (NT) is introduced as a way to trace effects of securitization efforts across narratives. Lastly, the chapter presents the ground plan for the case studies on *Al Qaeda*.

FROM DISCOURSE TO NARRATIVES

The dialectical–relational approach of CDA as introduced by Norman Fairclough particularly allows for the identification of various narratives in distinct social domains.[2] It connects different levels of analysis: texts, discursive practices of text production and consumption, and wider social practices that are situated in particular social structures.[3] Narratives (or discourses), as aggregations of texts in a particular context, reflect physical things, actions and the wider material world in a particular way. They are real in themselves, and have performative power, but they also reflect other aspects of reality and hence form a window to grasp such elements. There is a complex influence of social structures on events (and, over time, vice versa), which is shaped by all four types of causes. The challenge in discourse analysis is to recognise all of them and be open to working in an interdisciplinary or transdisciplinary way. This is not antithetical to Aristotle's views on the primacy of materiality, as was discussed in the Introduction. Rather, in indicating the significance of both material and discursive aspects of causal complexes, they balance each other, and unfold or stretch the theoretical framework to its full form.

It is beneficial to provide definitional clarity and use the concept of 'narrative' instead of 'discourse' to identify and analyse discursive data situated in particular social orders. One of the reasons for doing so is that the term 'discourse' is used in different ways within CDA. Narratives are the intertextual chains of utterances that relate to certain orders of discourse (language associated with a particular field or social practice).[4] A narrative combines basic elements, such as events, actors, time and locations, to form stories 'with a beginning, a middle and an end, containing a conclusion or some experience of the storyteller'.[5] Elements are selected and connected based on a certain logical and chronological order. Sequencing and presenting (or framing) elements in certain ways gives focus from particular points of view. Narratives have a referential and explanatory intention to describe actual (non-fictional) events, but are interpretative in nature due to selection, focus and salience attributed to their elements.[6]

Defining the boundaries of a narrative is ultimately a distinction that is determined not by subjects, but by the researcher. Any narrative is only a basic analytic narrative that is intertextually and interdiscursively linked beyond the boundaries of its definition. It is like trying to define the boundaries of light beams. Where do they end, or at what point do additional reflections change the beams to such an extent that 'original' characteristics are unrecognisable? Yet, looking at the middle of the beams, they are unquestionably there. Also, a narrative does not exist as a simple and separate stack of texts. In interpreting and contextualising texts, also by defining their audiences and producers, the basic core of narratives can be distinguished. The case studies presented in the following chapters each reflect both this narrative core and its inseparable research interpretation in terms of securitization. Different social practices function as prisms or looking-glasses that situate texts in narratives. The value of such a reflexive pluralism for the practice of intelligence analysis, analysing and contrasting different narratives, lies in embarking on the enriching divergent, cognitive and conceptual endeavour itself of seeking multiple meanings of events.

POWER, IDEOLOGY AND DIFFERENCE

Narratives not only reflect material and ideational conditions, but also teleological and efficient causes. They are tools that fulfil strategic functions by creating, maintaining, resisting or changing meaning, identities and relations of power. They not only describe stories, but 'do something' and have performative power. In this light, orders of discourse can be viewed as systems of power that are part of social practices which constitute a domain of struggle over power, while narratives (and counter-narratives) represent important tools of struggle for political, hegemonic or institutional continuity or change. Power and hegemony are processes or struggles that are always underway. They are relations defined by continuous interaction. In other words, narrative stasis would mean the end of institutions and identities.[7]

At the level of text, one could say that reality is reflected and (re)created while production and consumption are subject to relations of power. Who has the means and authority to say what about whom or what, or to keep others from speaking in this respect? Who has the ability and willingness to listen? Non-discursive power relations enable and constrain entities to produce, combine, reproduce or consume texts.

This section elaborates on the concepts of power, ideology and difference. Recognising the relationship between these concepts and narratives is valuable for understanding complex intelligence problems. However, as will be explained further on, what is not required is for researchers adopting the ACN methodology to have an explicit normative opinion about power relations in a particular social context. Structural power relations and the statements and actions through which difference is articulated can be thought of as a result of the various facilitating conditions and drivers that make up the causal complex. The discourse of those in power is often analysed as they are responsible for the existence of inequalities. The intertextual opportunity to realise unbounded creative imagination in texts on what might, could or should be, by combining new and old parts is in fact restrained by relations of power. To some extent, Fairclough draws on Michel Foucault's concept of *dispositif*, the system or apparatus consisting of heterogeneous semiotic and non-semiotic elements such as 'discourses, institutions, rules, laws, decisions, administrative measures, scientific statements, and philosophical, moral and philanthropic propositions – in short, the said as much as the unsaid'.[8] Although, Fairclough critiques Foucault for his lack of operationalisation of *dispositif*, and states that the imposing of power is not always successful;[9] because ultimately, over time, actors are able to influence power relations.

Various forms of power are distinguished by Fairclough. The power to do things (to act, to state) and having certain powers over people (to restrain) are distinct but dialectically related forms of power.[10] One form is necessary and of influence on the other. When legitimately attributed, power over people is not necessarily a negative thing either. When power is used in an illegitimate way, however, it becomes open to critique. As part of discourses, we can find two kinds of power over people. The first is power in discourse as an exercise of 'unequal encounters' in which the contribution of others is controlled. The most common examples are doctor–patient interviews and teaching in schools.[11] More hidden is power behind discourse, for example, the ability to standardise language use, to 'police' the boundaries of genre conventions, and to decide who has access to what kind of discourses.[12]

For intelligence agencies, news media and governmental advisory boards, hidden power resides in their ability to choose and select certain pieces of information over others. As their consumers are not co-present during this process, unlike in a doctor–patient interview or in a class, the effect of the power is less clear. Perhaps it is therefore more powerful than power in discourse. Power in discourse does not exclude power behind discourse. There is also hidden power behind medical examinations or lessons. A doctor is bound by genre conventions to ask only functional questions related to the problem at hand and can be disciplined for not conforming to this. In a sense, this hidden power lies behind the discourse of the interactions.

Fairclough acknowledges Antonio Gramsci's concept of hegemony, that is, 'one of the fundamental defined classes having leadership over society as a whole in alliance with other social forces'.[13] Hegemony is always partial, gradual and temporary. Integration of blocs into alliances is central and requires the consent and cooperation of the groups that are not in the lead rather than their submission to domination. The ideological process in which particular representations are naturalised and the manifestation of particular power relations in and through narratives are important aspects of hegemony.[14] As becomes apparent in the next section, securitization is in fact an ideological hegemonic process. Textual analysis offers a mode of entry to study this relation between ideology and power, and their enactment in ways of being and interaction in broader narratives.

Meaning becomes ideological if it is not just emphasising difference but also necessary to establish or maintain dominant power relations.[15] Whereas meaning can be local and specific, ideology is more stable, enduring and generic because of existing or emerging power relations. It is not the end of the spectrum, however, as 'common sense' is 'the consent to (or at least acceptance of) ruling-class attitudes and interests by the masses of a given social order as their own'.[16]

Meaning, ideology and common sense are overlapping stages on a continuum, and their applicability depends in part on the defined boundaries of the social reality. How much or how little resistance among 'the masses' makes a dominant ideology common sense? What are the boundaries of an ideology and how much resistance breaks a relatively stable set of unchallenged beliefs and values down to meaning? Resisting does not have to be a conscious decision. People might not necessarily be aware of the ideological dimension of their practice.[17] People, groups and institutional entities are ideologically positioned in socio-political contexts, but also able to shift, adapt and change these. The conceptual value of placing meaning, ideology and common sense on a scale or continuum, related through a process of naturalisation, is that it highlights the connection between different types of causes, most prominently efficient, final and formal causes. It illustrates how structure and agency are dialectical as both interact with and transform each other.

Power and ideology (as a form of hegemonic power) are important concepts for understanding social difference. They manifest through genres, discourse and styles. As rules for communication, certain genres enable and constrain actors to express themselves (or express themselves in certain ways) and allow or limit an audience to conceive expressions. The genre of giving an interview or press conference reflects underlying power relations. The social identity of actors enables and constrains these actors to speak with authority (or lack thereof). Being a head of state or a whistle-blower positions a speaker in such a way that comes with certain expectations of credibility. The everyday production of meaning, informed by ideology and constrained and enabled through power relations, is important for maintaining the social order. One could state that ideological processes and ultimately common sense inform a wider 'background context'.[18]

The theoretical concepts and themes introduced in the first part of this chapter inform the ACN methodology. When operationalising these into a method, some challenges will have to be met. Analytically, the concept of ideology is useful for its focus on power, but empirically it will be somewhat problematic for researchers to distinguish between less stable meanings and relatively more stable ideology or common sense (*zeitgeist*). In the case studies, consistency of utterances over time and signs of resonance among different types of audience serve as important indications of naturalisation. These indications show the extent to which the meanings in narratives become ideological and over time affect social practices.

While Fairclough's three-dimensional model and other concepts of discourse are valid, his idea of a normative critical agenda is not shared. From Fairclough's perspective, this book does not perform critical discourse analysis as he defines it. For that it is necessary to address social wrongs and find 'possible ways of righting or mitigating them' as CDA requires the researcher to not just be descriptive but also normative.[19] The normative aspect of addressing 'social wrongs' translates in this book as identifying processes of securitization and identification as potential or emerging 'social difference'. Researchers thus do not adopt a normative stance themselves to search for ways of undoing social inequality in a particular social order. However, the inherent nature of the development over time of contradictions, tensions and inequality in societies is accepted.[20] And another core theme in critical theory, the situatedness of entities, is an essential logic behind ACN. Researchers engage in comparative analysis, a narrative net assessment, of multiple perspectives as a means to widen understanding. As one of the narratives is part of the socio-political context that situates the researcher or intelligence analyst and the intelligence consumer, the analysis has an implicit emancipatory potential. There is self-reflection, but ACN moves beyond that to do research on other aspects. Do ideas on what constitutes a threat, or who can be perceived as an enemy have counterproductive or adverse effects?

Another question that comes to the surface when discussing the idea of 'critical' is: what separates narrative or discourse analysis from normal discourse, as any analysis is itself anything but discourse? The theoretical components provided by CDA enable us to ask why discourse is the way it is, and develops systematic analytical procedures to interpret the same resources as discourse participants. It is self-consciousness that separates the analyst from other participants when interpreting discourse. The analyst makes his or her observations and thoughts explicit. Research interprets meaning, but also studies the causal effect of discourse on other social elements (and vice versa) by making use of social science theorising. Narratives are systematically described, interpreted, evaluated, critiqued and explained in relation to non-semiotic conditions and events, and other narratives. In addition to influential narratives, additional smaller and less influential 'critical narratives' are studied that can serve as 'commentators' on discursive and non-discursive actions defined in other narratives. Narratives are explained with regard to how contradictions are (necessary) elements of the broader social reality of which they are part. As stated, there lies an implicit emancipatory potential in narrative net assessment. In the systematic use of theory, the researcher (or analyst) differs from discourse participants.

Securitization

The debate in critical security studies on securitization is highly significant to intelligence analysis. Security is not defined as an objective reality, but as a social construct or a form of interpretation manifested in the use of language. The traditional positivist paradigm limited security to the survival politics of states, primarily with a military focus. In general, the concept of securitization is associated with two generations of theorists. According to the Copenhagen

School, a political issue can be 'securitized' before a public audience by a 'securitizing actor' when a 'speech act' is uttered that a 'referent object' is existentially threatened.[21] This allows for extraordinary measures to be executed in order to deal with the threat. A condition for successful securitization is that the speech act has to be accepted by an audience, but there is no requirement in terms of causality for securitization itself to occur. Instances or processes of securitization are deemed to be 'discontinuous changes' or social 'quantum jumps' that have no preceding causal relations, for example, to non-discursive aspects of reality.[22] It hence becomes problematic to trace and explain how it is possible that securitization occurs, and what social elements are integrated and combined to generate effects. The discursive speech act approach omits the enabling or constraining of wider social conditions, underlying forces and non-discursive factors from the analysis.

A second generation of securitization scholars argue that securitization is more complex, dynamic and nuanced.[23] Belgian international relations professor Thierry Balzacq, a leading figure, argues that securitization is not a speech act, but a pragmatic act. This means that the use of language is explained within certain contexts, rather than as utterances of a sovereign speaker to a sovereign hearer. Furthermore, securitization can exist in practices other than words, such as bureaucratic procedures or technologies. An approach that clearly conforms more to the philosophical underpinnings of causal relations outlined in the Introduction of this book.

This contextual nature also implies that the status of various, differentiated audiences needs to be explicated. Balzacq proposes a distinction between formal and moral support of securitization.[24] Formal support comes from the audience that provides the necessary legitimate mandate to execute special measures to deal with the threat. Moral support conditions formal support, and securitizing actors strive to prompt a moral audience as large as possible to strengthen social relations and their position of authority. For this, the securitizing actor has to take into account the audience's frames of reference, their readiness to be convinced (depending on their trust in the securitizing actor), and the ability to (indirectly) grant or deny a formal mandate.

Other theorists, such as Finnish international politics professor Juha Vuori, have similarly argued that 'various types and parallel audiences' relate to the different (general or specific) functions of securitization processes, such as raising an issue on the agenda, reproducing a certain security status, or legitimising past and future actions.[25] Ultimately, audiences have to have the ability to somehow contribute to the underlying goal of the securitizing actor. This is a wider view of the role audiences can fulfil than the idea that they provide a mandate for deontological powers to the securitizing actor. Securitization maintains or strengthens processes of identification among general and specific audiences. In some instances, audiences might not even exist prior to securitization, as it is the effort itself that brings the awareness to people that they are part of a unified audience in relation to an issue.[26] For Vuori, predefining specific types of audience in theory is difficult because of the socio-historical, cultural and political conditions in which securitization takes place.[27]

In security studies, attempts to further operationalise audiences are primarily applicable to (democratic) institutionalised environments in which power relations have been established to a certain extent.[28] Based on the case studies in this book, the role of various types of audience in both an institutionalised national and a transnational social domain will be analysed. The aim is not to filter out singular essential characteristics, but to generate more insights into the nature and status of securitization audiences in these different contexts. Identifying audience assent and declaring securitization 'successful' is not necessary to adequately analyse the causal relations and effects involved in securitization efforts. Audiences are an essential component of securitization efforts, but not necessarily in terms of granting deontological powers to securitizing actors. Empirical evidence regarding audiences and their responses might be fragmentary or absent, but that does not a priori imply that no valid inferences can be reached based on alignment of securitization efforts with particular social structures and practices. As such, this research can also contribute to the debate on securitization within critical security studies in its analysis of various types of audience associated with the narratives or resonating with the securitization efforts.

The use of security modifies the context, yet to be 'effective' such use must be aligned with an external context that is independent from the use of language. In other words, there is a distinction between the situational context of the securitization effort and the background context or *zeitgeist*. Different audiences (both moral and formal) find themselves situated in various settings (for example, popular, elite, technocratic, scientific, religious).[29] Each of these settings can be characterised by particular expectations, specialised language, conventions and procedures. Hence, while a securitizing actor and his or her effort might resonate with some audiences in some settings, this might not be true for other audiences in other settings. The situational context can also be characterised by circumstances, such as a large-scale natural disaster, that make other securitized threats relatively less important. Ultimately, these more dynamic settings can be situated in more durable social structures. The concept of a background context positions these various and parallel audiences as part of a broader social domain, or particular social order. Discourses or narratives that encompass securitization efforts do so with respect to different audiences within an overarching social structure. This structure includes identities and power relations that manifest in and through the social position of the speaker and his or her unequal access and ability to use discursive resources. However, also the language itself has 'an intrinsic force that rests with the audience's scrutiny of truth claims, with regard to a threat, made by the speaker'.[30] Balzacq defines securitization as:

> an articulated assemblage of practices whereby heuristic artefacts (metaphors, policy tools, image repertoires, analogies, stereotypes, emotions, etc.) are contextually mobilized by a securitizing actor, who works to prompt an audience to build a coherent network of implications (feelings, sensations, thoughts, and intuitions), about the critical vulnerability of a referent object, that concurs with the securitizing actor's reasons for choices and actions, by investing the referent subject with such an aura of unprecedented threatening complexion that a customized policy must be undertaken immediately to block its development.[31]

In sum, three dimensions are central to securitization as defined above: agents, acts and context. The first level, agents, encompasses the various actors, including audiences, the personal and social identities, and the power relations involved. The discursive and non-discursive practices that endorse securitization are the focus of the second level: acts. This includes the type of language used, the strategic use of heuristic artefacts as social devices to generate the conditions that enable the mobilisation of audiences, the *dispositif* of (or generated by) the securitization process, and the customised policies generated by securitization. The third level, contexts, refers to the way securitization is situated socially and historically in situational and wider background contexts. Determining the status and response of the various audiences and therefore distinguishing whether securitization is 'successful' or 'unsuccessful' is difficult. The value of studying performative effects of securitization efforts in narratives lies in comparing, contrasting and tracing multi-consequentiality across various narratives. Among second-generation securitization theorists, academic debate is also ongoing about the nature of processes that reverse securitization efforts. There is always the potential for any securitization debate to 'open up', unmake, de-securitize, or transcend (for example, in the form of resistance, emancipation and societal, organisational or infrastructural resilience).[32] However, it is also recognised that the meaning of these logics or concepts and the way they relate is fragile and highly debated. ACN can generate insights on both securitization efforts and processes or ways of decreasing securitization momentum.

Balzacq's securitization theory and Fairclough's theoretical discourse model complement each other and enable one to identify and analyse distinct narratives. The differentiated critical realist view of reality and Aristotle's fourfold typology of causes provide a broader outline or philosophical theoretical foundation, grounding the theoretical components of ACN. One or more securitization efforts provide the logic that binds narratives. In and through narratives, securitization can be supported, challenged or transformed. It concerns the consistent attribution of a specific meaning of events regarding a possible existential threat. Emphasising difference between referent subject and referent object, and between threat and those threatened, lays the groundwork for the hegemonic practice of naturalisation in which meaning becomes a form of ideology (or even ultimately common sense). Although certain utterances are central to securitization, the whole process stretches over a series of events, statements and actions, forming intertextual chains at the discursive level. It concerns a more durable semiotic construal of aspects of the world in service of establishing and maintaining power relations.[33]

Despite its seemingly narrow definition, securitization is a broad concept as what constitutes the existential 'threat' and what is 'extraordinary' about the measures are ultimately defined by 'what actors have made of it' as they have combined narrative elements together.[34] Securitization efforts are multifaceted, multi-layered and situated in specific networks of social practices. Not every securitization effort has the same impact, as each is context-dependent and centred around different audiences. Securitization efforts must resonate with general background knowledge or the *zeitgeist* of audiences. For that a narrative can draw on and relate to other narratives or wider orders of discourse. For example, a narrative on the threat of terrorism can relate to a narrative on liberty and freedom. Through these interdiscursive links, the securitization narrative gains legitimacy with certain audiences in certain settings. A securitization narrative also represents and contributes to these other narratives and also affects (if only tacitly or marginally) other orders of discourse. It can affect the way liberty (and, for example, American citizenship) is perceived and defined.

Securitization efforts are also tied to the practice of security. The use of power to execute extraordinary measures that ensure the safety of a group of people is inherent. Studying securitization also involves taking the relation between discursive and non-discursive aspects of events as a central avenue of approach. This includes non-discursive action such as pre-emptive military strikes on foreign military installations or terrorist training camps, but also the actual terrorist bombings, the people killed and the damage done. Using this power to act strengthens the power base of the securitizing actor.

Processes of securitization also involve power over people. Non-discursive actions mix with discursive practices such as leadership statements before and after military strikes. The leadership's ability to comment on the timing, execution and effectiveness of the strikes represents the power that lies in discourse. During press conferences, the president has a conversation with journalists on the military strikes. The unequal nature of the encounter and the *power in* discourse becomes visible in the way the president is allowed to interrupt the journalists and hence control their contributions to the discourse. In case of mass media communication, such as a nationwide address, this power is more hidden from sight. The president appeals to the ideal type of patriotic citizen he chooses to represent. He can also select and emphasise certain aspects of social events over others. The same applies to the leader of a terrorist organisation or network, as he also addresses an ideal type of supporter and chooses to highlight a particular version of events.

Power behind discourse manifests more in the longer term. As language use becomes more standardised, it becomes more difficult to challenge basic assumptions without placing oneself outside the ongoing debate. Discussing communist ideals in the West during the Cold War became difficult at times of heightened tensions and increased threat perception, such as during the Cuba crisis in 1962. Right after a terrorist attack, it becomes inappropriate to consider whether there is any legitimacy to the motivations of the perpetrators. When this is transformed into more epic terms of good versus evil and us against them, this sense of inappropriateness becomes more standardised.

The ideological intent behind securitization efforts is key as power relations or hegemony depend on consent. Securitization emerges from the interplay of the status and psycho-cultural orientation of the audiences, the wider context or *zeitgeist*, and the differential power between speaker and listener. As conditions change and discourses evolve, relations of power are always dynamic. This implies that there is always the potential to change the momentum or effects of securitization efforts. Apart from being a narrative in its own right, any narrative can provide a form of critique to the naturalisation of meaning in other discourses or narratives. Its effectiveness depends on the extent to which narratives become interdiscursively linked in and through the occurrence of social events, such as text production.

Actively contesting security is a counter-practice often residing in smaller critical narratives that are suppressed by dominant institutional narratives. Entities associated with these critical narratives lack the power to act with similar means or in similar ways as those associated with dominant institutional discourses. Their main strength lies in challenging and critiquing relations of power over people, highlighting differences in the selection and availability of discursive resources, the standardisation of language use, and challenging genre conventions. The critical narrative identified in the third case study does not perform such a role, as it is situated in a distinct social order. However, in its critique, it widens understanding of the overall object of research for all case studies: *Al Qaeda*. Besides understanding other entities and adversaries, analysing such contrast between narratives also offers new insights that aid review of the dominant political strategic narrative in which intelligence organisations (or academic researchers) are encapsulated through their intimate relation with (intelligence) consumers.

ACN: From Methodology to Method

The ACN methodology consists of two phases. First, basic analytic narratives are identified and analysed in terms of securitization efforts. The narrative analysis framework (NAF) outlined in this section provides a method to accomplish this. As stated, it guides the case studies described in Chapters 2, 3 and 4. The second step is then to consider the multi-consequentiality of securitization efforts, both within and across social domains. To what extent is the development of macro narratives related? Narrative tracing (NT) extends the NAF method to focus on the second task.

A typical object of research for ACN is a complex intelligence problem characterised by 'sets of interacting issues such as themes, entities or activities, evolving in a dynamic social context'.[35] Examples include international terrorism, cyber security and proliferation of weapons of mass destruction, but also transnational and international (hybrid) conflicts. Each narrative relevant to a complex intelligence problem can be considered a separate case study focused on different bounded units of analysis, often at different levels (for example, individual, group, institution). Narratives are either part of different social orders (social structures, practices, events) or manifest at different levels within the same social order.

For example, a critical (personal) narrative from within an institution can provide new perspectives on the organisation and highlight possible alternatives to processes of naturalisation of meanings in the institutional narrative. In particular, identifying and studying critical narratives is a way of investigating inconsistencies and tensions in dominant narratives, and of increasing understanding of the construction of these dominant narratives. However, it is also essential that narratives be compared with and contrasted to other narratives situated in different orders of discourse (and wider social orders) to sufficiently widen the analytical spectrum. By integrating a narrative in the analysis that is associated with the intelligence consumer, assessment neutrality is improved in the initial stage of intelligence analysis. In this book, the terms 'macro narratives' and 'micro narratives' are used. Macro narratives relate to entities that have considerable discursive power over audiences and are able to engage in extraordinary security practices. Micro narratives concern accounts that often reflect critically on securitization efforts in the macro narratives, while the producing entities lack power to act in terms of security. It is possible, in case of a small country, for example, that the strategic narrative of the intelligence consumer is in fact a micro narrative compared with the narratives of great powers involved with the complex intelligence problem.

The basic and analytic character of all narratives implies that choices have to be made to define their core and boundaries. This is accomplished by focusing on key actors and entities involved with the production of key texts and relevant non-discursive actions. When investigating an institutional narrative, for example, data is selected from texts generated by or related to the institutional leadership. For a personal narrative, the focus is on texts produced by that person. Further sampling can then be guided by searching for key words in texts related to the issues defining the complex intelligence problem. For example, what (part of) speeches or which actions reflect (on) international terrorism?

As elements of (de)securitization are identified, further analysis puts them in the broader perspective of the other parts of the texts, the various settings and the wider context. Based on identification of these elements in the case studies, securitization efforts are central as neither social nor linguistic conditions can guarantee successful securitization for the initiating securitizing actors. The response of (moral and formal) audiences is equally relevant, but more difficult to grasp. It is assumed that reproduction and re-contextualisation in news media mirror the responses of audiences to some extent, as media outlets strive to maximise news consumption by aligning news frames with those of their audiences. This can be combined with other sources to contextually infer or study signs of resonance among various types of audience: for example, changes in voting, street protests or other social behaviour. Securitization is a process that involves moves (and counter-moves) and is not limited to a speech act or formula, much like a presidency is not limited to the swearing in, or a marriage to the wedding. Instead, it includes the continuous perception, workings and interactions of day-to-day activities and experiences. The three case studies represent various events and efforts that are stitched together into narratives.

Ultimately, once various narratives have been established, comparing and contrasting them can reveal additional insights into the complex nature of the intelligence problem. To what extent do the meanings attributed to events and processes of (de)securitization between the various basic analytical narratives relate? Does a securitization effort in one narrative correspond to a rally-round-the-flag effect or securitization effort in another, or in fact a critique?

But also, what is revealed about the relationship between the social structure, practice and events for each narrative? To what extent is the difference (us versus them) identified in narratives inherent to the social order of which each narrative is part? Ideology and meaning fuel processes of identification of others and self, and as such sustain domination and power relations. A perception of difference emerging from the (outside) threat of terrorism might constitute a process (or effort) of self-identification, just as much as the threat of terrorism presents an actual threat to the self. Conflicts between entities might reflect the shaping of entities, rather than a clash between them. This would be reflected in the extent of self-identification in securitization efforts. To what extent does *Al Qaeda* need the image of the United States that it propagates, or vice versa? Politicians, opinion leaders or news channels might, for example, portray groups of people in certain (negative) ways because of political, religious or economic social practices of trying to gain votes, maintain popular support or increase viewing rates.

Narrative analysis framework

The following derived framework offers a research focus that enables one to relate texts to core analytical categories and to identify narratives. However, the framework must not be taken for a simple checklist. The core analytical categories represent different perspectives and points of entry to analyse texts. Every text is different and has a different function in different narratives. Some can be considered as key texts signifying social change, while others can be grouped as reproductions or minor re-contextualisations of other key texts. As such, the analytical framework offered here might be considered as a sort of versatile Swiss knife that enables the researcher to shift focus between the core analytical categories while studying texts as part of a particular narrative. To some extent all categories remain relevant for studying texts, but it is impossible to take all aspects of texts into account all of the time. Analysing texts word for word takes an enormous amount of time and can result in relatively little gain. Hence, it is necessary to focus on elements of securitization efforts in key parts of texts. The researcher must make explicit what aspects are most relevant for understanding and explaining the function of texts as part of the particular narrative.

The core analytical categories concentrate on: (A) the manifestation of securitization efforts in narratives through meanings in texts; (B) textual analysis of key texts; (C) the setting or situational context of text production and text consumption; and (D) the wider external (non-semiotic) context. These categories partly overlap as meanings arise from the interplay of genres, discourses and styles of intra-textual aspects within extra-textual settings, and against the backdrop of wider background contexts.

(A) Meanings and narratives: securitization

The first and most central analytical category focuses on meaning (or semiosis) that emerges in texts, discourses and orders of discourse as one of the elements of social practice. *Meanings* arise from the way events are represented in situated texts, and how these events are woven together with other events within situated texts. How does the text producer experience the natural and social world? What social relations are enacted via the text in the discourse? And how does the text producer evaluate subjects? Fairclough suggests a series of questions for analysis; the following remarks are a derivate.[36]

What elements (aspects of events, voices/perspectives on events) are prominent or absent? How does the level of abstraction in texts vary (general, specific)? In what way are the various social entities portrayed? What discourses are drawn upon or mixed in the text? Does the text constitute 'an openness to, acceptance/ recognition or an explanation of difference by means of dialogue'? Is it 'an accentuation of conflict and struggle over meaning, ideology and power'? Or, in contrast, is it 'an effort to overcome difference by focusing on commonality and solidarity'? Is there 'normalisation and acceptance of differences of power which suppresses differences of meaning and differences over norms'?

Central to the research is the concept of *securitization*. Securitization efforts aim to classify something as an existential threat and establish an ultimate form of difference. What processes of securitization and identification, and critiques of them, can be distinguished? What discursive and non-discursive elements constitute securitization efforts? How do securitization efforts reflect and relate to underlying power relations and social roles? The unprecedented and imminent nature of the threat aims to legitimise an extreme exercise of power that supersedes normal politics. An exception to the norm is proposed. This does not mean normal politics is not concerned with difference and social change, or security and threats for that matter. Nor does it mean that securitization efforts necessarily achieve such an aim. However, researching such moves or efforts offers more focus and is theoretically the most promising approach to finding contrast between different narratives. Analysis concentrates on the securitization elements of heuristic artefacts, securitizing actor, audiences, referent object, referent subject and customised policy.[37]

The concept of securitization emphasises the role of various types of and parallel audiences, a wider context, and social power relations in establishing and maintaining perceptions of otherness and difference. The definition of the referent object implies that the entity is a (potential) audience. In addition, the 'consumers' of the statements or actions that constitute securitization efforts might include other groups. The efforts and their effects can resonate with these audiences in different ways. Here there is overlap regarding the concept of audiences, as the analytic category of 'settings' in the NAF and narrative tracing also further explicate the term. Another aspect of interest is the multi-consequentiality of securitization efforts. How does the securitization effort relate to processes of identification in other (contrasting) narratives? For example, what narrative is produced by the defined referent subject, and before what audience? Do the efforts of the securitizing actor (either statements or security practices) affect the referent subject's rhetoric or actions? Is perhaps a form of polarization or rally-round-the-flag occurring on the side of the referent subject? In other words, does securitization lead to securitization?

Not all narratives encompass securitization efforts themselves. The ACN methodology explicitly seeks to include one or several narratives that reflect a perspective critical of securitization efforts in other narratives. For critical perspectives, the definition of securitization serves as an analytical starting point to reference how and against what critique is uttered.

(B) Communicative event: text

Textual analysis of key data concerns a functional approach to the internal relations of language in *text* elements. What do key paragraphs and phrases mean, what do they do? As 'texts' also include non-textual communicative events such as signs and sounds, analysis can include visual and phonological aspects. Broadening the concept of texts beyond written texts enables a thicker description of events and social practices that fits Balzacq's conceptual ideas of sociological securitization. Most images and audio include a form of written or spoken language, making grammatical and lexical cohesion of the language used the most important elements of this category. Primary building-blocks of texts are clauses: textual elements that consist of words and phrases. Clauses can configure three functional components of meanings; they have three meta-functions.[38] Textually, clauses have a theme or subject that forms the central perspective: what is the clause about? Interpersonally, clauses express interactions (the exchange): is the clause a question or a declaration? And ultimately, ideationally, clauses reflect the experience of processes, participants and circumstances: what is happening? For instance, in the clause 'we were attacked by terrorists', the 'we' represents the theme or perspective, while 'were attacked by' corresponds to the indicative and declarative process as an aspect of both the subject ('we') and the active participant or actor ('terrorists'). Elements of clauses can have multiple functions as texts can mean multiple things at the same time. An imperative function of the clause 'we were attacked by terrorists' might emerge from other text elements, settings or wider contexts. The clause effectively means 'we must do something' or 'it is us against them'.

Meanings of clauses arise from the total configuration of their functions, but also from part–whole relations, as several clauses can form clause complexes or sentences. The significance of individual words or phrases, clauses and clause complexes not only varies per text, but can also vary between different instances of consumption of the same text. Of relevance in this respect is also the location in time (tense), fabric of time (aspect) and spatial dimensions. Is something currently relevant or imminent? Where and on what scale? In Fairclough's terms, the logic of securitization represents a semantic problem–solution relation and implies causal and conditional semantic relations between clauses and sentences.[39] Clauses involve statements of facts and predictions (speech functions), and have a declarative nature. Because there is a problem, action is required.

The meaning in selected key parts of texts emerges through grammar, lexicon and non-textual aspects. *Grammar* can bind text together in various ways. Certain parts within a text, such as groups and phrases, clauses or clause complexes, are held more strongly together than others, affecting their interpretation. Reference is 'the act of using referring expressions to refer to referents in the context' and can link with preceding (anaphora) or following (cataphora) elements in the text (endophoric reference). When text elements relate to elements outside the text itself (exophoric reference), this is not considered part of grammatical cohesion.[40] Typical words are 'them' and 'we'. Another grammatical device is substitution, a way of replacing one word for another to avoid repetition. For example, replacing 'cup' with 'one' in 'it's the last cup/one'. A third form of grammatical cohesion is maintained by ellipsis, leaving out certain words or a clause in a sentence that is nevertheless understood because of the remaining text. An example is the way a lover can respond with 'I do too'. Substitution and ellipsis are forms that can be used effectively only when it is sufficiently clear what is being substituted or left out. To some audiences, leaving out what is obvious to them is a powerful rhetorical tool, while for other audiences such a socio-cultural silential dimension might not resonate.

Lexical cohesion is achieved through the selection of particular vocabulary. Most importantly, the use of metaphors, synonyms and superordinates influence interpretation.[41] Metaphors are figures of speech that connect descriptions (words, phrases) to an entity, object or action though they do not have literally identical meanings (describing locations or situations as 'paradise', defining countries and organisations as 'evil'). Synonyms are broadly accepted substitutes. Superordinates are generalisations that can link an event to a phenomenon, or an entity to a category: a cow is an animal, and an animal is a living creature. Similarly, one could state a terrorist attack is a form of terrorism, and terrorism is related to terror. When responding to a terrorist attack, declaring a global war against 'terror' or defining an 'axis of evil' is of a different nature than starting a case-specific criminal investigation. Synonyms and superordinates are different from metaphors because of higher levels of intersubjectivity. In texts and discourses, a connection is often sought between synonyms, superordinates and metaphors, for example, in stereotyping entities. Although certain vocabulary can serve as a device for lexical cohesion within certain settings and a wider context, it may not in other situations.

Visual images and other *non-textual* signs and signals influence interpretation in specific ways. Despite the possibilities of manipulating visual recordings, images are historically associated with truth and objectivity and have primacy over words.[42] Objects placed in the background while giving a speech can underline the statements made, hence, becoming symbols for the message. A Soviet rifle resting against a wall in the background while Osama bin Laden records a speech on video in which he threatens the United States underlines his determination, fits his war rhetoric and adds to his status for some audiences.

Studying the interplay of grammatical and lexical cohesion within and between clauses with visual and phonologic relations indicates the level of text consistency and the force or strength with which meanings are signified. Focusing on textual aspects in these terms enables one to better explain and substantiate the function of text elements with regard to securitization coding categories and the other elements of the NAF: settings and the wider background. In this regard, intertextuality is understood as 'the property that texts have of being full snatches of other texts, which may be demarcated or merged in, and which the text may assimilate, contradict, ironically echo and so forth'.[43] This book refers to intertextuality in terms of both reproduction and re-contextualisation of texts to emphasise the extent meaning-making in narratives changes over time. Reproduction of statements by others is seldom exact. For example, news media are forced to select fragments and summarise statements in commentary. It is more a matter of degrees of re-contextualisation than analysing texts in terms of either/or with regard to intertextual aspects. The concept of intertextuality emphasises historicity in texts and signifies how several texts, and in particular securitization efforts identified in them, relate to each other and shape the wider basic analytic narrative.

(C) Settings

Meanings are also shaped by extra-textual aspects, such as the *setting* or situational context of text production and consumption. This is one of the central aspects of sociological securitization that distinguishes the pragmatic act of securitization from its speech act predecessors. Settings partly shape the nature and status of various types of parallel audiences. What types of *audience* (formal and moral, institutionalised or not) can be identified within the same setting, or in different ones? A formal audience could be thought of as a nation's parliament or congress, while the moral audience might be a nation's population, which expresses itself through opinion polls on presidential popularity. Both affect securitization processes in different ways, as formal audiences can be influenced by moral audiences. Other types of less institutionalised or formalised moral audiences could be a supportive global community of some sort ousting their backing via (social) media, rallies or protests. Posters, graffiti or music can also provide anecdotal evidence indicating resonance with securitizing efforts. Securitizing actors and audiences relate in a causally adequate manner: without one or the other, there can be no securitization. However, it is unnecessary for formal audiences to grant deontological powers before statements or actions can be viewed in terms of securitization.

The situational context of the production and consumption of texts (the discursive practice) is strongly related to genre, discourse and style. Genres are categories of ways of (inter)acting characterised by specific rules for communication, such as a job interview, a parliamentary debate or written memoirs. Conventions are reflected in communicative forms, and temporal and spatial dimensions. This includes the type of medium used, the practical constraints and institutional formalities or roles that come with the use of these mediums, and the emergence of idealised audiences. Settings can constrain meaning-making. As a US presidential candidate, Barack Obama had to use the Bush-type language of a 'global war on terror' (GWOT) to avoid placing himself outside the debate in the run-up to the elections. Yet as soon as Obama was in office, the US government stopped using this term.[44] Discourse construes representations of reality from a particular perspective that corresponds with particular groups of social actors (what is good or bad, strange or normal, noteworthy or not to whom). Style concerns ways of being that relate to the semiotic aspects of social identities. A king, president or business executive is expected to abide by the credo *noblesse oblige*, international aid workers or Buddhist monks commonly demonstrate altruism, and independent journalists generally have a critical and investigative posture.

Over time, discourse in narratives can in some cases become 'enacted as new ways of (inter)acting, inculcated as new ways of being (identities), and may be physically materialized as new ways of organizing space'.[45] A new informal (or even blunt/improper) political discourse introduced by a popular party might (incrementally) change parliamentary debate or press conference genre conventions. The discourse of a large-scale stock exchange scam can unite 'victims' in a collective of which they were previously unaware. A security discourse on the threat of terrorism can cause public buildings such as airports and railway stations to undergo architectural changes to limit public access to certain areas, affecting the wider order of discourse and social practice.

Reproduction and re-contextualisation of texts are also influenced by situational context. This has important consequences for the various audiences that are actually reached. For example, a US presidential speech in the White House Rose Garden only has a small physical audience, yet news media choose to broadcast (parts of) it live, adding comments on screen, introducing or summarising it by a news anchor, or asking experts to comment on it.

A text or communicative event rarely reaches only a single (type of) audience. In different settings, there are different expectations, or logics of persuasion. The relations of power 'in' and 'behind' discourse vary. There is a particular yet also dynamic local 'regime of truth' among audiences.[46] Hence, securitization operates differently within these different settings. The speaker's social position and unequal access and ability to use resources influence this truth, but language also has an intrinsic value to audiences. An audience considers the extent to which information is available and perceived to be credible at a certain moment in time. Speakers must use words, signs and symbols that fit the reference frames of audiences within particular settings. The semiotic and non-semiotic aspects of the medium used in communicating the message also influence this. Who has the knowledge to access certain modes of communication like satellite TV or chat applications on computers and smartphones, and what technological constraints or possibilities are tied to certain (new) media?

Ideally, studying settings requires that a researcher or intelligence analyst performs as a 'situated critical interpreter'.[47] He cannot be an objective observer because it is necessary to absorb the specific language and the customs of the situational context, but, at the same time, he must maintain enough distance to be able to rise above the setting and offer an outside view. In practice, this will be a challenge for scholars and intelligence analysts, and necessitate the knowledge of various experts.

(D) Wider background: non-semiotic elements

Apart from discourse (or semiosis), non-semiotic elements shape the social practice within which a securitization effort manifests. Securitization can be effective only if it is sufficiently aligned with the *external context* or *zeitgeist*. Fairclough primarily identifies four non-semiotic elements: action and interaction; social relations; persons (with beliefs, attitudes, histories, etc.); and the material world.[48] The distinct properties of these elements are researched on different theoretical bases than the way this study researches language and discourse. However, as partly explained in the previous section, these non-semiotic elements also relate dialectically to each other and to semiotic elements. They internalise or contain parts of the other elements without being reducible to them, as 'social relations are partly discoursal in nature and discourse (or narrative) is partly social relations'.[49] Processes of identification are relational, and relations manifest in narratives.

For example, the politics of nations can be seen as a social practice that involves diplomatic, military or economic action and (friendly, neutral or hostile) interaction, defined by and defining various national and international organisations and institutions, along with people's citizenship and the organisation of geographical space. These aspects can be studied with theories of international relations, economics, war studies, organizational studies, ethnography, anthropology, social identity theory, etc. Yet all these aspects are also reflected in discourse and all gain or maintain meaning through it. It is often in the national security strategy that one can find the clearest references to what values define the nation. Threats that need to be countered point to these values and hence underline national identity. In a similar way, securitization efforts (re)create or (re)define various types of audiences, and lead to (preventive) action or the restructuring of physical space. Thus, important questions are: how are securitization efforts affected by non-semiotic elements (including material security practices and actions), and in what way do securitization efforts affect these elements? To what extent do they influence (networks of) social practices?

Some background knowledge or fundamental existential/social beliefs are undetectable in texts. They relate to a *silential dimension* of things that remain unsaid. The unsaid is presupposed for audiences and becomes apparent as intertextual chains are formed and interdiscursive links are identified. This core analytic category relates to social structures like culture, religion, institutions and power relations that manifest in and are shaped by social practices. Suggestions on what is 'normal' or on what types of people are socially less valued are good indicators of presuppositions.

How can we separate discourse from scientific theories on non-semiotic elements in other disciplines? Similar to the distinction between discourse and discourse analysis, it is the specific nature of these other scientific theories that distinguishes them from other discourses. Scientific theory is situated, but the systematic and transparent nature of the approach makes underlying knowledge explicit.

Through the framework of analysing social events, settings, meanings and the wider background, texts relating to specific actors and audiences constitute the building-blocks for drawing up distinctive narratives around processes of securitization, and also for critiquing them.

Narrative tracing

Stories reflect reality but they can also 'do something', have performative power. For the case studies, securitization efforts lie at the heart of performative effects. The NAF accommodates the study of this social influence on various types of audience. In an institutionalised setting, various formal and moral audiences can be distinguished that hold different perceptions on policies. Some might be convinced of the need to trade some privacy for security, while others might oppose proposed policies. In an open democratic society, for example, physical protective measures might be taken in the public space as a result of a terrorist threat. Whereas this might make some citizens feel more secure, others could feel less so as they are constantly reminded of the threat by barriers and armed security personnel. For less institutionalised entities, such as social movements or networks, other differentiations of audiences can be made, for example, between active supporters or followers, more indirect sympathisers, and those with a general understanding of some of the anger and grievances that bind followers. Some 'audiences' might not necessarily agree with all a movement stands for, but in general align with feelings of anger or demands for freedom from interference.

But apart from influencing various audiences in a particular social domain in different ways, securitization efforts can also be multi-consequential across social domains. These 'consequences' of narratives can be intended or unintended, direct or indirect. Whereas a promise by national leaders to aggressively deal with a terrorist threat might be expected by their constituents, this might also provide the antagonist status and recognition among his or her own followers. Taking the discursive performative effects of security measures and policies into account in such a way seems especially fitting for the complex problem of international terrorism represented by *Al Qaeda*. Based on historic research, although focused on a different (domestic) context and a different timeframe, some have tentatively concluded that the expressive aggressive statements and actions that served to mobilise the population against terrorism actually nourished a climate favoured by terrorists.[50] This leads to interesting questions: to what extent do one entity's securitization efforts lead to securitization efforts by the defined referent subject? Do securitization efforts enhance self-identification and a sense of purpose among the antagonist's audiences? What is the role of leadership or the securitization actor? How do bureaucratic practices or (uncoordinated) sub-government institutional statements and actions affect the security problem? Since threat articulation seeks to enable an extraordinary response to deal with the threat, it would be antithetical if associated statements and actions also further actualised the threat.

In addition to the NAF, NT involves focusing on multi-consequentiality of securitization efforts and linking the development of distinct narratives. Using the term 'process tracing' is deliberately circumvented to avoid any suggestion that NT involves focusing on the most dominant or singular causal relation that explains particular social effects. Rather, NT entails focusing on the (potentially counterproductive) effects of securitization efforts in other narratives. It proceeds along the following questions:

- What is the analytical beginning and end of each macro narrative? The NAF is instrumental in defining and outlining the three case studies (introduced in the last section of this chapter).
- What facilitating conditions and drivers, or factors and events, account for the overall transformation of the narrative trajectories between these points? Identification of the patterns and dynamics that explain the development of the two macro narratives is a precondition for comparing and contrasting the narratives in terms of multi-consequentiality. Micro narratives serve to enhance, contrast or highlight additional aspects of facilitating conditions and drivers.
- How do macro narratives incorporate statements and actions that are reflected in (or are part of) other macro narratives? This question relates to both the qualitative and quantitative extent to which this type of re-contextualisation occurs. The significance lies in the interdiscursive nature of these narrative elements, and less in their impact on narrative content. The latter is also relative to other factors and events influencing the development of a macro narrative.
- How do such statements and actions resonate (add or remove momentum) among the various audiences of a narrative? This can be derived from explicit audience responses such as polling data and voting behaviour, or street protests and public debate. However, additional study of the alignment of audiences with the ideational background and situational context

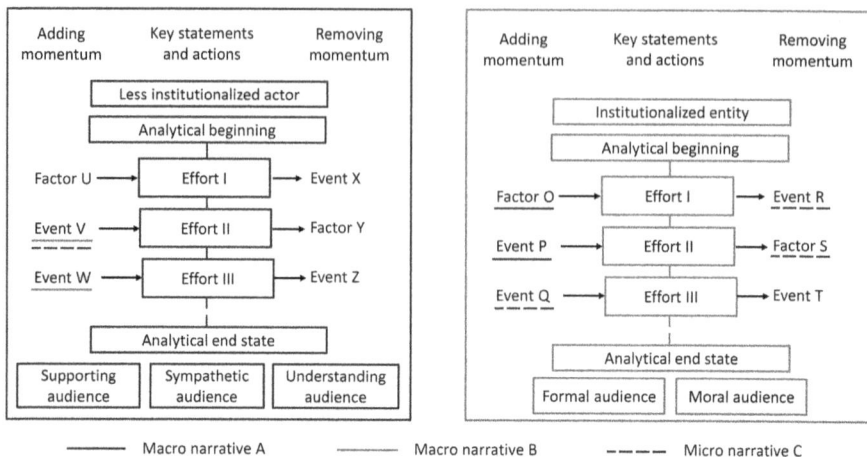

Figure 1.1 Schematic overview of narrative tracing

of the narrative can also be performed. Which audiences are addressed in the narrative content; who is characterised as referent object; and which audiences actually consume the texts that make up the narrative? It is also possible for external factors or events to strengthen or weaken alignment of audiences to particular narratives. Terrorist attacks, military strikes, scandals or hypes can have more fluctuating effects, whereas deteriorating socio-economic conditions could have a more gradual impact on shifts in the alignment of audiences.

The approach can be graphically summarised as in Figure 1.1. Now that the theory, methodology and method for ACN have been discussed, the remainder of the chapter presents the object of research and the plan for the case studies.

The Complex Intelligence Problem of Al Qaeda

The organisation, network and ideology represented by *Al Qaeda*, and more particularly the evolution of meanings of *Al Qaeda* over time and the meanings of actions associated with it, serve as object of research. The term *Al Qaeda* refers to the group of people and social network that associate themselves with the name *Al Qaeda*, the leadership of Osama bin Laden, the world view, beliefs and values of a *jihad* against a far (Western) enemy, and public representations and non-discursive (violent) activities of *Al Qaeda* members. For ACN this provides appropriate cases as narratives clearly play a highly significant role. Non-discursive attacks need narratives to provide meaning in context. More-over, threats made in video messages or manifestos are strongly discursive in nature. The name *Al Qaeda* connects and represents inter- and transnational phenomena that in different ways are part of separate yet partially overlapping narratives that manifest at different levels.

It is also a case with which many people (scientists, intelligence professionals, politicians, citizens, etc.) are familiar and to which they can thus relate. In the last fifteen years, an extensive number of original documents found with *Al Qaeda*'s leader Osama bin Laden in Pakistan have become publicly available. Partly as a consequence, much scientific research has been conducted on *Al Qaeda*, based on different theories. In contrast to the analysis of narratives as projected here, quantitative pattern-seeking approaches have mostly originated from an outside perspective.[51] They have a tendency to think about what could possibly pose a threat, and thus include the most dangerous scenarios: can terrorists acquire weapons of mass destruction or nuclear material? Are our borders secured? What financial resources enable terrorist activities? Is there a pattern so we can predict future attacks? Such questions echo the positivist zero sum games and prisoner's dilemmas that guided Western policymakers during the Cold War. Most conveniently, one is able to calculate the most preferable policy or the extent to which taking out a leader will 'degrade' the organisation. However, this level of certainty is a mirage if various meanings, settings and contexts of social events are insufficiently taken into account.

The relevance of basic analytic narratives is closely related to the scope, aim and object of research. While its primary focus is on *Al Qaeda* on a global (international) scale, analysis at other levels, such as the US national level, can equally be of value. One of the three narratives identified in this book is a (nationwide) *United States institutional terrorism narrative*. However, at times it can become clear how a basic analytic narrative at the national level is difficult to obtain due to ideological struggles at a subnational level. A good illustration was the debate on *Al Qaeda* between Republicans and Democrats in the United States that followed after an attack on 11 September 2012 on the US Embassy in Benghazi, Libya. Republicans were convinced the attack in Benghazi had been 'a coordinated, military style commando-type raid' organised by *Al Qaeda*.[52] They were keen to criticise President Obama's counterterrorism record. Democrats made every effort to question *Al Qaeda* involvement and downplay the organised character of the attack: it was a street protest that had gotten out of hand.[53] Both parties were preparing for the upcoming presidential elections and lacked any will to find common ground on what had happened. Hence, with ACN, it remains important to adopt an abductive attitude during research and reflect on whether the level of analysis, timeframe and scope of the identified narratives are the most adequate.

Central to the research in this book was the identification of actors and their fundamentally different narratives in which '*Al Qaeda*' was articulated between 1994 and 2001. Instrumental in this process was distinguishing between different social and discursive practices that situate narratives. These were different overlays that could be placed over a map formed by landmark events such as attacks or declarations. Chapter 2 presents the 'counter-colonial' or 'global jihad' *Al Qaeda* narrative, as situated in the social practice of *Salafi-jihadism*. This is a violent form of Islamic fundamentalism or fanaticism, also referred to as Islamism, which manifests at the transnational and global levels within the social structure of Islamic society.[54] Communicative events that constituted the narrative embodied violent and kinetic acts or terrorist attacks, along with the public statements made by Osama bin Laden on behalf of or generally attributed to *Al Qaeda*. As discussed in Chapter 3, the discursive practice relating to the second narrative, the *US institutional terrorism narrative*, was institutional communication and execution of national policy by the US administration under President Bill Clinton. From a US policy perspective security threats like *Al Qaeda* related to the social practice of the international politics of nations as part of the broader national security order of discourse.

These first two narratives could be considered macro narratives in that they demonstrate a considerable performative power (or social influence) with respect to their audiences and power to act with regard to the security problem. In comparison, the third narrative is more that of a commentator at the micro or personal level, providing additional insights by reflecting on the securitization efforts and dynamics identified in the macro narratives from a micro perspective. The *critical terrorism narrative* discussed in Chapter 4 was identified in a different manner than the previous two. After the case studies on the US and *Al Qaeda* narratives were concluded, a social practice or space was identified that could cultivate a relevant narrative with a potentially critical perspective on the preceding case studies: the information society. It has enabled individuals, groups, organisations and institutions to network together around streams of information, bypassing traditional social and institutional borders.[55] The information revolution has enabled critics to make their views public and hold governments or other powerful actors accountable for their actions. Robert Fisk, a British journalist and correspondent in the Middle East for the London-based newspaper *The Independent*, was selected as a central contributor for this critical narrative. Unlike any other journalist, Fisk interviewed Bin Laden in Arabic three times in both Sudan and Afghanistan. Furthermore, he had been recognised by a relevant former US intelligence officer as a reputable and reliable.[56] However, contrary to other English-speaking reporters, Fisk did not extensively use American official sources in his reports on *Al Qaeda* and Bin Laden. Other British and American journalists who interviewed and reported on Bin Laden were included in the research for comparison and showed significant parallels. It was not the impact or performative power, but the potential of the meanings attributed to events in the third narrative to reveal tensions and inconsistencies in other narratives that analytically served the methodology of ACN.

Events and Text Selection

Narratives take shape around social events that are manifested in texts. The identification of relevant events emerges from data in the selected texts, but the analysis of these events is also informed by other sources, such as the review of literature and general news reporting. Gathering data and identifying events and core elements of narratives is in fact a dialectical process that gains focus as available literature and data accumulate and key events emerge. A mixture of different types and a sufficient amount of texts are needed to ensure an adequate intertextual level to represent a narrative. Selected texts for the narratives included public statements like press conferences, institutional reports, news articles, open letters, online video statements, reporting on terrorist attacks, memoirs, historical research and discussions on television. An overview of the key and general texts selected for the narratives in chapters 2, 3 and 4 is provided online at https://edinburghuniversitypress.com/book-us-intelligence-and-al-qaeda.html. Further research was conducted on (sometimes declassified) studies that were informative for analysing settings and the wider background context of narratives.

As a first step, significant events were identified in generally available literature and news media, and chronologically ordered in a timeline. From this timeline, themes and events were clustered. The focus lies between 1994 and early 2001, as this period reflects the emergence of *Al Qaeda* (as an organisation, network or ideology). Events included Osama bin Laden's statements in that timeframe, with a special emphasis on his 1996 declaration, the 1998 World Islamic Front statement and interviews in Western media. Other important events were the 1998 attacks on US embassies in Kenya and Tanzania, and the consequential US military strikes in Afghanistan and Sudan. The foiled millennium plots and the attack on the USS *Cole* in 2000 were also highlighted as key occurrences.

Empirical limitations of the research were twofold. First, only a selection of texts was studied. The selected texts were combined into basic analytic narratives. This always leaves open the possibility of expanding or adapting narratives. Furthermore, among the selected texts, a distinction was made between key texts and other texts. Key texts were those that were extensively reproduced and contextualised in other texts and as such signified social change or action to a greater extent. They were selected over other texts that had less impact on narratives, as the latter merely added to what had already been said. Secondly, the research was based on publicly available data. This left out classified information that could have affected further analysis. It should be emphasised here that the ACN methodology is itself not limited to public discourse. Classified information collected by means of signals intelligence, human intelligence or imagery intelligence will only improve and enrich narratives and their settings and contexts. Constructing these narratives solely on secretly obtained information is a less productive approach, however. Securitization efforts require audiences. Terrorists aim to spread fear

Table 1.1 An overview of the three narratives

Narrative	Social practice	Order of discourse	Text examples
Chapter 2: *Al Qaeda narrative* (macro)	(Global) Salafi jihad	Salafi jihadi order of discourse	Osama bin Laden's 1996 speech and newspaper article (Ladenese epistle) and related newspaper interviews
Chapter 3: *US institutional terrorism narrative* (macro)	International politics of nations	National security order of discourse	Presidential speech and re-contextualisation in US news broadcasts
Chapter 4: *Critical terrorism narrative* (micro)	The information society	News correspondent reporting	Robert Fisk's interviews with Bin Laden

with their actions and mobilise support. A public dimension hence forms a crucial aspect for narratives. All in all, the two limitations did not conflict with the overall purpose of the research, as the primary aim is to demonstrate ACN. The texts selected for the identified basic analytic narratives provided ample material to achieve this. For Chapters 2, 3 and 4, the NAF was central. In the last chapter, based on NT, more insights are generated by comparing and contrasting all narratives in terms of discursive and non-discursive action, identity, power and social orders. In addition, the ACN methodology is evaluated and organisational and practical concerns are described relating to the implementation of a derived method in intelligence organisations.

NOTES

1. Agrell and Treverton, *National Intelligence and Science.*
2. Fairclough's approach to discourse has been adopted to study (aspects of) intelligence as part of a single (US or Swedish) social domain, but not to distinguish and study multiple social domains. For example, see Bean, *No More Secrets*; Eriksson, *Swedish Military Intelligence.*
3. Norman Fairclough, *Critical Discourse Analysis* (Boston, MA: Addison Wesley, 1995); Norman Fairclough, *Analysing Discourse: Textual Analysis for Social Research* (London: Routledge, 2003); Fairclough, *Critical Discourse Analysis*, 2nd edn.
4. Fairclough, *Discourse and Social Change*; Montessori, *A Discursive Analysis of a Struggle for Hegemony in Mexico*, 147.
5. Montessori, *A Discursive Analysis of a Struggle for Hegemony in Mexico*, 147–8.
6. Mieke Bal, *Narratology: Introduction to the Theory of Narrative* (Toronto: University of Toronto Press, 1997).

7. After 'Stasis is death really seems to be the general law of the World', as in David Campbell, *Writing Security: United States' Foreign Policy and the Politics of Identity* (Minneapolis, MN: University of Minnesota Press, 1992), 11–12.

8. Michel Foucault, *Power/Knowledge: Selected Interviews 1972–1977*, ed. and trans. Colin Gordon et al. (New York: Pantheon Books, 1980), 194–228; Balzacq, *Securitization Theory*, 22, 37.

9. Fairclough, *Discourse and Social Change*.

10. Fairclough, *Language and Power*, 3rd edn (New York: Routledge, 2015), 26.

11. Ibid., 27.

12. Ibid., 73–100.

13. Fairclough, *Critical Discourse Analysis*, 2nd edn, 61.

14. Fairclough, *Analysing Discourse*, 218.

15. Fairclough, *Critical Discourse Analysis*, 2nd edn, 9.

16. Ibid., 67; A. Gramsci, *Selections from Prison Notebooks* (London: Lawrence & Wishart, 1971).

17. Marianne Jørgensen and Louise Phillips, *Discourse Analysis as Theory and Method* (London: Sage, 2002), 70–1, 76.

18. Fairclough opposes the term 'background knowledge' as the notion of 'knowledge' obscures the ideological process involved. However, in this book the critical realist epistemological approach to knowledge sufficiently explains the relativity of 'knowledge' as a form of theory. Hence, it is not necessary to reject the term 'background knowledge' as it is similar to common sense. Both common sense and background knowledge are relatively stable beliefs, although all knowledge is ultimately dynamic. Fairclough, *Critical Discourse Analysis*, 2nd edn, 26, 46.

19. Fairclough, *Critical Discourse Analysis*, 2nd edn, 10–11.

20. A core theme in critical theory in general. See, for example, Aradau et al., *Critical Security Methods*, 1–22.

21. Barry Buzan, Ole Wæver and Jaap de Wilde, *Security: a New Framework for Analysis* (London: Lynne Rienner, 1998), 1–47.

22. Ole Wæver, 'Politics, Security, Theory', *Security Dialogue* 42(4/5) (2011): 476. It must be noted that Barry Buzan has developed a different view in this regard. Further discussion of this distinction lies beyond the scope of this book.

23. Holger Stritzel, 'Towards a Theory of Securitization, Copenhagen and Beyond', *European Journal of International Relations* 13(3) (2007): 375–83.

24. Thierry Balzacq, 'The Three Faces of Securitization: Political Agency, Audience and Context', *European Journal of International Relations* 11(2) (2005): 171–201. A point developed further by Paul Roe, 'Actor, Audience(s) and Emergency Measures, Securitization and the UK's Decision to Invade Iraq', *Security Dialogue* 39(6) (2008): 615–35.

25. Juha Vuori, 'Illocutionary Logic and Strands of Securitization: Applying the Theory of Securitization to the Study of Non-democratic Political Orders', *European Journal of International Relations* 14(1) (2008): 65–99.

26. Michael C. Williams, 'The Continuing Evolution of Securitization Theory', in Thierry Balzacq (ed.), *Securitization Theory: How Security Problems Emerge and Dissolve* (Abingdon: Routledge, 2011), 215.

27. Vuori, 'Illocutionary Logic and Strands of Securitization', 72.
28. Sarah Léonard and Christian Kaunert, 'Reconceptualizing the Audience in Securitization Theory', in Thierry Balzacq (ed.), *Securitization Theory: How Security Problems Emerge and Dissolve* (Abingdon: Routledge, 2011), 57–76; Adam Côté, 'Agents Without Agency: Assessing the Role of the Audience in Securitization Theory', *Security Dialogue* 47(6) (2016): 541–58; Lee Jarvis and Tim Legrand, '"I Am Somewhat Puzzled": Questions, Audiences and Securitization in the Proscription of Terrorist Organizations', *Security Dialogue* 48(2) (2017): 149–67.
29. Mark Salter, 'Securitization and Desecuritization: a Dramaturgical Analysis of the Canadian Air Transport Security Authority', *Journal of International Relations and Development* 11(4) (2008): 321–49.
30. Balzacq, 'The Three Faces of Securitization', 173.
31. Balzacq, *Securitization Theory*, 3.
32. Thierry Balzacq (ed.), *Contesting Security* (New York: Routledge, 2015).
33. Norman Fairclough, 'A Dialectical–Relational Approach', in *Critical Discourse Analysis*, 1995, 163–4.
34. Rita Floyd, 'Just and Unjust Desecuritization', in Thierry Balzacq (ed.), *Contesting Security: Strategies and Logics*, PRIO New Security Studies (London: Routledge, 2014), 126.
35. Agrell and Treverton, *National Intelligence and Science*, 34.
36. Fairclough, *Analysing Discourse*, 191–4.
37. Balzacq, *Securitization Theory*, 3; see also Balzacq's full definition in the previous section.
38. M. A. K. Halliday and C. M. I. M. Matthiessen, *Halliday's Introduction to Functional Grammar*, 4th edn (London: Routledge, 2014).
39. Fairclough, *Analysing Discourse*, 89.
40. Joan Cutting, *Pragmatics and Discourse: a Resource Book for Students* (Florence, KY: Routledge, 2002), 9.
41. Ibid., 9.
42. Available at: http://www.strath.ac.uk/aer/materials/6furtherqualitativeresearchdesignandanalysis/unit3/howtodocda-languageaspects; Fairclough, *Critical Discourse Analysis*, 7.
43. Fairclough, *Language and Power*, 37.
44. Hodges, *The 'War on Terror' Narrative*.
45. Fairclough, 'A Dialectical–Relational Approach', 165.
46. Ibid.; Foucault, *Power/Knowledge*, 109–133.
47. Colin Wilkinson, 'The Limits of Spoken Words: From Meta-narratives to Experiences of Security', in Thierry Balzacq (ed.), *Securitization Theory: How Security Problems Emerge and Dissolve* (Abingdon: Routledge, 2011), 100.
48. Norman Fairclough, 'The Discourse of New Labour: Critical Discourse Analysis', in Margaret Wetherell, Stephanie Taylor and Simeon Yates (eds), *Discourse as Data: a Guide for Analysis* (London: Sage, 2014), 234.
49. Fairclough, *Analysing Discourse*, 25.
50. Beatrice A. de Graaf, *Theater van de Angst, De strijd tegen terrorisme in Nederland, Duitsland, Italië en Amerika* (Amsterdam: Boom, 2010); Beatrice, A. de Graaf and

Bob G. J. de Graaff, 'Bringing Politics Back In: the Introduction of the 'Performative Power' of Counterterrorism', *Critical Studies on Terrorism* 3(2) (2010): 272.

51. For example, Jonathan D. Farley, 'Breaking Al Qaeda Cells: a Mathematical Analysis of Counterterrorism Operations (A Guide for Risk Assessment and Decision Making)', *Studies in Conflict and Terrorism* 26(6) (2003): 399–411.

52 Catherine Herridge, 'House Intelligence chair, Benghazi attack 'Al Qaeda-led event", *Fox News*, 29 December 2013.

53. Mark Morgenstein and Chelsea J. Carter, 'New York Times Report Casts Doubt on al Qaeda Involvement in Benghazi', CNN, 28 December 2013.

54. For example, see Gilles Kepel, *Jihad: the Trail of Political Islam*, trans. Anthony F. Roberts, 4th edn (London: I. B. Tauris, 2006).

55. See, for example, Robin Mansell (ed.), *The Information Society: Critical Concepts in Sociology* (London: Routledge, 2009).

56. Michael Scheuer, *Osama Bin Laden* (Oxford: Oxford University Press, 2011), 225.

2

AL QAEDA NARRATIVE

INTRODUCTION

The first case study relates to Bin Laden and his network, the entity that would receive the most attention from any intelligence effort on *Al Qaeda* regardless of method. The *Al Qaeda* narrative has a significantly different character than the *US institutional terrorism narrative* presented in the next chapter. This is, first, because it concerns a far less institutionalised (in the 1990s even diffuse) entity. There are no institutional genre conventions or strict formal structures, roles or practices like those in the United States. Furthermore, the *Al Qaeda* narrative has a more emotional character than the US institutional terrorism narrative, which includes more rational explanations of policy. Bin Laden sought to enhance a sense of solidarity among various intended audiences. Moreover, the narrative was based on grievances that accumulated over time, instead of being sparked by a high-impact non-discursive event.

Although the timeframe for this study is set between 1994 and early 2001, texts and non-discursive actions are clearly related to discourse and events preceding this timeframe. Making matters more complex are differences regarding the moment *Al Qaeda* 'came into being'. American writer Lawrence Wright states *Al Qaeda* was born as a terrorist organisation in late 1991 and early 1992, as Osama bin Laden moved to Sudan and the East Africa cell that would bomb the US embassies was formed.[1] Former FBI agent Ali Soufan, who was involved with the Bin Laden investigation, describes how the East Africa cell was operational in early 1994.[2] The Lebanese-American academic Fawaz

Gerges identifies May 1996 as the moment Bin Laden started to systematically operationalise *Al Qaeda*, and notes how there was a significant shift in *Al Qaeda*'s focus in the mid-1990s.[3] British journalist and author Jason Burke concurs that it was between 1996 and 2001 that *Al Qaeda* 'matured', although 'it was still far from a structured terrorist group'.[4] In contrast, according to American journalist and scholar Peter Bergen and investigative reporter Paul Cruickshank, *Al Qaeda* already existed as 'a military base' in the late 1980s.[5] American religious studies scholar Flagg Miller appears to counter this notion most radically, stating that only after 2001 was the term *Al Qaeda* used by militants to 'signify a worldwide organization'.[6]

What this illustrates is the extent to which authors choose to highlight different aspects, stages or phases of '*Al Qaeda*'. At any point in time between the 1970s and the present, between the time Arabs joined the Afghan mujahedeen in the fight against Soviet troops and the 'post-Bin Laden era', *Al Qaeda* has existed in some form at the level of networks of people, hard-core organisation and ideology. The '*Al Qaeda* narrative' between 1990 and 2001 thus needs to grasp these different aspects as they developed.

For the *Al Qaeda* narrative as defined in this book, one must start by focusing on the Saudi businessman and jihadi leader Osama bin Laden amidst his developing group of followers and associates. As this group evolved, especially during the late 1990s and early 2000, it becomes more applicable to speak of a 'central leadership' that served as the most suitable mode of entry into the narrative, consisting not only of Osama bin Laden but also from the mid-1990s the Egyptian doctor who joined him, Ayman al-Zawahiri. During the selected timeframe it was mostly Bin Laden that made public statements.

Hence, data for analysis primarily includes the statements of Bin Laden, as well as (violent) non-discursive actions associated with these *Al Qaeda* leaders in either an inspirational or organisational sense. Public statements have been collected from various sources and databases.[7] Western and Arab news media such as the London-based *Al Hayat* and *Al-Quds Al-Arabi* provide data on reproduction and re-contextualisation of the public statements before various audiences. Video reporting, photographs and other news reports offer context regarding non-discursive aspects of violent attacks and other events. Flagg Miller's analysis of Bin Laden's extensive collection of audio-cassettes captured in Kandahar in 2002 also adds valuable context. The value of audio-cassettes to Arab culture compared with printed or digital media is discussed further on in this chapter.

Focal points for analysis of the *Al Qaeda* narrative are key texts: discursive and non-discursive events that signify social change, in terms of either narrative or mode of action. Important nodes in the *Al Qaeda* narrative are the 1996 Ladenese memorandum and the 1998 World Islamic Front declaration. Especially in the latter text, the tone became more aggressive and the focus narrower. Activities employed to prepare and execute attacks were mostly covert and only partially revealed by post-attack declarations, criminal investigations and intelligence gathering. Therefore, the centre of gravity of the *Al Qaeda* narrative described in this chapter leans towards the public dimension. Still, as it includes descriptions of non-discursive actions and studies on non-public statements, this is distinctly different from other approaches. For example, British international relations scholar Donald Holbrook's analysis of 'the Al-Qaeda doctrine' is limited to public addresses.[8] This chapter maintains a wider view and discusses 'propagandists' and 'planners'.

Analysing translations of Arab texts implies that a part of the meaning is literally lost in translation. There is a tendency in translations to 'unpack' complex constructions and enhance simplification.[9] However, there are a number of similarities between Arabic and English that enable adequate analysis of English translations.[10] In addition to text analysis, various academic studies of key texts have been incorporated in this analysis as they relate to either meanings, text, settings or the wider background. The main theoretical focus in the narrative is the phenomenon of securitization. Language and culture together set the scene and provide messages to resonate within specific contexts. As Middle Eastern scholar at Duke University Mbaye Lo notes, Quranic or classical Arabic is mystified and elevated as a sacred language.[11] It is an Arabic tradition to equate good grammar with good morals.[12] Communicating in classical Arabic creates a religious setting and enhances Arab cultural identity, as the language is the primary vehicle of Islam.[13] The wider context provided to situate the texts is rooted in an array of studies on Al Qaeda, jihadism and Salafism. They put the analysed key texts and events in perspective.

BIN LADEN'S BASE

To provide an understanding of the wider context, this chapter starts with a brief overview of preceding historical events and circumstances that are relevant to the narrative. A natural epoch in which to situate the *Al Qaeda* narrative is the Afghan war in the 1970s and 1980s, when Bin Laden and his followers and the United States fought on the same side against the 'godless' communist regime. It is during this period that Bin Laden gained social status through his religious knowledge, his fighting reputation, the size and nature of his group of followers, and his moral standing.

Osama bin Laden held no formal religious degree. He was the son of an illiterate Yemeni who gained the trust of the al-Saud family and earned billions with building contracts, most notably for doing work on the Holy Sanctuaries in Jerusalem, Mecca and Medina. Later, he studied economics at King Abd al-Aziz University in Jeddah in the 1970s. It gave him the chance to attend courses in Islamic studies taught by Muhammad Qutb and Abdullah Azzam, both members of the Egyptian Muslim Brotherhood.[14] Muhammed Qutb

Social structures

Social practices

Discursive practice

Texts | Texts | Texts

e.g. Bin Laden statements

Translations (e.g. FBIS, CTC, Lawrence, Kepel and Milelli, MSA)

Reproduction and recontextualization in Arab news media, e.g. Al Hayat, Al-Quds Al-Arabi, Al Jazeera (translations)

Interpretations (e.g. Miller, Gergez)

Formal audience

Moral audience

General texts (translations)

Key texts (translations)

The World Islamic Front, February 23 1998

All these American crimes and sins are a clear proclamation of war against God, his messenger, and the Muslims.

Religious scholars throughout Islamic history have agreed that *jihad* is an individual duty when an enemy attacks Muslim countries. This was related by the Imam ibn Qudama in "The Resource," by Imam al-Kisa'I in "The Marvels," by al-Qurtubi in his exegesis, and by the Sheikh of Islam when he states in his chronicles that "As for fighting to repel an enemy, which is the strongest way to defend freedom and religion, it is agreed that this is a duty. After faith, there is no greater duty than fighting an enemy who is corrupting religion and the world."

On this basis, and in accordance with God's will, we pronounce to all Muslims the following judgement: To kill the Americans and their allies – civilians and military – is an individual duty incumbent upon every Muslim in all countries, in order to liberate the al-Aqsa Mosque and the Holy Mosque from their grip, so that their armies leave all the territory of Islam, defeated, broken, and unable to threaten any Muslim.

This is in accordance with the words of God Almighty: "Fight the idolators at any time, if they first fight you;" "Fight them until there is no more persecution and until worship is devoted to God;" "Why should you not fight in God's cause and for those oppressed men, women, and children who cry out: 'Lord, rescue us from this town whose people are oppressors! By Your grace, give us a protector and a helper!?"

Key sections

Securitization elements (securitizing actor, referent subject, referent object, customized policy)

On this basis, and in accordance with God's will, we pronounce to all Muslims the following judgement: To kill the Americans and their allies – civilians and military – is an individual duty incumbent upon every Muslim in all countries, in order to liberate the al-Aqsa Mosque and the Holy Mosque from their grip, so that their armies leave all the territory of Islam, defeated, broken, and unable to threaten any Muslim.

Limited textual analysis

Sentence, clause, lexicon, grammar

Wider background context literature

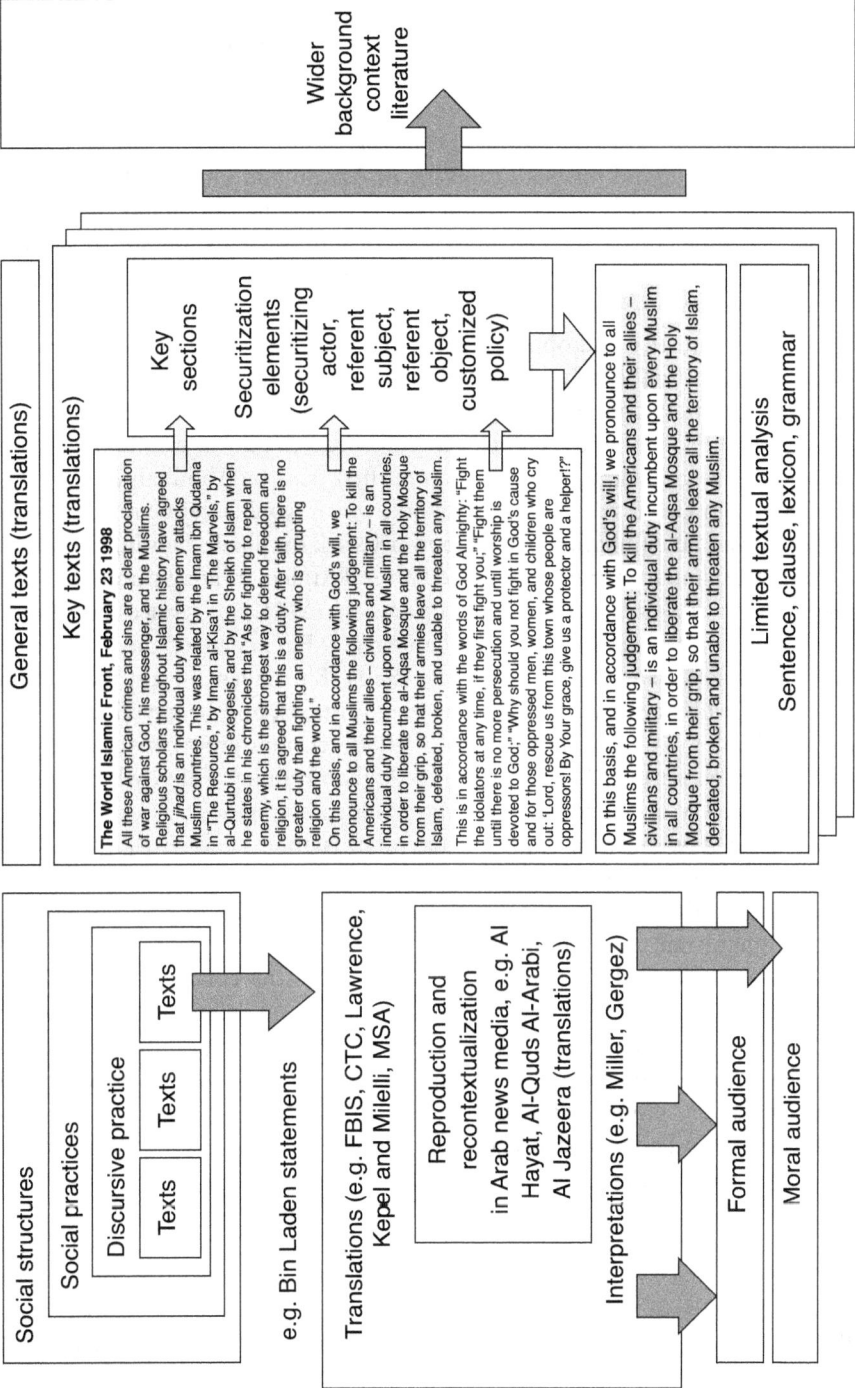

Figure 2.1 Schematic overview of text selection and analysis

was a brother of Sayyid Qutb, the highly influential Egyptian scholar who was executed in 1966 for being one of the main voices of the radical Islamist movement that threatened Arab nationalism. Abdullah Azzam was a professor of Palestinian origin who lived in Jordan before he was forced to relocate to Jeddah in 1973 because of his radical thought.

The ideological and religious thinking of Azzam and Qutb with which Bin Laden interacted would prove to influence him for the remainder of his life. This will become apparent when analysing some of the texts that are key to the *Al Qaeda* narrative. In the poetry of both Sayyid Qutb and Bin Laden, death for the sake of Allah appears as an honourable alternative for the oppressed. Humiliation, injustice and oppression are central themes that necessitate resistance and prioritise the holy struggle of *jihad* against other enemies. Bin Laden admired Azzam's uncompromising attitude on armed struggle as an individual duty for Muslims. He left university without a degree and was eventually drawn to the war in Afghanistan, facilitated on his first trips by Abdullah Azzam.[15]

Initially, Bin Laden's developing network, which would later be referred to as *Al Qaeda*, was a continuation of a support network for jihadis fighting the Soviet invaders. The support network facilitated several Afghan training camps and was called *Maktab al-Khadamat al-Mujahidin al-Arab* (MAK), or services bureau for Arab mujahidin.[16] Together with Abdullah Azzam, Bin Laden led the MAK from Peshawar in Pakistan. During the early 1980s, Bin Laden mostly focused on establishing a library of Arab-language religious texts, and he gave Islamic history and theology classes. However, as of 1986, tensions grew between the two men. Bin Laden set up *Al-Faruq*, his own Afghan training camp, which hosted more advanced weapons training and more in-depth religious classes.

Ayman al-Zawahiri, the leader of Egyptian Islamic Jihad (EIJ), also joined the network. He and Bin Laden increasingly thought of spending MAK funds beyond Afghanistan.[17] On the other hand, Azzam wanted to limit spending to Afghanistan, possibly including Palestine at a later date, but opposed using MAK funds in Egypt. Abdullah Azzam saw the concept of *Al Qaeda al-sulba* as a 'solid base' formed by actual territory and defended militarily. He thus opposed Bin Laden and al-Zawahiri's notion of a revolution instigated by a small clandestine group. This was contrary to al-Zawahiri's interests. In November 1989, months after the Soviets had left Afghanistan, Azzam was assassinated. Bin Laden and al-Zawahiri continued to coordinate communication in the international network as jihadis left Afghanistan to fight elsewhere, such as in Bosnia, Chechnya, Algeria and the Philippines.

During the late 1980s, Bin Laden had established his credentials as a jihadi fighting the Soviet forces in Afghanistan, something that would continue to be illustrated in later interviews, picturing Bin Laden with captured Kalashnikov rifles. A myth founding his reputation describes a battle near the town of Jaji in 1987: outnumbered *jihad* fighters led by Osama bin Laden fought against Soviet special forces; Bin Laden had organised a training camp there and was able to defend it for a week.[18] Bin Laden became notorious especially for choosing to endure the harsh conditions in the camp despite being the descendant of a wealthy Saudi family. Many present-day Western scholars and journalists have pointed out that it was useless for a few hundred Arab fighters to attempt to contribute to the war in Afghanistan from a small camp within range of Soviet forces. But from Bin Laden's perspective, such reasoning surpassed the true value of the experience there. The name of the camp, *Ma'sadat al-Ansar*, or 'Lion's den of the supporters', refers to the early days of Islam and is associated with courage and open defiance.[19] Although the camp was of very limited use from a military perspective, it proved to be invaluable in symbolic terms for decades to come.[20]

After returning to Saudi Arabia in 1989, Bin Laden became a famous speaker in public places. Some of his speeches on audio-cassette were sold hundreds of thousands of times.[21] These were loved not only because of Bin Laden's reputation, but perhaps even more because of his eloquent use of classical Arabic.[22] As the traditional language of Islam, anyone who masters the language (*fasaha*) and the art of good rhetoric (*balagha*) in such a high degree is held in high esteem.[23] Audio-cassettes have a significant role in Arab culture as a decentralised medium to transfer messages among the population, including a large illiterate audience.[24] In addition to putting across a message, it also enables the transfer of more emotion, sincerity and refinement of the arguments through the sound and intonation of the speaker's voice.

It is mainly through audio-cassettes and Arab newspapers that Bin Laden was able to present himself as a war hero with a testament of faith before a vastly superior Soviet enemy, and to advocate a purer and ascetic Arabian Islam.[25] The central theme of his speeches in the 1980s was the necessity to take up arms against the Soviets. It is significant that even in his early addresses to his Saudi audience, Bin Laden noted how 'Jerusalem has been taken' from the Muslims and how 'Arabs have been shamed and disgraced'.[26]

In 1990, Iraq invaded Kuwait, giving the Saudi government reason to be somewhat concerned for their security. Bin Laden offered them his international network of jihadi fighters to protect the Saudi borders, as they had 'successfully' fought against the Soviets in Afghanistan. After the Soviets withdrew, funding for the mujahedeen decreased drastically, and attention on the Arab fighters there also faded. The recent developments in Kuwait provided a new sense of purpose for Bin Laden and his followers. However, the Saudi king rejected the suggestion as a grotesque idea. Instead, he accepted an offer from the United States to host their troops in defence of further aggression by Iraqi President Saddam Hussein. This was insulting for Osama bin Laden at a personal and a religious level. To be patronised by a regime that allowed a non-Muslim military force in the land of the two Holy Places (*Al-Masjid al-Haram* in Mecca and *Al-Masjid an-Nabawi* in Medina) remained a source of aggravation as US troops remained in the country after the Gulf War was over in 1991.

After becoming increasingly publicly critical of the Saudi government, Bin Laden was placed under house arrest and lost access to a significant part of his family wealth. With the help of his family, he fled to Africa, where he accepted an invitation from the Sudanese leader of the National Islamic Front, Hassan al-Turabi. Al-Turabi sought to establish a pan-Islamic network that could support his efforts against his domestic (Christian) enemies, and also welcomed Bin Laden's investments. With an estimated number of more than a thousand jihadi fighters associated with the *Al Qaeda* network, Bin Laden settled in Sudan in 1991 to train Sudanese forces in guerrilla tactics.[27] In the early 1990s, Bin Laden's religious and socio-political ideas took further shape. He also managed to transform his network into a more corporate-type organisation. By setting up agricultural companies and other businesses, Bin Laden was able to ensure funding for his religious and socio-political activities and communiqués. As discussed further in Chapter 4, in interviews Bin Laden denied supporting any form of terrorism.

Bin Laden was probably providing some support to groups fighting against US troops in Somalia, although to what extent is subject to debate.[28] Hence, the precise relationship between Bin Laden and his followers, and Arab Afghan fighters in Somalia has remained unclear. At various levels, they had shared experiences, acquaintances and worldviews. However, Bin Laden never publicly claimed responsibility for attacks there, and only pointed more generally to how Muslims in Somalia cooperated with 'Arab Mujahedeen'.[29] However, Bin Laden did refer in his rhetoric to how the US operation in Somalia had led to the death of tens of thousands of Muslims. Together with some of his close followers, he also issued statements in 1992 in which people were ordered to attack US troops in Saudi Arabia.[30] Years later, in 1998 and 1999, it was the bombings of the Mövenpick Hotel and the Gold Mohur Hotel in Aden on 29 December 1992 that Bin Laden claimed to be the 'first operational victory of *Al Qaeda* against the crusaders'.[31] An Austrian and a hotel employee were killed and seven others wounded. US soldiers had been staying at the hotels before the attacks, but no Americans were present during the bombings. The attacks occurred only weeks after the US operation 'Restore Hope' had begun to support the United Nations Operation in Somalia (UNOSOM).

Bin Laden and his closest followers viewed the battle of Mogadishu as another move by the United States to strengthen its grip on the region and impose its will on Muslims. These sentiments resonated with the wider Islamist movement represented across the Arab and Muslim world, of which the diverse leadership was brought together by Sudanese President Hassan al-Turabi during several conferences.[32] There was a perception among Bin Laden's closest follow-ers that the battle was 'the second claw of a pincer movement' after the United States had already stationed troops in Saudi Arabia, the land of the two Holy Places.[33] For them, the US humanitarian relief operation was possibly only the beginning of an increasing American involvement in the region. In Sudan, the United States could come to assist Christians against the Muslims, threatening the Islamist regime in Khartoum.

On 26 February 1993, a truck bomb exploded under the north tower of the World Trade Center (WTC). The organizer of the attack, Ramzi Youssef, devel-oped his plan in Afghan training camps in the early 1990s. His uncle, Khalid Sheikh Mohammed (KSM), provided some funding for the attack. A non-gov-ernmental organisation run by KSM had supported fighters in Afghanistan and Pakistan in cooperation with Abdullah Azzam. Despite this link to the MAK and Bin Laden, Yousef sent several letters to New York newspapers claiming he belonged to the 'Liberation Army, Fifth Battalion' and by no means referred to anything like 'Al Qaeda'.[34] During the investigation into the WTC bomb-ing, the FBI connected the perpetrators to the Blind Sheikh.[35] There was social interconnectedness of the people in Bin Laden's network with other radical Islamists, including the Blind Sheikh, but nothing like direction or some chain of command.[36]

The Egyptians

In the early 1990s, 'the Egyptians' belonging to the EIJ increasingly gained influence over Osama bin Laden. EIJ was a derivate of the Cairo faction within *Tanzin Al-Jihad*, a radical political Islamic (or Islamist) organisation that emerged in the 1970s under Egyptian President Sadat and was allowed to counter the Marxist movement. This Islamist thinking was based on the ideas of Abu al-A'la Mawdudi, Sayyid Qutb and Ibn Taymiyya that Muslims had dis-carded traditional moral values (*jahiliyya*).[37] Muslim societies were no longer considered Islamic. After the Yom Kippur War, Sadat signed a peace treaty with Israel in 1979 that returned the Sinai to Egypt. The radical Islamists accused him of giving up Palestine and a rift occurred. Sadat was eventually assassi-nated in 1981 by *Al-Jihad* members hoping to start mass protests and instigate a Sunni revolution similar to the Iranian revolution in 1979. Vigorously battled by Sadat's successor Hosni Mubarak in the 1980s, the *Al-Jihad* leadership was arrested, and most radical Islamists went underground. Many of the Cairo fac-tion fled to Pakistan and formed the EIJ. This was how their ideas inspired a wider movement across the region, including in Pakistan. Nominally still led by Abbud al-Zumur, who was imprisoned in Egypt, it was de facto Sayyed Imam al-Sharif (also known as Dr Fadl) who headed the EIJ group. In 1988, in Peshawar, al-Sharif wrote 'The Essential Guide for Preparation (for Jihad)', in which he pointed out that defeating the Soviets was not the real victory:

ultimately, that was eternal salvation and martyrdom.[38] This book would continue to have influence among EIJ and Bin Laden followers, even after al-Sharif stepped down as a de facto leader of EIJ.

In 1991, Ayman al-Zawahiri autocratically took control of the group and broke with al-Zumur. It was al-Zawahiri who wanted to train and build the group in Afghanistan and Sudan to eventually create an Islamic state in Egypt, and from there to launch a jihad to liberate Jerusalem from the Jews (and fight Western influence). This resonated with Bin Laden's ideas of confronting the West or 'head of the snake', and contrasted those of Abdullah Azzam, who primarily wanted to rebuild Afghanistan.[39] The divide between al-Zawahiri and Azzam was of a deeper nature, as Azzam had been a prominent Muslim Brotherhood member. In his 1992 book *The Bitter Harvest*, al-Zawahiri critically reflected on sixty years of Muslim Brotherhood history.[40] He denounced the movement for an array of reasons, such as recognising and allying rulers who did not govern 'according to revealed law', legitimising the constitution as the proper way to establish change, and rejecting the use of violence.[41] Al-Zawahiri noted that *Al-Jihad* expected Muslim Brothers to repent their errors publicly, to condemn the apostasy of tyrants, to 'disavow these tyrants and their impious laws', and to believe and act according to the individual duty of jihad.[42] This was because if someone refused to wage a violent jihad, he would be punished by God and replaced by someone else. As terrorism consultant and former US foreign service officer Marc Sageman notes, when al-Zawahiri took control, the EIJ became 'a free-floating network without any real ties to its original or its surrounding society'.[43]

Bin Laden and al-Zawahiri found a common interest in sharing and combining Bin Laden's wealth and network with al-Zawahiri's experience and rigid directions. This also resulted in the installation of an Egyptian security detail, limiting access to Bin Laden to the extent that it even became more difficult for Abdullah Azzam to speak with him in private. This caused friction among other followers of Bin Laden such as those of Arab origin and from other African countries.[44] The Egyptians also increasingly strained Bin Laden's relationship with the Sudanese government. The EIJ perpetrators of an assassination attempt on Mubarak (during his visit to Eritrea) were allowed to hide with Bin Laden in Sudan.[45] This led to increased international pressure on Sudan to expel them. On another occasion, Egyptian intelligence officers were able to blackmail the son of an EIJ member into spying. As this came out, EIJ members tried and executed the boy.[46] This led to an unforgiving response from the Sudanese government. EIJ members were welcome, but not allowed to judge and execute sentences. Also complicating the relations between the Sudanese government and Bin Laden were some associated members of the Libyan Islamic Fighting Group. Under pressure from Libya, the Sudanese government was forced to oust all Libyan Bin Laden followers belonging to this group. However, as stated, despite these internal formal and informal shifts of influence, Bin Laden still remained the public face. As of late 2000 the podium was shared more explicitly with al-Zawahiri and others.[47] This falls outside the scope of this book.

SHAPES OF AL QAEDA

Different sources have highlighted various aspects of Bin Laden's messages and the activities of his followers in the early 1990s. In other words, different accounts have focused on discursive or non-discursive actions. While some public accounts have highlighted a non-violent (rhetorical) direction, other sources have pointed to initiatives and covert preparations for more violent actions that supported an international *jihad*. It was in these accounts of non-discursive actions that the outline of an organisation, or a 'hard core *Al Qaeda* element', emerged, in addition to the wider social network of which Bin Laden was part. The increase in Bin Laden's discursive practices reflected the development of his ideas and intention to reach an increasing Arab and Western audience.

The National Commission on Terrorist Attacks upon the United States' (the '9/11 Commission') extensive two-year inquiry contextualised the events and circumstances related to Bin Laden in the light of the attacks on the United States on 11 September 2001. Its final report mentioned how Bin Laden's offices in Cyprus, Zagreb, Sarajevo and Baku covertly 'provided financial and other support for terrorist activities' as he simultaneously built an 'Islamic army' by joining forces with Islamist groups across the Arab world, Africa and Asia.[48] Because of his links with these other groups, the report associated Bin Laden with several attacks occurring in the 1990s. He was reportedly involved in transporting weapons across the region and unsuccessfully sought the 'capability to kill on a mass scale' by attempting to acquire uranium.[49] This episode was also described in detail by Ali Soufan.[50]

In contrast, Mbaye Lo states that Bin Laden was predominantly a passive businessman during his Sudan years, involved with road building and agricultural activities. He 'only became active as a Jihadi when the French and the Americans engaged the Sudanese government to surrender him'.[51] Between 1992 and 1994, Bin Laden coordinated his activities with the Saudi opposition Committee for the Defence of Islamic Rights and even attempted to establish 'a proxy political party in Saudi Arabia'.[52] It was after the committee released a 'Memorandum of Advice' in 1992 which was critical of the Saudi regime that the 107 signatories were harassed and jailed, forcing several of them to flee to London.

Bin Laden started to gain a profile in Western and Arab media in the early 1990s as a critic of the Saudi government and US foreign policies in the region.[53] The presence of US troops in the land of the two Holy Places was disgraceful; Saudi man-made laws that contradicted fundamental Islamic values indicated the lack of religious legitimacy; and incidents during the annual pilgrimage in Mecca, the *Hajj*, illustrated the inability of the Saudi government to function as the protector of the Holy Places. He was not alone: in 1992, a group of 109 religious scholars and clerics forwarded an extensive declaration with similar points to the Saudi king.[54] Many of the 1992 memorandum signatories were arrested and tortured. Bin Laden was stripped of his Saudi nationality. Over the next few years, the Saudi government arrested 200 junior and senior scholars for supporting *jihad* and challenging the American footprint in the country.[55]

These developments motivated Bin Laden to set up the Advice and Reform Committee (ARC) in London in 1994. The office professionalised and simplified the worldwide circulation of communiqués. The ARC became an important node in the international network of Saudi oppositionists. Through the media office's use of faxes and the developing internet, Bin Laden was able to circumvent Saudi state media control and publish freely to reach a global Arabic-speaking audience. Starting satellite TV stations like Al Jazeera were an addition to the internet. Furthermore, as an alternative to newspaper articles, speeches were distributed on audio-tapes across the Arab world. Consequently, the number of his communiqués increased starkly. Between April 1994 and May 1996, at least sixteen open letters were released, and one interview held. Repeatedly, Bin Laden discussed the legitimacy of Saudi social, religious and security policies, warning Saudi security officials and raising objections on the rulings of Sheikh Bin Baz, the country's highest religious authority.[56]

In November 1995, a US-operated military training centre in Riyadh was attacked with two truck bombs. Five Americans and two Indians were killed. Another attack on US military personnel occurred in Saudi Arabia seven months later. On 25 June 1996, a truck exploded before an apartment building in Khobar, killing nineteen US airmen and wounding almost 500 other people of various backgrounds. The attacks marked heightened tensions in Saudi Arabia. In open letters Bin Laden emphasised the constellation of a submissive power relation to the United States that characterised Saudi foreign policies such as the peace process. This power relation served American interests and enabled them to project a military capability in the region.

Although the incidents in Saudi Arabia fit with Bin Laden's views and statements, he did not publicly claim responsibility for the attacks. At the time, the United States did not hold him directly responsible. The bombings in Khobar occurred one month after Bin Laden was forced to relocate to Afghanistan following heavy international pressure on the Sudanese government to stop hosting him. As mentioned, apart from the Riyadh attack and Bin Laden's statements, there was also the failed attempt to assassinate Egyptian President Hosni Mubarak in Addis Ababa that was linked to some of the Egyptians in Sudan. In May 1996, the political pressure increased to such an extent that Bin Laden was not only asked to leave the country, but also stripped of his Sudanese nationality.

As a stateless person, he and his family left for Afghanistan. It was an area he knew well, and Bin Laden was successful in gaining the trust of the Taliban by offering investments and equipment in support of their fight for control over the country. Despite this, however, Miller notes that this was a time when he was 'confronting the bleakest prospects of his career'.[57] He was stateless, accompanied by only several hundred followers, deprived of millions in family funding, and unable to retrieve his immense investments from the Sudanese government.

By examining Bin Laden through the various prisms offered by Flagg Miller, Fawaz Gerges, the 9/11 Commission, Mbaye Lo and others, it becomes clear that his presence and activities in Saudi Arabia, Afghanistan and Sudan up to 1996 were multifaceted, and not all in light of financing or organising terrorist activities against the United States. Moreover, it was not until after his 1996 declaration that the United States became a more prominent (or as some say, the most prominent) evil to target.[58] But for all the anti-American language used, it was still the 'Islamic community's own weakest link', the Muslims themselves and the corrupt regional Muslim regimes, against which the messages were directed.

Ultimately, the communiqués of the early 1990s culminated in the 'Ladenese Epistle', the comprehensive and key text distributed on audio-cassette to tens of thousands of people, published in *Al-Quds Al-Arabi* on 23 August 1996, and translated into English by Saudi oppositionist Al-Mas'ari, the CIA's Foreign Broadcast Information Service and others.[59] Partly as a consequence, between late 1996 and early 1998, there was a period of extensive international news media exposure for Bin Laden. The following section presents the textual and contextual analysis of this key text.

Bin Laden's Speech in 1996

Genre and style

The 1996 speech was recorded and printed in various forms. Tens of thousands of these copied recordings probably circulated throughout the Arab world.[60] The medium allowed for a decentralised distribution of a message that contained not only the words, but also the sound and emotion of the speaker, emphasising certain parts of the speech over others. It was a genre with which Bin Laden was quite familiar. Partially helped and promoted by the Saudi government, an earlier recorded speech of Bin Laden in 1990 had sold over 250,000 copies in the kingdom.[61] That was at a time when Bin Laden mostly reflected on the deeds of the Saudi-supported Arab Afghan mujahedeen. The favourable Saudi attitude towards Bin Laden had shifted gradually as he became increasingly critical of the Saudi regime.

The 1996 key speech was submitted via Bin Laden's London-based media office, the ARC, to the London-based Pan-Arabic newspaper *Al-Quds Al-Arabi*.

However, in contrast to earlier statements, it was emphasised that this text came from Bin Laden personally, not the ARC.[62] On 23 August 1996, a 750-word summary was published in *Al-Quds Al-Arabi*. With an estimated circulation of 15,000 or more, the article reached a significant literate Pan-Arab audience spread over major cities in the world.[63] It was the leading story of that edition, titled 'Bin Laden Calls for Guerrilla War to Expel "The American Occupiers" from Saudi Arabia' ('Bin Ladin Yadú li-Harb 'Isbat li-Ikhraj 'Al-Muhtallin Al-Amrikiyin'min Al-Sa'udiyyah').[64] Taking into account the elements that were left out of the *Al-Quds Al-Arabi* summary, it would be more adequate to balance the focus on the United States in the headline with a critique on the Saudi regime, and to include other types of resistance than guerrilla warfare against the regime and the occupier. Miller, Lo and Holbrook have argued that it is mostly through this printed publication that Bin Laden's message became known in the Arab world.[65] However, despite the difference in the circulation speed between audio-cassettes and printed newspapers, it is also the audio-cassettes that had a major impact in the Arab world as a medium, especially among illiterate Arabs hearing messages in a taxi, cassette shop, cafe or other public place. Thus, the impact of the Bin Laden speech on audio-cassette should not be underestimated.

It is insightful to problematise the genre of Bin Laden's 1996 speech. English translations are most commonly titled a 'declaration of war' or defined as an Islamic juridical decree (*fatwa*). A *fatwa* is characterised by a lack of political motives, however, and such motives were not missing in the text. The speech also deviated from the *fatwa* tradition as it did not relate to a specific question with a narrow and specific response. According to Islamic intellectual tradition, what was allowed for Muslims was to conduct prayer to Allah, the Prophet Muhammed and his companions (*basmalah*), and to remind other Muslims of their individual religious duties (*tadhkiir*), even without a formal religious degree.[66] Bin Laden translated this individual duty to economic resistance and physical *jihad* against the corrupt Saudi regime and the 'Zionist Crusader occupation' in Saudi Arabia. The Saudi regime was oppressive and increasingly following man-made laws instead of Islamic law. To motivate this view, Bin Laden provided an array of political and religious arguments.

Also illustrative of the extent to which the speech deviated from a carefully crafted *fatwa* was Bin Laden's selective reciting of the Quran and the Prophet Muhammed's deeds (*ahadith*) to suit his argument. Most notably, Bin Laden selectively recited a Medinan verse on repentance (*surah At-Tawbah*):

> The most Exalted said in the verse of As-Sayef, The Sword 'so when the sacred months have passed away, then slay the idolaters where ever you find them, and take them captives and besiege them and lie in wait for them in every ambush'. (At-Tawbah 9:5)[67]

The second part of the phrase on repentance was excluded:

> . . . But if they should repent, establish prayer, and give zakah, let them [go] on their way. Indeed, Allah is Forgiving and Merciful. (At Tawbah 9:5)[68]

Characterisations of the text as *fatwa* or declaration of war were also some-what problematic as they implied that Bin Laden was a leader of a defined group of followers, and had the legal and religious credentials and the moral authority to declare a war. In the mid-1990s, this was not the case. However, through his epistle and previous publications, Bin Laden's legitimacy as a scholar of the moral intent of Islamic law was beginning to emerge. In December 1994, he had written a letter to the Saudi Chief Mufti Abd al-Aziz ibn Baz critiquing his endorsement of the Oslo agreement between Israel and Palestine. In 1995, he wrote a letter to the Saudi King Fahd objecting to his decisions to invite American troops to Saudi Arabia and to adopt man-made laws. This 1996 Ladenese Epistle was his third major statement intended for a wider audience.

Bin Laden's leadership status initially came from his family's status and his fund-raising ability, which in part also relied on his connections with the Saudi elite. In the Saudi and wider Arab public eye, Bin Laden had managed to present himself as a courageous leader of Arab Afghan mujahedeen fighters. Illustrative was that in Afghanistan and Sudan, Bin Laden was photographed many times riding a horse: in Muslim tradition, this is an important symbol of courage and heroism.[69] The closing statement of the Ladenese Epistle also appealed to this symbol and projected an image of Bin Laden leading the 'cavalry of Islam'.[70] The actual size of his group of followers at the time was less important in the epistle than the location where the group resided. Bin Laden also explicitly referred to 'myself and my group' once in the text as he explained that they had suffered from injustice like others.[71] There was no mention of the name *Al Qaeda* or anything resembling an organisation in the epistle. But it was from the mountains of Khurasan that the group began the work of 'talking and discussing the ways of correcting what has happened'.[72] For jihadis, Khurasan was a highly symbolic base from which to operate. Several Islamic *hadith*s refer to an army led by the Mahdi, a descendant of the Prophet Mohammed, marching from Khurasan to Jerusalem to liberate all Muslims.[73] The Madhi was a redeemer at the end of times. Bin Laden was respected for his deeds against the Soviets in Afghanistan, his influence, net-work and financial resources. But in the mid-1990s he was deprived of most of that when he had been forced to leave Sudan.

Given cultural and religious norms and values, his deprived situation in 1996 did not degrade the strength of Bin Laden's message before Arab and Muslim audiences. One of the most powerful and inspiring aspects of Bin Laden's public image was that he had traded the possibility of a luxurious life for caves and trenches in Afghanistan out of principled beliefs. Self-abnegation or asceticism (*zuhd*) is an important and powerful idiom in Islam;[74] it has been practised by historic figures and exemplary Muslims. Leaving wealth and belongings aside enables one to practise self-discipline and prepare for the afterlife.

Depicting the text as a memorandum (*mudhakkira*), instead of a declaration of war or *fatwa*, expresses how especially the audio recording was a more versatile message.[75] In a memorandum, an author attempts to give his or her advice or 'legal opinion' to the audience in a dignified way. According to Miller, the extensive epistle articulates eloquence and provided Bin Laden with ample opportunity to 'artfully combine colourful pleasantries, competitive verbal jousts, and political wrangling'.[76] Miller notes how it was especially Bin Laden's extensive use of poetry (*qasidah*) that strengthened the emotional appeal of specific topics in the message. It increased the passion rather than the ideas in the texts.[77] As an example, Miller highlights the poem about 'Amru Ibn Hind, a Nestorian Christian regent whose dynasty capitulated to Persian conquerors. The poem was produced by 'Amru Ibn Kulthum Al-Taghlibi, king of a powerful Arab tribe in pre-Islamic times who felt humiliated and killed 'Amru Ibn Hind.[78] It was positioned in the part where Bin Laden directly addressed US Secretary of Defense William Perry about the spirit and willingness of the Muslim youths to fight.

Among Arabs familiar with the well-known poem, it caused or resonated with feelings of resistance and the rejection of a regent who was illegitimate. As such, even though it was cited while addressing William Perry, it underlined Bin Laden's argument against the Saudi regime that allowed US forces onto the land of the two Holy Sanctuaries and followed man-made laws instead of Islamic law. What this indicates is that the argument against the Saudi regime was the primary argument in the 1996 text, and of greater significance than arguments made against the United States. For an important part, this was strengthened by the moral resonance of the poetry that made up roughly a third of the speech on the audio-cassette – a part that was left out of most English translations and to some extent the *Al-Quds Al-Arabi* article.

Regarding this aspect, Fawaz Gerges even states that 'stripped of its anti-US rhetoric and drama, transnational jihad was Bin Laden's fig leaf, masking a desire to seize power in his native land'.[79] Flagg Miller obviously shares a similar opinion: anti-US rhetoric provided the necessary stepping stone to rally support for this objective in the long term. Others like Donald Holbrook and Dutch Middle Eastern studies scholar Pieter Nanninga have acknowledged critical references to the house of Saud, but argue that the focus of the text is in fact on the United States.[80] However, when taking into account his 1995 open letter to King Fahd, many of the themes reoccurred and the form of both texts was quite similar.[81] Moreover, the *qasidah* poetry made the opposition to the Saudi regime more prominent (at least equal to rejecting the United States) before Arab audiences.[82]

Audiences: identifying and relating self and other

The memorandum began by addressing all Muslim believers around the world.[83] The *ummah*, or the global community of Muslims, represented the idealised broader audience of the text in the widest sense. Substitutes such as 'my Muslim brothers' or 'the people of Islam' all related to the community of which Bin Laden and 'his group' felt they were part. Bin Laden also portrayed himself specifically as being among the group of Islamic scholars (*ulema*), highlighting how they had suffered oppression in Saudi Arabia and were unable to express their legitimate critical opinions as 'advocates of correction'. He subsequently added how he had himself been pursued in Pakistan, Sudan and Afghanistan by the Saudi government and its allies.[84] Finally, after a long absence, he found a 'safe base' in the Hindu Kush mountains in 'Khurasan'.[85] Miller emphasises how in the speech recording, Bin Laden's voice reached its highest pitch the moment he mentioned this, signalling relief and gratitude.[86] From there, he and his group began 'the work, talking and discussing the ways of correcting'. Bin Laden went to great lengths to highlight the intellectual and non-violent nature of the efforts made by the *ulema*, as they were merely trying to provide 'polite' advice to the Saudi regime.

In terms of action, a prominent audience of the memorandum was the Saudi population. Saudi Muslims were addressed as Bin Laden attributed the deteriorating economic situation of the country to Saudi government corruption, mismanagement, and US policy and presence. In addition to poetry, the frequency of terms referring to the Saudi 'regime' indicated its central position in the text, as that was what the Saudi population had to oppose. The Saudi regime adopted man-made laws over religious laws, controlled the news media, neglected social services, and insufficiently invested in infrastructure and security forces. The regime was unable to facilitate and protect visitors of the pilgrimage to Mecca (the *Hajj*), while Saudi officials gave priority to American oil interests and personal gain over the wellbeing and living conditions of the people. As stated, these complaints were also raised by Bin Laden and other Saudi scholars in earlier open letters to the Saudi regime.

The reason for action was suppression. The regime 'had closed all peaceful routes and pushed the people to armed action'.[87] They had betrayed the *ummah* and joined the unbelievers or polytheists who did not believe in the oneness (*tahwid*) of God. Bin Laden called upon the Saudi Muslim population to reject the legitimacy of the Saudi regime and fight the occupation by all means. American goods had to be boycotted. Before Arab audiences, the strength of the reasoning for this boycott was enhanced through its reference to asceticism (*zuhd*) and the broader style in which Bin Laden presented himself.

Moreover, Bin Laden warned Saudi security personnel that the regime wanted to play civilians and military personnel against each other, and warned them not to act against people resisting oppression.

Mentioned almost as much in the texts as the Saudi regime was the 'Zionist–Crusader Alliance' (ZCA) and its regional allies in the broader Arab world. The United States was portrayed as the main or 'greatest unbeliever' (*Kufr*) that unrightfully controlled the Islamic countries, as it led the alliance with the Jewish people. The terms 'crusader' and 'Zionist' were metaphors for the United States, Israel and other allies, with a connotation to the history of Islam. In general Arab discourse, these terms have a negative connotation. Other derogatory terms used frequently in a related manner in the memorandum were 'iniquitous', 'enemies', 'occupiers', 'horrifying', 'massacres', 'a clear conspiracy' and 'propaganda'. They added to processes of identification of self (the Muslim *ummah*) and other (ZCA).

According to the memorandum, the people of Islam had 'suffered from the aggression, iniquity and injustice imposed on them by the ZCA and its collaborators' in Palestine, Iraq, Lebanon, Tajikistan, Burma, Kashmir, Assam, Malaysia, the Philippines, Somalia, Eritrea, Chechnya and Bosnia-Herzegovina.[88] A 'clear conspiracy' between the United States and its allies 'under the cover of the iniquitous United Nations' prevented the people from obtaining arms to defend themselves.[89] The most recent and gravest of the 'aggressions' described was the 'occupation' of Saudi Arabia, the land of the two Holy Places, by the armies of the American crusaders. As long as the country was under control of the ZCA, it was useless to act against the Saudi regime. The use of the word 'occupation' as superlative of control was extensive.

It was in relation to this 'greatest unbeliever' that Bin Laden's main focus on the youths of Islam, the 'men of the bright future of Mohammed's nation', became clear.[90] As a subgroup of both the global Muslim community (*ummah*) and the Saudi population, Bin Laden devoted roughly a quarter of the memorandum to very explicitly addressing the heroic deeds of the courageous 'youth of Islam'. These youths, or 'sons' of the land of the two Holy Places, had come out to fight and defend Afghanistan against the Soviets, Bosnia-Herzegovina against the Serbs, and Chechnya against the Russians. As Bin Laden reminded the youths, the battle they fought was not finished yet; and he also claimed they were prepared to die to defend the Holy Land.[91] Ultimately, the appropriate remedy for the threat against the Muslim *ummah* lay in the hands of the youths: 'explosions and jihad'.[92] Bin Laden addressed US Secretary of Defense William Perry directly as he threatened the United States:

> The youths also reciting the All Mighty words of: 'so when you meet in battle those who disbelieve, then smite the necks . . .' (Muhammad; 47:[4]). Those youths will not ask you (William Perry) for explanations,

they will tell you singing there is nothing between us need to be explained, there is only killing and neck smiting. And they will say to you what their grandfather, Haroon Ar-Rasheed, Ameer-ul-Mu'meneen, replied to your grandfather, Nagfoor, the Byzantine emperor, when he threatened the Muslims: 'from Haroon Ar-Rasheed, Ameer-ul-Mu'meneen, to Nagfoor, the dog of the Romans; the answer is what you will see not what you hear'. Haroon El-Rasheed led the armies of Islam to the battle and handed Nagfoor a devastating defeat. The youths you called cowards are competing among themselves for fighting and killing you. Reciting what one of them said: The crusader army became dust when we detonated al-Khobar. [93]

They love death as much as you like life; they inherited honor, generosity, truthfulness, courage, and sacrifice from generation to generation.[94]

Two things stand out in these phrases. First, a parallel was drawn between Muslims battling Byzantines in the eighth century, and the current youths of Islam opposing the United States and the ZCA. Secondly, Bin Laden used 'youths' as a superordinate for the Khobar attackers. Even though Bin Laden had not claimed responsibility for the attack at the time, he 'connected' with the attackers through his plea in the text; he understood and supported them. A 'blessed awakening' was sweeping the Islamic world.[95] As a metaphor, the explosions in Riyadh and Khobar were compared with 'warning signs a volcanic eruption was emerging'. It was through reference to the Muslim youths and the ZCA, an 'us versus them' relation, that the distinct social identity of his audiences took further shape.

The section in which William Perry was mentioned did not per se indicate the US government as an audience. Addressing William Perry was a rhetorical form mirroring the heroic attitude of the seventh century Islamic knight Qatari in facing enemies in a direct manner. From the perspective of his idealised Muslim audiences, doing so added to Bin Laden's prestige. It also contributed to the bipolar identification of 'the *ummah*' against the Saudi regime and the 'Zionist–Crusader Alliance' led by the United States. While Muslims abided by the divine will of Allah, the United States only intended to serve its own interest. In the memorandum, Bin Laden referred to a speech given by Perry after the Khobar bombings in which Perry stated that US troops were in Saudi Arabia to serve US national interests. Bin Laden's message was also a form of self-identification. He characterised himself and his group in the speech and its reproductions. In contrast to the criticised state officials, Bin Laden did not lead and represent an institution. He placed himself among other groups and amidst the social scenery he painted in the memorandum through his rhetoric. An obvious conclusion from a Western perspective could be that Bin Laden positioned himself primarily in opposition to the ZCA. However, this could also be seen as a means to an end, because ultimately Bin Laden opposed and aimed to oust the Saudi regime.

All in all, the 1996 memorandum was thus in fact more of a mixed message. It contested illegitimate and un-Islamic domestic and foreign policies, and called upon Saudi Muslims, Saudi security personnel and, most prominently, the (Saudi) youths of Islam to engage in (irregular) armed action against US military forces (though not civilians) by any means possible. But it also called for mass protests, economic boycotts and other non-violent approaches such as debate to attempt to correct these mistakes. The significance of non-violent approaches became even more prominent in the way the *Al-Quds Al-Arabi* newspaper characterised Bin Laden: as 'one of the most prominent members of the Saudi Opposition, not a religious figure, organizational leader, financial executive or proponent of global jihad against the West'.[96]

In the Arabic speech recording, religious and poetic aspects of the original message were significantly more prominent than in other versions of the text. The key words and groups of words not only highlighted social identities and relations among the most important actors and elements because of their frequency and lexical and grammatical cohesion, they also related to symbolic, historic, cultural and religious meanings rooted in wider contexts.

The wider background: a social practice of Islamic militancy and Salafi jihadism

Bin Laden's speech and the article published in *Al-Quds Al-Arabi* were rooted in a form of Salafi jihadism, and situated in the social and political contexts of Saudi Arabia. In academia, Salafism is characterised as a school of thought that emerged as a reaction to the spread of Western ideas in the second half of the nineteenth century.[97] For the Salafists themselves, they represented the true, literal and traditional understanding of the rulings in the sacred texts. Dutch Islamic studies scholar Joas Wagemakers defines Salafism as referring to Muslims who try to live their life as narrowly as possible in the same manner as the pious predecessors (*al-salaf al-salih*), the first three generations of Islam.[98] He identifies monotheism, or the unity of God (*tawhid*), as the most central concept to Salafism. The concept has three components: 'God is the sole creator and sovereign of the universe, God is supreme and entirely unique, and God alone has the right to be worshipped'.[99] In the strict Salafi interpretation any deviation from this core concept, such as the worshipping of saints or secularism (accepting man-made laws over God), is seen as a form of polytheism (*shirk*) and unbelief (*kufr*).[100] People guilty of polytheism or unbelief have to be excommunicated (*takfir*) as they can no longer be seen as Muslims.

Religious innovations (*bid'a*) such as regional and cultural deviations not enjoined by the Quran or the Prophet's deeds have to be avoided and reversed as much as possible. The application of the human intellect and logic to the original sources (rationalism) is a dangerous challenge to Islam as it will lead to religious pluralism. This is different from the Salafism movement that emerged in the late nineteenth century out of a desire to rid Islam of its historic burden, which holds that returning to its ancient foundation enables the reconstruction of Islam to function better in modern times. Attempts aimed only at purifying and not modernising Islam are deemed contemporary Salafism.[101] This is the Salafism discussed in this chapter.

Rejecting deviations from ancient Islam includes declining the four major Sunni legal schools or interpretations of Islam: the Hanafi, Shaf'i, Maliki and Hanbali schools. While each of these schools recognises the other three, Salafists consider the Quran and the *hadith*s to be the only two original sources of Islam that could inform any further independent reasoning. This is why the relatively new movement of Salafism was strongly influenced by the eighth-century Medinan movement *ahl al-Hadith* of Muslims searching to expand the number of *hadith*s instead of relying on reasoning, legal opinions and other non-scriptural sources.[102] As a widely accepted source, however, the *ahl al-Hadith* movement also influenced the four legal schools, particularly the Hanbali School, of which, for example, Ibn Taymiyya was a prominent scholar as well.

The creeds (*'aqida*) of reading sources literally and finding textual evidence instead of relying on reasoning are mostly agreed upon by Salafists. As American Islamic studies scholar and senior intelligence analyst Quintan Wiktorowicz notes, it is the assumed appropriateness of the method (*manhaj*) of applying creeds that significantly separates various types of Salafists.[103] It is not belief that divides them, but the contextual analysis and the selected strategy: what is the current state of affairs? Are Muslims under attack? If so, by whom? Then what is to be done?

First, those emphasising propagation (*da'wa*) of the message through teaching and preaching are 'purists'. They avoid taking part in politics or violent activity and view politics as something that deviates from faith. Because of the great emphasis on literally following the Quran and the *hadith*s, studying and student–teacher relations are of great importance for purist Salafists. This also applies to the other two types of Salafists. Secondly, 'politicos' engage in political debate and sometimes even in elections or political institutions. For them, it is ultimately in the political arena that they can make a significant impact on society, advocating their perspectives on social justice and the right of God alone to legislate. Lastly, and for this chapter most importantly, 'jihadis' hold the militant view that the current context requires a violent revolution. Wagemakers notes that jihadism is perhaps the least defined Salafi subgroup in scholarly literature.[104] This is in part because in principle, all Salafists view both the greater and lesser holy struggle (*jihad*), or the internal fight against temptations and sins and the external fight against invading non-Muslim enemies, as legitimate concepts. A difference lies in the contextual analysis of situations and the practical objections to actually pursuing war. Whether a Salafist becomes a non-violent or violent extremist is more a matter of political views than one of radical religious beliefs. It is the substantial difference between violent and non-violent forms of Salafism that results in the distinct social practices to which this and other potential (political) Salafi narratives relate.

The Salafi jihadi faction arose from the Afghan war against the Soviet Union. They advanced the concept of jihad beyond a classical fight against external enemies and saw it as legitimate to wage a revolutionary war within Muslim societies to oust unjust or unbelieving rulers.[105] In the context of the military training offered and the ongoing fighting, the Arab Afghans or Saudi Salafists fused their ideas with some of the Egyptian groups present, such as Islamic Jihad. It was this new type of reasoning that inspired the Salafi jihadi Islamist movement on various fronts in Bosnia, Algeria and Egypt after the Afghan war ended in 1979. For those who had gained experience as Arab Afghan mujahedeen and had continued to fight elsewhere, the 1996 Bin Laden speech and memorandum came at a moment of declining success at the various fronts.

Several Islamist leaders, ideologists and intellectuals sought a break from waging war and pursued their goals through political means as politicos. The concentration in London of radical and militant Islamist groups such as the Algerian Gamaa Islamiya and factions of the Egyptian *Al-Jihad* had grown over the last two decades because of the city's relatively permissive discursive climate. By the mid-1990s, all groups represented in 'Londonistan', including Bin Laden's ARC, still benefited from being able to spread their ideas to a global Arab audience through the daily newspapers *Al-Quds Al-Arabi* and *Al Hayat*.[106] This enabled Bin Laden to propagate his critical views on the Saudi government at a time when political dissidents in the country were heavily repressed. Although the Saudi Chief Mufti Abd Al Aziz Bin Baz was a purist in Salafi terms, Bin Laden accused him of either being ignorant or consciously hiding the truth of the state of affairs in the country from the people.[107]

The discursive practices in the *Al Qaeda* narrative that link events to the Salafi jihadi social practice are the doctrine and justifications for the threat of conducting attacks in texts. For Bin Laden, justifications such as those in the 1996 memorandum were rooted in the Quran and *hadith*s, but also supplemented by an array of other Islamic and Arab literature, such as the works of Qatari and Ibn Taymiyya. It is through references in the text to their work that Bin Laden's specific interpretation of Islam and Islamic duties in relation to jihadism emerge.

Qatari lived during the first Islamic century, the seventh century AD, and was appointed caliph of the nomadic Khawarij rebel group in Khurasan (Afghanistan nowadays). He corresponded directly with political opponents, glorifying death and war in the name of Allah.[108] Qatari's interpretation of Islam and Islamic scriptures was literal, and those Muslims who failed to literally follow the Quran became enemies. Bin Laden often cited Qatari's poems and spoke of his followers in terms of 'knights'. In the Ladenese memorandum, he referred to his exile in a safe base in the 'high Hindu Kush mountains in Khurasan'.[109] Identifying with such a historical persona, who had no respect for central authority and was willing to die in pursuit of his strict interpretation of Islam, legitimised Bin Laden's call for *jihad*. In this light, as mentioned, Bin Laden's direct address to US Secretary of Defense William Perry was a courageous act of confronting an enemy directly, rather than an effort to seek his attention as an audience. In the 1996 text, Bin Laden also projected historic examples onto the current 'occupation' of Saudi Arabia, emphasising the important role for the Islamic youth. He recited a well-known *hadith* from Bukhari that described two youths eagerly killing Abu Jahl, a seventh-century Meccan Quraysh leader who opposed Mohammed.[110] By connecting the historic example to the current context, Bin Laden also implicitly identified with Abdul-Rahman, as through the text he pointed eager youths of Islam towards the *kufr* ZCA and the Saudi regime.

Bin Laden cited Taqi al-Din Ibn Taymiyya several times in the memorandum, a thirteenth-/fourteenth-century Syrian Hanbali scholar who stands unquestionably as an authoritative Islamic figure to many orthodox Muslims in the Salafi, Wahhabi and wider Sunni movements, and also to Muslim Sufis. Ibn Taymiyya was a leading theologian in the days when Mongols invaded Muslim lands. He stated that even Mongol leaders converted to Islam could be seen as unbelievers based on their deeds. Like Ibn Taymiyya, Bin Laden projected the concept of *kufr* on rulers. The government of Saudi Arabia, in particular the king, was not adhering to the oneness of God (*tahwid*) and upholding his law: the Saudi king allowed man-made laws and invited US servicemen into the land of the two Holy Places. It was the dicta of Ibn Taymiyya's ruling (*fatwa*) resonating in the Ladenese text that 'it is the first obligation after the profession of Faith to repel the enemy aggressors who assault both sanctity and security'.[111] This reasoning allowed Bin Laden to declare it an individual duty of every Muslim to fight a defensive *jihad* against the *kufr* regime and the ZCA with its allies. Bin Laden compared ancestral scholars of Islam such as Ibn Taymiyya to current scholars, as both had the intent of instigating the *ummah*.

The notion that minor differences between Muslims needed to be set aside to fight a greater danger underscored the main focus of the memorandum: the necessity to fight and resist the Saudi regime, the United States and their allies. It gave a collective character to the individual duty of every Muslim to fight a defensive jihad.[112] Citing Ibn Taymiyya, Bin Laden even stated that, if necessary, it was acceptable to fight the major danger to the religion with the help of non-righteous rulers, military personnel and commanders.[113]

Salafists have drawn heavily on Ibn Taymiyya because he rejected the 'rationalism' (the application of human intellect and logic) that was also dominant among Muslims in his time.[114] Due to his reference to Ibn Taymiyya, the audience of Salafi jihadis were more receptive to Bin Laden's message. It also created the opportunity for Bin Laden to insert himself into the equation. In a subtle way, he added himself and his group to the category of oppressed Muslim scholars by underlining how he had gone into exile in the Hindu Kush after migrating to Sudan to avoid persecution in Saudi Arabia. For Muslims, migration (*hijrah*) was considered compulsory when persecuted and unable to practice the faith. Another subtlety was that Ibn Taymiyya had also emphasised the supremacy and importance to Islam of classical Arabic (*Fusha*), the language that Bin Laden was so skilled at eloquently using in a highly precise manner.[115]

The religious arguments in the memorandum were situated in the social, political and also religious contexts of Saudi Arabia. The Saudi state-sponsored movement can be traced to the preaching of Mohammed ibn Abd al-Wahhab in the eighteenth century and embodies an effort to purify Islam from religious innovations and polytheism. Wahhabism follows the Hanbali Islamic legal school (*fiqh*), which is one of four, and the official school of interpretation in Saudi Arabia. Salafism also advocates for Muslims to revive Islam by studying its primary sources, but in contrast rejects all four schools of interpretation. Bin Laden drew on widely known religious sources and referred to events that were part of the history of Islam, but did so to depart from and criticise the Saudi state. All in all, the Ladenese memorandum was firmly situated in the Salafi jihadis' social practice, relating also to the Saudi political and social context.

Meaning in Bin Laden's 1996 speech

The Ladenese memorandum (or epistle) and speech primarily served three purposes. First, it was a comprehensive attempt to publicly strengthen Bin Laden's legitimacy as a leader. In the recorded speech, this was more related to *jihad*, while in the *Al-Quds Al-Arabi* article he was also characterised as an opposition leader. Secondly, with this call for religiously inspired action against primarily the Saudi regime, he tried to recruit new (young) followers. Thirdly, to this end, Osama bin Laden threatened the United States. Noteworthy for their meaning are the differences between the Ladenese speech, memorandum and English translations. The recorded speech was the most complete text including poetry and many references to resisting the Saudi regime, whereas the *Al-Quds Al-Arabi* article title pointed more towards a declaration of war against the United States and its allies, something that was even more prominent in English translations of the text.

The 1996 speech was a key node for the hegemonic practice of naturalisation that formed the foundation of this analytical *Al Qaeda* narrative. It was an effort by Bin Laden to lift meanings attributed to events and circumstances to the level of ideology. The publishing network of the ARC in London enhanced Bin Laden's ability to make his point (power in discourse). Through his rhetoric and language skills, he also had inspirational power over the Arab audiences of his recorded speech and newspaper articles, but he lacked the power to execute the proposed solution for the problem with the means and number of followers he had at that time. With the texts, Bin Laden was shaping his ideology and building his power base.

In terms of meaning, the speech and articles were an accentuation of conflict, struggle and difference. They separated from the normal practice of (political) opposition to national and foreign or international policymaking. The level of abstraction varied between local and global, specific and general. As a result, in terms of securitization, the referent object can be perceived as a global Muslim community or *ummah* and the Saudi population. Bin Laden worked to strengthen the sense of solidarity for both. Similarly, in an abstract sense, the referent subject can be viewed as a global ZCA with its allies, or the oppressive Saudi regime. As illustrated, according to Bin Laden the threat came as much from the latter as from the former. The level of abstraction also varied with the appropriate actions that needed to be taken to reach that state. The attacks in Khobar and Riyadh were portrayed as a first sign of 'an erupting volcano'. The substantial portion of the text directed at the (Saudi) 'youths of Islam' who were called to action signified a process of identification of Salafi jihadi youths whom Bin Laden was willing to lead.

The speech and memorandum were multifaceted lamentations of a varying tone that did contain elements of securitization, but did not represent a single, unified effort of securitization. This was due to the complex structure of the texts, the abstract definition of the referent object, the multi-layered referent subject, and the customised policy of waging *jihad* with bomb attacks, guerrilla tactics and economic boycott. This leads to the questioning and further investigation of whether Bin Laden did covertly provide and plan for a customised policy in the sense of organising attacks. Moreover, how was the message in the 1996 speech and memorandum reproduced and re-contextualised in the statements and media reports that followed?

Subsequent statements: reproduction and re-contextualisation of the memorandum message

Between 1996 and 1998, Bin Laden worked to expand and organise his network of followers, pledged allegiance to the Taliban, and also facilitated and coordinated planning for the 1998 attacks against the US embassies in Kenya and Tanzania. Meanwhile, he was interviewed by several English, Arab and Urdu news media, significantly increasing his public exposure during those years. The developments and activities sometimes contradicted each other and caused friction with supporters and among those who had pledged allegiance to Bin Laden.

A considerable effort was made to counter any form of critique as, on several occasions, Bin Laden used interviews to deny negative rumours and thoughts. According to him, they were accusations to weaken and disperse the jihadi movement and his personal reputation. Bin Laden denied there were any problems with him continuing his stay in Afghanistan, and stated that relations with the Taliban were good. He stressed the legitimacy of the Taliban in metaphorical terms and asked all Muslims to support and assist them.[116] Bin Laden's support for the movement continued, although it was not made clear in what way exactly. Sometimes, Bin Laden was asked why nothing had happened along the lines of the 'Khobar operation' since he had 'declared jihad against US forces and demanded the boycott of Washington goods'.[117] His response was that 'major operations require time, in contrast with small operations' and 'the nature of the battle requires good preparation'.[118] It was a lexicon of warfare that aligned with the duty of *jihad*.

Compared with the Ladenese speech or memorandum, the interviews and statements in Arab and Urdu newspapers had a more action-oriented perspective, explicitly covering attacks on US and allied forces. They also served to connect to audiences in Sudan, the Arabian Peninsula, Pakistan and Afghanistan, also by emphasising differences with the United States. For example, Bin Laden spoke of his substantial contribution to the battle of Mogadishu, while at the same time explaining how any Pakistani UN soldiers who had died in Somalia were killed because they were sent to a mined area by the United States.[119] He was careful not to criticise Pakistan and draw a distinction with the referent subject: the United States and the ZCA. In general, attacks on US forces in Yemen and Somalia in the early 1990s were presented as good examples of how to force the United States to retreat. Bin Laden resisted the view that attacks, such as in Khobar and Riyadh, were acts of terrorism, and emphasised that it was an honour for Muslims to defend their *qiblah* and protect it from 'plundering'.

More than a state or national institution, Bin Laden depended on the reproduction and re-contextualisation of his message for the development and prominence of his social identity. Hence, for Bin Laden the *Al Qaeda* narrative embodied his primary occupation, while the Saudi and US governments were involved with an array of national and foreign policy issues and responsibilities. In all publications, Bin Laden continued to challenge the Saudi regime and the United States. However, the perceived preoccupation with the media caused friction with his closest advisers and was against the explicit wishes of his host, Taliban leader Mullah Omar.[120]

Like Bin Laden, Omar had fought the Soviets during the 1980s. Their common history proved to be one of only few similarities. Another was their push for a conservative Wahhabi or Salafi form of Islam. Yet the two leaders had starkly contrasting goals. While the Taliban was mostly concerned with controlling and stabilising Afghanistan under its rule, Bin Laden primarily wished to incite the global Muslim community to wage a transnational *jihad*. He was welcome in Afghanistan because of logistical and financial support, and his pledge of allegiance to Omar.[121] But for Omar, using Afghanistan as a base for Bin Laden's activities and staging ground for international attacks only endangered the stability sought by the Taliban. The relationship between Bin Laden and the Taliban had never been easy, and the divergent goals provided a certain bandwidth in which Bin Laden could operate without losing the Taliban's hospitality. The interviews and statements increasingly put the relationship under pressure.

Bin Laden's allegiance to the Taliban and focus on the advancement of the transnational agenda also led internally to divisions among his followers. First, there were those who disagreed with pledging allegiance to Mullah Omar and the Taliban. The Islamic law or *shariah* the Taliban claimed to implement was actually more related to the Afghan Pashtun tribal code, Pashtunwali.[122] According to some of Bin Laden's followers, pledging allegiance to this was heretical as there were several indicators of polytheism, such as shrines in mosques. In the background, tensions between Arabs and Afghans continued to have an effect, as Arabs looked down on the local population and their primitive and remote living conditions. Secondly, several of his senior associates were critical of Bin Laden's eagerness to invite journalists and participate in interviews in which his persona became almost as prominent as his message. Thirdly, there were those who still agreed with the initial orientation of Ayman al-Zawahiri and Sayyed Imam al-Sharif (or Dr Fadl), and who worked to avoid too much of a transnational focus on the United States and Saudi Arabia in favour of more momentum to first continue the fight on other fronts, such as Egypt.[123] This discussion went back to the days of Bin Laden's cooperation with Abdullah Azzam in Afghanistan and Pakistan.

Because of the deteriorating permissiveness of the Egyptian societal climate, the options of Ayman al-Zawahiri and the other Egyptian followers were limited. They had become highly dependent on Bin Laden's funding, and in choosing this direction he had burned his bridges to the majority of *Al-Jihad* members. Because of their experience, those *Al-Jihad* fighters who did accompany al-Zawahiri were able to secure positions as some of Bin Laden's most trusted associates. In the late 1990s, they joined the former Arab Afghan fighters to form the inner circle or *shura* council that was at the core of what had become *Al Qaeda*; a network that transformed into an organisation that not all followers seemed to support.

The Taliban followed a dual strategy to contain the negative consequences of Bin Laden's public statements as much as possible. He was allowed to set up and run training camps to host the young Muslims who sought training for *jihad* in Afghanistan, but was also asked to refrain from making explicit public statements on international *jihad*. However, it proved to be impossible to silence Bin Laden. On 23 February 1998, the World Islamic Front (WIF) issued a religious decree, often referred to as a *fatwa* by Western media, 'against the Jews and the

Crusaders'.[124] It summarised Bin Laden's recent interviews and statements in a powerful, more focused, and more aggressive manifesto.

WORLD ISLAMIC FRONT DECLARATION 1998

Genre and style

The manifesto was published in the pan-Arab newspaper *Al-Quds Al-Arabi*, titled 'Declaration of the World Islamic Front for Jihad against the Jews and the Crusaders' (*Nass Bayan al-Jabhah al-Islamiyah al-Alamiyah li-Jihad al-Yahud wa-al-Salibiyin*).[125] The main differences compared with the Ladenese memorandum in 1996 were that the 1998 declaration was significantly shorter, that it was not only signed by Bin Laden but also by four co-signatories, and that it had a much narrower focus on the role of the United States in the Middle East. Furthermore, not only military and security personnel were threatened but also civilians, and not only on the Arabian Peninsula but in 'all countries'. The problem was defined in fewer words but with a similar pejorative and politically charged lexicon as in 1996. The Muslim people suffered from America's 'excessive aggression', 'horrific massacres' and the 'devastation inflicted upon them'. The American 'crimes and sins' were a 'proclamation of war' against Islam. The ZCA had attacked Muslim countries in the Islamic world, most recently in the Arabian Peninsula, and the Saudi regime had failed to follow God's will and protect the land of the two Holy Places. The introduction of the 1998 text recited the first half of the Quranic verse on repentance (*Surah At-Tawbah*, 9:5). Similar to the 1996 text, it was the first phrase on 'slaying the idolaters', also referred to as the verse of the sword (*surah As-Sayef*), that was narrated.[126] The subsequent phrase on how Allah could be merciful if these idolaters 'should repent' was not recited. [127]

Compared with the 1996 memorandum, it seems more appropriate to characterise this text as a focused religious decree on a specific issue. Most English translations adopted the term *fatwa*. Several of the signatories were established leaders of known groups, and Bin Laden's moral authority certainly had increased as a widely recognised Saudi oppositionist. But did the WIF actually declare a *fatwa* against the United States? The term 'judgement' used in the text referred to a 'considered judgement' (*hukm*) in contrast to a 'juridical decree' (*fatwa*).[128] The difference is subtle but of interest. In contrast to the universally applicable *fatwa*, a considered judgement is issued by an authoritative leadership in the light of specific prevailing conditions. The *hukm* remains in place as long as those conditions prevail.[129] So compared with *fatwa*, the term *hukm* had a more political connotation. In the text, the US 'occupation' or foreign policy in the Middle East shaped the specific conditions on the Arabian Peninsula. Although criticised, it was not the American 'way of life' that the authors sought to destroy per se.

A key aspect was the name of the entity producing the text, the 'World Islamic Front for Jihad against the Jews and the Crusaders'. In addition to the 1996 Ladenese memorandum, 'World' signified the large scale of the 'front for jihad' that had allegedly been founded, whereas 'Islamic' specified the character of the inclusiveness as opposed to others, the 'Jews and the Crusaders'. By choosing this title, the authors sought to underline collaboration and unity over a cause amidst diversity. The signatories were presented in the text as:

Sheikh Osama bin Muhammed bin Laden
Ayman al-Zawahiri, amir of the Jihad Group in Egypt
Abu-Yasir Rif'ai Ahmad Taha, Egyptian Islamic Group
Sheikh Mir Hamzah, secretary of the Jamiat-ul-Ulema-e-Pakistan
Fazlur Rahman, amir of the Jihad Movement in Bangladesh[130]

Yet the global and united character of the front could be questioned. First, the WIF represented only a fraction of the jihadi groups around the world. Illustrative was how even Yemeni jihadis of the Aden-Abyan Islamic Army who were associated with Bin Laden were piqued that they were not consulted before publication of the text.[131] After publication, Bin Laden made efforts to increase support for the publication in Yemen by discussing revisions. Also, the Taliban, to which Bin Laden had pledged allegiance (as the 'pious caliphate would begin from Afghanistan'), did not support the WIF statement, and tried to limit Bin Laden's ability to make public statements.[132] Some Afghan factions deemed Bin Laden's behaviour to be so reckless that they accused him of being an agent of the United States who wanted to destroy the Taliban Islamic Emirate.[133] Further on, this chapter will describe how the strong shift in focus from a 'near enemy' (or a local regime) towards a 'far enemy' (or global enemy) was a major dividing factor among Salafi jihadi groups.

Secondly, there were internal differences among the jihadi groups 'represented' by the signatories, also concerning the international or global orientation of the top priority. Even among Bin Laden's closest Afghan Arab followers, there had been long-standing fundamental discussions on goals and strategies since the 1980s. But discussions among all groups were now taken to a new level. Al-Zawahiri had declared support for Bin Laden against the will of the majority of the EIJ. He had faced internal problems with the *shura* council, the executive decision-making body of his EIJ, on whether a transnational *jihad* was in the interest of the organisation. Among EIJ senior members, a debate was ongoing over whether the costs of militant jihadism to the *ummah* were too high, and whether teaching and preaching (*dawa*) would not be a better way to Islamise Egyptian and the wider Muslim society. It seemed al-Zawahiri wanted to pursue a new jihadi agenda to substitute for a losing old one. At a personal level, this new text marked al-Zawahiri's definitive departure from prioritising the struggle against the Egyptian government, the near enemy. Eventually, only eight lieutenants followed al-Zawahiri in joining the WIF, and the EIJ *shura* council released a statement in which al-Zawahiri and those loyal to him were all expelled, sealing the discussion within EIJ with the split.[134]

Similarly, Abu-Yasir Rif'ai Ahmad Taha (or Abu Nasir of Egypt) had appeared to sign on behalf of the Egyptian Islamic Group (EIG, *Al-Gamaa Al-Islamiyya*), but also only represented a faction. He had not consulted the wider EIG leadership and was later forced to release a disclaimer in which he denied the EIG was 'a party in any front against Americans'.[135] The vast majority of the EIG supported an announced cease-fire and pursued a political debate with the Egyptian government. Later, EIG leader Sheikh Omar Abdul Rahman (the Blind Sheikh) circulated a written statement supporting the formation of another world Islamic front to spread and defend Islam, but by means of peaceful action only.[136] This was also after the Embassy bombings that will be described further on in this chapter.

Representing the Sunni Hanafi Barelvi religio-political party Jamiat-ul-Ulema-e-Pakistan (JUP) was secretary-general Sheikh Mir Hamzah. As an opposition party, the JUP was represented in the national parliament, which brings the political dimension in the 1998 WIF declaration more to the forefront. From a religious perspective, the Barelvi differ from Deobandi schools in Pakistan and India because of their personal devotion to the Prophet Mohammed and their adoption of Sufi practices of worshipping saints. From an international perspective, the bond between the Barelvi and the Iraqi regime of Saddam Hussein had traditionally been strong, as the movement's patron saint had been buried near Baghdad. Still, when Iraq invaded Kuwait in 1990, most Islamists, including the Pakistani JUP, condemned the action of invading another Muslim country. However, disagreement soon transformed and shifted to anger towards the Saudi regime that allowed American troops on its lands.[137]

Fazlur Rahman, also known as Sheikh Abd al-Salam Muhammad Khan, was the ideologue of the Deobandi Jihad Movement in Bangladesh, known as *Harakat-ul-Jihad-al-Islami Bangladesh* (HUJI-B). HUJI-B was founded in 1992, and in terms of rhetoric and attacks became an active branch of the wider Pakistan-based militant jihadi HUJI organisation. The creed of HUJI-B was for 'all to become Taliban (or Muslim students) and turn Bangladesh into Afghanistan'.[138] After signing the 1998 text, the HUJI-B became increasingly involved in violent attacks against Hindus and progressive intellectuals in Bangladesh.[139] With the support of Fazlur Rahman for the WIF and its first declaration, the symbolic reach of the message in the Muslim world stretched further into Asia. Still, compared with other militant Islamic organisations in the Arab world and Asia, HUJI-B remained a relatively minor group.[140]

Examining the WIF declaration in terms of text production, the various signatories claimed to represent several Islamic organisations in the Middle East and Asia comprising a 'World Islamic Front'. However, the WIF was far from encompassing a global Salafi jihadi movement. Moreover, the authority of the signatories to declare *jihad* on behalf of 'their' groups was highly questionable. The WIF was somewhat of a bricolage of small groups of Salafi jihadis. This brings back to the forefront the discussion in the introduction of the chapter on the nature of *Al Qaeda* with respect to the WIF: was *Al Qaeda* more of an ideology, a network or a coordinated group? Analysing the signatories of the WIF declaration points towards the perspective of a 'loose network of networks' of individuals and minority groups that were affiliated.[141] Although Bin Laden's followers had pledged allegiance, there were frustrations and differences among them. Defining *Al Qaeda* at this stage is thus more a matter of perspective. It seems the common cause of fighting 'the Jews and the Crusaders' was primarily an effort to bring diverse and divided groups of jihadis closer together.[142]

The text: focusing the argument of the *Al Qaeda* narrative

After religious introductions and a focused arrangement of some of the arguments presented earlier in the 1996 Ladenese text, the sentence carrying the considered judgement (*hukm*) was the central message of the 1998 text:

> On this basis, and in accordance with God's will, we pronounce to all Muslims the following judgement: To kill the Americans and their allies – civilians and military – is an individual duty incumbent upon every Muslim in all countries, in order to liberate the al-Aqsa Mosque and the Holy Mosque from their grip, so that their armies leave all the territory of Islam, defeated, broken, and unable to threaten any Muslim.[143]

It was an extreme standpoint to kill servicemen and civilians, regionally and globally, that required strong argumentation, especially as the WIF statement intended to appeal to a diverse Muslim community. God was praised as in the Quran (*basmallah*) and presented as 'defeater of factionalism', a reference to the various contrasting strands, schools, traditions, views and opinions in Islam, and specifically Salafism.[144] It illustrated how Bin Laden and the co-signatories strived to unite the *ummah*, address their audiences and incite them to adopt their cause of 'liberating' the land of the two Holy Places. Never in its history had the Arabian Peninsula

> . . . suffered such a calamity as these Crusader hordes that have spread like locusts, consuming its wealth and destroying its fertility. All this at a time when nations have joined forces against the Muslims as if fighting over a bowl of food. When the matter is this grave and support is scarce, we must discuss current events and agree collectively on how best to settle the issue.[145]

According to the statement, for seven years the United States had projected its power and 'excessive aggression' through US military bases in the region, for example, against the people of Iraq. They had come 'to annihilate what was left of the Iraqi people and humiliate their Muslim neighbours' while ensuring the survival of Israel. The situation served US religious and economic purposes, but also diverted attention from the Jewish occupation of Jerusalem. These actions were a 'clear proclamation of war against God, his messenger, and the Muslims'. The text cited religious authorities and scholars as stating that *jihad* was an individual duty when Muslim countries were attacked. Of note is that 'Muslim' referred to the people, whereas 'Islamic' would have referred to the 'state'. Among the cited works were Muwaffaq al-Din ibn Qudama's book *The Resource* (*Al-Mughni*, primary Hanbali jurisprudence), Al-Qurtubi's exegesis of the Quran, and the remarks of Ibn Taymiyya (often referred to as 'the Sheikh of Islam') that after faith there was no greater duty than fighting to defend the religion and the world from corruption.[146] In line with the audiences and actors identified in the Ladenese memorandum, scholars, leaders, youths and security personnel were called upon to kill Americans and seize their money wherever they found them. However, the 1998 text was more explicitly focused on the United States as the root cause of the problem. Furthermore, highly significantly, instead of limiting the threat to US military troops in the region, US civilians and servicemen around the world were also included explicitly as a target in the text.

When analysing the meaning of the message's content that emerged from the language used, it becomes clear that the declaration itself had a powerful coherence. The 1998 WIF statement served as a landmark declaration in the *Al Qaeda* narrative because it increased focus on the United Sates, the far enemy.

The near and far enemy

Throughout history, Salafist scholars have debated the meaning of Islamic concepts such as *jihad*, *kufr* (or unbelief) and *kaffirs* (or unbelievers). Pivotal in Salafi thinking is defending the concept of *tawhid*, the notion of the oneness of God as he is the sole divine creator. Throughout history, *jihad* has had various meanings among Muslims, not necessarily referring to armed struggle. In traditional Islamic jurisprudence, the 'greater *jihad*' referred to an inward struggle in which every Muslim engaged to live in accordance with Islam, while the 'lesser *jihad*' was the duty of Muslims to defend Islam against threats.[147] Violent (lesser) *jihad* has been an important Islamic concept throughout history, consisting of two dimensions: defensive and offensive.[148] Defensive *jihad* is defined as an individual duty (*fard ayn*) in which all Muslims are required to engage when a community is attacked, while offensive *jihad* is the collective requirement (*fard kafiya*) of Muslims to spread Islam. Only a specific group of trained and experienced Muslim fighters are to engage in spreading Islam by conquering lands and implementing God's rule (*shariah*). This sets the condition for communities to convert to Islam, although forced conversion is not allowed. Another, less violent, way to spread Islam's reach is by preaching (*dawa*).

For jihadis, Sayyid Qutb was one of the most influential modern Islamic scholars, introducing in 1965 the new *jihad* paradigm of attacking the 'near enemy'.[149] The repression by Nasser's socialist regime of the Muslim Brotherhood in Egypt and the imprisonment of Qutb as one of its prominent ideologues created the conditions in which the thinking based on historic figures such as Ibn Taymiyya ripened. *Jihad* was an 'eternal struggle against any obstacle that came in the way of worshipping God and the implementation of the divine authority on earth', Qutb concluded.[150] Every Muslim had to honour the universal role of Islam in the world and the sovereignty of God. Rulers who did not follow the strictest form of Islam were identified as *kaffir*s who had to be removed from power. This included any ruler who deemed himself a Muslim or Islamic leader, as the only true leader of Muslims was *Allah*.[151] Instead of a limited and offensive collective fight against foreign enemies, the situation in Egypt required Muslims to perform their individual defensive duty against the *kufr* regime. Omar Abdul Rahman built on these ideas to legitimise his role in the killing of Egyptian President Sadat, stating that 'Muslim rulers must not change a single letter'.[152]

Another important contribution was EIJ member Mohammed Abd al-Salam Faraj's coining of the term 'far enemy' (*al-Adou al-Baeed*) in contrast to 'near enemy' (*al-Adou al-Qareeb*). His pamphlet, 'The Neglected Duty' (*Al-Farida Al-Gha'eba*), circulated among Egyptian jihadis in the early 1980s and contributed to the elevation of the status of *jihad*.[153] It was more expansionist in its underlying motivation than Qutb's *Milestones*. Also inspired by Ibn Taymiyya, Faraj concluded that unbelievers or Muslims not adhering to Islamic law (*shariah*) must be fought to re-establish the Islamic caliphate from which the world could be conquered. Although the ultimate aim was to 'liberate' Jerusalem from the Jews, whom Faraj characterised as the 'far enemy', the route to accomplish this went through national capitals such as Cairo, Amman and Riyadh. According to Faraj, modern Muslim rulers were apostates who had been brought up 'at the tables of colonialism' as they allied with (Western) unbelievers.[154] Faraj propagated the idea that defeating the near enemy was the first priority as it served as a precondition for liberating Jerusalem and ending the colonial presence in Muslim lands. Both Qutb and Faraj informed the thinking among Salafi jihadis that attacking the near enemy was necessary.

Given the divisions in the Salafi jihadi landscape, how did the stance of attacking American military and civilians, locally and globally, fit in the wider context of the Salafi jihadi order of discourse? The WIF declaration marked a radical or strategic ideological transformation of the concept of defensive *jihad*, away from the focus on the near enemy. The latter was a traditional focus that al-Zawahiri himself had defended for decades, for example, in Afghanistan while discussing it with Abdullah Azzam. After the Soviet withdrawal from Afghanistan in 1989, Abdullah Azzam had been an advocate of turning attention towards liberating Palestine, instead of taking the *jihad* to Egypt and other local Muslim regimes.[155] This had led to serious disagreements with other members of the Afghan MAK support network such as al-Zawahiri and Omar Rahman. Long after Azzam's death, and with the situation in Egypt changed dramatically, the 1998 WIF declaration now marked a shift in focus from fighting the 'apostate near enemy' to the 'greater power' behind the local regimes: the ZCA.

The WIF intended to aggregate highly diverse groups of Salafi jihadis. But among the various strands of Salafi jihadi thought that had developed over the last century, the WIF declaration was an extreme standpoint, unparalleled in this form. A radical creed and method of *jihad* was advanced in which it was the duty of individuals to proactively attack the ZCA enemy in all its forms and in every place on earth. Its global scope contrasted to the local concerns of most of the Salafi jihadi groups that the message sought to address.[156] It was a direction that was anything but widely supported among Salafi jihadis.[157] Yet underneath the radical innovation of *jihad* lay the grievances adequately captured by Bin Laden's earlier rhetoric, which resonated widely among Salafists and broader Muslim communities.[158]

To partially deal with negative sentiments among Muslims, the Saudi ruling family sought to advance foreign and domestic policies along two contrasting lines. Since the foundation of the country, the House of Saud had cooperated with strict Wahhabi Muslims to maintain regional influence. Islamic fundamentalists had proven to be a useful instrument in the fight against the Soviets in Afghanistan and to counter Iranian regional influence after the Islamic revolution in 1979. Saudi Arabia was also one of the few supporters of the Taliban. As a concession to the strict Saudi Wahhabi scholars (*ulema*), the decision to allow the stationing of 500,000 American troops on Saudi soil was accompanied by a decree that gave Islamic religious police (*mutaween*) officers and volunteers more competence to oversee and enforce conformity to *shariah* in the country.[159] This did not negate US–Saudi relations. Hence, despite the radical nature of the approach to *jihad* propagated by the WIF, in a broader sense an increasing number of Muslims were somewhat sympathetic to some of the sentiments in the 1998 WIF declaration.

Meaning in the 1998 declaration

It was the 1998 WIF declaration that accelerated and focused the *Al Qaeda* narrative, which had been marked comprehensively for the first time in the 1996 memorandum. As securitizing actors, Bin Laden and the co-signatories presented themselves as united leaders of a vanguard for all Muslims. This was potentially more powerful than if Bin Laden had only sought to improve his authority and position by increasing his profile and media exposure. The primary referent subject was more clearly defined as the United States, represented by both military and civilian Americans, and the Jews and their allies. This was also a result of the customised policy projected: kill them and seize their money whenever and wherever it is possible.

However, it was the referent object that perhaps formed the weakest aspect of this securitization effort. Despite negative sentiments among Muslims regarding Iraqi population casualties, or the situation of the Palestinians and Jerusalem, there appeared to be a lack of congruence between the frame of reference and the strategy of the securitizing actor, and the various frames of reference among the audience, the Muslim *ummah*. The argument in the text was that in the history of the Arabian Peninsula, the calamity at hand had never been greater and required violent resistance. However, transnational militant jihadism resonated with only a small Salafi minority within the global Muslim community. Although other Salafists agreed with the specific context that situated the *hukm*, politicos and quietist Salafists pursued non-violent methods to reach their goals. Thus, among more moderate Sunni, Shia and Sufi Muslim communities in Saudi Arabia, Palestine, Iraq and the wider Arab world, some of the grievances described were felt but failed to rally support for the WIF statement. The considered judgement caused significant debate among the readers of the pan-Arab newspaper *Al-Quds Al-Arabi* and the various Muslim groups, instead of all-out unity and incitement. Of the twenty groups operating in Afghanistan, only three had supported the statement.[160] For a small group of Salafi jihadi followers, the text would prove to offer a natural fit with their beliefs and legitimise an operation in Africa that would catch the attention of the US president.

The statement marked yet another step in the development of the network into an organisation that would become known as *Al Qaeda*. At its core was Osama bin Laden, surrounded by his *shura* council of closest associates. In London, the ARC represented the executive element of *Al Qaeda*'s media committee, which was led by chief propagandist Khalid al-Fawwaz. Other *shura* members and related subgroups focused on funding and conducting business, or on scholarly research on Islamic law (*shariah*). Abu Ubaidah was *Al Qaeda*'s chief planner and military commander until he died in a ferry accident in Africa on 21 May 1996. Then, Abu Hafs al-Masri (also known as Mohammed Atef) took over preparing and coordinating the execution of several operations against the adversaries defined in Bin Laden's statements. After Ubaidah's death, Abdullah Ahmed Abdullah (also known as Abu Mohammed al-Masri or Saleh) headed the *Al Qaeda* cells that would execute the bombings of the American embassies in Kenya and Tanzania a few months later.

Among those who disagreed with the 1998 text, and who were quite unpleasantly surprised by this latest statement made by Bin Laden, were Taliban leader Mullah Omar and Foreign Minister Maulana Muttawakil.[161] For his efforts to gain international credibility, Bin Laden's behaviour and statements continued to cause frustration. In response, several of the Afghan training camps that facilitated training for fighters and followers associated with Bin Laden were shut down. As a reprisal, the Taliban leadership also told Bin Laden to move from Jalalabad to the more remote city of Kandahar in March 1998. They confiscated his satellite phones, hoping to reduce his ability to communicate. Nevertheless, he continued to actively seek and find the attention of Arab, Urdu and English news media.

Between 23 February and 7 August 1998, Bin Laden held several interviews discussing the WIF declaration, resulting in eleven substantial articles. Bin Laden responded laughingly to rumours that the US CIA had been sent to capture him as a consequence of the WIF statement.[162] He defended and explained his core message. Furthermore, he commended the Taliban for their 'certificate of good conduct'. They had been added to the US list of states sponsoring terrorism because of their continued support for Bin Laden and his followers.[163] He also widened the focus of the WIF from the United States back to the ZCA and stated that 'the US Jews and Christians are using Israel to bring Muslims to their knees', hoping to increase the group that was attracted to the cause.[164] The apotheosis of Bin Laden's efforts came on 26 May 1998, as he held a major press conference in one of his training camps in Khost discussing the WIF declaration, resulting in three articles and a television interview with US news channel ABC.[165]

With the efforts of the Taliban leadership to limit Bin Laden's rhetoric remaining fruitless, and with that rhetoric negatively affecting their own goals of internal stability, they were willing to discuss other options. In June 1998, the head of Saudi intelligence Prince Turki al-Faisal was able to make a secret deal with the Taliban to have Bin Laden expelled from Afghanistan.[166] The '*fatwa*' and press conference were decisive signs for the Taliban leadership that it was simply impossible to keep their Arab guest silent and prevent international problems.[167] However, as a consequence of the US military strikes on Afghanistan that followed the Embassy bombings in Africa, the deal would not be executed.[168]

Embassy Bombings in Kenya and Tanzania and US Missile Strikes

At 10.39 am on 7 August 1998, a Toyota Dyna truck detonated in front of the US Embassy in Nairobi, Kenya. Ten minutes later, a Nissan truck exploded at the US Embassy in Dar es Salaam, Tanzania. In total, 224 people were killed and over 4,700 people wounded. Most of the 4,500 wounded in Nairobi were civilian bystanders who stopped in the street or came to the windows of their civilian offices in response to the stun grenades thrown by the attackers. The stun grenades drew people near out of curiosity and did not scare civilians away, as *Al Qaeda* members would later testify to be the intent. It was Friday, and around that time the mosques in the vicinity were holding their religious services – an argument that would surface later among Bin Laden's followers to justify that the civilian casualties were either not true Muslims or would be accepted by God as martyrs.[169]

The Nairobi embassy, which was the largest US embassy in the region, was severely damaged by the blast, although not as much as the weaker civilian office building next to it, which had collapsed and housed 400 people daily. The windows of the nearby Cooperative Bank, a Nairobi landmark, were shattered. Among the rubble and twisted steel were scattered human remains and burnt corpses. As aid workers and news agencies rushed to the scene, hundreds of wounded were filmed walking to receive treatment in the street. In Tanzania, a water truck had blocked and absorbed part of the explosion as it was thrown from its place at the gate towards the embassy. The bomb still caused substantial damage to two-thirds of the embassy, and a significant number of people were killed and wounded. However, probably because of the scale of the first blast in Nairobi, most video material was made and broadcast from Kenya.

Two claims of responsibility were made by 'platoons' belonging to 'the Islamic Army for the Liberation of the Holy Places'.[170] One platoon from the Arabian Peninsula was named after Martyr Khalid al-Saeed, who was behind the attack at Al-Khobar; the other was named after Abdullah Azzam. They had almost identical words and were distributed to various Arab media outlets.[171] Initially, Bin Laden denied any personal involvement. According to the Hong Kong office of AFP, Bin Laden relayed a message via Ayman al-Zawahiri to the Pakistani newspaper *The News* on 20 August, 'calling upon the Muslim *ummah* to continue jihad against Jews and Americans' while 'denying any involvement in the Nairobi and Dar es Salam bombings'.[172] Of note, in the AFP report al-Zawahiri

Figure 2.2 The damaged US embassies in Nairobi, Kenya (left) and Dar es Salam, Tanzania (right)

Sources: Left: K24TV (YouTube publisher), 'Kenya Remembers 1998 Terror Attack I', 7 August 2013; Right: National Security Archive, Associated Press image, NSAEBB253.

was introduced as the 'head of the Egyptian Islamic Jihad Organization', not as a leader of Bin Laden's group or *Al Qaeda*. Later, Afghan Islamic Press also quoted Bin Laden as categorically denying any involvement in the attacks, while feeling no sorrow over the blasts.[173] However, the actions of Bin Laden's associates demonstrated how he was in fact involved.[174]

As described in the next chapter, US President Clinton responded by ordering missile strikes on targets related to Bin Laden and *Al Qaeda* in Afghanistan and Sudan. The Khost training camp Al-Badr, scene of Bin Laden's 26 May press conference, was one of the targets, as were the Al-Farouq training camp near Kandahar and the Al-Shifa pharmaceutical factory in Sudan. United States' companies were among the international businesses that delivered parts for the Sudanese factory that now allegedly produced and stored chemical weapons. The seventy-five cruise missiles failed to kill Bin Laden or any of his senior followers. Bin Laden had left the Al-Farouq training camp and other *Al Qaeda* members had been ordered to move as well. Among those killed were militants of Pakistani, Egyptian, Saudi and Yemeni origin. A few buildings were damaged, but complete camps were not destroyed. The attacks failed to strike or intimidate Bin Laden and his followers, or other jihadi groups and those aspiring to join the *jihad*.

But more important was how Muslims' distaste for the civilian casualties of the embassy bombings was diminished by anger over the missile strikes, and a genuine wider feeling that the United States was pursuing self-interest in the Middle East and was unconcerned with Muslim suffering.[175] The strikes resulted in several mass protests in the Muslim world, especially in Pakistan and Sudan. In Islamabad, hundreds of protesters burned an American flag before the US Information Service Center, and in Karachi thousands gathered and Clinton cartoons were burned while others held pictures of Bin Laden.[176] The Pakistani government denounced the attacks. The Taliban denounced the bombing as having been aimed at and showing enmity towards the Afghan people. In Sudan, thousands gathered in the streets of Khartoum in protest under the leadership of President Omar al-Bashir.[177] The Arab League, at the time chaired by Sudan, unanimously demanded an investigation into the targeting of the pharmaceutical factory. As a prominent target of the strikes, Bin Laden became more widely known in the Arab and Muslim world as a heroic figure.[178]

Securitization after the US missile strikes, not the embassy bombings

The events that occurred in Kenya and Tanzania on 7 August 1998 were lethal attacks that led to damage and destruction, killed 224 people and wounded thousands. Many of the victims were not related to the US embassies. One of the 'suicide attackers' (or *martyrs*) was not among the dead as he had survived the bomb blast and fled the scene after the attack. The timing of the events, within 10 minutes of each other, combined with the spatial (geographical) separation of the locations highlighted the coordinated and regional or international character of the events.

The day of the attacks marked the eighth anniversary of the arrival of US troops in Saudi Arabia. However, in the weeks after the bombings Bin Laden did not make efforts to enhance his securitization of the ZCA occupation. Possibly, the denial of Bin Laden's personal involvement was of a tactical nature, to avoid losing the support of the Taliban regime due to involvement with planning or facilitating the violent operation. More strategically, it also served to strengthen the *Al Qaeda* narrative that the youths of Islam were answering the call made by Bin Laden, even though one of the attackers failed to kill (or *martyr*) himself. As Bin Laden anticipated the United States would respond militarily, it is possible that he wanted to wait for this as the best opportunity to exploit feelings of hostility among jihadis and other Muslims. After all, the Afghan training camps were also used by other jihadi groups that had not pledged loyalty to Bin Laden. Lastly, the high number of civilian casualties could also have prevented Bin Laden from making securitization efforts. Among Muslims and Arabs in Africa, the Middle East and other regions, there was dismay over the extensive number of casualties who were ordinary Africans.

However, any doubts or reservations among Bin Laden's audiences were pushed to the background after and in the context of the US missile strikes on 17 August 1998 that followed as a reprisal. After that, Bin Laden used the bomb attacks in Kenya and Tanzania more explicitly to illustrate the rising spirit of *jihad* among the global Muslim *ummah* against the ZCA led by the United States.[179] The US missile strikes had a limited physical impact, but a significant symbolic one. They brought Bin Laden's rhetoric on US foreign policy and the military occupation of the Arabian Peninsula to life, and as such enhanced his ability to contextually mobilise the emotions and images he had presented. It offered a sentimental wave for Bin Laden to ride, which naturally enhanced his status as a securitizing actor. The strikes were 'an expression of enmity against Muslims and the Islamic world'.[180] The United States was 'scared of the implementation of the Islamic system in Islamic countries'.[181] Because 'the youths of Islam' were 'determined to implement Islam in their countries' and were waging *jihad* in Kashmir, Palestine and Afghanistan, they all belonged 'to the same breed'.[182] According to *Al-Quds Al-Arabi*, in the light of the missile strikes Bin Laden was becoming an 'Islamic symbol' for more and more Muslims.[183] The US attacks in Afghanistan also caused a shift in Taliban policy towards Bin Laden. The deal with the head of Saudi intelligence was off the table; Bin Laden claimed in an *Al-Quds Al-Arabi* interview that Mullah Omar had vowed that he would not extradite him.[184] For his part, Bin Laden renewed his allegiance to the Taliban leader in mid-September and increased his public support of the Taliban. In an open letter to its spiritual leader, Bin Laden connected the Taliban to the 'sacred struggle' and stated supporting the Taliban was a similar duty to waging *jihad*.[185]

Reproduction and re-contextualisation and the role of new media: Al Jazeera

The late 1990s saw a significant development of new media platforms in the Arab world, which came in addition to the spread of audio-cassettes and pan-Arab newspapers. Arab satellite television stations such as Al Jazeera and Al-Arabiya were setting up and expanding their broadcasting activities. Major events such as Operation Desert Fox, the US-led bombing campaign over Iraq in 1998, provided the stepping-stone for Al Jazeera to become the primary news channel in the Arab world. Viewers were able to express their outrage over the militarisation of American interventionism in the region during TV call-in shows. The Qatari government allowed Al Jazeera to broadcast documentaries, editorials and news reports with critical perspectives that previously could not reach Arab audiences on such a global scale. Furthermore, the number of jihadi websites on the internet, such as azzam.com, was increasing. Satellite technology and the internet enabled a new, more critical, social dynamic in the Arab world. It empowered Bin Laden to reach larger and broader audiences in a shorter time, using the ARC in London, the jihadi website run by his confidant Yusuf al-ʿAyiri www.alneda.com, the newly founded Al-Sahab media office, and Al Jazeera.[186] These platforms also allowed him to evade Saudi state censorship and the Taliban's ban on giving interviews.

A highly significant Arab text in which the 1998 embassy bombings were discussed and re-contextualised was a 90-minute Al Jazeera interview with Bin Laden conducted in mid-December 1998.[187] Parts of the interview were rebroadcasted by other Arab and Western media over the following months, illustrating the significance of the text. Al Jazeera reran the entire interview in 2001, after the attacks on 11 September. The interview confirmed Bin Laden's leadership position and covered a highly diverse array of topics. The visual introduction produced by Al Jazeera featured Bin Laden on the back of a horse, indicating his status as a respected leader. Other imagery showed him firing a Kalashnikov rifle, thus demonstrating his fighting skills, and operating an excavator, which emphasised his knowledge and capability to improve infrastructure and build constructions. During the interview, Bin Laden was seen sitting in a tent with a Kalashnikov rifle by his side, wearing a camouflage jacket and a white turban. The Kalashnikov and jacket referred to his experience as a jihadi fighter against the Soviets in Afghanistan, and also to his description of the current state, or occupation, of the *ummah*. The white robe and turban indicated his eloquence and moral standing as a leader.

Bin Laden mostly sat still during the interview, spoke calmly and measuredly, looked to the side several times, and occasionally lifted his hands while answering. The emphasis was on his words. The wide-ranging topics addressed were both a consequence of the questions asked and Bin Laden's own initiative.

Figure 2.3 Al Jazeera video imagery introducing Osama bin Laden prior to the interview, December 1998

Figure 2.4 Al Jazeera, Bin Laden interview with imagery of Operation Desert Fox (right), December 1998

Source: AbuOsamaBinLaden (YouTube publisher), 'Al Jazeera, Osama Bin Laden Interview 1998' (in Arabic), 12 September 2010.

He approached topics from various angles. It is assumed that in general the production of this in-depth interview represented the intent and consent of both Al Jazeera and Bin Laden to broadcast it in this way.

In the interview, the most prominent re-contextualisation of the embassy attacks was Operation Desert Fox, a four-day American and British bombing campaign against Iraqi military and regime targets in mid-December 1998. The operation started on 16 December, an hour after the head of the United Nations Special Commission inspectors declared before the UN Security Council that Iraq was not cooperating with the inspections. The aim of the operation was to target the Iraqi weapons of mass destruction programme. In the Arab world, the attacks triggered much criticism, and public protests were held across the region in Syria, Jordan, Egypt, Sudan, Yemen and the Palestinian territories.[188] Several regional US allies denied the use of local bases to conduct airstrikes. Also within the UN Security Council, China, France and Russia, the other permanent members, expressed criticism and in response pleaded for the lifting of Iraqi oil sanctions. Iraqi government officials had already accused UN weapons inspectors of spying for the United States, and in early 1999 the UN acknowledged that this had occasionally happened. Furthermore, because a significant part of the targets was related to the Iraqi (Air) Defence structure, there was widespread criticism on the actual goal of the operation, not least in the Arab world. The feelings of anger over the military bombings added to the negative sentiment among large groups of Arabs regarding the earlier US cruise missile strikes on Afghanistan and Sudan. Also, in that same timeframe (late 1998–early 1999), several interviews with Bin Laden were also (partly) published or broadcasted in American and British news media. Compared with those interviews, in the Al Jazeera interview Bin Laden was asked and also chose to comment significantly more extensively on the recent US military interventions in Iraq.

The formulation of the opening questions from the Al Jazeera correspondent reflected the wider anger and resentment among Arab audiences against the recent bombing campaign.[189] Bin Laden noted how these were not attacks on Iraqi President Saddam Hussein, but against the growing power of the Arab and Islamic world. He pointed out that weapons of mass destruction were not the actual issue. According to Bin Laden, America had accused Iraq of using poison gas against the Kurds and lethal weapons against Iran, while actually supporting Iraq in those days. He stated that it was the United States that had really used weapons of mass destruction against Japan during the Second World War. Now that Iraq had become too great a power and a threat to Israel, the 'Jews were able to employ American and British Christians to do the job of attacking Iraq'.[190] As an illustration, Bin Laden named various US government officials who were Jewish. Because Israel possessed nuclear weapons, it was a right and duty for Muslims to acquire the same. Bin Laden praised Pakistan, the Muslim state that had been able to test five nuclear devices in May 1998. By doing this, he avoided answering whether *Al Qaeda* was actively acquiring nuclear weapons itself.

Similar to Bin Laden's 1996 and 1998 statements, the Al Jazeera interview served to strengthen the legitimacy of his ideas and persona, to threaten the United States, and recruit or inspire young followers. Contributing to all of these goals was Bin Laden's discussion of the value and symbolism of money as the antithesis of asceticism. For Bin Laden, the US reward of US$5 million for information leading to his capture merely illustrated the contrast between the values of the fighters who abandoned the material world as they came to the Afghan camps, and the US pursuit of self-interest, the adultery of American leadership and its general lack of moral values. For some of the more ordinary illiterate followers, it would have been virtually impossible to imagine the magnitude of such an amount of money. US attempts to drain Bin Laden's financial resources with sanctions were only partially effective. With respect to American goods, Bin Laden had already called for a boycott himself in the 1996 memorandum. He stated that instances in which 'countries on our side ordered us to stop attacking America' were a test of faith beyond the understanding of the 'hypocrites'.[191] 'Hypocrites' was used as a key synonym for the enemies of Islam, the ZCA, and their regional allies that pursued self-interest and personal wealth. This referred to the Quranic verse on hypocrites (*Surah Al-Munafiqun*) recited by Bin Laden in the interview.[192]

Other religious and historic references included the recurring referrals to Ibn Taymiyya, and in this case also one of his students, Ibn Kathir. As stated, after faith and prayers, *jihad* was the most important individual duty of every Muslim. Moreover, *hadith*s from the widely accepted volumes of al-Bukhari and Muslim, and Quranic verses such as the verse on the spoils of war (*Surah al-Anfal*, Quran 8:5) and the one on repentance (*Surah at-Tawbah*, Quran 9:118), underlined that there was no alternative but to rely on God. The interview focused on interpreting current events, Bin Laden's intentions, and the state of his efforts in a general sense, speaking to the Al Jazeera audiences.

Flagg Miller has noted that some of the 'divisive implications' of Bin Laden's Salafist background and Arabian ethnic-privileging were downplayed in the interview.[193] In a general sense, this was the case, though at one point the *Al Jazeera* correspondent did ask whether Bin Laden's position was contrary to the wider current of the Islamic movement, since many Islamist organisations had become more sympathetic towards democracy.[194] Bin Laden used this question to distinguish several groups of Muslims within the *ummah*. He stated that if circumstances prevented Muslims from gaining military knowledge, then it was sometimes impossible to wage *jihad* as an individual duty. Furthermore, Bin Laden again singled out the Muslim youths aged between fifteen and twenty-five years old: they were old enough to gain knowledge and young enough not to be committed to families and children. Older Muslims, who had done their share of fighting, for example, in Afghanistan, now had the different and important role of inciting and guiding (with their voices and pens) the young and energetic. Because of the US and allied Arab governments' power over the media, many youths had not learned about the true nature of the occupation in the early 1990s. In general, Bin Laden stated that Muslims should take care not to be 'afflicted by the disease of holding back'.[195]

At times, Bin Laden's answers appeared diffuse or conflicting. When asked why nothing had been heard from the WIF since its founding declaration, he replied that 'these months' could not 'be considered a long time in the renaissance of the *ummah* and resistance against the biggest enemy in the world'. Bin Laden further outlined how not all activities were advertised. Yet he also tried to highlight a sense of urgency with respect to Palestine, stating 'I don't know what people are waiting for after this clearest of betrayals' as Arab rulers had acted in the interest of the Jews in America.[196] Asked about the position of the EIJ within the WIF, Bin Laden stated, 'they have links to us'. He clarified that they had signed and supported the declaration but were not part of the WIF. There had been 'some confusion over an administrative issue' because 'the issuing of the ruling coincided with the founding of the Front'.[197]

The interviewer appeared to formulate his questions in a critical way now and then, making Bin Laden deny several issues. He denied any involvement in the killing of Abdullah Azzam in 1989 and underlined that they had greatly relied on each other. Rumours about the Arab Afghan mujahedeen receiving funds from the CIA or American government were refuted. He also rejected reports on his being in bad health, and contrasted them to his status as the most dangerous man in the world. Any doubts about his good relationship with the Taliban and scenarios of leaving the country were countered, as Bin Laden used the powerful and historic synonym 'Commander of the Faithful' (*amir al-muminin*) to describe Taliban leader Mullah Omar as leader of Muslims.[198] However, a critical point of the collateral damage done by followers (or himself) was not addressed: the victims of the 1998 embassy bombings were not subject to debate. Bin Laden mentioned that people were 'sorry to see the killing of innocents', but in the same breath stated that his efforts to incite the *ummah* with declarations had 'brought happiness to Muslims in the Islamic world' and underlined 'the extent of the sympathy in the Islamic world for strikes against Americans'.[199] The attacks were 'a popular response from young men who have put themselves forward and are striving to please God', according to Bin Laden.

Less prominent in the interview was the economic and security situation in Saudi Arabia that was so central to the 1996 Ladenese memorandum. On the other hand, some new topics were introduced, like North Korea's position on the international stage as a country with wise non-Muslim men resisting international organisations such as the UN. After the specific 1998 WIF declaration, this interview perpetuated the focus of the *Al Qaeda* narrative on the United States as the greater enemy. Gulf states were blamed for falling into the trap of deceit set for them by the United States. The securitization of the United States as an existential threat for the Islamic world that was central to the *Al Qaeda* narrative was reproduced in the Al Jazeera interview and hence amplified before a greater audience. It resonated well with wider Muslim sentiments and allowed Bin Laden to benefit from growing anti-American feeling among the greater Al Jazeera Arab audiences. The interview strengthened his position and image as a prominent opinion leader whose doings were in the service of activating young Muslims. The dual aim was to recruit them to join the Afghan training camps, and also spark violent activities beyond the direct capability of his networked organisation.

More interviews and documentaries on Bin Laden followed, providing a pan-Arab and Urdu forum for Bin Laden's message. In Pakistani news reports on Bin Laden regional topics were also re-contextualised, such as the threat from India and the situation in Kashmir, as waging *jihad* in terms of the *Al Qaeda* narrative. Two weeks before the press conference, India had tested five nuclear bombs, while Pakistan had yet to do the same. Several months later in June, as the war between India and Pakistan over control of the Kashmiri Kargil district was ongoing, *Wahdat* reported on Bin Laden's open letter in support of *jihad* in Kashmir.[200] Two Urdu reports in June and September outlined that Bin Laden was expecting US commandos. His order to 'shoot them on sight' and disdain for financial rewards stressed his confidence in the loyalty of his followers.[201] Between 1998 and 2001, many thousands of recruits joined the Afghan training camps.[202]

THE FOILED MILLENNIUM PLOTS

The turn of the millennium was not a prominent episode in Bin Laden's *Al Qaeda* narrative. There was a lack of statements. In the United States, the last months of 1999 were a phase in which fear of terrorist attacks was widespread. One of scarce references by Bin Laden to this timeframe was made in an Urdu newspaper in June 1999:

> [T]he United States' journey towards destruction will start before the arrival of the 21st century because this is the century of Islam and therefore the Muslim *ummah* should declare a jihad against the United States.[203]

It seems an opportunistic argument to make a reference with the 'century of Islam' to the twenty-first century on the Gregorian calendar. No major terrorist attack occurred as the (Western) world changed from 1999 to 2000, but two plots were thwarted. In late November 1999, sixteen suspects were arrested on terrorism charges in Jordan. Among them were several Arab Americans; they had been planning attacks on an SAS Radisson Hotel in Amman and several tourist sites in the country to target Westerners. In December, the Algerian Ahmed Ressam was arrested in Port Angeles, Washington, with a stack of explosives hidden in his car. His nervous behaviour while leaving the ferry from Canada had apparently caught the attention of one of the border guards. The investigation that followed revealed the intended target as Los Angeles international airport.

Those directly involved with the plots had sought support and received training in the Afghan training camps facilitated by Bin Laden and others. Ressam was not an actual 'Al Qaeda operative', but had received training to make bombs in a camp facilitated by Bin Laden in Afghanistan.[204] Similarly, some of the Jordanian cell members received explosives training at al-Farooq training camp in Afghanistan. One of them, Raeed Hijazi, was born in California and grew up in Saudi Arabia. He had met Abu Zubaydah, who was responsible for running training camps for Bin Laden, and pledged allegiance (bayat) to Bin Laden in return for the training and support he had received. It was reportedly the call from Abu Zubaydah to Jordanian cell leader Abu Hoshar that 'training was over' that led to the arrest of the sixteen cell members.[205] As a consequence of the training, Bin Laden, Abu Zubaydah, Mohammed Atef and Ayman al-Zawahiri all probably knew of the foiled millennium plots in advance.

Another failed attack was the attempt to bomb the USS The Sullivans in the Yemeni port of Aden on 3 January 2000. A small boat was loaded with so many explosives that it sank before reaching the US Navy vessel. This would remain hidden from the public eye until a second attempt against the USS Cole succeeded.

The USS Cole

On 12 October 2000, the small sunken boat had been recovered and was piloted alongside the American destroyer USS Cole which was arriving for a refuel stop in the port of Aden. After making friendly gestures on approach, the attackers detonated the boat, killing seventeen and wounding thirty-nine US sailors waiting for lunch aboard the ship. An Al Qaeda operative tasked to videotape the attack for propaganda purposes, Fahd al-Quso, had overslept and failed to accomplish his task. Yet soon images of the damaged destroyer were broadcasted globally by Western and Arab news media such as CNN and Al Jazeera. These pictures would later be used extensively as propaganda or dawa outreach recruitment material by Al Qaeda.

The attack marked the end of years of preparation that had involved Bin Laden directly. The intended target was initially a commercial vessel, but Bin Laden had shifted the focus to US military ships. The USS The Sullivans and

USS *Cole* represented the type of vessel used in the retaliatory strikes with cruise missiles on Afghanistan and Sudan. Bin Laden knew the operational coordinators and attackers well.[206] In November 2000, Bin Laden confided before a small audience of trusted aides and Al Jazeera reporter Ahmed Zaidan that he had been involved in the planning for the USS *Cole* attack.[207] Later, Zaidan commented critically how, contrary to the perception of many Al Jazeera viewers, Bin Laden was not only 'talking about religion' but was also using it to prove his ideas on world affairs.[208] Bin Laden wanted and anticipated a reprisal attack by US forces on Afghanistan, like the missile strikes in 1998 that had caused so much anger in the Arab world. If the United States was to invade Afghanistan on the ground, it would situate them in the same position as the Soviet forces during the Cold War. It would set them up for defeat from jihadi mujahedeen.

Reproduction and re-contextualisation: *As Sahab* video productions

Bin Laden made another statement on the USS *Cole* attack during his son Muhammad's wedding to the daughter of Al Qaeda's military commander Abu Hafs al-Masri (or Mohammed Atef) in Kandahar. The wedding consisted of two ceremonies held in January 2001. Again, Al Jazeera reporter Ahmed Zaidan was present, and the news channel broadcasted on the event.[209] During the first ceremony, most speakers, including Bin Laden, commented on the situation in Palestine. It was in the second ceremony that Bin Laden delivered a poetic speech that clearly referred to and praised the attack on the USS *Cole*. He was also seen wearing a Yemeni dagger (*jambiya*) as he stood before a large world map. Bin Laden was purportedly not content with his initial address and arranged another rehearsal before camera in the same hall the next day. He was highly thoughtful of his media presence: his image management included asking people to take new pictures when his appearance did not satisfy him.[210]

The internet increasingly enabled decentralised distribution of propaganda videos. Despite the failure to record the attack on the USS *Cole* itself, Al Qaeda's media office *As Sahab*, under the direction of Khalid Sheikh Mohammed, produced a video titled 'The Destruction of the American Destroyer USS *Cole*'. It featured fragments of Bin Laden's speeches, such as at the wedding, images from CNN and Al Jazeera, and clips from jihadi training camps in Afghanistan. It also addressed Muslim suffering in Palestine, Kashmir and Chechnya. The propaganda video would circulate widely on jihadi websites, among those training in Afghan camps, and youths in Saudi Arabia and Yemen. Some parts of the video material were broadcasted on Western and Arab news channels.

Featuring prominently in the fragments is the aspect of how a tiny boat can 'destroy a destroyer'. The most recent attack on the USS *Cole* was situated in line with legendary Islamic leaders and battles, such as Sultan Sallahudin who successfully fought the Crusaders in Jerusalem during the battle of Hitteen in

Figure 2.5 The *As Sahab* video

Source: *As Sahab*, 'The Destruction of the American Destroyer USS Cole',
June 2001, as in US Military Videos (YouTube publisher), 'The Al Qaida Plan,
videos by the terrorist, for the terrorist', 31 May 2012.

1187; the divine intervention that influenced the battle of Badr in favour of
the Prophet Mohammed in 624; and the battle of Khaybar against the Jews
near Medina in 629. The tiny boat or dinghy versus the slow-moving mighty
destroyer represented the asymmetrical relationship between the Muslim youth
of the *ummah* who 'sprung forward for jihad' versus the large US occupation
force. Like the battle of Badr, the attack on the USS *Cole* could be viewed as a
turning point and demonstration of heroism and success. In Yemen and Pakistan, Bin Laden's name was written on walls, sales of T-shirts with Bin Laden
prints and audio-cassettes of his speeches peaked, and he appeared on magazine covers like an icon.[211] According to Bin Laden, the attack demystified the
false competence and illusion of power, similarly to how US troops proved to
be a paper tiger as they withdrew from Somalia after a few casualties, and how
Soviet Special Forces were forced out of Afghanistan. Bin Laden's efforts to
activate and lead the Muslim youths into waging *jihad* against Americans, the
wider ZCA and their regional allies appeared to have been effective.

The wedding of Bin Laden's son as setting for the speech was illustrative of how the tight family bond between father and son, and between the offspring of the two jihadi leaders, was used as a symbolic projection of the nature of *Al Qaeda* as a jihadi organisation or movement, and the wider Muslim *ummah*. During the wedding ceremony, another of Bin Laden's sons, Hamza, addressed the audience. His complaint against the United States mirrored a text from Bin Laden published later by daily newspaper *Ausaf* in Urdu in March 2001. It consisted of a conversation between a father and his son. The son complained about why the United States continued to pursue Bin Laden only because 'you want to sacrifice yourself for the respect and magnificence of the Holy Kaaba and the eminence of Islam'.[212]

The attack and the propaganda outreach or preaching (*dawa*) that followed generated financial donations and spurred *Al Qaeda*'s recruitment efforts, resulting in many new young fighters.[213] On a broader scale, the video helped to strengthen the pre-eminence of Bin Laden and *Al Qaeda* among the population in various Arab and Muslim countries and specifically other jihadi groups. Some stated that a Bin Laden cult or hype was occurring in the Islamic world that resonated with wider feelings of anger and resentment against Western, and specifically US, economic involvement and military intervention in the Arab and Muslim world.[214]

For the *Al Qaeda* narrative, developments in Israel and the Palestinian territories at the time of the attack on the USS *Cole* provided a regional context that illustrated and amplified the wider meaning of the bombing in Yemen. The visit of Israeli opposition leader Ariel Sharon on 28 September 2000 to the *al-Haram al-Sharif* complex in Jerusalem where the *Al Aqsa* mosque was located, referred to by Jews as the Temple Mount, provoked anger among Palestinians and caused riots in Jerusalem. Just ten days before, the Palestinians had remembered the massacre of Palestinians and Lebanese Shiites in Beirut's Sabra and Shatila neighbourhoods. Sharon was held personally responsible by the Palestinians as he was the Israeli Defence Minister at the time. Following the visit, a second Palestinian uprising (*intifada*) broke out, with riots spreading across Israel and the Palestinian territories. On 12 October, the day the USS *Cole* was attacked, Israeli reservists were arrested after accidentally entering the Palestinian city of Ramallah. An angry mob lynched them while the recordings of an Italian television crew were broadcasted across the globe. The *Al Qaeda* narrative on fighting the far enemy focused on the United States as the 'head of the snake', but Israel was very much part of the ZCA too. Bin Laden sought to also recruit Palestinian youths by stating that liberating Jerusalem was one of his ultimate aims.

By now, *Al Qaeda* consisted of an executive *shura* council headed by Bin Laden, and several committees occupied with religious, political, military, administrative, media and security affairs.[215] In addition to some of the rigid structure overviews of *Al Qaeda* that have been presented, it is important to recognise how multifaceted *Al Qaeda* has always been. As groups and individuals still maintained multiple links and associations regarding ideology, logistical support and social networks, it is perhaps most accurate to describe Bin Laden's *Al Qaeda* as a networked organisation consisting of close associates, advisers and personal security confidants, wider groups of followers, and associated organisations that had received training to varying degrees.[216] Furthermore, there was disagreement over various issues among *Al Qaeda* members and associates, leading them to leave, and there was criticism among those who trained in the camps.[217] Nevertheless, it is apparent that the senior *Al Qaeda* leadership was able to coordinate and facilitate the planning and execution of complex terrorist attacks on US embassies in Africa, the USS *Cole* in Yemen, and not least the attacks on Washington and New York on 11 September 2001.

SECURITIZATION, POWER AND IDENTITY IN THE AL QAEDA NARRATIVE

This chapter has produced a situated and developing *Al Qaeda* narrative. As a key text, the 1996 memorandum represented the analytical beginning for this book, while marking its end were the *As Sahab* video and interviews which described the attack on the USS *Cole* in Yemen on 12 October 2000. Over the years, Bin Laden and *Al Qaeda* adjusted to the new media environment. Via a network of media offices and representatives, they were able to use satellite news channel Al Jazeera and the internet, which empowered them to reach larger and broader audiences in the Arab and Muslim world. The selected data in this study comprises translated Bin Laden speeches and statements that were either reproduced or re-contextualised by Arab and Urdu news media, and on the internet. Discursive practices of text production and consumption were situated in Arab culture, Islam and an Islamist Salafi jihadi order of discourse. To perform adequate textual and contextual analysis of the translations, a body of scholarly work on many of these texts was studied. The following now offers an analysis of the *Al Qaeda* narrative in terms of securitization, power and identity.

Bin Laden made various securitization efforts over the course of the *Al Qaeda* narrative. They built on and enforced each other, while also gradually transforming and developing the overall focus and meaning of Bin Laden's strategic message. For Bin Laden and the close associates who formed the core of what had become known as the networked organisation *Al Qaeda*, the institutionalisation of structure, roles and activities was developing. This was unlike the relatively stable structures and conventions that lie at the basis of a nation-state. More than in the US institutional narrative described in the next chapter, the *Al Qaeda* narrative was as much a reflection of its institutionalisation process as it was an element of its institutional development. By examining the constituent elements of securitization over time, the transformation of the *Al Qaeda* narrative could be mapped.

As *securitizing actor*, Bin Laden fulfilled the central role throughout the *Al Qaeda* narrative. This is not a conclusion based upon the analysis of the narrative (that would be rather tautological), but a result of the data selection for this study: statements and news reports on Osama bin Laden between 1992 and 2001. Yet, as various sources have indicated, the 1990s marked a 'golden age' or high tide for *Al Qaeda* in which Bin Laden *was* the central figure.[218] The narrative analysis framework, in addition, highlighted some nuances that were valuable when studying the process of securitization. In the early 1990s, Bin Laden's activities in Sudan were multifaceted, including setting up agricultural businesses and infrastructural projects while writing critical letters to the Saudi regime. He was also involved in providing guerrilla training to the Sudanese military and some of his own followers and associated groups. In the 1996 memorandum, Bin Laden introduced himself and his group as 'a concerned element' within the community of Muslim scholars (*ulema*). He was presented in the mid-1990s in political terms as an 'oppositionist leader', but also with religious knowledge and credentials, and relevant fighting experience. This positioned him to criticise the situation in Saudi Arabia and the Arabian Peninsula, to challenge the wrongdoings of the Saudi regime, and to denounce US regional military interventions and foreign policy. Bin Laden connected socio-economic, political and security problems with Islamic literature and jihadism, although contrary to several English translations of the 1996 memo-randum, the text could not be equated to a formal religious decree (*fatwa*). His position, power and responsibilities were ill-structured in the beginning. Hence, Bin Laden 'grew' into the role of securitizing actor who consistently worked to communicate his message.

In exploiting the opportunities new media offered to present his person-ality, Bin Laden also caused tensions among his followers and some of the associated groups. In 1998, the WIF against the Jews and the Crusaders was launched, formally decentralising Bin Laden to one of the five (although the first) signatories while allegedly signifying the growth of a movement. It proved difficult to expand and formalise coalitions such as the WIF, however. The front represented only a fraction of the Salafi jihadi groups around the world, and several of the signatories had to confront internal differences in the groups they represented. Al-Zawahiri's decision to sign without consulting the EIJ's *shura* council resulted in an organisational split. Following the foundation of the WIF and al-Zawahiri's personal shift of focus primarily on the far instead of the near enemy, he and some loyal supporters officially merged with *Al Qaeda*. Because of this, al-Zawahiri gained more prominence as a leading figure in *Al Qaeda* at the cost of the influence of others. Overall, the WIF declaration marked a strategic ideological transformation with respect to the existing Salafi jihadi order of discourse, separating Bin Laden, al-Zawahiri and other loyal followers from other Salafi jihadis.

The transformation was also strategic in that it unquestionably provided Bin Laden and his followers with a unique profile, which they strengthened further over the years as part of a distinct strand within the Salafi jihadi order of discourse. The Taliban wanted Bin Laden to maintain a low profile while residing in Afghanistan, but Bin Laden chose to continue publishing statements and holding press conferences and interviews. Several of Bin Laden's followers were critical of his allegiance to the Taliban and his eagerness to be interviewed. Thus, many personal and organisational fault lines fractured the 'front', whose global character was rather disputable too. Yet, as a consequence of the dynamic caused by the WIF declaration, the '*Al Qaeda* core' also grew, and in a way some of the former EIJ members became closer to Bin Laden as they institutionalised further.

Bin Laden used attempts by the United States to target him to increase his status and moral stance. The US economic sanctions against Bin Laden and Afghanistan, and the reward issued for information on him were in fact used as clear examples of the false, egocentric and material US values. For Bin Laden and his followers, these developments provided an opportunity to stress how Bin Laden had left behind his family fortune to engage in *jihad*, accentuate the value of asceticism and confirm their faith. Assertions that Bin Laden was being hunted by the CIA or targeted by the US missile strikes on Afghanistan also provided him with additional legitimacy. In general, Arab and Urdu news media enabled Bin Laden to express his views and at times provided textual or visual introductions that underlined his status as a leader.

According to Bin Laden, the *referent object* threatened was essentially the global Muslim world (*ummah*). It was more an ideological, cultural and religious entity than an institutionalised nation. Bin Laden used examples of suppression of Muslims, and specifically scholars, to illustrate how the essence of the *ummah* was under attack. Local illustrations of this wider threat were violence and aggression against Muslims in Palestine and Jerusalem, Egypt, Iraq, Chechnya, Bosnia, Kashmir, Indonesia, Somalia and Sudan. The Arab world, and specifically the Arabian Peninsula or the land of the two Holy Places, were of special prominence to all Muslims. The stationing of US troops in Saudi Arabia in 1990 represented clear and alarming proof of the growing involvement and intervention, or occupation, of the Americans in this holy region. This gave the Saudi population and particularly the Saudi youths a special status within the *ummah*. The critical vulnerability of the referent object lay in its physical and social security, as well as the protection of its values. In Saudi Arabia, the Holy Places were threatened by the combination of adopting 'man-made' laws over the law of God, the inability of the Saudi regime to fulfil its religious duty of protecting the Holy Places, the oppression of any resistance from Islamic scholars, and also the poor socio-economic conditions of minorities and the power and influence of international oil concerns on the Saudi regime. As such, the *ummah* as a whole was threatened.

Bin Laden also 'localised' the broader concept of the *ummah* as referent object before various other regional audiences. This was sometimes driven by aspirations to demonstrate the relevance of the message as the *Al Qaeda* coalition expanded, while in other cases it was given by the setting of text production, such as newspaper interviews, or out of a necessity to ensure support. In the case of Pakistan, newspapers were used frequently as an outlet for statements from Afghanistan, in parallel to and as a substitute for media contacts in London. Two of the signatories of the WIF declaration, Mir Hamzah and Fazlur Rahman, represented jihadi movements in Pakistan and Bangladesh. Responding to topical issues in Pakistan, Bin Laden congratulated the country for its successful nuclear tests in 1998. According to him, Pakistan had provided Muslims with an 'Islamic nuclear bomb'. Earlier tests by India were a cause for concern as India's alliance with Israel threatened the Muslim world. During the major Kargil war between India and Pakistan, Bin Laden compared the Pakistani-backed jihadi fighters with the Afghan mujahedeen. He also spoke repeatedly of the Iraqi people who suffered from the indiscriminate US aggression during the Gulf War in 1990, through UN and US economic sanctions against Iraq, and through Operation Desert Fox in 1998. Many references were made to the dire conditions in which the Palestinian people lived. According to Bin Laden, the Jews supported by the United States suppressed them and occupied Jerusalem.

Despite the efforts to relate *jihad* to local contexts, as noted there were many fault lines to overcome. Bin Laden's message resonated only with a small part of the Salafi jihadi groups, themselves a small minority among Muslims. There was an ideological gap regarding the nature of the referent subject between the Salafi jihadis willing to confront the near enemy (by either preaching, politics or violence) and the small group that supported Bin Laden's focus on the far enemy. This translated to weaknesses in the definition of the referent object. Who was threatened and by whom? Even though Salafi jihadis might have shared feelings of hostility towards the United States, many held different opinions on defining them as the primary enemy, or even explicitly declaring war.

Another issue causing friction among Salafi jihadis was Bin Laden's relationship with the Taliban. According to Bin Laden, the Taliban regime in Afghanistan had established the pious Islamic caliphate based on God's law (*shariah*). After the attacks on the US embassies in Africa, Bin Laden increased his show of support for the host on which he depended. Bin Laden announced that Taliban leader Mullah Omar was the Commander of the Faithful (*amir al-muminin*) and that supporting him was a religious duty. This statement was contested among some of his followers, but also deviated from the essence of Bin Laden's developing securitization effort. Therefore, attributing Omar with such symbolic Islamic credentials was probably a pragmatic move to maintain the support of his host. According to Bin Laden, the fact that the United States had added Afghanistan to the list of sponsors of terrorism was 'a sign of good conduct'.

Opposing and threatening the *ummah* was the *referent subject*, the ZCA and its regional allies, of which one of the most prominent was Saudi Arabia. In the early 1990s, Bin Laden's focus was on both the threat posed by policies and practices of the corrupt Saudi regime and the American troops that occupied the Arabian Peninsula. For Bin Laden, this occupation was the greatest and gravest of all ZCA aggressions. The 1996 memorandum published in *Al Quds Al Arabi* pointed more towards the United States as leader of the ZCA than the recorded speech did, which considered the threat posed by the oppressive activities of the Saudi regime as being more equal to that posed by the United States. The 1998 WIF declaration, with its more aggressive tone towards both the military and civilians, narrowed the focus on the Americans who were leading the alliance. As mentioned, this signified a distinct ideological shift or variation within the Salafi jihadi order of discourse.

According to Bin Laden, the 'crusader hordes acted like locusts, draining the region of its wealth and fertility', and (as a result) the Saudi regime was unable to fulfil its religious and social duties. Moreover, he stated, it was this acquired wealth that was used to buy the bullets that killed Muslims. According to Bin Laden, the ZCA was also responsible for killing mujahedeen, like Abdullah Azzam, and US Jews and Christians were using Israel to bring Muslims in Palestine to their knees. But also, it was under the influence of the Jews that the United States acted on behalf of Israel. In the context of Operation Desert Fox, Bin Laden noted in 1999 that Iraq had gained too much power and posed a threat to Israel, leading the Jews to employ American and British Christians to do the job of attacking Iraq.

Although several members of the UN Security Council objected to the US–UK bombing campaign over Iraq, Bin Laden continued to portray the UN as a cover for US and ZCA activities. In the early 1990s, it was the UN sanctions that prevented Muslims from obtaining arms, such as in Bosnia, and it was a UN umbrella that covered the US invasion of Somalia. Clear proof of how the UN was an instrument to the United States, Bin Laden stated, was that UN weapon inspectors were spying for the United States during their duties for the UN in Iraq.

The negative connotation of 'crusader' and 'Zionist' in the Muslim and Arab world resonated especially well with public resentment over US missile strikes in Afghanistan and Sudan, Operation Desert Fox and the presence of US troops in the Arab world. The visits to Yemen by the USS *The Sullivans* and USS *Cole* were presented as clear proof of US military involvement and intervention in a central Islamic region. Other powerful synonyms, such as 'hypocrites' and great unbeliever (*kufr*), strongly situated the referent subject in Islamic and historic terms as the enemy.

The *customized policy* aired the dicta of Ibn Taymiyya that the first individual obligation after faith and prayer was to defend Islam against intruders who assaulted sanctity or security. However, as the definition of the referent subject developed over the years, the character of this 'defence' changed. From expelling the ZCA presence from the Arabian Peninsula and ousting the Saudi regime with bomb attacks, guerrilla warfare and boycotting American goods, it altered to a *jihad* against primarily American servicemen and civilians all over the world. In the early 1990s, the bombings in Khobar and Riyadh served as clear indications for the ZCA to leave. Because of the large number of civilian casualties, the attacks on the US embassies in Africa were at first less symbolic for the *jihad* Bin Laden and *Al Qaeda* sought to instigate against the aggression of the ZCA; Bin Laden denied personal involvement in the attack. Yet, as distaste among Muslims for civilian casualties diminished through anger over the US missile strikes, Bin Laden stated he felt no sorrow for the embassy attacks.

Although not emphasised or exploited in the *Al Qaeda* narrative, the people arrested for plotting attacks at the turn of the millennium did embody the customised policy of an inspired Muslim vanguard taking the initiative to conduct assaults. The bombing of the USS *Cole* was in many respects the most symbolic illustration of how a courageous front of Muslim youths could defy the illusion of American military superpower. The asymmetrical character of the small boat versus a colossal military vessel was emphasised in *As Sahab* media publications. Bin Laden was screened expressing the key words and phrases that marked his earlier securitization efforts. Similar to the historic battle of Badr in 624 AD, the attack was presented as a turning point that could lure the United States into a losing ground war in Afghanistan.

Resonance with the identified audiences

The *Al Qaeda* narrative worked to inspire and incite, offering a framework for others to adopt and on which to base their actions. Ultimately, the goal was to (re)establish *shariah* in the land of Islam, free the sacred places from the ZCA, and liberate oppressed Muslim scholars (*ulema*) around the world. This was to be accomplished by mobilising a wide Muslim movement, including and beyond the direct capability of *Al Qaeda* and its associated groups, to engage in *jihad* with word and deed. Publicly, Bin Laden chose to deny his personal involvement in the various attacks after they had occurred, while welcoming the efforts. It is possible he needed to avoid losing the support of his host in Afghanistan, the Taliban. Yet such a stance also strengthened the narrative that Bin Laden was primarily offering his leadership to a vanguard of youths expressing the will of the *ummah*. What has become clear from US investigations following the attacks on the US embassies in Africa and the USS *Cole*, however, is that Bin Laden and his associates were closely involved in planning these actions.

Over the years, Bin Laden sought to establish, activate and expand various types audiences of the *Al Qaeda* narrative in parallel. Since his activities in Afghanistan in the 1980s, he had become a public figure. Across the Muslim world, pictures and posters of Bin Laden could be found in bazaars and religious schools, and audio-cassettes of his speeches were among those played in taxis or cafes, as he was deemed in many circles to be an inspirational ascetic figure.[219] Initially, the Saudi population was a key audience for the 1996 memorandum, while the wider global Muslim community remained more in the background. Bin Laden specifically sought to address the Muslim (and specifically Saudi) youths as potential followers who could become inspired and form a vanguard of the *ummah* to take action. He also addressed Saudi security personnel encouraging them to rise up against the Saudi regime. His primary audience consisted of young men aged between fifteen and twenty-five-years-old. According to Bin Laden, it was because some of them had not experienced the start of the ZCA occupation in 1990 that it became so important to educate and lead them. In later interviews and news reports, other regional audiences were also addressed, such as in Sudan, Pakistan and Afghanistan.

The 1996 speech and memorandum, and the 1998 WIF declaration were key texts in the development of securitization within the *Al Qaeda* narrative. However, it was also the reproduction and re-contextualisation of these texts in international news media, accelerated by the technological developments in the media environment, that amplified the narrative. Highly prominent was the 1998 Al Jazeera interview, which served to improve the legitimacy and status of Bin Laden's ideas and his persona. Satellite television brought not only Bin Laden's words, but also his pronunciation, tone, gestures and facial expressions as part of the message, directly to Al Jazeera's Arab viewers around the world. Thus, the securitization effort of the 1998 WIF declaration was reproduced and amplified before a greater audience. The ARC office in London and media contacts in Pakistan also gave Bin Laden power in discourse and enabled him to similarly circumvent Saudi state control. Through his eloquent language use and leadership status, Bin Laden had authority and a potential form of power over Arab and Muslim audiences to inspire.

As the attacks on the US embassies in 1998 and the USS *Cole* in 2001 demonstrated, Bin Laden also had the power to instigate and facilitate executive action. Publicly, Bin Laden often denied direct involvement and sought to advance the notion of a vanguard of Muslim youths as the engine for such attacks. But until the US missile strikes in 1998 that followed the embassy attacks in Africa, Bin Laden had only been able to a limited extent to inspire a broad popular audience and extend or mobilise his loyal followers with the developing (and strategically innovative) *Al Qaeda* narrative. His efforts went against the dominant current of Islamist or Salafi movements, such as in Egypt, which were turning away from violence. Moreover, although many in the Arab and Muslim world felt the grievances addressed by Bin Laden, only those belonging to a small segment of Salafi jihadis agreed with the proposed strategies. In terms of organisation, it is fair to characterise this small group of people who had pledged allegiance to Bin Laden as '*Al Qaeda*' in its early organisational form. At one end of the spectrum, they could be considered his *formal audience* (or perhaps more accurately, clusters of formal audiences) who were willing to plan, facilitate or conduct attacks.

After the US missile strikes on a pharmaceutical factory in Sudan and several jihadi training camps in Afghanistan (Operation Infinite Reach), popular protests occurred in Pakistan, Afghanistan and Sudan. Protesters expressed their anger over the killing of innocent Muslims by the United States, and some carried posters of Bin Laden. As a prominent target of the strikes, Bin Laden became better known to groups of Arabs and Muslims. The protesters could be considered part of his *moral audience*, as they strengthened Bin Laden's position of authority and indirectly or potentially influenced opinions among Salafi jihadis about his securitization efforts.

The bombing campaign over Iraq (Operation Desert Fox) resulted in further resentment in the Arab and Muslim world over US economic involvement and military intervention or 'occupation' in the region. It increasingly aligned Bin Laden's securitization efforts with the situational perception of these wider populations, not just his group of loyal followers. To a certain extent, doubts and reservations regarding the African civilians who had been killed in the embassy attacks were backgrounded. The successful bombing of the USS *Cole* with a small dinghy only added to this backgrounding effect. The video of the attack produced by *As Sahab* was a powerful tool for inspiration and recruitment that aligned with Muslim discontent and resentment against the United States. As mentioned, the imposing of economic sanctions against Bin Laden, his followers and the Taliban only confirmed and substantiated the *Al Qaeda* narrative. In 1996, Bin Laden had called for a boycott on American goods in Saudi Arabia, and for Salafi jihadis, asceticism was an essential way of life that contrasted to Western materialism. Practically, the sanctions had a highly limited effect on Bin Laden's funds or US–Afghan trade. Efforts by the United States to target Bin Laden and offer rewards were perceived as proof of US materialism and power politics.

The character of the narrative

The elements above described the transformation of Bin Laden's proactive securitization efforts between the early 1990s and early 2001. Bin Laden increasingly dedicated his time and effort to the single cause of securitizing the 'far enemy' that he had come to define so explicitly during the late 1990s. The narrative highlighted the gradual development of characterisations of entities in texts as an ideological process of naturalisation. Some of the early efforts were complex or diffuse, but later ones were accelerated by clear statements and powerful events. In the narrative, US foreign policies in Saudi Arabia, Israel and Palestine, Iraq, and the wider Middle East were a central concern. This provided the basic condition of 'occupation', which transformed the nature of the *jihad* and legitimised attacking US servicemen and civilians around the globe as an individual duty for Muslims. Any peaceful intentions Americans might have had, and any positive effects of their influence in the region were not considered.

In terms of power, Bin Laden employed his discursive ability to establish and maintain a narrative against the dominant Salafi jihadi current. In a way, this involved working cautiously around the power 'behind discourse' of established mainstream Muslim scholars to standardise language use and to decide on genre conventions. For example, questions were raised regarding whether the signatories of the 1998 WIF declaration were in fact authorised to make the statement, and with that, what the nature or character of the declaration was in terms of genre. Because of Bin Laden's moral and somewhat mythical status, his eloquent use of Arabic, and more practically his ARC platform, he had the power in discourse to declare what he wanted before a wide Arabic-speaking audience – at some stage even in spite of attempts by his host in Afghanistan, the Taliban, to keep him silent.

Financial and physical resources allowed Bin Laden to employ power to instigate and facilitate actual attacks. However, these attacks required only the consent of those engaged in their planning and execution. There was compartmentalisation of attack plans, and the network structure of individuals and groups gave Bin Laden's formal audience of loyal followers a fragmented character; Bin Laden did not need the consent of his formal audience as a whole. In a wider sense, given the unconventional direction of his efforts (against the 'far enemy'), gaining momentum with the narrative among broader (moral) audiences was at times something of an uphill battle. The narrative struggled to gain assent among Muslims, against more traditional Salafi jihadi and wider Arab and Muslim philosophical, moral and institutional propositions. For securitization efforts, audiences are as necessary an element as the securitizing actor, but what this *Al Qaeda* narrative has shown is that in the case of Bin Laden and *Al Qaeda*, defining the nature, status, and function of moral and formal audiences was complex. This issue is addressed further in Chapter 5.

The US missile strikes on Afghanistan and Sudan; the US indictment, reward and sanctions against Bin Laden and *Al Qaeda*; the US sanctions against the Taliban; Operation Desert Fox; and the attack on the USS *Cole* were just as crucial as Bin Laden's numerous media performances for the momentum or progress of the narrative. It was because of the combination of these events and circumstances that the late 1990s and early 2000s became the glory days for Bin Laden and the *Al Qaeda* narrative. It signified a process of the naturalisation of Bin Laden's Salafi jihadi message among small but growing formal and larger moral audiences. Meanings attributed to statements, events and circumstances resonated with feelings of outrage and resentment, and became more ideological to an increasing number of new followers.

For *Al Qaeda*, the 1996–2001 timeframe simultaneously marked a process of self-identification. As narrative and events took shape, social roles became more institutionalised, and so did *Al Qaeda* as an organisation. Over time, a limited number of other jihadis joined Bin Laden's effort, and he started to share the public stage with some of them, such as Ayman al-Zawahiri. *Al Qaeda*'s *shura* council and the various military, political, religious, administrative, security and media subcommittees developed as they coordinated and facilitated activities in support of the proposed customised policy. *Al Qaeda* was reflected in the narrative, but also became more of an organisation because of and through the narrative as securitization efforts and attacks escalated.

REFLECTION

How adequate is the basic analytic narrative captured in this chapter? The selected key texts generated a strong anchor for the *Al Qaeda* narrative, complemented by the analysis and interpretation that followed from the narrative analysis framework. The introductory and descriptive sections that provided the background and outline for the narrative were also essential. Identifying audiences was more difficult, however, and determining resonance of the securitization efforts was challenging. Nevertheless, the narrative has provided clues, such as referent object definition, text reproduction and anecdotal evidence of resonance. These will be used in the last chapter to more comprehensively position audiences and discuss their nature and significance for the securitization efforts.

Limiting the research, though not making it impossible, was the necessary use of (multiple) English translations of texts. As a result, linguistic analysis was restricted. By contrasting English translations, some irregularities could be identified and excluded from analysis. For example, two respected academic sources identified Fazlur Rehman, one of the WIF declaration signatories, as a different person.[220] English translations classified both the 1996 Ladenese memorandum and the 1998 WIF declaration as *fatwa*s (formal religious decrees), whereas from detailed analysis and a discussion of the literature, it became apparent that neither text could be characterised as such. Furthermore, by taking Arab poetry (*qasidah*) and other religious references in the 1996 speech recording and text more explicitly into account, another conclusion of this study was that the Saudi regime was a more equal part of the referent subject compared with the United States or ZCA than several English translations of the memorandum had indicated.

Some of the extensive available literature on Bin Laden, *Al Qaeda*, jihadism and Islam was invaluable for interpreting and contextualising the texts.[221] All in all, the *Al Qaeda* narrative has highlighted how this case study as part of the wider ACN methodology could not be performed in a vacuum. Using translated texts and various linguistic, cultural, and religious interpretations of various renowned scholars and writers proved to be an adequate approach to capture this basic analytic narrative in this book.

NOTES

1. Lawrence Wright, *The Looming Tower: Al-Qaeda and the Road to 9/11* (New York: Vintage Books, 2006), 193; Tod Hoffman, *Al Qaeda Declares War: the African Embassy Bombings and America's Search for Justice* (Lebanon, NH: University Press of New England, 2014), 16.
2. Ali Soufan, *The Black Banners: Inside the Hunt for Al-Qaeda* (London: Penguin, 2011), 75.
3. Fawaz Gerges, *The Rise and Fall of Al-Qaeda* (Oxford: Oxford University Press, 2011), 60.
4. Jason Burke, *Al Qaeda* (London: Penguin, 2007), 8.
5. Peter Bergen and Paul Cruickshank, 'Revisiting the Early Al Qaeda: Updated Account of its Formative Years', *Studies in Conflict and Terrorism* 35(1) (2012): 1–36; Holbrook, *The Al-Qaeda Doctrine*, 12.
6. Flagg Miller, 'Al-Qaida as a "Pragmatic Base": Contributions of Area Studies to Sociolinguistics', *Journal of Language and Communication* 28 (2008): 388. The term *Al Qaeda* has been used in an Islamic context as early as the eighth century.
7. For example, Bruce Lawrence (ed.), *Messages to the World: the Statements of Osama Bin Laden* (London: Verso, 2005); Gilles Kepel and Jean-Pierre Milelli, *Al Qaeda in Its Own Words*, trans. Pascale Ghazaleh (Cambridge, MA: Harvard University Press, 2008); FBIS, 'Compilation of Usama bin Laden statements 1994–January 2004'.
8. Holbrook, *The Al-Qaeda Doctrine*.
9. Ashraf Abdul-Fatah, 'A Corpus-based Study of Conjunctive Explicitation in Arabic Translated and Non-translated Texts Written by the Same Translators/Authors', PhD thesis, University of Manchester, 2010.
10. Mohammed Ali Bardi, 'A Systemic Functional Description of the Grammar of Arabic', PhD thesis, Macquarie University, Sydney, 2008.
11. Mbaye Lo, *Understanding Muslim Discourse: Language, Tradition, and the Message of Bin Laden* (New York: University Press of America, 2009), 10.
12. Ibid., 9.
13. Ibid., 6; Abu 'Uthman Al-Jahiz, *Al-Bayan wa al-Tabyin* (Lebanon: Dar al-Jil, 1965), 98.
14. Lawrence, *Messages to the World*, xii.
15. Rohan Gunaratna, *Inside Al Qaeda: Global Network of Terror* (New York: Berkeley, 2003), 17.
16. Flagg Miller, *The Audacious Ascetic: What the Bin Laden Tapes Reveal about Al-Qaeda*, Kindle edition (Oxford: Oxford University Press, 2015), 80.
17. G. J de Graaff, *Op Weg Naar Armageddon, De Evolutie van Fanatisme* (Den Haag: Boom, 2012), 531–45.
18. Peter Bergen, *The Osama bin Laden I Know* (New York: Simon & Schuster, 2006), 49–74.

19. Miller, *The Audacious Ascetic*, location 1480–1929, 3568.
20. Peter Nanninga, 'Jihadism and Suicide Attacks, al-Qaeda, al-Sahab and the Meanings of Martyrdom', PhD thesis, University of Groningen, 13.
21. De Graaff, *Op Weg Naar Armageddon*, 534.
22. Lo, *Understanding Muslim Discourse*, 3.
23. Ibid., 92–108.
24. Flagg Miller, *The Moral Resonance of Arab Media: Audiocassette Poetry and Culture in Yemen* (Cambridge, MA: Harvard University Press, 2007).
25. Jamal Khashoggi, 'Arab Youths Fight Shoulder to Shoulder with Mujahedeen', *Al Majallah*, No. 430, 4 May 1988.
26. Miller, *The Audacious Ascetic*, 77.
27. Gunaratna, *Inside Al Qaeda*, 30–1.
28. Gunaratna, *Inside Al Qaeda*, 206; Burke, *Al Qaeda*, 148–9; Soufan, *The Black Banners*, 41; Gerges, *The Rise and Fall of Al-Qaeda*, 94.
29. Bernard Shaw (TV anchor), 'Impact, Holy Terror?, Osama bin Ladin', interview by Peter Arnett for *CNN Impact*, CNN, 10 August 1997.
30. Soufan, *The Black Banners*, 51; Miller, *The Audacious Ascetic*, 161.
31. Abu Shiraz, 'May 1998 Interview with Bin Laden Reported', *Pakistan*, 20 February 1999, 10, as translated in FBIS, 111–17.
32. Kepel, *Jihad*, 316–17.
33. Hoffman, *Al Qaeda Declares War*, 17.
34. Steve Coll, *Ghost Wars: the Secret History of the CIA, Afghanistan, and Bin Laden, from the Soviet Invasion to September 10, 2001* (New York: Penguin, 2004).
35. Soufan, *The Black Banners*, 48–50.
36. For example, Hoffman, *Al Qaeda Declares War*, 17.
37. Kepel, *Jihad*, 84; Nanninga, 'Jihadism and Suicide Attacks', 54.
38. As discussed in Ḍiyā' Rashwān (ed.), *The Spectrum of Islamist Movements*, vol. 1 (Berlin: Verlag Hans Schiler, 2007), 429–40.
39. Soufan, *The Black Banners*, 30–2.
40. Laura Mansfield, *His Own Words: a Translation of the Writings of Dr Ayman Al Zawahiri* (London: LTG Publications, 2006), 160–3.
41. Kepel and Milelli, *Al Qaeda in Its Own Words*, 171–81.
42. Ibid.
43. Marc Sageman, *Understanding Terror Networks* (Philadelphia, PA: University of Pennsylvania Press, 2004), 148.
44. Soufan, *The Black Banners*, 30, 65, 122.
45. Ibid., 52.
46. Bergen, *The Osama bin Laden I Know*, 125.
47. Jamal al-Rayyan (TV anchor), 'Bin Ladin, Others Pledge "Jihad" to Release Prisoners in US, Saudi Jails', *Today's Harvest*, Al Jazeera, 21 September 2000, as translated in FBIS, 144–6.
48. 9/11 Commission Report, 58.
49. Ibid., 60.
50. Soufan, *The Black Banners*, 33–55.
51. Lo, *Understanding Muslim Discourse*, 84–5.

52. Ibid., 85.
53. Ali Abd-al-Karim and Ahmad Al-Nur, 'Usama Bin Ladin Denies "Terrorism" Link', *Al-Quds Al-Arabi*, 9 March 1994, 4, as translated in FBIS, 1–3.
54. Abdul Bari Atwan, *The Secret History of Al Qaeda*, Kindle edition (London: Saqi Books, 2008), location 2957.
55. Ibid., location 3051.
56. See Annex 'Selection of Texts' under Chapter 3.
57. Miller, *The Audacious Ascetic*, 19.
58. Ibid., 34, location 735, Kindle edition.
59. Osama bin Ladin, 'Ladenese Epistle', 23 August 1996, multiple translations.
60. Miller, 'Al-Qaida as a "Pragmatic Base"'.
61. Miller, *The Audacious Ascetic*, 21.
62. Atwan, *The Secret History of Al Qaeda*, location 818.
63. William A. Rugh, *Arab Mass Media: Newspapers, Radio, and Television in Arab Politics* (Westport, CT: Praeger, 2004), 173.
64. Miller, *The Audacious Ascetic*, 244.
65. Ibid.; Lo, *Understanding Muslim Discourse*, 16; Holbrook, *The Al-Qaeda Doctrine*, 65.
66. Lo, *Understanding Muslim Discourse*, 20–4.
67. MSANEWS, 'The Ladenese Epistle, Declaration of War against the Americans Occupying the Land of the Two Holy Places', 2 October 1996.
68. Sahih International, 'Surah At-Tawbah'.
69. Lo, *Understanding Muslim Discourse*, 86.
70. Lawrence, *Messages to the World*, 30.
71. MSANEWS, 'The Ladenese Epistle'.
72. Lawrence, *Messages to the World*, 27; MSANEWS, 'The Ladenese Epistle'.
73. Soufan, *The Black Banners*, xvii–xix.
74. Miller, *The Audacious Ascetic*, location 631.
75. Ibid., location 5215.
76. Ibid.
77. For example, Behnam Said, 'Hymns (Nasheeds): a Contribution to the Study of the Jihadist Culture', *Studies in Conflict & Terrorism* 35(12) (2012): 863–79.
78. Miller, *The Audacious Ascetic*, 236.
79. Gerges, *The Rise and Fall of Al-Qaeda*, 79.
80. Holbrook, *The Al-Qaeda Doctrine*, 15; Nanninga, 'Jihadism and Suicide Attacks', 55–7.
81. Bin Laden, 'Open Letter to King Fahd'; Lawrence, *Messages to the World*, 23.
82. Miller, *The Audacious Ascetic*, 253, location 5361, Kindle edition.
83. MSANEWS, 'The Ladenese Epistle', Sahih International, 'Surah Ali'Imran'.
84. MSANEWS, 'The Ladenese Epistle'.
85. Ibid.
86. Miller, *The Audacious Ascetic*, location 5226.
87. MSANEWS, 'The Ladenese Epistle'.
88. Ibid.
89. Ibid.

90. Ibid., Osama Bin Laden, 'Declaration of War', 1996, translated by CTC West Point.
91. MSANEWS, 'The Ladenese Epistle'.
92. Ibid.
93. Ibid.
94. Ibid., Bin Laden, 'Declaration of War'.
95. MSANEWS, 'The Ladenese Epistle'.
96. Miller, *The Audacious Ascetic*, 245.
97. See, for example, Kepel, *Jihad*, 219.
98. Joas Wagemakers, *A Quietist Jihadi: the Ideology and Influence of Abu Muhammad al-Maqdisi* (Cambridge: Cambridge University Press, 2012), 2–10.
99. Quintan Wiktorowicz, 'Anatomy of the Salafi Movement', *Studies in Conflict and Terrorism* 29(3) (2006): 208.
100. Wagemakers, *A Quietist Jihadi*, 4.
101. Ibid., 6.
102. Ibid., 5.
103. Wiktorowicz, 'Anatomy of the Salafi Movement', 207–40.
104. Wagemakers, *A Quietist Jihadi*, 9.
105. Ibid., 9.
106. Kepel, *Jihad*, 304.
107. For example, Osama Bin Laden, 'Open Letter for Shaykh Bin Baz on the Invalidity of his Fatwa on Peace with the Jews', 29 December 1994.
108. Lo, *Understanding Muslim Discourse*, 57.
109. MSANEWS, 'The Ladenese Epistle'.
110. Bukhari, Vol. 4, Book 53, No. 369.
111. Lawrence, *Messages to the World*, xx.
112. MSANEWS, 'The Ladenese Epistle'.
113. Ibid.
114. Wiktorowicz, 'Anatomy of the Salafi Movement', 211.
115. Lo, *Understanding Muslim Discourse*, 6–14.
116. Hamid Mir, 'Pakistan Interviews Usama Bin Ladin', 18 March 1997, as translated in FBIS, 41–8
117. Abdul Bari Atwan, 'Bin Laden Interviewed on Jihad Against US', *Al-Quds Al-Arabi*, 27 November 1996, as translated in FBIS, 28–36.
118. Ibid., 28–36.
119. Mir, 'Pakistan Interviews Usama Bin Ladin'.
120. *Asharq al-Awsat*, 'The Afghan-Arabs Part One', 29 June 2005; Gerges, *The Rise and Fall of Al-Qaeda*, 64–72.
121. Burke, *Al Qaeda*, 183; Wright, *The Looming Tower*, 284.
122. For example, Vahid Brown, *Cracks in the Foundation: Leadership Schisms in Al-Qa'ida from 1989–2006*, CTC Harmony Project (West Point, NY: CTC West Point, 2007), 12–18.
123. Gerges, *The Rise and Fall of Al-Qaeda*, 46.
124. Lawrence, *Messages to the World*, 58–62.
125. Miller, *The Audacious Ascetic*, location 8908.

126. Lawrence, *Messages to the World*, 58–62.
127. Sahih International, 'Surah At-Tawbah'.
128. Lawrence, *Messages to the World*, 61, fn. 10.
129. 'Hukm', *The Oxford Dictionary of Islam*; 'Aḥkām (plural of hukm)', *The Encyclopedia of Islam*.
130. Lawrence, *Messages to the World*, 60–1.
131. Camille Tawil, *Brothers in Arms: The Story of al-Qa'ida and the Arab Jihadists* (London: Saqi, 2010), 153–4.
132. Mir, 'Pakistan Interviews Usama Bin Ladin'.
133. Gerges, *The Rise and Fall of Al-Qaeda*, 65.
134. Tawil, *Brothers in Arms*.
135. Salah, Al Hayat, 28 December 1998, as in Gerges, *The Rise and Fall of Al-Qaeda*, 69.
136. Alison Pargeter, *The New Frontiers of Jihad: Radical Islam in Europe* (Philadelphia, PA: University of Pennsylvania Press, 2013), 75.
137. Ibid., 218.
138. Stanford University, 'Harkat-ul-Jihadi al-Islami'.
139. Subir Bhaumik, 'Jihad or Joi Bangla, Bangladesh in Peril', in Jaideep Saikia and Ekatarina Stepanova (eds), *Terrorism: Patterns of Internationalization* (London: Sage, 2009), 84.
140. Kepel and Milelli, *Al Qaeda in Its Own Words*, 282, n. 18.
141. Burke, *Al Qaeda*, 13.
142. Lawrence, *Messages to the World*, 60.
143. Ibid., 61.
144. Ibid., 59.
145. Ibid., 59.
146. Ibid., 60–1.
147. Kepel, *Jihad*; David Cook, *Understanding Jihad*, 2nd edn (Berkeley, CA: University of California Press, 2015); Richard Bonney, *Jihad: From Qur'an to Bin Laden* (London: Palgrave Macmillan 2004); Rudolph Peters, *Jihad in Classical and Modern Islam: a Reader* (Princeton, NJ: Marcus Wiener, 1996).
148. For example, Anne-Marie Delcambre, *Inside Islam* (Milwaukee, WI: Marquette University Press, 2005).
149. Sayyid Qutb, *Milestones (Ma'alim fi-l-Tariq)*, translation (SIME Journal, [1965] 2005).
150. Qutb, *Milestones*, 45.
151. De Graaff, *Op Weg Naar Armageddon*, 503–21.
152. Omar Abdel Rahman, *A Word of Truth: Dr. Omar Abdul Rahman's Legal Summation in the Jihad Case* (in Arabic) (n.p.: n.d.), 75, as in Fawaz Gerges, *The Far Enemy: Why Jihad Went Global*, 2nd edn (Cambridge: Cambridge University Press, 2010), 5.
153. Steven Brooke, 'Jihadist Strategic Debates before 9/11', *Studies in Conflict and Terrorism* 31(3) (2008): 205.
154. R. Sayed (ed.), *The Militant Prophet: the Revolutionaries*, vol. II (in Arabic) (London: Riad El-Rayyes Books, 1991), 130, as in Gerges, *The Far Enemy*, 10.

155. Abdullah Azzam, 'From Kabul to Jerusalem', *Al Jihad* 52 (February–March 1989), as in Brooke, 'Jihadist Strategic Debates before 9/11'.
156. Vahid Brown, 'Classical and Global Jihad: Al-Qa'ida's Franchising Frustrations', in Assaf Moghadam and Brian Fishman (eds), *Fault Lines in Global Jihad: Organizational, Strategic, and Ideological Fissures* (New York: Routledge, 2011), 88–9.
157. Gerges, *The Far Enemy*, 27–8.
158. Maha Azzam, 'The Gulf Crisis: Perceptions in the Muslim World', *International Affairs* 67(3) (1991): 473–85.
159. Milton Viorst, 'The Storm and the Citadel', *Foreign Affairs* 75(1) (1996): 93–107.
160. Miller, *The Audacious Ascetic*, location 5150.
161. Bergen, *The Osama bin Laden I Know*, 250.
162. Azeem Siddiqui, 'Interview with Usama Bin Ladin Reported', *Al-Akhbar*, 31 March 1998, 1, 8, as translated in FBIS, 61–2.
163. *Al-Quds Al-Arabi*, 'Bin Ladin: Afghanistan's Inclusion on US "Terrorism List" is "Certificate of Good Conduct" for Taliban', 18 May 1998, 3, as translated in FBIS, 66–7.
164. Muhammed Salah, 'World Islamic Front Backs "Intifadah of Palestine's Sons"'.
165. Muhammad Dalbah, 'United States Admits that Keeping its Troops in the Gulf is Causing Dissatisfaction, Bin Ladin Threatens to Launch Attack Soon', *Al-Quds Al-Arabi*, 28 May 1998, 1, as in FBIS, 70–1.
166. Burke, *Al Qaeda*, 185.
167. Rahimullah Yusufzai, 'Taliban let Bin Ladin Break His Silence', *The News*, 6 January 1999, internet version, as translated in FBIS, 79–82.
168. Wright, *The Looming Tower*, 244.
169. Soufan, *The Black Banners*, 78, 319.
170. Gus Martin (ed.), *The SAGE Encyclopedia of Terrorism*, 2nd edn (Thousand Oaks, CA: Sage, 2011), 307–8.
171. Soufan, *The Black Banners*, 85.
172. Ayman Al-Zawahiri, 'Bin Ladin Calls on Moslem Ummah (Nation) to Continue Jihad against Jews and Americans to Liberate their Holy Places', *The News/ Agence France Presse*, 21 August 1998, as translated in FBIS, 74–5.
173. Agence France Presse, 'Bin Ladin Denies Role in Bombings of US Missions', 24 December 1998, as in FBIS, 78–9.
174. For example, Soufan, *The Black Banners*, 75.
175. Burke, *Al Qaeda*, 181; Wright, *The Looming Tower*, 309.
176. For example, CNN, 'Muslims, Yeltsin Denounce Attack', 21 August 1998.
177. CNN, 'Thousands Stage anti-U.S. Protest in Sudan', 22 August 1998.
178. Michael Scheuer, *Through Our Enemies' Eyes: Osama bin Laden, Radical Islam, and the Future of America*, rev. edn (Washington, DC: Potomac Books, 2007), 311–12.
179. For example Abdul Bari Atwan, 'Bin Ladin Tells al-Quds al-'Arabi, "The Battle Has Not Yet Started, We Will Reply to Clinton in Deeds"', *Al-Quds Al-Arabi*, 22/23 August 1998, 1.
180. *Al-Akhbar*, 'Usama Bin Ladin Sends Message to Anti-US Conference'.
181. Ibid.

182. Ibid.
183. *Abdul Bari Atwan*, '"The Battle Has Not Yet Started"'.
184. Ibid.
185. Jamil Khan, 'Bin Ladin, Expel Jews, Christians From Holy Places', *Rawalpindi Jang*, 18 November 1998, 1, 7, as translated in FBIS, 78.
186. Nanninga, 'Jihadism and Suicide Attacks', 69.
187. Lawrence, *Messages to the World*, 65–94.
188. For example, Daniel Williams, 'Protests, Violence Flare in Arab World', *The Washington Post*, 20 December 1998.
189. Lawrence, *Messages to the World*, 66, 68.
190. Ibid., 67.
191. Ibid., 78.
192. Sahih International, 'Surah Al-Munafiqun'.
193. Miller, *The Audacious Ascetic*, location 6355.
194. Lawrence, *Messages to the World*, 79.
195. Ibid., 80.
196. Ibid., 75.
197. Ibid., 88.
198. Ibid., 86.
199. Ibid., 74.
200. *Wahdat*, 'Usama Bin Ladin Pens Letter in Support of Kashmir Jihad', 8 June 1999, 1, 5, as translated in FBIS, 118–19.
201. *Rawalpindi Jang*, 'Bin Ladin Calls on Muslims to Declare Jihad Against US', 25 June 1999, 1, 6, as translated in FBIS, 133–4; *Islamabad Khabrain*, 'UBL Orders Mujahidin to Shoot US Commandos "on Sight"', 12 September 1999, 1, 6, as translated in FBIS, 134–5.
202. Atwan, *The Secret History of Al Qaeda*, location 3069.
203. *Rawalpindi Jang*, 'Bin Ladin Calls on Muslims to Declare Jihad Against US'.
204. Burke, *Al Qaeda*, 199; Wright, *The Looming Tower*, 336.
205. 9/11 Commission Report, 174–5.
206. For example, Soufan, *The Black Banners*, 562–3.
207. Bergen, *The Osama bin Laden I Know*, 254–7.
208. Ibid.
209. Ahmad Zaidan, 'Al Jazeera's A. Zaidan, I am a Journalist not Terrorist, 15 May 2015.
210. Wright, *The Looming Tower*, 377.
211. Scheuer, *Through Our Enemies' Eyes*, 307.
212. *Islamabad Ausaf*, 'Ausaf Receives Bin Ladin's Poem on Resolve to Continue Jihad', 3 March 2001, 1, 7, FBIS, 147–8.
213. Wright, *The Looming Tower*, 331, 374; Thomas Hegghammer, 'Terrorist Recruitment and Radicalization in Saudi Arabia', *Middle East Policy* 8(4) (2006): 39–60; Atwan, *The Secret History of Al Qaeda*, location 3083.
214. For example, Miller, *The Audacious Ascetic*, 302, location 6338; Burke, *Al Qaeda*, 181.
215. See, for example, Rohan Gunaratna and Aviv Oreg, *Global Jihad Movement* (Washington, DC: Rowman & Littlefield, 2015), 58.

216. Bruce Hoffman, 'Rethinking Terrorism and Counterterrorism since 9/11', *Studies in Conflict and Terrorism* 25(5) (2002): 309–10.
217. US CIA, AFGP-2002-003251.
218. For example, see Marc Sageman, *Leaderless Jihad: Terror Networks in the Twenty-First Century* (Philadelphia, PA: University of Pennsylvania Press, 2008), 49–50.
219. Scheuer, *Through Our Enemies' Eyes*, 306–7.
220. Kepel and Milelli, *Al Qaeda in Its Own Words* versus Lawrence, *Messages to the World*.
221. Especially Miller, *The Audacious Ascetic*; Gerges, *The Rise and Fall of Al-Qaeda*; Gerges, *The Far Enemy*; Kepel, *Jihad*.

3

US INSTITUTIONAL TERRORISM NARRATIVE ON BIN LADEN AND *AL QAEDA*

INTRODUCTION

Like the previous chapter, this one serves both a descriptive and an analytical purpose. In portraying US institutional statements on Bin Laden and *Al Qaeda*, and their reproduction and re-contextualisation in US media, common themes emerge from the narrative. Several securitization efforts can be identified, along with more indirect strategies to manage the threat of terrorism. Since its foundation, the United States has experienced terrorist acts of various kinds, with various motivations. However, this study deliberately limits terrorism to Bin Laden or *Al Qaeda*. The strategic narrative of the intelligence consumer is something traditionally kept separate from intelligence analysis, yet considering that this perspective is key to examining the multi-consequentiality of US and *Al Qaeda* securitization efforts across social domains.

The following chronologically describes the *US institutional terrorism narrative* on Osama bin Laden and *Al Qaeda* during the 1990s and 2000. Situated in the social practice of the politics of nations, the narrative is based on source material that embodies a wide variety of US government statements: ad hoc and planned press meetings; formal declarations to the US Congress and international fora such as the UN; weekly radio addresses from the White House; and live televised presidential statements. Furthermore, other official US government communiqués such as annual reports on terrorism have also been studied. Texts were selected based on a set of search queries of key words relating to President Clinton, the US government, Osama bin Laden, *Al Qaeda* and various significant events, such as the US embassy bombings in Kenya and Tanzania, foiled plots at the turn of the millennium, and arrests of terrorist suspects by US law enforcement agencies. Most central to the narrative are statements made by President Clinton.

Some investigative reports and publications that were declassified or published years after the events of the 1990s occurred are incorporated in the analysis. In the intelligence practice, the ACN methodology would entail cooperation between intelligence professionals, working-level policymakers, and possibly trusted outside experts with access to an array of classified information, especially regarding national security policymaking. For this case study, post mortem evaluations, such as the 9/11 Commission Report, represent the attribution of meaning to social events that was relevant at that time but only became publicly accessible through interviews and research conducted years later. Both types of documents improve interpretation and situate the US institutional terrorism narrative.

The analysis also includes reproduction and re-contextualisation of the speeches and communiqués in US televised and printed news reports. Television broadcasts embody various news genres, including news bulletins, live recordings of official statements, documentaries, infotainment programmes and in-depth interviews. Broadcasts represent a form of communication that responds in an extremely timely manner to social events such as presidential speeches. In addition, the visual nature of the information enables the quick switch between an anchor introducing the topic and a correspondent, research journalist, expert, (former) government official or (oppositional) politician explaining his or her views on the matter. By nature, news programmes make a selection of available information and repetitively summarise previous broadcasts as topics develop. In contrast to written texts in newspapers, images and sounds accompany texts on screen. In and through institutional texts and their reproduction and re-contextualisation the basic analytic US institutional terrorism narrative emerges.

The social practice of the 'politics of nations' occurs within the social structure of states, international organisations and regimes. Regardless of any domestic politico-administrative dynamics, states are articulated on the international stage in a relatively equal sense as entities that represent a territory, a population and a legitimate government. Conducting foreign policy through diplomacy, trade or military intervention reflects and merges the semiotic and non-semiotic elements of the social practice (and at the level of social events the discursive and non-discursive). Despite the effects of the information revolution and processes of globalisation, the international system is still mostly characterised by the treaties among and actions of nation-states. To a limited extent, the social practice of international politics is also shaped by the US institutional narrative on international terrorism as a stimulant for cooperation among nations. For example, cooperation with the United States and other states and international organisations intensified at the turn of the millennium

In the 1990s, the United States dominated the international system. In terms of the national security order of discourse, the nexus between defence and security had significantly shifted after the end of the Cold War towards managing risks and vulnerabilities instead of countering threats. National security was defined more extensively in wider (non-military) terms. In this new political reality, US policy priorities and preferences mattered significantly to other countries and international organisations. Throughout history, the protection of national security and the defence of national interests were always central to American foreign policymaking, and the United States relied significantly on 'hard' military power projection for defence, deterrence and compellence.[1] However, a debate on what exactly constitutes American national interests and how to pursue them evolved within the United States, especially after the end of the Cold War.[2] Security and national interests were increasingly perceived in broader terms. Drug smuggling and the environment featured more prominently on the agenda, as did economic policies. In this wider context, views on terrorism also changed.

Domestically, the US Constitution traditionally invites a struggle between the US president and Congress. At the level of structural policies, which, for example, covers the allocation of resources for defence spending, members of Congress are keen to exert influence and benefit from stimulating the economies of their constituencies. Strategic foreign policies are left more to foreign policy specialists and those interested in a particular policy for a specific region. As Commander-in-Chief of the Armed Forces and recipient of intelligence updates such as the President's Daily Brief, the president is best equipped to respond at the level of crisis policies. Yet, while the president can declare threats to national security, it is constitutionally up to Congress to declare a war.[3] Because of the struggle that is inherent to the American political system, institutional narratives have a significant role in the formulation of US foreign policy.

After briefly describing early efforts by intelligence analysts to place Bin Laden on the national security agenda, the US institutional terrorism narrative takes shape around the described key events. How were they reflected in Clinton's statements, and in what way did news media report on them? Then, processes of securitization and identification that emerge from the narrative are discussed. Lastly, the concluding remarks address the nature of the narrative: what are its strengths and weaknesses? What can be learned about the narrative analysis framework from applying it? The attacks on 11 September 2001 are not part of the analysis because this study seeks to emphasise the formative period of the US institutional terrorism narrative on *Al Qaeda* at an early stage. This period is more of a terra incognita. Furthermore, it is the exploration of this formative period that has the greatest potential for developing ACN, as it concerns the emergence of the security problem.

Social structures

Social practices

Discursive practice

| Texts | Texts | Texts |

e.g. Presidential statements

Search queries (entities, themes, events)
e.g. "Bin L*", "Al Q*", "Terroris*", "Embass*", "USS Cole", "Millennium"

Reproduction and recontextualization in US news media
e.g. CNN, ABC, CBS, PBS

Formal audience

Moral audience

General texts

Key texts

Address to the Nation on Military Action Against Terrorist Sites in Afghanistan and Sudan August 20, 1998

Good afternoon. Today I ordered our Armed Forces to strike at terrorist-related facilities in Afghanistan and Sudan because of the imminent threat they presented to our national security. I want to speak with you about the objective of this action and why it was necessary. Our target was terror; our mission was clear: to strike at the network of radical groups affiliated with and funded by Usama bin Ladin, perhaps the preeminent organizer and financier of international terrorism in the world today.

The groups associated with him come from diverse places but share a hatred for democracy, a fanatical glorification of violence, and a horrible distortion of their religion to justify the murder of innocents. They have made the United States their adversary precisely because of what we stand for and what we stand against.

A few months ago, and again this week, bin Ladin publicly vowed to wage a terrorist war against America, saying, and I quote, "We do not differentiate between those dressed in military uniforms and civilians. They're all targets." Their mission is murder and their history is bloody.

In recent years, they killed American, Belgian, and Pakistani peacekeepers in Somalia. They plotted to assassinate the President of Egypt and the Pope. They planned to bomb six United States 747s over the Pacific. They bombed the Egyptian Embassy in Pakistan. They gunned down German tourists in Egypt. The most recent terrorist events are fresh in our memory.

Key sections

Securitization elements (securitizing actor, referent subject, referent object, customized policy)

Today I ordered our Armed Forces to strike at terrorist-related facilities in Afghanistan and Sudan because of the imminent threat that they presented to our national security. I want to speak with you about the objective of this action and why it was necessary. Our target was terror; our mission was clear: to strike at the network of radical groups affiliated with and funded by Usama bin Ladin, perhaps the preeminent organizer and financier of international terrorism in the world today.

Additional textual analysis

Sentence, clause, lexicon, grammar

Wider background context literature

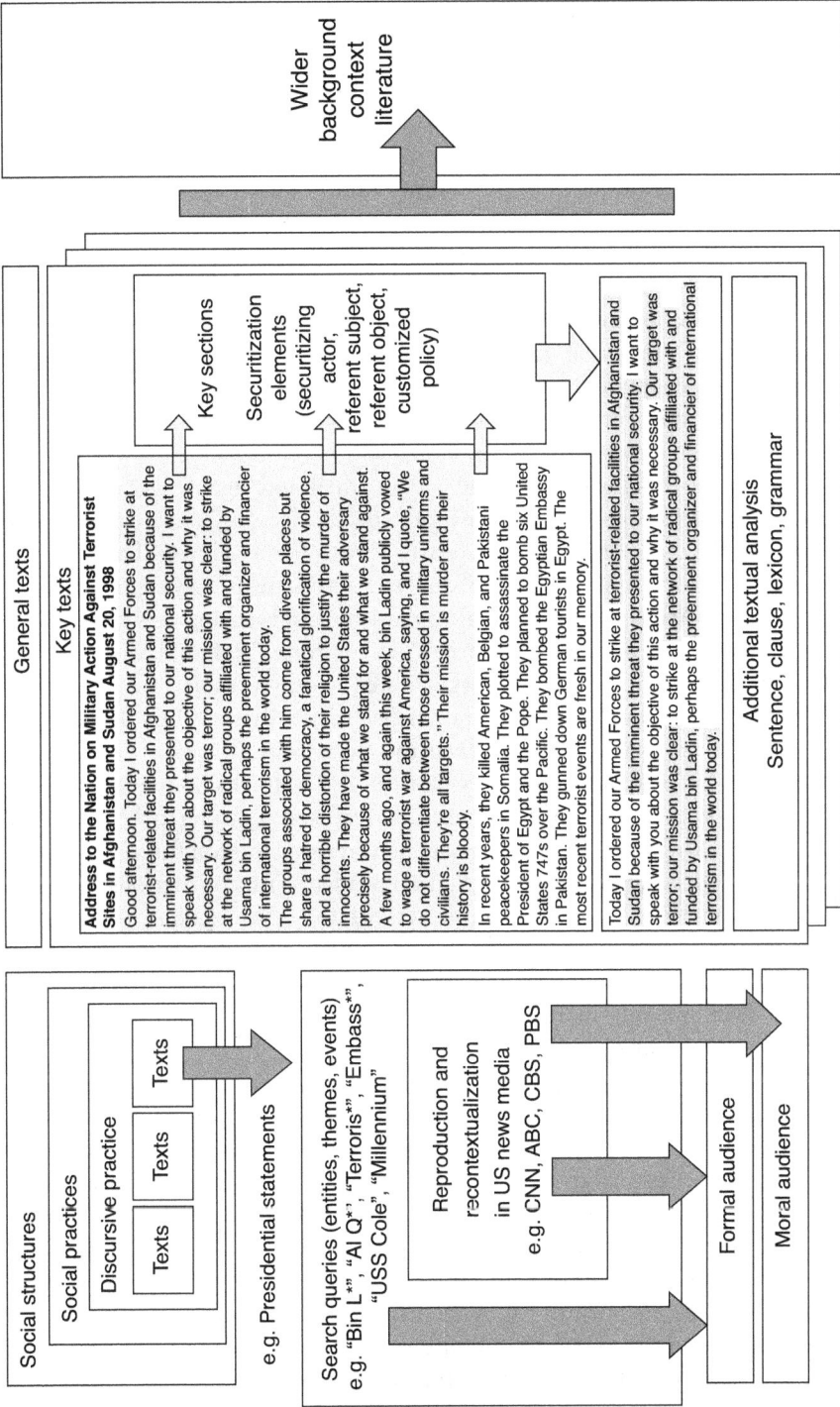

Figure 3.1 Schematic overview of text selection and analysis

EARLY EFFORTS TO PUT BIN LADEN ON THE NATIONAL SECURITY AGENDA

On 23 February 1993, a car bomb detonated in the parking garage below the World Trade Center (WTC) in New York. It signalled a new kind of religiously inspired catastrophic terrorism in the United States that was about killing large numbers of people, rather than putting pressure on political decision-makers regarding a specific agenda. The perpetrators were inspired by an Islamic fundamentalist belief and aimed to destroy symbolic American targets to express their grievances. The extent to which the organisational forms, methods, means, fields of action and scale of this new kind of terrorism contrasted to the classical (political) terrorism that had been dominant during the Cold War has been subject to debate in academia.[4] In general, however, the religious (Islamic) extremism that motivated fundamentalists was distinct from the separatist drives of political activists.

There is some disagreement on the way in which intelligence assessments of this new kind of terrorism, and later more specifically *Al Qaeda*, evolved and were part of the policy agenda in the early 1990s. Some scholars have argued that it was an effort by 'a hand full of analysts across the IC' trying to sell their ideas on 'young Arabs departing from Afghanistan and seeking new battlefields to the intelligence community at large'.[5] In contrast, National Coordinator for Counter-Terrorism Richard Clarke[6] notes in his memoir how by 1994, he, President Bill Clinton, and National Security Advisor Tony Lake were convinced that terrorism 'would shape the post-Cold War world'.[7] Clinton emphasises in his own autobiography that the 1993 attacks on the WTC demonstrated 'the vulnerability of the open American society to terror'.[8] Although Bin Laden (or *Al Qaeda*) was not yet at the forefront for Clinton, Clarke and other senior officials, they recognised in a broader sense connections between 'terrorists from the Middle East' and acts of terrorism against Americans, such as the WTC bombing.[9] However, it is important to recognise that there were other significant policy and intelligence priorities for the United States, including developments in Russia, the security situation in the Balkans and Indo-Pakistan nuclear tensions.

In the mid-1990s, several policy documents reflected the US government concerns over a 'new kind of terrorism'.[10] The US Department of State mentioned the name Osama bin Laden for the first time in its 1995 annual report to the US Congress on international terrorism; in this report, Bin Laden was characterised as a 'Khartoum-based major private financier of terrorism with radical Muslim followers'.[11] He was positioned as a logistical enabler, not an inspirer. In January 1996, the CIA's Counterterrorism Center (CTC) dedicated a station to Osama bin Laden and his network of followers named Alec Station. It was partly the result of the CIA's wish to test an in-house virtual station that focused on a topic in a similar manner as CIA stations in the field. Unable to recruit an operations officer and guided by National Security Advisor Anthony Lake's interest in terrorist finance, a CIA analyst with a special interest in Afghanistan was recruited as station chief. The analyst, Michael Scheuer, proposed to focus on Bin Laden. From that moment, US intelligence efforts grew steadily, strengthened in mid-1996 by the testimony of Jamal Ahmed Mohamed al-Fadl, a defecting long-time member of Bin Laden's network.[12] A translation of Bin Laden's 1996 memorandum emphasised what was said about the United States over how it was said: all poetry was removed and religious references were reduced. This stimulated an anti-US interpretation of the text over the anti-Saudi sentiments expressed.

There has been some disagreement among US officials about the influence of Bin Laden's 1996 memorandum on US threat perceptions.[13] Nevertheless, in the margin of other international policy and intelligence priorities, the US government pursued a policy of obstruction towards Bin Laden in Sudan.

Three UN Security Council resolutions in 1996 increased international pressure, and eventually the Sudanese government decided to expel Bin Laden from Sudan.[14] In May 1996, Bin Laden migrated from Sudan to Afghanistan. One month later, the bombing of an apartment building in al-Khobar, Saudi Arabia, killed nineteen US airmen. This attack followed an earlier one on an American-run military training centre in Riyadh in November 1995. In both cases, the attackers had gained experience in 'translating their anti-Saudi, anti-American extremism into violence' during the Afghan *jihad* and were now associated with Bin Laden.[15] United States' intelligence analysts were also researching connections to an attempted bombing of US troops in Yemen in 1992, the 1993 bombing of the WTC in New York, or attacks against US and UN troops in Somalia in 1993.

In 1997 and early 1998, several US intelligence and law enforcement agencies increasingly began to perceive Bin Laden not just as an extremist financier, but as a capable and central figure of *Al Qaeda*, a network or organisation planning operations against US interests worldwide. They had reason to believe *Al Qaeda* was actively trying to obtain nuclear material.[16] On occasion, US government agencies such as the FBI and CIA worked together, for example, in searching the house of suspected *Al Qaeda* member Wadith el Hage in Nairobi in August 1997. This was an attempt to find evidence linking el Hage to the 1993 WTC bombing.[17] In general, however, each agency pursued its own approach to dealing with Osama bin Laden. In 1998, the New York Field Office of the FBI successfully worked to build a case with the US Attorney's office to have Bin Laden indicted for the involvement of *Al Qaeda* in international terrorism and conspiring to attack US defence installations.[18] Parallel to the legal case, the CIA's CTC discussed operational plans with the White House to grab Bin Laden from his residence in Afghanistan, conduct sabotage attacks in Afghanistan and Sudan, and gather intelligence to support military strikes.[19] To no avail, as the possibility of collateral damage to US citizens or the risk of exposing US intelligence capabilities in the process was weighed as being more important.[20] For those analysts who had followed Bin Laden and still had any doubt about his intentions against the United States, the 1998 WIF declaration convinced them. In English translations it was explicitly framed in English as a religious juridical ruling (*fatwa*). However, it still remained difficult to establish a unity of effort at the US institutional level in relation to this threat.

US Embassy Bombings in Kenya and Tanzania

The size of the attacks on the US embassies in Kenya and Tanzania, and the large number of casualties among US and local officials and civilians significantly impacted news reporting worldwide in August 1998. Information gathered during the investigation by US law enforcement and intelligence officers over the following weeks pointed to the involvement of Osama bin Laden and *Al Qaeda*.[21] The events gave reason for US President Bill Clinton to respond with a series of statements that substantiated two significant securitization efforts as part of the US institutional terrorism narrative. The nature of both efforts differed because several aspects of the securitization varied in scale, such as shifting settings, the type of audiences, the referent object and the proposed customised policy.

First, one securitization effort was a cluster of speeches in which Osama bin Laden's terrorist network was presented as a clear threat to the United States. This included the weekly presidential radio address on 8 August; the remarks President Clinton made in Martha's Vineyard on 20 August 1998; his nationwide address later that day; formal writings to the US Congress on 20 and 21 August that legitimised the US military response; and the radio address on 22 August. Secondly, Clinton's address to the 53rd United Nations General Assembly on 21 September 1998 embodied an effort to securitize terrorism as a threat to the world and 'the world's problem'. Both efforts related to the embassy bombings and contributed to a wider terrorism narrative in the United States.

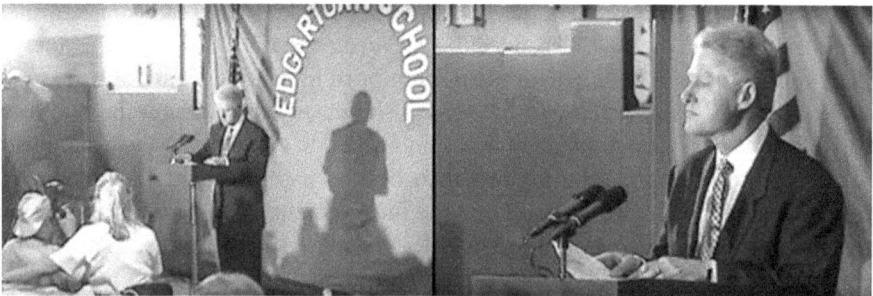

Figure 3.2 President Clinton's initial remarks at the improvised press conference location in Edgartown on Martha's Vineyard, 20 August 1998

Figure 3.3 Later address to the nation from the White House in Washington on 20 August 1998. The camera zooms in as Clinton emphasises 'we will persist, and we will prevail'.

Source: Clinton Digital Library, 'Statement to Press on Military Strikes Against Sudan & Afghanistan (1998)'

Osama bin Laden's network as a threat to national security

In Clinton's radio addresses to the American people on 8 August, the attacks on the US embassies in Kenya and Tanzania were characterised as terrorism, using both the lexicon of crime and war. Clinton declared that he would bring the perpetrators of the 'criminal act' 'to justice', providing law enforcement 'the best counterterrorism tools available'. Moreover, he also underlined that he had intensified efforts on all fronts in 'the battle' against terrorism.[22] As US law enforcement and intelligence agencies acquired more information, suspects were identified. On August 20, Clinton determined the referent subject by stating US national security was imminently threatened by Bin Laden. It was the first time a US president mentioned Osama bin Laden by name. According to Clinton, associated terrorists 'were planning additional terrorist attacks against US citizens and others, and they were seeking new dangerous weapons'.[23] The military action against the terrorist sites in Afghanistan and Sudan, two weeks after the terrorist attacks, were presented as the necessary response (customised policy) to counter the threat. Clinton was clear on this necessity as the 'national security was challenged, and the US government had to take extraordinary steps to protect the safety of its citizens'.[24] According to Clinton, the military strikes destroyed terrorist infrastructure and sent a clear message to terrorists around the world. The president also amended an executive order that prohibited American citizens and businesses from having financial transactions with Osama bin Laden or his group.[25]

All statements, whether they focused on the victims, perpetrators, or both, related to the general phenomenon of terrorism. As securitizing actor, President Clinton articulated to all Americans that the terrorist attacks in Africa in fact targeted the United States through its global interests. America became a vulnerable target (referent object) as it strived to openly engage in a dialogue to promote peace, freedom and democracy around the world. By contrasting the terrorists and the attacks to peaceful US foreign policy aims, this built on a wider background context of US cultural presuppositions. The most extensive text that comprised all elements of securitization was Clinton's address to the nation delivered from the White House on 20 August. It functioned primarily to explain and justify the military strikes before Clinton's moral audience, the American people, as they were also the referent object of the 'imminent threat'.[26]

By executing his powers, President Clinton became more of a president, strengthening the institution by confirming genres and styles. In the speech he depicted the motivations of the terrorists:

> The groups associated with him come from diverse places but share a hatred for democracy, a fanatical glorification of violence, and a horrible distortion of their religion to justify the murder of innocents. They have made the United States their adversary precisely because of what we stand for and what we stand against. A few months ago, and again this week, bin Ladin publicly vowed to wage a terrorist war against America, saying, and I quote, 'We do not differentiate between those dressed in military uniforms and civilians. They're all targets.' Their mission is murder and their history is bloody.[27]

Not only did the president name Bin Laden, but he also quoted him. In this way, President Clinton granted Bin Laden a high level of attention. Recognising Bin Laden as a potent adversary improved the latter's leadership status among his followers. This negative effect was also recognised by the senior advisers who formed Clinton's Principals Committee on national security.[28] Although these members agreed to refrain from using Bin Laden's name as much as possible, they found it difficult to do so in practice.

Apart from the more generic goal of striking 'terror', the final part of his address emphasised the temporal aspect of urgency. There was 'compelling evidence' that new attacks were being planned. As the term 'evidence' referred to classified intelligence that the president was not allowed to share with the public, this phrase became a call for trust in Clinton fulfilling his duties as president in protecting national security by ordering the military strikes. Adding 'the unanimous recommendation of my national security team' worked to strengthen the institutional character of the decision. It made Clinton's order less of a personal choice. Further on, this chapter will discuss in more detail how, at the time of this address, Clinton was politically and personally weakened by an investigation into his relationship with intern Monica Lewinsky.

Of note is that, depending on setting and audience, Bin Laden and his followers were characterised in slightly different ways in the various statements as referent subject. In the initial statement on the military strikes at Martha's Vineyard on 20 August 1998, Clinton indicated that the military targeted 'one of the most active terrorist bases in the world' in Afghanistan, 'operated by groups affiliated with Osama bin Laden, a network not sponsored by any state but as dangerous as we face'. In Sudan, a 'chemical weapons-related facility' was targeted. After returning to Washington DC the same day, Clinton stated in a nationwide address that the targets were 'terrorist-related facilities in Afghanistan and Sudan' as 'the network of radical groups affiliated with and funded by Osama bin Laden, perhaps the preeminent organizer and financier of international terrorism in the world today', posed 'an imminent threat to US national security'.[29] In the same address, Clinton stated that there was 'convincing information from our intelligence community that the bin Laden terrorist network was responsible for these bombings'.[30] It now appeared that 'the network' was the entity, not 'several groups' affiliated with Bin Laden. Clinton made this nuance even more distinct when he claimed, 'we have high confidence that [the embassy] bombings were planned, financed, and carried out by the organization bin Laden leads'.[31] Further on in the nationwide address, Clinton again referred several times to 'the Bin Laden network of terrorist groups'. The Afghan training camp 'contained key elements of Bin Laden's network's infrastructure' and 'served as training camp for thousands of terrorists from around the globe'. A gathering of key terrorist leaders was supposedly about to take place there. In Clinton's words, the actions were aimed at 'fanatics and killers who wrap murder in the cloak of righteousness and in so doing profane the great religion in whose name they claim to act'.[32]

Clinton's letters on 20 and 21 August to the US Congress, his formal audience, contained a similar message but show some interesting differences. Military targets struck in Afghanistan were 'a series of camps and installations used by the Osama bin Laden organization and facilities that are being used for terrorist training', and in Sudan 'where the bin Laden organization has facilities and extensive ties to the government'.[33] It was stated that the Bin Laden organisation was responsible for the embassy bombings. The word network or group was not used in either formal letter. A day later, during the weekly presidential radio address before his moral audience, Clinton projected 'the bin Laden network of radical groups' as the most dangerous non-state terrorist actor in the world, targeting all Americans and responsible for a number of attacks (in Somalia and against US airliners) and assassination plots.[34]

Distinctions between a network, a group and an organization were subtle, but important to the securitization effort before Clinton's formal audience. Formal letters to Congress indicated that Bin Laden 'leads an organization', and the words network or group were not used. In the formal written communiqués, the threat to US lives was addressed highly explicitly. Speaking in terms of an organisation instead of a fuzzier network or social movement helped to better legitimise the use of force and the financial measures against Bin Laden and his followers.[35] Both letters served an informative purpose, as the president did not have to ask for permission from the US Congress to conduct the military strikes. Yet the letters were also aimed at increasing bipartisan support since the Republicans had the majority in both the House of Representatives and the Senate at that time.

In his public statements, Clinton emphasised several times how the military strikes 'were not aimed against Islam, the faith of hundreds of millions of good, peace-loving people all around the world, including the United States'. The targets were 'fanatics and killers' and the 'battle against terrorism' had been and continued to be ongoing. He stated it was a long battle between 'freedom and fanaticism', and 'the rule of law and terrorism'. The word 'freedom' referred to a wider context of American values such as peace, democracy, human rights and the entrepreneurial spirit. This pointed to the ideological thought that formed a basis for, and was also enhanced by, the securitization efforts. A severe terrorist threat articulated by the president not only lifted the political narrative on terrorism to a new level, but also gave reason to highlight basic assumptions on national and institutional identities, norms, and values that underlay and supported US institutional power relations. American strategic goals were 'good' and US foreign policy aimed to further that cause; any threat to its execution was a threat to national security. The US foreign policy in the Middle East or the Arabian Peninsula at that time was not questioned in the US institutional narrative on terrorism and *Al Qaeda*. A stronger narrative on terrorism and threat led to a stronger sense of the identity of the United States for its citizens and officials.

Securitization of a new kind of international terrorism

During the 53rd Session of the United Nations General Assembly (UNGA), Clinton pleaded that international terrorism had 'a new face in the 1990's'.[36] Mobility, openness, information and weapons technology were misused to threaten all of humanity. In general, Clinton was rather inclusive with regard to the events and actors he deemed to be part of this new terrorism. For example, referencing the Real IRA, Aum Shirikyo, and violence in Kashmir and Sri Lanka. In the speech, he underlined that this new terrorism was not the manifestation of a 'clash of civilizations', of Islam against the West; however, he noted that there were violent people who wanted the world to believe this. He defined terrorism instead in terms of a 'clash between the forces of the past and the forces of the future, between those who tear down and those who build up, between hope and fear, chaos and community'.[37]

The scale of the elements of Clinton's securitization effort varied (that is, securitizing actor, referent object, referent subject, customised policy). He was still a securitizing actor, although in the new setting his authority was based on moral leadership instead of a formal position as commander-in-chief. Textual analysis predominantly shows the repetitive use of inclusive words such as 'people' and other references to human identity. In his speech, Clinton tried to build a bridge by providing a framework to examine terrorism. In doing so, the notions of 'terror' and 'terrorism' became more abstract and general compared with the recent securitization efforts before the US audience.

The global impact of Clinton's speech was limited, as the General Assembly served as a forum for member states to deliver messages on a wide range of topics. Apart from that, terrorism was not the only topic on Clinton's mind. His address started with the conclusion that the world 'had much to celebrate, as peace had come in Northern Ireland and Bosnia held free elections'.[38] Clinton also held three bilateral meetings in the margin of the UNGA, discussing the situation in Kosovo and Albania with Italy, nuclear proliferation with Pakistan, and the necessity of economic reform and the North Koreans' missile capability with the Japanese prime minister.[39] Perhaps an important goal of the speech was to explain the recent US missile strikes in Afghanistan and Sudan as an act against terrorism, especially improving support and understanding among Muslim countries. After the strikes, several national leaders had criticised the legitimacy of the actions.

The wider scale of the threat image articulated before the UN in terms of this new kind of terrorism, as most recently represented by Osama bin Laden's threats, only added to the momentum of the US domestic securitization effort building against Bin Laden. They strengthened the same understanding of good versus evil, or peace and security versus terror, and strengthened US identity.

Reproduction and re-contextualisation in the media

News media perform a crucial function in American society. Despite all the powers vested in the US government, much depended on how media chose, selected, introduced, broadcast and commented on the nationwide addresses and other statements made by Clinton. However, there was a mutual dependency here, as the media also needed authoritative statements as content for their reports. With respect to the embassy attacks in Africa and the military strikes that followed, news media reproduced official statements, for example, by including citations of President Clinton in news reports or broadcasting his weekly radio address entirely. Clinton was physically at the White House as he gave his weekly radio address; the residence symbolised the office of the president, with all its domestic and international prestige. As president, Clinton had access to the privileged knowledge produced by the US intelligence community. This power was maintained by legislation and institutional rules that had to be respected by US media.

Initially, the lexicon of crime used by Clinton was maintained in the media; the perpetrators needed to be 'brought to justice'.[40] On 20 August, as 'America struck back' militarily, all news programmes reproduced President Clinton's claim to success. Several of them broadcast the presidential statement live.[41] The US government claimed to have 'compelling evidence that the bin Laden network was poised to strike at us again soon'.[42] The media was simply not in a position to question the underlying classified information, such as a soil sample from near the *Al-Shifa* factory.[43] Characterisations of Bin Laden and his followers in US national media paralleled institutional statements.

The reason presented in the media for acting militarily now was 'clear evidence that Bin Laden's followers were ready to strike again'.[44] National Security Advisor Sandy Berger and Secretary of State Madeleine Albright supported Clinton's statement that this was but a successful operation in a long-term battle.[45] It shifted attention from the embassy attacks and the present threat to the wider ongoing fight against terrorism that had entered a 'new age'. This also placed less emphasis on the level of success achieved by the military strikes. Terrorism experts in the media confirmed that terrorists were becoming increasingly mobile, had access to information, and intended to strike the United States with chemical and biological weapons.[46] This was not just speculation: a terrorist attack with chemical or biological agents had already occurred in the Tokyo subway in 1995.

Despite the high level of reproduction, all television broadcasts were in fact also re-contextualisations of the presidential communicative events. A clear example of media coming to their own conclusions was that most national news media were ahead of the US government in identifying Bin Laden as early as 8 August.[47] Bin Laden had made no secret of waging a 'Holy War' against the United States.[48] It was this Holy War that had provided the media with a frame of reference that fit the narrative on a new age of terrorism. He was also one of the few with the money and expertise to conduct the kind of terrorist attacks that had occurred. Military experts in news shows initially warned against 'leaping to the easiest label or the label of what we dislike' when assuming at that stage that it was an Islamic group.[49] However, as a man tied to the attacks was arrested in Pakistan while trying to flee to Afghanistan, the alleged hiding place of Osama bin Laden, speculation in the media on the involvement of Bin Laden intensified.[50]

On a critical note, some news reports questioned the feasibility of the government's effort to find the perpetrators.[51] And days after the military strikes on 20 August some correspondents investigated the targets, putting the effectiveness of the strike in Afghanistan into perspective. ABC News interviewed a Pakistani journalist who had visited the six targeted camps.[52] Local villagers stated a gathering of (terrorist) leaders was not taking place, but some people related to Osama bin Laden had been killed. Some buildings were damaged or destroyed, but the camps were not 'wiped out'. Two little mosques were also hit, fuelling anti-US sentiments in the area. The legitimacy of the attack on a facility in Sudan was also subject to debate in the media. Bin Laden's ties to the Sudanese government and the activities at the targeted pharmaceutical factory were questioned. United States' officials confirmed that Bin Laden and his organisation were attempting to acquire chemical weapons.

However, news media questioned the evidence the CIA had provided and stated the pharmaceutical plant was producing the majority of the drugs for Sudan.[53] The Sudanese government was furious and called, to no avail, for UN experts to verify that no chemical weapons were produced there.[54] In Khartoum, protesters gathered in front of the American Embassy. Other reactions around the globe that were reported in US media varied. Russian President Yeltsin denounced the military strikes, but an aide to Yeltsin later stated that the United States and Russia were 'in the same boat' in the struggle against terrorism.[55] Leaders from the United Kingdom, France, Germany and Israel were quoted as supporting the strikes, while Japan and China withheld their final judgement.[56] Taliban leaders and members of the Iraqi Revolution Command Council firmly condemned the US strikes.[57]

Despite an agreement among the members of the National Security Principals Committee that they should refrain from referring publicly to Bin Laden and focus on the wider *Al Qaeda* network, few government officials did so.[58] This was also due to news media demand. After the Clinton administration publicly referred to Osama bin Laden as a suspect on 20 August, news media provided additional context on his background, personality, motives and, most importantly, his capabilities. The media focused on Bin Laden as an individual; his photograph was repetitively screened to quickly familiarise audiences with the topic. According to the media, there had been no doubt all along that Osama bin Laden was behind the attacks. Former US counterterrorism officials recognised that the US military strikes were not 'a knock-out blow' but part of a series of military, diplomatic and economic initiatives, suggesting a large reward would make followers hand in Bin Laden.[59]

A highly significant re-contextualisation of Clinton's securitization, especially for his formal institutional audience, had little to do with the contextual mobilisation of heuristic artefacts, or with any aura of unprecedented threatening complexion, but with the securitizing actor himself. The timing of the customised policy to conduct the military strikes gave reason to major national news channels to discuss Clinton's motives. As of January 1998, Clinton was confronted with major personal and therefore domestic political problems.[60] Some media referred to it as 'the major domestic story' or 'sex scandal'.[61] In August 1998, speculation soared in the media about a connection between the legal investigation into the alleged intimate affair of Clinton with White House intern Monica Lewinsky and the missile strikes.

The speculation gained more weight as the decision-making process and execution of the military attacks were debated in the media.[62] Some of President

Clinton's closest staff members had allegedly not been informed of the strikes in advance.[63] US personnel investigating the embassy bombings were not briefed prior to the strikes, leaving them unable to take additional protective measures.[64] The government of Pakistan was also not informed, while the cruise missiles flew over Pakistani territory. To make matters worse, a cruise missile came down unexpectedly in Pakistan, killing six people.[65] The decision not to inform several relevant parties gave some the impression that President Clinton was pressed for time, even though planning the strikes took over a week. It fuelled speculation about what other (personal) motives the president might have had to order the strikes.

An element that implicitly influenced the public debate on the timing and motivation of the strikes was the release of a movie called 'Wag the Dog' in December 1997. In it, a spin-doctor and a Hollywood producer worked to fabricate a war to divert attention from the president's personal problems concerning a sex scandal in the run-up to elections. Yet, according to Clinton's own account and some of his close associates at the time, there was never any doubt that this was a purely professional decision based on the intelligence that was available.[66] It was emphasised that the planning process was done thoroughly, and with all relevant stakeholders involved.

As Clinton denied allegations the public opinion polls indicated that many American citizens did not care about the Lewinsky affair.[67] Support for the president among his moral audience remained high.[68] Although polling indicated that the affair had affected his moral stance, about two-thirds of respondents still viewed Clinton as compassionate and a strong leader.[69] The booming economy gave people reason to overlook his moral behaviour.[70] Eventually, news media criticised themselves for focusing so extensively on the Lewinsky affair. Nevertheless, the whole process had substantially damaged Clinton's authority and troubled his relationship with Congress. He barely avoided impeachment by the Republican-led House and Senate, significantly limiting his bandwidth to operate freely and proactive as US president.

Managing the Threat of Terrorism

President Clinton's securitization efforts before the American people and the United Nations in the months after the embassy bombings reflected how he had put Bin Laden and the network *Al Qaeda* high on the US national security agenda. Besides the rapid military strikes in Sudan and Afghanistan, a comprehensive politico-military plan codenamed 'Delenda' (Latin for 'to be destroyed') was drafted to eliminate *Al Qaeda* as an organisation. It involved an extensive array of intelligence, military, law enforcement, financial and diplomatic instruments that were available to the US administration. The various intelligence and law enforcement agencies were tasked to deal with the threat in both covert and overt ways, such as identifying and arresting cells, finding financial resources and seizing funds, training and equipping adversary groups, and neutralising or eliminating the leadership. On the other hand, Clinton and several senior US officials objected to conducting additional missile strikes in Afghanistan without reliable and verified intelligence for fear of increasing negative sentiment around the world.[71] Accounts varied on the extent to which their combined efforts constituted an effective practice. FBI special agent Ali Soufan, CIA station chief Michael Scheuer, and Counterterrorism Security Group Chair Richard Clarke all recognised that there were institutional or bureaucratic problems in sharing and understanding available information, aligning efforts and shifting momentum away from other intelligence problems to the threat of terrorism at hand.[72]

The ascribed priority was reflected in public government reports. In 1998, the annual State Department report 'Patterns of Global Terrorism' included 'Al Qaeda' for the first time.[73] It summarised its goal to 're-establish the Muslim State throughout the world', referred to the 1998 fatwa issued by the WIF, and linked Al Qaeda to the 1998 bombing of the US embassies and various plans to conduct high-profile assassinations and terrorist attacks. The report stated that the organisation 'claimed to have shot down US helicopters and killed US troops in Somalia in 1993, and conducted bombings against US troops in Yemen in 1992'.[74]According to the State Department, Al Qaeda resided in Afghanistan yet had a global reach.

Several of the measures taken centralised Bin Laden, despite the administration's intention to refrain from concentrating too much on him as a person and to focus on the wider network instead. Senior US officials at the time recognised that capturing or killing Bin Laden would not end the threat from Al Qaeda and could even grant Bin Laden a heroic martyr status.[75] Still, it was decided that one of the first steps to tackle the problem and confront the threat was to go after the Al Qaeda leader. Bin Laden unquestionably performed an important unifying function among the diverse people who had joined him. One of the measures that targeted Bin Laden personally, as well as Al Qaeda, was the sanctions issued against him by Clinton on the same day as the military strikes in Sudan and Afghanistan.[76] In his nationwide radio address, Clinton mentioned that this was part of his determined efforts to 'use all the tools' available against terrorism.[77]

In addition, in November 1998, the Court of the Southern District of New York publicly indicted Osama bin Laden and twenty associated members of Al Qaeda on 238 counts.[78] Most prominent was the count of conspiring to kill US nationals. This followed a secret indictment against Bin Laden for his role in Somalia that had been issued earlier that year.[79] Over the next two years, the public indictment was expanded to 319 counts, comprising over 150 pages. Parallel to the initial release in November 1998, the US Department of State offered a then-record US$5 million reward for any actionable information on Bin Laden. Using the interdepartmental Rewards for Justice Program was part of the administration's efforts to do everything possible to counter the threat of terrorism and hold perpetrators accountable. Later, in June 1999, Bin Laden was added to the list of the FBI's ten most wanted fugitives.

Apart from the practical purpose of generating investigative leads, the reward and FBI list also had an important symbolic articulative effect on the American people and people friendly to the United States worldwide. The FBI list was a publicity programme originally founded in conjunction with the media. Its publication served to garner nationwide attention to America's most dangerous fugitives, to inform the public of the threat they posed, and to alert people to report relevant information. Apart from being included in this notorious selection, at the time the reward against Bin Laden was the highest ever issued by the State Department. In the US context, it symbolised his significance as referent subject.

In his own public statements in 1999, President Clinton widened the scope when referring to terrorism.[80] He frequently associated terrorist groups with criminals and narcotics traffickers; they had all become increasingly interdependent. Processes of globalisation and the development of new technologies enabled international terrorists to conduct more sophisticated attacks, such as bio-terrorism, chemical terrorism, nuclear terrorism or cyberterrorism. In one of Clinton's few references to Bin Laden's network in the first months of 1999, he discussed with reporters *Al Qaeda*'s efforts to acquire chemical weapons.[81] This fit the message Clinton had been consistently spreading before and since the 1998 embassy attacks on new threats to US security in the twenty-first century. According to Clinton, the United States had to reduce vulnerabilities and be prepared to deal with these more sophisticated threats posed by the enemies of peace, democracy and freedom.

In 1999, Clinton did not make direct additional discursive securitization efforts with respect to the Bin Laden network. But indirectly, two events were relevant in terms of securitization theory, as they represented ways of dealing with the threat. First, he made an effort to manage the Bin Laden threat by securitizing the Taliban for harbouring Bin Laden. Essentially, the executive order was an extension of the sanctions Clinton had imposed earlier on Bin Laden. However, Clinton articulated and motivated the sanctions against the Taliban more explicitly, and there was more news reporting on it. Through this, he shifted focus and broadened the scope of his public securitization efforts on Bin Laden and *Al Qaeda*. Secondly, in late December 1999, he highlighted the efforts made by the US government to protect the American people from terrorist attacks. In assuring US citizens that the authorities were doing all they could, Clinton worked to establish positive securitization. In other words, the existence of the threat was not denied (and was even confirmed), but the emphasis was on the efforts to manage the threat of terrorist attacks occurring at the turn of the millennium. This was about self-determination and openness, rather than fear of threats and enmity, as Clinton did not intend to terrify US citizens.[82]

Securitizing the Taliban

In early 1999, efforts by the US government to convince the Taliban to expel Bin Laden from Afghanistan remained fruitless. From March to June 1999, US foreign policy focused on the Balkans as US warplanes flew missions over Serbia and Kosovo, participating in the NATO operation 'Allied Force'. In July, the Clinton administration decided it was time to raise the pressure on the Afghan Taliban regime. By offering Bin Laden a safe haven, the Taliban had become an 'unusual and extraordinary threat' to the United States. A letter to the leaders of the US Congress on 4 July 1999 embodied the securitization of the Taliban before Clinton's formal institutional audience. Its power stemmed from the strict rules of communication to which it adhered: the securitization followed the formal procedure of the National Emergencies Act (NEA) 1976. The NEA authorises the president to declare a national emergency, which activates emergency powers that are described in other statutes. In this case, it related to the International Emergency Economic Powers Act 1977. After declaring a national emergency before the US Congress, the president was authorised to block or limit trading with related foreign entities and confiscate their property.

Clinton presented the executive order as a vigorous and precise instrument that targeted the Taliban, not the Afghan people. In demonstrating 'the need to conform to accepted norms of international behavior' and stressing the aim of deepening 'international isolation', the president highlighted the social practice that situated the US institutional narrative on Bin Laden and *Al Qaeda*. Clinton was dealing with the threat with the means he had at his disposal. These were situated in the social domain of the politics of nations. However, despite some tough language, the lexicon in the executive order also sent a somewhat mixed message regarding the nature of Bin Laden's followers as a referent subject for securitization. In both his letter to Congress and his address to the nation, Clinton deemed 'Bin Laden and the *Al Qaeda* organization' as the main threat, but also referred to 'Bin Laden's network'. He intended to 'bring Bin Laden to justice for his crimes', while classifying Mohammed Atef in the letter to Congress as Bin Laden's 'military commander'.[83] The latter characterisation underlined some sort of chain of command and placed *Al Qaeda*'s terrorist acts in the realm of military operations. In addition, the more Clinton emphasised the current threat posed by Bin Laden and the Taliban, the more he undermined the perceived success of previous US policies, such as the military strikes in Afghanistan and Sudan. Clinton concluded that Bin Laden and his network had been provided with a safe haven, had been able to operate freely in Afghanistan since 1998, and were planning additional attacks against US targets.

The focus shifted from the terrorists to those who nurtured terrorism. By sanctioning Afghanistan, the Taliban became the link between the transnational movement of jihadi extremists and international politics. Regardless of the rhetorical thrust provided by the public address on the order, however, its practical effect was in fact rather limited because of the minor trading activities between the two countries. It was also a slight shift from (military) action to symbolism. According to some, Clinton's presidential stance among US military leaders also had its limits. Within the walls of the White House and the Pentagon, Clinton's lack of a military record and his earlier critique of the Vietnam War had decreased his status and power to convince US military commanders to become involved in (covert) military operations targeting Bin Laden, against which they had advised.[84] Because of the limited practical impact, news reporters re-contextualised the effect of the sanctions in a critical manner.[85]

Unites States' diplomatic efforts at the level of the United Nations resulted in the Security Council unanimously adopting resolution 1267 in October 1999. It was an initiative to install economic sanctions against Afghanistan and the Taliban parallel to the unilateral US measures. The UN sanctions added some weight to the sanctions on the Afghan economy, but to no avail as the Taliban did not alter their position and Bin Laden remained able to operate freely. Moreover, while the focus on Bin Laden had increased in the United States, a hostage crisis in December 1999 at Kandahar airfield in Afghanistan had internationally put the securitization effort of the Taliban into a slightly different perspective. On 24 December, an Indian Airlines plane was hijacked by Islamist extremists and forced to land in Afghanistan. For the next seven days, the Taliban put pressure on the hijackers to release the hostages and give up on their demands. United Nations officials commended the Taliban regime for bringing the situation to an end without any casualties. Countering Clinton's Taliban securitization effort, US media affirmed this was an opportunity for the pariah state 'to show the world a different face' and gain a small amount of international credibility.[86]

On the same day that Clinton imposed sanctions on the Taliban, there was also another international dimension at play. On 4 July 1999, Clinton had met with Pakistani Prime Minister Sharif at the latter's request to discuss the emerging crisis between India and Pakistan over skirmishes in India's Kargil district. The sanctions against the Taliban also demonstrated Clinton's determination to Sharif, as the latter had come to the United States requesting help. Clinton was determined to discuss increasing Pakistan's efforts against the Taliban in the meeting. An agreement was reached that the United States would train sixty Pakistani commandos to capture Bin Laden in Afghanistan. Despite being sceptical over working relations between the Pakistani intelligence agency ISI and the Taliban, Clinton wanted to explore every option.[87] His concerns were not unfounded: as described in the previous chapter, Bin Laden had endorsed the *jihad* in Kargil against India and had also mentioned in Pakistani newspapers how he knew of efforts by US commandos to capture him.

Millennium plots and positive securitization

Days before the end of the millennium, media reports thrived on all that could go wrong. Would computers be able to handle the change of digits? Would vital information infrastructure systems crash? Amidst this speculation, the possibility of terrorists conducting attacks was not ruled out either. On 14 December 1999, US Customs had arrested Ahmed Ressam at the US–Canadian border. He was an Algerian living in Montreal and had intended to detonate bombs at Los Angeles airport. Two days earlier, security services in Jordan had arrested dozens of suspects accused of preparing terrorist attacks on various tourist and religious sites in the country. In late December 1999, President Clinton answered some questions on this 'Year 2000 terrorism' in interviews, advising American citizens to go about their business and 'call the authorities if they see something suspicious'.[88] No link to Bin Laden was made at the time. There was no guarantee in advance that nothing would happen, but the law enforcement and intelligence agencies were doing all they could to 'maximize protection'.[89] In an interview with CNN anchor Larry King, President Clinton emphasised this:

> *Larry King*: And how about the terrorism threat, where people are asked to be careful, especially overseas, and we have these arrests occurring in Washington and Vermont?
> *President Clinton*: Well, what I would say to the American people about that is that we know that at the millennium, a lot of people who may even be a little crazy by our standards or may have a political point to make, may try to take advantage of it. So we are on a heightened state of alert. We're working very hard on it. No one can guarantee that nothing will happen. But all I can say is we're working very hard. And my advice to the American people would be to go on about their business and do what they would intend to do at the holiday season but to be a little more aware of people and places where they find themselves. And if you see something suspicious, well, call us and let us know. Call the authorities. We're working very, very hard on this. And if it were me, I would not just refrain from activities. I'm going to go out and do my Christmas shopping. I'm going to do what I normally do.[90]

Clinton's calming words 'I'm going to do what I normally do' are not to be mistaken for de-securitization, since the threat of a terrorist attack remained. In this interview, emphasis lay on 'working very hard', 'make sure', 'everything we possibly can' and 'maximize our protection'. It was an act to convince US citizens that the state was protecting them by stressing the effort made, a form of positive securitization. Apart from repeated references to this effort, such as 'we're working very hard', Clinton also empowered the American people by giving them responsibility to report suspicious activity and 'call us', 'call the authorities'. Furthermore, by emphasising that he would continue to 'act as normal', Clinton showed his intention to lead by example and expressed self-determination.

In late 1999 and the first months of 2000, Clinton did not relate arrested suspects or foiled plots to Bin Laden. In January 2000, news media cited anonymous US officials as stating that following the arrest of Ahmed Ressam, a related suspect under investigation in Senegal had indirect ties to Bin Laden.[91] However, at that time, the media reported that there was no proof that Bin Laden had directed the failed plot in Jordan. For law enforcement and intelligence agencies, Bin Laden had been among their top priorities since the 1998 embassy bombings, and every possible link to Bin Laden remained subject to analysis. On 17 May 2000, Clinton gave more details about the millennium plots before US Coast Guard personnel at the Coast Guard Academy in New London. He now publicly linked both the arrests in Jordan and in Seattle to Bin Laden and the organisation Bin Laden had created, and he emphasised the importance of international cooperation for the United States.[92]

At the turn of the millennium, Clinton's intent was very much to inform and prepare, but not frighten the public.[93] In secret, the government effort to detect threats and prevent terrorist attacks at the time was all-encompassing.[94] Clinton's cabinet was on high alert and meeting nearly daily after intelligence agencies saw an increase in reporting on terrorist threats to the United States. Interagency exercises were held, coordination centres set up, warnings issued, and international partners of the US pressured to pre-emptively conduct raids on possible cells. As Ahmed Ressam was arrested at the Canadian border and a plot in Jordan was foiled, National Security Advisor Sandy Berger channelled Clinton's words to the members of the US Principals Committee, saying, 'this is it, nothing more important, all assets. We stop this fucker.'[95]

In a general sense, the self-determination associated with positive securitization and foiling of the millennium plots increased the credibility and authority of the US government before the American people and their representatives in Congress. The Larry King interview also worked to strengthen US national identity. Clinton's remarks about 'people who may be a bit crazy by our standards' or people 'who have a political point to make' were subtle references to American norms and values. The United States saw itself as a leading nation promoting peace, prosperity, freedom and human rights.[96]

For Clinton, the turn of the millennium was a public opportunity to reflect on the past decade of transformation and look ahead with a positive vision. The world had moved from the industrial age into the global information age.[97] In his address to the UN General Assembly, he had called upon the world's leaders to use their resources, knowledge and institutions to make the millennium a 'true changing of times and gateway to greater peace and prosperity, not just a change of digits'.[98] This effort was threatened by 'primitive claims of racial, ethnic, or religious superiority, when married to advanced weaponry and terrorism', as they made 'a wasteland of the soul'.[99] It underlined the otherness and difference of radical elements, whose threats and actions contrasted to Clinton's personal belief and striving to bring people in the world together.[100] As the American president, Clinton worked to bring 'more hope for peace, freedom, security and prosperity all over the world', and tried to promote 'faith, hope and love'.[101] In his memoir, also reflecting on the terrorist attacks on the United States on 11 September 2001, he states that it was important that fighting the threat of terrorism did 'not compromise the character of our country' and the belief in common humanity at the global level.[102] Overall, the Clinton administration had sought to improve defensive measures and act on terrorist threats, but also to enhance international cooperation, share wealth, and to improve living conditions with development aid as a means to combat terrorism.

THE ATTACK ON THE USS *COLE*

In his initial response to the USS *Cole* bombing before the American press in the Rose Garden of the White House, President Clinton condemned the 'cowardly act' and affirmed that 'those responsible will be held accountable'.[103] Days later, in a direct radio address to the American people, the president elucidated that the US sailors in Yemen 'were doing their duty by standing guard for peace'.[104] He stated that the US military not only represented military might, but also exemplified how men and women from very different backgrounds could stand united to promote peace and freedom around the world. Significantly, Clinton mentioned that 'America is not at war', a fundamental characterisation of the context for the attack on the USS *Cole*.[105] He mentioned 'risk' and 'dangers' in the world, but underlined how 'our military' was guarding the peace, preventing 'wars', 'losses' and 'tears'. The US military symbolised the concepts of community and freedom, according to Clinton.

In the context of the lack of war and the American quest for peace, the attack on the USS *Cole* represented the action of a 'hate-filled' other. It was a demonstration of the divide between 'we' (or us) and 'them', although Clinton did not make the 'other' more specific here. According to Clinton, it required that the United States continued to lead the world by sharing its values, celebrating diversity and affirming 'our common humanity'.[106] Themes that were also reflected in several speeches that followed.

No securitization effort

Clinton did not make a securitization effort following the attack on the USS *Cole*; indeed, he took limited public actions in response to the USS *Cole* attack compared with the aftermath of the 1998 embassy attacks. A formal letter to

Congress on 14 October explained the deployment of approximately a hundred troops and two US Navy vessels to provide security, disaster response and medical assistance. United States' forces would 'redeploy as soon as the additional security is deemed unnecessary'.[107]

Unlike the military response following the US embassy bombings in 1998, Clinton did not discuss any customised policy response in public. Since the 1998 missile attacks, US senior government officials had become more hesitant to respond with military strikes. This was partly because of Clinton's past personal problems and a lack of accurate and credible intelligence.[108] With regard to Bin Laden and *Al Qaeda*, the indictment, reward and position on the most wanted list remained in place. Moreover, in secret, Clinton had given the CIA, FBI and military the authority to go after Bin Laden and *Al Qaeda*, a programme that involved frequent use of Predator unmanned aerial vehicles scanning for any signs of Bin Laden in Afghanistan, and submarines armed with Cruise missiles on standby.[109] However, it proved difficult to build enough confidence on the intelligence gathered to engage possible targets. In November 2000, an FBI agent found a link between the perpetrators and a known *Al Qaeda* member, Tawfiq bin Attash (also known as Khallad), although it was not until 2002 that the United States had evidence connecting Bin Laden personally to the attack on the USS *Cole*.[110] Publicly the US government refrained from holding Bin Laden responsible for the attack.

The Middle East powder keg and US presidential elections

The context of other world events taking place, in addition to US domestic developments, is crucial to interpreting the meaning of Clinton's statements on the USS *Cole* attack for his formal and moral audiences. Days before the USS *Cole* was attacked, the Israeli–Palestinian conflict resembled a powder keg exploding. As described in the previous chapter, the visit of Israeli opposition leader Ariel Sharon to the Temple Mount in Jerusalem led to a second Palestinian uprising. On 12 October 2000, Palestinians lynched Israeli reservists who had entered Ramallah. President Clinton had been personally committed to the Israeli–Palestinian peace process right from his early days as president. He now saw the carefully reached Oslo Accords, signed in 1993 by Yitzchak Rabin and Yasser Arafat, nullified in weeks. Right from his first response to the USS *Cole* attack on 12 October, Clinton also mentioned the situation in the Middle East in his speeches. According to Clinton, like the visit of the USS *Cole* to Yemen, US involvement in the Middle East was necessary precisely to try to end violence and promote peace.

Another element influencing the content and settings of the president's public statements were upcoming elections and the consequential ending of Clinton's last term in office. Vice-President Al Gore was running against Governor George W. Bush. In late 2000 and early 2001, Clinton often publicly reflected on his past two terms, summing up his successes and emphasising the prosperous state of the country.

Optimism and hope overruled the fear of international terrorism. Although it was still 'a dangerous world', according to Clinton, there was an 'absence of severe external threat'.[111] He stated American society was as 'free as we have ever been'. The address was made in a Baptist church before the smaller audience of a congregation, a week before the presidential elections. Terrorism was not the only issue outduelled by optimism. The attack on the USS *Cole* was one among many other foreign policy priorities: the security situation in Israel and Palestine, Russia, the Balkans, Sudan, North Korea, Iraq, Iran and Afghanistan were all on the US foreign policy agenda as declared national emergencies.

Reproduction and re-contextualisation in the media

What mostly surfaced in the media reporting on the USS *Cole* attack was the difference in character between law enforcement and intelligence. Criminal investigators emphasised the lack of evidence for the involvement of one of their prime suspects, Osama bin Laden, whereas from an intelligence perspective the potential threat posed by Bin Laden and his organisation stood at the forefront. In the months after the attack on the USS *Cole*, the US government issued several threat warnings to US servicemen and civilians worldwide which news media connected to Bin Laden.

From the very first moment, reporters and terrorism experts re-contextualised official statements on the USS *Cole* attack in news reports by speculating on the involvement of *Al Qaeda* and the EIJ.[112] Compared with news reports following the 1998 embassy attacks, questions of Bin Laden's background were less prominent; a general frame of reference had already been established among audiences. Bin Laden was described as the 'United States' number one terror suspect' and deemed among 'America's most wanted'.[113] Reporting was more about what Bin Laden and his network or organisation were responsible for, and what the current potential threat was. Public discussions on the lack of a US military response highlighted difficulties in deterring and containing terrorists.

Other events, such as developments in the Middle East and the Balkans, influenced reproduction and re-contextualisation of US government statements on terrorism mostly indirectly. Domestically, the run-up to the US presidential election in late 2000 was naturally a major topic in news reports. The campaign focused mostly on domestic issues such as social security and Medicare. News media did not relate the lack of a military response to the elections themselves. This was unlike what had occurred with the presidential decision to conduct missile strikes in 1998.

Overall, how did the narrative reflect elements of securitization, the use of discursive and non-discursive power, and the shaping of US identity? And what can be learned about the narrative itself from the analysis?

Power, Securitization and Identity in the
US Institutional Terrorism Narrative

This section summarises and analyses key findings in the US institutional terrorism narrative on Bin Laden and *Al Qaeda*. The narrative begins in the mid-1990s, as Bin Laden (and later *Al Qaeda*) emerged on the US national security agenda, and is characterised by President Clinton's fluctuating initiative to engage in securitization efforts. The embassy attacks in 1998 were followed by the clearest securitization effort and execution of extraordinary measures. In part, Clinton justified the legitimacy of military strikes *ex post* because presidential powers enabled him to do so. Overall, several consequential discursive and non-discursive events added to the developing narrative on *Al Qaeda*'s representation of a new kind of terrorism.

The US government, structure, roles and social practices were highly institutionalised. Unites States' institutions were reflected in the settings in which texts were produced and consumed. As *securitizing actor*, the US president (directing his staff) had the power to do certain things by giving orders, but also had power over the American people which he exercised in or behind discourse. As a means of power in discourse, for example, he could influence the genre of press briefings. He controlled the timing, the character of attendees and the extent of their contributions to the questions asked. When speaking, he selected the location and setting for these addresses. Different genres, such as a presidential nationwide address, an interview on television or a letter to the US Congress, involved distinct (historic, institutionalized) rules of communication. The office of the US president granted an aura of authority and legitimacy to text production that enabled Clinton to influence these genres. As a form of power behind discourse, he was also able to set a standard for the language that was used with regard to security topics. However, declaring something an extraordinary threat by invoking the National Security Act was only partly of influence on the effect of securitization efforts. It was the wider configuration of circumstances of the power relations between speaker and listener, but also the nature of audiences and the context that influenced the subsequent development of culminating securitization efforts.

It was also through addressing various types of audiences that the presidential position was shaped and authority for securitization was generated. Support among Clinton's *formal audience*, the US Congress, was reflected by votes in favour of legislation and policy. In 1995, Clinton's Democratic Party lost its majority position in Congress. Republicans had the majority vote in both the House of Representatives and Senate until 2000, limiting Clinton's options to formulate policy as Republican support was required. As commander-in-chief of the armed forces, the US president had the power to conduct foreign policy and declare threats to national security. This included ordering military strikes, blocking trade, and seeking various forms of cooperation with other nations such as Kenya and Tanzania. However, the power to declare war lay with Congress. Clinton's troubled relationship with Congress became even more strained after the Lewinsky affair: the impeachment attempt had caused profound damage.

Besides the formal institutionalised relationship between the president and Congress, as organised in the US constitution, the president has an electoral and moral obligation to represent all American citizens: his *moral audience*. During President Clinton's time in office, technological developments caused a shift in the media landscape of Clinton's audiences. The internet and the growing number of television stations reduced the influence of the US government on news media and hence its ability to shape public opinion.[114] However, as the focus of these new media outlets was increasingly on the presidential personage instead of the office of the presidency, the influence of the presidential rhetoric increased.[115] Developing a good relationship with the American people became more important as a basis for authority than institutional rituals such as an inauguration.[116]

Measuring the relationship between the US government and its citizens is more complex than measuring that with Congress. Since the 1930s, news media have reported on presidential approval rates, yet researchers and journalists have debated the value contributed to the outcome of the polls.[117] Some journalists have tended to use the polls as a fever chart, linking outcomes to public opinion on recent developments, whereas other scientific research has identified more deeply rooted feelings such as party affiliation as important factors.[118] Clinton's presidential approval rates were rather stable, even during the turbulent years of 1998 and 1999, supporting the latter position.[119] Between 1995 and 2000, the overall trust in the US government increased.[120] Trust in the ability of the national government to deal with domestic problems rose relatively more than for international problems.[121] Among respondents, trust in various American institutions between 1995 and 2000 remained relatively stable (Congress 24 per cent, Supreme Court 48 per cent, the presidency 46 per cent, the military 64 per cent).[122] Variations were less than five percent points from average, except for the presidency, which varied from 39 per cent in 1996 to 53 per cent in 1998.[123] An important reason for Clinton's popular support was the sound state of the American economy.[124]

With regard to the perceived threat of terrorism against family members, polling indicated a steady decrease in concern ('very or somewhat worried') among American citizens from 42 per cent in April 1995, to 32 per cent on 20 August 1998 (after the embassy bombings), and 24 per cent in April 2000.[125] Other polling in 1994 and 1998 indicated that the 'international terrorist' threat against US vital national interests was increasingly perceived as 'critical' by respondents (from under 70 per cent to 84 per cent).[126] Notably, only 38 per cent of respondents perceived Islamic fundamentalism as a threat to US vital interests in October/November 1998.[127] The percentage, comparable with polling between 2004 and 2014, was a basic indication of how the threats of both new international terrorism and Islamist motivations were perceived in different ways.

In a general sense, these trends correspond to Clinton's securitization efforts in 1998 and 2000. After the embassy attacks, he emphasised the threat of Bin Laden's organisation and network for US interests. At the turn of the millennium, Clinton's positive securitization effort served to decrease perceptions of the terrorist threat against the US public during the millennial festivities. In 2001, Clinton also refrained from making a securitization effort after the USS *Cole* bombing, emphasising optimism about the state of the world. However, what these rudimentary numbers lack is a closer examination of respondents' perception on the worry and fear articulated in US news media in late 1999.

As an intermediate, US national news media also had a certain power in and behind discourse over their audiences. Presidential statements were quoted literally or broadcast live, but also introduced and commented on by news anchors and subject-matter experts. Some experts were invited more frequently than others, depending on their expertise and the way they were able to contribute to the developing frames in a meaningful way. Because of the power invested in the American president to act and his power in and behind discourse, reproduction and re-contextualisation was extensive. United States' media closely followed Clinton's rhetoric. Differences in re-contextualisation had different potential effects on the already fluctuating development of securitization of *Al Qaeda*-related terrorism. The size of network news audiences, the circulation of newspapers, and increasing numbers of views of news websites indicated substantial consumption of news topics among American citizens, although domestic topics garnered more interest than international politics.[128]

But at the same time, what people viewed or read and what they thought or perceived were two different things. This was emphasised by reporting on the Lewinsky affair. Despite high television network viewing rates regarding Lewinsky, public polling indicated that viewers wanted to be informed more about domestic and foreign policy topics than about Clinton's personal affairs.[129] Surveyed Americans found the US missile strikes on Iraq, Afghanistan and Sudan to be more significant events than the Lewinsky affair.[130] Furthermore, between 1995 and 2000, public trust in news media remained relatively stable, varying no more than five percent points from average (newspapers 33 per cent, television news 35 per cent).[131] To some extent, public polling could validate whether securitization efforts and reproduction or re-contextualisation in news media had an effect on the opinion of moral audiences. It provided a voice to Clinton's primary moral audience, similar to the political voting behaviour among his formal audience.

Does this render reproduction and re-contextualisation in news media obsolete as a sign of resonance of securitization efforts among the moral audience? Not exactly. It can also be argued that the frame of reference of Clinton's moral audience and their readiness to be convinced were partially reflected by the tone in these media reports, as news media sought to maximise their audience by accommodating viewers. High viewing rates and self-reflection with regard to the Lewinsky affair could also be seen as a sign in that respect. In sum, there was a triangular relation between the securitizing actor, various types of audiences and the media. The media partly reflected the efforts of the securitization actor, and to a certain extent the media were a generative force of their own. In some respects, however, they also reflected audience preferences.

Securitization efforts

At different times in the 1990s and early 2000, the threat posed by Osama bin Laden and *Al Qaeda* was encompassed by securitization efforts, as highlighted by Clinton in the narrative. Most clearly, following the 1998 embassy attacks, Clinton characterised Osama bin Laden as *referent subject* and deemed him and his followers to be the most dangerous non-state terrorist threat to the United States. Clinton's depiction of the referent subject's support base differed somewhat as the genre, setting and audience of statements changed. In his remarks before his moral audience, Clinton referred to 'the network of radical groups affiliated with and funded by Bin Laden' and to 'the Bin Laden terrorist network', but also to how 'the organization' Bin Laden led had 'planned, financed, and carried out' the embassy bombings. The characterisation and demarcation of the referent subject was stricter for Clinton's formal audience, justifying (*ex post*) the legitimacy of the securitization effort and the customised policy.

In contrast, most early descriptions of Bin Laden between 1995 and 1998 did not characterise him as a typical referent subject. Before 1998, he was defined as a 'private financier' and an 'enabler' of attacks. He was an 'extremist' with radical 'Muslim followers'. In general, the emphasis was on his capabilities. Details on his motivation and the fact that he inspired people were less prominent in the selected texts. It was the non-discursive action of the attacks that triggered Clinton's response and provided the powerful setting. The *referent object* was characterised in general terms as 'the United States' or 'America', and more specifically as 'US citizens' or 'those dressed in military uniforms and civilians'. All were targets, putting the national security of the country at stake. For Clinton's formal audience, all variations of the referent object were encompassed by the umbrella term of 'national security'.

The administration had 'compelling evidence' that the terrorists were ready to strike again soon. According to them, a successful military strike and financial measures constituted the necessary *customised policy* to counter the immediate threat. For the execution of the customised policy, the audiences were not formally required to accept the speeches and letters, yet in a wider moral sense they were asked to accept the threat image presented to them. The Clinton administration stated that the military strikes were but steps in a wider battle against terrorism. This battle also highlighted the national identity, norms and values against which terrorism was aimed, and as such strengthened the power base of US institutions such as the presidency. A second, broader, securitization effort was made before the UN General Assembly on 'new terrorism' aiming to be inclusive to all nations, and emphasising there was no clash of civilisations or religions. Given the text, setting and context, it did not seem to have significant international impact. At the US national level, the securitization effort fitted with the wider US institutional terrorism narrative, and strengthened US national identity and the genre of US presidential statements.

Of significant influence on both securitization efforts, in terms of meaning, was the reproduction and re-contextualisation in US national news media. In general, the primary securitization elements were reproduced. When referring to US identity in terms of promoting peace and security in particular, President Clinton's statements were quoted literally in most cases. This was also the case when the victims of the terrorist attacks in Kenya and Tanzania were commemorated. Three forms of *re-contextualisation* stand out in US news media following the 1998 embassy attacks. First, the capabilities and personality of the referent subject were emphasised. More than in Clinton's own statements, news reports focused on the money and expertise that Osama bin Laden possessed. He was characterised as an 'exiled Saudi millionaire', and some suggested that the best way to deal with the threat was to 'go after his money, cut his money off'. Although occasionally described as 'charismatic' and as 'instigating', he was mostly referred to in functional terms such as a 'skilled businessman', 'fundraiser' or 'organizer'. Bin Laden's motivations were mentioned to a lesser extent. Furthermore, the media focused more on 'the man' Bin Laden was than on the people who surrounded him. Bin Laden's picture was shown repetitively on television sets across the United States and the rest of the world. The US$5 million reward and Bin Laden's inclusion on the list of most wanted American fugitives aligned with such a focus. The media enforced Clinton's securitization effort in this regard. In broader terms, Bin Laden and his followers represented the 'enemies of peace' to whom Clinton referred before the UN General Assembly.

However, secondly, news reports emphasised the limited effects of the military strikes in Sudan and Afghanistan. Even though seventy-five cruise missiles were used, the targets had not been killed, or were not totally destroyed. The public damage assessment nuanced the American people's thinking on the success of the strike, and by doing so questioned the value and accuracy of classified intelligence. Partly related, there was also a discussion on the legitimacy of striking the targets, especially the pharmaceutical factory in Sudan. In a general sense, when classified intelligence is questioned by public media reporting, it is an uneven challenge. Nothing can be made public about the intelligence without endangering sources and methods, and hampering future intelligence work. To some extent, the discussion on the effectiveness of the strikes weakened the authority of the Clinton administration. The media nevertheless reproduced the threat of new terrorist attacks without much question, as they did not have access to the government's 'compelling evidence' on this matter. Putting the strikes in a broader perspective rather than a win-or-lose assessment, most media reports stated that the strikes were but the beginning of an effort to counter this new kind of non-state terrorism.

Thirdly, other domestic and foreign political developments tended to shift public attention away from terrorism. Speculation on Clinton's motives for ordering the military strikes reduced the strength of both securitization efforts that followed the embassy attacks, especially before his formal audience. A conflict between Clinton's personal identity and the social identity of the presidency emerged and weakened his position. Republicans underlined in the media that the office of the president had been damaged by the Lewinsky affair as it had altered the president's personal identity in a way that did not match national norms and values. Furthermore, at the global level, other issues dominated international relations at the time, such as developments in Kosovo. Still, Bin Laden and the threats he made to the United States became a framework for terrorism in news reports, and hence among formal and moral US audiences (to some extent). Bin Laden was projected as the most dangerous man in the world.

Later, in an effort to manage the threat of terrorism and limit Bin Laden's freedom of action, Clinton identified the Taliban, who facilitated and harboured Bin Laden in Afghanistan, as part of the referent subject. Declaring the Afghan Taliban a threat to US national security in July 1999 was a mostly symbolic and mixed signal, and only had a limited effect in financial terms. It also called into question the level of success of the US military strikes conducted in August 1998. The securitization of the Taliban represented an additional focus on supporters of terrorism, and a move away from a military reaction towards a more symbolic diplomatic and economic public response. In diplomatic terms, this effort became more relative as well, as several months later the Taliban even gained some international credibility by successfully mediating with the hijackers who had landed an Indian Airlines plane in Afghanistan. Hidden from the public eye, intelligence operations and criminal investigations against Bin Laden and *Al Qaeda* were ongoing.

Another way in which the Clinton administration dealt with terrorism was positive securitization of its preventive actions at the turn of the millennium. This was less related to Bin Laden at the time. Days before the festivities, the media reported extensively on all that could go wrong, including the possibility of terrorist attacks. This caused Clinton to respond in a reassuring manner that stressed self-determination. He stated that the US government was doing all it could to offer Americans maximum protection from harm. This practice confirmed and strengthened the authority of the US government and the presidency; offering protection is part of the very essence of the state.

Lastly, following the USS *Cole* attack in 2000, Clinton did not make an explicit securitization effort. The context he provided for the attacks was that 'America was not at war', and in general 'it was a time of peace'. The initial official US response mostly underlined the need to gather evidence and refrained from accusing Osama bin Laden or *Al Qaeda* of the attack. In media reports, however, experts and anonymous US officials involved with the investigation instantly linked the USS *Cole* attack to Osama bin Laden and *Al Qaeda*, emphasising what Bin Laden was responsible for, and with what capabilities and where the organisation could strike next. In the background, the US government continued to plan covert operations against Bin Laden.

What became apparent from analysing the selected texts was that Clinton also sought to emphasise feelings of optimism. In 1999 and 2000, the US national identity, norms and values that defined the referent object became increasingly prominent in the narrative. Reflecting on the past decade of transformation, Clinton noted that the turn of the millennium marked an opportunity to establish a true changing of times and to realise greater peace, prosperity, freedom and human rights. In the context of the run-up to the presidential elections in November 2000, Clinton repeatedly elaborated on these values as a driving force for his foreign policy. In the light of the attack on the USS *Cole*, Clinton emphasised that the killed US sailors were 'standing guard for peace', exemplifying how people with widely different backgrounds could unite. He stated that their goal was to 'build harmony' and 'bring people together', 'celebrating diversity while recognizing universal human rights' to show the world that the United States led 'to share its values'. The use of US military means across the world expressed commitment to a US foreign policy aimed at establishing such peace and stability. Hence, it was important to continue US policies in the Middle East. His broader main message was that although it was still a dangerous world, the United States was as free from external threat to security and internal crisis as ever before. In the late 1990s, public opinion polling broadly indicated that the American people shared Clinton's views and satisfaction about the general state of affairs in the United States was high.[132] Active US involvement in the world was also supported.[133] In this regard, military might was viewed as more important than economic power, especially with regard to critical threats such as international terrorism.[134]

Most visible in the US institutional terrorism narrative was the way the violent non-discursive action of the embassy attacks reactively triggered discursive events, and how justification for the legitimacy of extraordinary responsive measures were offered *ex post*. The production and consumption of texts related to non-discursive action, such as the use of the US diplomatic, economic and military power against the capabilities of Osama bin Laden and his followers. Furthermore, this narrative also highlighted several strands of identification, most prominently self-identification. Bin Laden and *Al Qaeda* embodied the antithesis of American identity.

Lastly, it appeared from media reporting and public opinion polling that US citizens found Bin Laden's motivations and grievances vague and difficult to grasp. Bin Laden's 1996 declaration of *jihad*, the 1998 declaration by the WIF and several interviews, along with developments in Afghanistan, Africa and the Middle East, were incidentally referenced in the US institutional terrorism narrative on Bin Laden and *Al Qaeda*. However, they were also discussed in terms of the wider background context of US culture and national security.

Reflection

As a prelude to the last chapter, the following reflects on strengths, weaknesses and limitations of the US institutional terrorism narrative on Bin Laden and *Al Qaeda*. What can be learned about the narrative analysis framework from applying it?

The narrative that emerged is a descriptive representation of the selected texts. Compared with the *Al Qaeda* narrative, there was much more information available for the US institutional terrorism narrative and no issues with translating. The availability of all public presidential statements and the accessibility of a large body of media reporting (primarily through LexisNexis) enabled the thorough selection of adequate data for the narrative. Several US polling institutions, such as Gallup, Pew Research Center and the Chicago Council on Global Affairs, were able to provide (rudimentary) polling information on perceptions among Clinton's moral audience. However, although institutions such as Gallup have a lengthy scientific track record of polling Americans, it was only after the attacks on 11 September 2001 that detailed questions with regard to Bin Laden, *Al Qaeda*, Islamic fundamentalism and international terrorism were asked on a frequent basis.

Memoirs and other literature were used in addition to the primary data of selected texts to provide context and fill in some of the gaps on covert action that were not described in public statements. The *ex post* use of memoirs does not imply that narrative analysis as part of *ex durante* intelligence analysis is impossible. In a collaborative environment, intelligence analysis should involve dialogue with working-level policymakers on the strategic narrative and implemented security measures and policies. Furthermore, detailed knowledge of secret policies and covert actions or other security practices could enable even better contrastive analysis of how these actions would be reflected in other narratives, such as those of adversaries, and to what effect.

On the other hand, it is possible that *ex post* findings on *Al Qaeda* and Bin Laden that have influenced accounts on events and circumstances enabled a more comprehensive composition of the US institutional terrorism narrative. These findings include, for instance, those reflected in the 9/11 Commission Report, and those in some of the literature by Jason Burke, Ali Soufan, Michael Scheuer, Lawrence Wright and others. In practice, ACN will always be an imperfect striving to provide the most optimal basic analytic narratives. In case of *ex durante* intelligence analysis or research, this imperfect nature will become even more apparent. However, the reality of information gaps or distortions does not render the use of the ACN methodology impossible. It offers a way to process, position and analyse public texts on discursive and non-discursive action and the raw intelligence reporting collected from human and technical sources. Most *ex durante* secret intelligence reporting is not made available *ex post* for academic research, and certainly not on short notice. Thus, in that respect, intelligence practitioners would have an advantage.

A challenge for the US narrative was to decide to what extent other (domestic and foreign policy) topics had to be taken into account to properly contextualise and situate Clinton's statements. While this narrative concentrated on *Al Qaeda*, an overly narrow focus on Bin Laden and *Al Qaeda* would have led to the disregard of the extent to which other entities were also deemed part of the 'new terrorism'. Furthermore, were the sanctions against the Taliban partly imposed to send a signal to Pakistani Prime Minister Sharif? If Clinton recognised Bin Laden as a significant threat to US national security, why was it also important to state after the USS *Cole* bombing that the United States was in a time of peace and not at war?

In contrast to the *Al Qaeda* narrative, identifying the moral and formal audiences was less of a challenge. The domestic and international position, formal powers and responsibilities of the US president were structured to a large extent by laws and related genre conventions. This provided a natural fit with the role of the securitizing actor within the securitization framework as described in Chapter 1. There is a certain inverse logic to the two challenges of determining the (contextual) relevance of issues, and identifying audiences in the narrative analysis. The formal and moral audiences for Clinton's securitization efforts were more clearly distinguishable than in the case of the *Al Qaeda* narrative because of the institutionalisation of the United States. In and through the various practices of the state and its citizens with regard to a multitude of domestic and international issues, social roles had been defined and confirmed. In contrast, the *Al Qaeda* narrative was more centred around the single issue of *jihad* against the far enemy, trying to expand the reach of the idea and establish and confirm social roles in the process.

Another potential issue of concern was the distinction between the institutional and the personal when analysing narratives. By speaking, President

Clinton brought institutional authority to the topics discussed. However, the president is also human. Making a distinction between more personal idiosyncratic rhetorical elements and the institutional discursive practice of the administration and US government institutions was difficult as the timeframe of this narrative limited analysis to the Clinton administration only. With additional research on other cases or timeframes, this aspect in the analysis should be addressed more fully. Based on this research, no conclusions can be drawn on the continuity of the US institutional terrorism narrative on Bin Laden and *Al Qaeda* across different presidencies. However, all-in-all the narrative analysis framework provided an adequate tool to identify and contextualise securitization efforts for the given timeframe.

NOTES

1. James Sperling, 'United States: a Full Spectrum Contributor to Governance?', Emile J. Kirchner and James Sperling (eds), *National Security Cultures: Patterns of Global Governance* (New York: Routledge, 2010), 172–209.
2. Walter R. Mead, *Special Providence: American Foreign Policy and How It Changed the World* (New York: Alfred Knopf, 2001); Walter R. Mead, *Power, Terror, Peace and War: America's Grand Strategy in a World at Risk*, reprint (New York: Vintage, 2005); Joseph S. Nye, *The Paradox of American Power: Why the World's Only Superpower Can't Go It Alone* (Oxford: Oxford University Press, 2002).
3. Underneath the bipartisan political landscape of Republicans and Democrats, and the various isolationist or interventionist traditions of American foreign policy, there lie some fundamental American values and views that attribute a special status to the United States as a nation. This is often referred to in terms of 'American exceptionalism' and 'Americanism'. For example, see Seymour M. Lipset, *American Exceptionalism: a Double-Edged Sword* (New York: W. W. Norton, 1996).
4. For example, see Walter Laqueur, 'Terror's New Face: the Radicalization and Escalation of Modern Terrorism', *Harvard International Review* 20(4) (1998): 48–51; Isabelle Duyvesteyn, 'How New Is the New Terrorism?' *Studies in Conflict and Terrorism* 27(5) (2004): 439–54.
5. Mark E. Stout, 'The Evolution of Intelligence Assessments of al-Qaeda to 2011', in Lorry M. Fenner, Mark E. Stout and Jessica L. Goldings (eds), *9.11 Ten Years Later: Insights on al-Qaeda's Past and Future Through Captured Records*, Conference Proceedings, (Washington, DC: Johns Hopkins University Center for Advanced Governmental Studies, 2011), 28.
6. Chairman of the Counter-terrorism Security Group (CSG) of the National Security Council (NSC).
7. Richard A. Clarke, *Against All Enemies* (London: Free Press, 2004), 90.
8. Bill Clinton, *My Life*, Kindle edn (New York: Knopf, 2004), location 10303.
9. Ibid.
10. Federation of American Scientists, 'PDD-39 U.S. Policy on Counterterrorism', 21 June 1995.
11. US Department of State, 'Patterns of Global Terrorism', 1995.

12. 9/11 Commission Report, 62, 109.
13. Clarke, *Against All Enemies*; Scheuer, *Imperial Hubris*; Hoffman, *Al Qaeda Declares War*.
14. UNs Security Council, resolutions 1044, 1054 and 1070.
15. Philip Shanon, 'The World, Holy War is Home to Haunt the Saudis', *The New York Times*, 14 July 1996.
16. US District Court Southern District of New York, 'Indictment 98 Cr.', retrieved from Federation of American Scientists.
17. Hoffman, *Al Qaeda Declares War*, 34; Soufan, *The Black Banners*, 45–50.
18. US District Court NYSD, 'Indictment 98 Cr.' and 'Indictment S(9). 98 Cr. 1023 (LBS)'.
19. 9/11 Commission Report, 112, 481; Clarke, *Against All Enemies*, 149.
20. Hoffman, *Al Qaeda Declares War*, 34.
21. FBI, 'Interview of Mohamed Sadiq Odeh'.
22. Bill Clinton, 'The President's Radio Address 8 August 1998', *Public Papers of the Presidents of the United States*, 1998 II (Washington, DC: Office of the Federal Register, 2000), 1415.
23. Bill Clinton, 'Remarks in Martha's Vineyard, Massachusetts, on Military Action Against Terrorist Sites in Afghanistan and Sudan', 20 August 1998, *Public Papers*, 1998 II, 1460.
24. Bill Clinton, 'Address to the Nation on Military Action Against Terrorist Sites in Afghanistan and Sudan', 20 August 1998, *Public Papers*, 1998 II, 1460–1462.
25. Bill Clinton, 'Letter to Congressional Leaders on Terrorists Who Threaten to Disrupt the Middle East Peace Process', 20 August 1998, *Public Papers*, 1998 II, 1463.
26. Clinton, 'Address to the Nation on Military Action Against Terrorist Sites in Afghanistan and Sudan'.
27. Ibid.
28. Clarke, *Against All Enemies*, 198.
29. Clinton, 'Address to the Nation on Military Action Against Terrorist Sites in Afghanistan and Sudan'.
30. Ibid.
31. Ibid.
32. Ibid.
33. Bill Clinton, 'Letter to Congressional Leaders Reporting on Military Action Against Terrorist Sites in Afghanistan and Sudan', 21 August 1998, *Public Papers*, 1998 II, 1464.
34. Bill Clinton, 'The President's Radio Address', 22 August 1998, *Public Papers*, 1998 II, 1464–1465.
35. Sageman, *Leaderless Jihad*, 29.
36. Bill Clinton, 'Remarks to the 53d Session of the United Nations General Assembly in New York City', 21 September 1998, *Public Papers*, 1998 II, 1629–1633.
37. Ibid., 1632.
38. Ibid.
39. Wendy S. Ross, 'Fight Against Terrorism Focus of Clinton Speech to UNGA', *United States Information Office*, 18 September 1998.

40. Jane Robelot (TV anchor), 'Battle Plans for US Missile Strike Were in Effect Last Week', *CBS This Morning*, CBS News, 21 August 1998.
41. Dan Rather (TV anchor), 'President Clinton Addresses The Nation Regarding Today's US Military Strikes on Terrorist Sites in Afghanistan and Sudan', *CBS News Special Report*, CBS News, 20 August 1998.
42. Clinton, Bill, 'President Clinton's Weekly Radio Address', radio broadcast, *White House Briefing*, Washington, DC, Federal News Service, 22 August 1998.
43. Clarke, *Against All Enemies*, 189.
44. Lou Dobbs (TV host), 'America Strikes Back, Markets Unmoved', CNN.
45. Leon Harris (TV anchor), 'America Strikes Back, U.S. Citizens Abroad Urged to Exercise Greater Caution, Stray Missile Hits Pakistan', *CNN Early Edition*, CNN, 21 August 1998; Dobbs, 'America Strikes Back, Markets Unmoved'.
46. Dan Rather (TV anchor), 'The Decision', CBS News.
47. Julie Chen (TV anchor), 'The Hunt Continues for an International Gang of Mass Murderers Following the East African Bombings', CBS News.
48. Laurie Dhue (TV anchor), 'Dual Objectives in U.S. Embassy Bombings, Treat the Injured, Find Who's Responsible', *CNN Saturday*, CNN, 8 August 1998.
49. Ibid.
50. Marina Kolbe (TV anchor), 'Man Arrested in Pakistan in Connection with Embassy Bombings', *CNN Saturday*, CNN, 15 August 1998.
51. Gene Randall (TV anchor), 'Finding Culprits Responsible for Bombings May be Difficult', *CNN Worldview*, CNN, 8 August 1998.
52. Peter Jennings (TV host), 'A Closer Look', *World News Tonight with Peter Jennings*, ABC News, 4 September 1998.
53. Jeanne Meserve (TV anchor), 'Just in Time, Combating International Terrorism, Quickly', *CNN Newsday*, CNN, 31 August 1998.
54. Lisa McRee (TV host), 'America Strikes Back', *ABC Good Morning America*, ABC News, 21 August 1998.
55. Ibid.
56. Ibid.
57. Henderson (TV co-host), 'Newsroom Worldview'.
58. Clarke, *Against All Enemies*, 198.
59. Gene Randall (TV anchor), 'America Strikes Back, What are the Capabilities of Osama bin Laden?' *CNN Saturday*, CNN, 22 August 1998.
60. Richard A. Posner, *An Affair of State: the Investigation, Impeachment, and Trial of President Clinton* (Cambridge, MA: Harvard University Press, 1999).
61. For example, Kevin Newman (TV host), 'Kenya Bombing Investigation', *ABC Good Morning America*, ABC News, 13 August 1998; Ted Koppel (TV anchor), 'What in the World is Going On?', *ABC Nightline*, ABC News, 24 September 1998.
62. Dan Rather (TV anchor), 'Timing of the Attack Against Terrorists in Afghanistan and Sudan', *CBS Evening News*, CBS News, 20 August 1998.
63. McRee, 'America Strikes Back'.
64. Jane Robelot (TV co-host), 'Orlando Family's Reaction to US Bombing in Retaliation for Embassies being Bombed in Africa', *CBS This Morning*, CBS News, 21 August 1998.

65. Chen, 'U.S. Air Strikes Catch Many by Surprise and Leaves Questions'.
66. Clinton, *My Life*, location 16666; Clarke, *Against All Enemies*, 186.
67. Jim Lehrer (TV anchor), 'The NewsHour with Jim Lehrer, Staying the Course, Swissair Crash, Cancer War, the President and the Press, Should He Resign?', *PBS News Hour*, PBS, 3 September 1998; Jim Lehrer (TV anchor), 'The NewsHour with Jim Lehrer, Going Public?, Wall Street Wrap, Reporting on Race, Dialogue', *PBS News Hour*, PBS, 18 September 1998; Koppel, 'What in the World is Going On?'.
68. The American Presidency Project, 'Presidential Job Approval Rates', University of California, Santa Barbara, CA; Pew Research Center, 'Support for Clinton Unchanged By Judiciary Vote, Public's Good Mood and Optimism Undeterred by Latest Developments', Washington, DC.
69. Arthur H. Miller, 'Sex, Politics, and Public Opinion: What Political Scientists Really Learned from the Clinton–Lewinsky Scandal', *Political Science and Politics* 32(4) (1999): 721–9.
70. Ibid., 725.
71. Clarke, *Against All Enemies*, 200–2.
72. Soufan, *The Black Banners*; Scheuer, *Imperial Hubris*; Clarke, *Against All Enemies*; Hoffman, *Al Qaeda Declares War*.
73. US Department of State, 'Patterns of Global Terrorism', Washington DC, 1998.
74. Ibid.
75. Clarke, *Against All Enemies*, 198.
76. Clinton, 'Letter to Congressional Leaders on Terrorists Who Threaten to Disrupt the Middle East Peace Process'; The American Presidency Project, 'Executive Order 13099', 20 August 1998.
77. Ibid.
78. US District Court NYSD, 'Indictment 98 Cr.', 'Indictment S(9). 98 Cr. 1023 (LBS)'.
79. US District Court NYSD, 'Indictment 98 Cr. 539'.
80. Bill Clinton, 'Address Before a Joint Session of the Congress on the State of the Union', 19 January 1999, *Public Papers of the Presidents of the United States*, 1999 I (Washington, DC: Office of the Federal Register 2000), 62–71; Bill Clinton, 'Remarks at the National Academy of Sciences', 22 January 1999, *Public Papers*, 1999 I, 85–8.
81. Bill Clinton, 'Interview with Judith Miller and William J. Broad of the New York Times', 21 January 1999, *Public Papers*, 1999 I, 90–96.
82. Clarke, *Against All Enemies*, 177.
83. Bill Clinton, 'Statement on the National Emergency with Respect to the Taliban', 6 July 1999, *Public Papers*, 1999 II, 1136.
84. Clarke, *Against All Enemies*, 225.
85. For example, James Foley, 'State Department Regular Briefing by James Foley, Deputy Spokesman', *Federal News Service*, 6 July 1999.
86. Jonathan Mann (TV anchor), 'Millennium 2000, UN Officials Praise Taliban's Handling of Hostage Crisis', *CNN Live Event/Special*, CNN, 31 December 1999.
87. Clinton, *My Life*, locations 17945, 17968.
88. Bill Clinton, 'Interview with Larry King of CNN's "Larry King Live"' and 'Interview with Charlie Rose of CBS' "60 Minutes II"', 22 December 1999, *Public Papers*, 1999 II, 2331–2339, 2343–2349.
89. Ibid., 2331–2339, 2343–2349.

90. Clinton, 'Interview with Larry King of CNN's "Larry King Live"', 2332–2333.
91. Donna Kelley (TV anchor), 'U.S. Investigators Uncover Ties Between bin Laden and Suspects Under Investigation for Smuggling Explosives into U.S.', *CNN Early Edition*, CNN, 27 January 2000.
92. Bill Clinton, 'Commencement Address at the United States Coast Guard Academy in New London, Connecticut', 17 May 2000, *Public Papers of the Presidents of the United States*, 2000 I (Washington, DC: Office of the Federal Register, 2001), 950–951.
93. Clarke, *Against All Enemies*, 177.
94. Ibid., 211–14.
95. Ibid., 212.
96. Bill Clinton, 'Remarks to the 54th Session of the United Nations General Assembly in New York City', 21 September 1999, *Public Papers*, 1999 II, 1563.
97. Clinton, *My Life*, location 19791.
98. Clinton, 'Remarks to the 54th Session of the United Nations General Assembly'.
99. Ibid.
100. Clinton, *My Life*, location 19791.
101. Ibid., location 19791, 19829.
102. Ibid., location 19829.
103. Bill Clinton, 'Remarks on the Attack on the U.S.S. Cole and the Situation in the Middle East', 12 October 2000, *Public Papers of the Presidents of the United States*, 2000 III (Washington, DC: Office of the Federal Register, 2002), 2165.
104. Bill Clinton, 'The President's Radio Address', 14 October 2000, *Public Papers*, 2000 III, 2176–2177.
105. Ibid., 2176–2177.
106. For example, Bill Clinton, 'Remarks at a Reception for Hillary Clinton in Flushing, New York', 23 October 2000, *Public Papers*, 2000 III, 2292.
107. Bill Clinton, 'Letter to Congressional Leaders Reporting on the Deployment of United States Forces in Response to the attack on the U.S.S. Cole', 14 October 2000, *Public Papers*, 2000 III, 2191.
108. Richard Clarke, *Your Government Failed You: Breaking the Cycle of National Security Disasters* (New York: HarperCollins, 2008), 161.
109. Clarke, *Against All Enemies*, 222–5.
110. 9/11 Commission Report, 192.
111. Bill Clinton, 'Remarks to the Congregation of Alfred Street Baptist Church in Alexandria, Virginia', 29 October 2000, *Public Papers*, 2000 III, 2373.
112. Bob Schieffer (TV anchor), 'President Clinton Comments on the Terrorist Attack on the USS Cole in Yemen', *Face the Nation*, CBS, 15 October 2000.
113. Bill Hemmer (TV anchor), 'Osama bin Laden's Organization No. 1 Suspect in USS Cole Bombing', CNN, 14 October 2000.
114. 'Report of the National Task Force on Presidential Rhetoric in Times of Crisis', in James Aune and Martin J. Medhurst (eds), *The Prospect of Presidential Rhetoric* (Austin, TX: A&M University Press, 2008), 363.
115. 'Report of the National Task Force on Presidential Communication to Congress', in James Aune and Martin J. Medhurst (eds), *The Prospect of Presidential Rhetoric* (Austin, TX: A&M University Press, 2008), 283.

116. John M. Murphy, 'Power and Authority in a Postmodern Presidency' in James Aune and Martin J. Medhurst (eds), *The Prospect of Presidential Rhetoric* (Austin, TX: A&M University Press, 2008), 33.

117. James Aune and Martin J. Medhurst (eds), *The Prospect of Presidential Rhetoric* (Austin, TX: A&M University Press, 2008), 305.

118. George C. Edwards, *Presidential Approval: a Sourcebook* (Baltimore, MD: Johns Hopkins University Press, 1990), 134–52.

119. Gallup, 'Presidential Job Approval, Bill Clinton's High Ratings in the Midst of Crisis, 1998', Gallup, 'Presidential Approval Ratings, Bill Clinton'.

120. Pew Research Center, 'Public Trust in Government: 1958–2017', 3 May 2017, Washington DC.

121. Gallup, 'Trust in Government'.

122. Gallup, 'Confidence in Institutions', available at: http://news.gallup.com/poll/1597/confidence-institutions.aspx, last accessed 7 February 2018.

123. Ibid.

124. Pew Research Center, 'Public Trust in Government: 1958–2017'; Miller, 'Sex, Politics, and Public Opinion', 725.

125. John Mueller and Mark Stewart, *Chasing Ghosts: the Policing of Terrorism* (Oxford: Oxford University Press, 2016), 81; Gallup, 'Concern about Being a Victim of Terrorism'.

126. Ibid., 88; Gallup, 'Americans Support Active Role for U.S. in World Affairs', 1 April 1999.

127. Gallup, 'Americans Support Active Role for U.S. in World Affairs'; Chicago Council on Global Affairs, 'Poll, Republicans Fear Islamic Fundamentalism Even More Than after 9/11', 22 August 2016.

128. See, for example, Pew Research Center, 'Internet News Takes Off', 8 June 1998, Washington DC.

129. Ted Koppel (TV anchor), 'What in the World is Going On?' ABC News; Stephen Earl Bennett, 'Another Lesson about Public Opinion during the Clinton–Lewinsky Scandal', *Presidential Studies Quarterly* 32(2) (2002): 276–92.

130. Felicity Barringer, 'Impeachment, the Media, in Poll, Public Says Clinton Scandal Wasn't ' 98's Most Compelling Event', *The New York Times*, 23 December 1998.

131. Gallup, 'Confidence in Institutions'.

132. Gallup, 'Satisfaction with the United States'.

133. Gallup, 'US Position in the World'.

134. Lydia Saad, 'Americans Support Active Role for U.S. in World Affairs', Gallup News Service: Barbara A. Bardes and Robert W. Oldendick, *Public Opinion Measuring the American Mind*, 5th edn (London: Rowman & Littlefield, 2017), 247.

4

CRITICAL TERRORISM NARRATIVE

INTRODUCTION

The rationale behind the *critical terrorism narrative* must be explained and emphasised. This third narrative is not some 'verdict' from an 'independent' third party, nor is the perspective outlined in this chapter necessarily a highly influential narrative. On the contrary, the *Al Qaeda* narrative and the US institutional terrorism narrative can be viewed as discourses at the macro level. They involved people who were in the social position to produce texts with explicit performative power: President Clinton could sign laws and decrees that were binding for US citizens, and Bin Laden's directives carried meaning for those who had pledged loyalty (*bayat*) to him. In contrast, this critical terrorism narrative manifested more at a micro (individual or personal) level, due to the actors and the nature of their relationship with audiences involved. To a certain extent, journalists are free to report what they want, but so are audiences to read or view what they desire. The performative power of these texts is limited. In the intelligence practice (and among securitization scholars), studying such critical micro narratives is unconventional.

Within the broader framework of ACN, the narrative described in this chapter is therefore of a different value and performs a different function. A methodological difference compared with the previous two chapters is that the elements of securitization efforts identified in the macro narratives (that is, securitizing actor, referent subject, referent object, audiences, heuristic artefacts, customised policies) served as point of departure for critical reflections (on tensions and inconsistencies) in this micro narrative. The narrative points from outside both the dominant social practices of the politics of nations and Salafi jihadism to how notions of difference feature in the way these social spaces are organised. Rather than the researcher (or intelligence analyst) advocating for alternative views in a normative way, this function could in principle be performed by an unlimited number of critical narratives. The narrative presented in this chapter could be characterised as one of many commentators on discursive and non-discursive displays of the macro narratives. To what extent did the United States and *Al Qaeda* narratives respond to or even need each other? To use a metaphor, was some sort of tennis match going on between them? Capturing the nature and potential of the critique generates additional questions and could inform further research (or intelligence activity) on *Al Qaeda*. It could also provide insights on broader US security practices and policies, but the ultimate focus in all narratives lies on *Al Qaeda* as the intelligence problem.

More than the two previous chapters, the selection of this narrative was the researcher's choice, though it was an informed decision based on argumentation and theoretical considerations. The narrative is situated in a distinctly different social structure and practice compared with the previous chapters: the social space of the network society and the information society. Principal discursive practices are investigative journalism and mass-media reporting, but also writing books and memoirs. These are distinct in terms of genres and settings from primary discursive practices in the US institutional terrorism narrative (for example, Clinton statements) and the *Al Qaeda* narrative (for example, Bin Laden statements). Especially the US institutional terrorism narrative was influenced by reproduction and re-contextualisation of official statements in news media, mostly mass media. However, it is possible and valuable to separate this from the reporting part of this narrative. Thus, this chapter analyses specific journalists' news media reporting as part of a distinct narrative. The open information society allows investigative journalists and news correspondents to report and comment on social events and circumstances in their own way, surpassing 'official' narratives. This opens up possibilities to critically highlight the use of power by others: to perform actions, to control the availability and selection of discursive resources, to maintain genre conventions, and to standardise language use. By itself, the critical terrorism narrative described in this chapter lacks the large and adequate audience and, hence, the weight to be of significant influence on the macro narratives. Nevertheless, as stated, it has the potential to provide an ideology critique of the naturalisation of meaning through processes of securitization, thereby broadening the understanding of social or intelligence problems.

ACN on *Al Qaeda* is not finished with this third narrative. In fact, comparing narratives of complex, dynamic and ambiguous (intelligence) problems is never finished. Already within the social practice of the information society, a vast number of (critical terrorism) narratives can be identified. These can be related to either other journalists or other entities that are active in the social space of the information society, such as think tanks or non-governmental organisations. Compared with the latter two, the work of journalists offers a more detailed discourse that is more responsive to the various social events in the macro narratives. The general impression that journalists are also more independent and objective in their work than (political) think tanks is in fact more nuanced.[1] The next sections elaborate on the information society and explicate how the critical terrorism narrative has been further narrowed down.

The social practice of the information society

The social practice of the information society and the network society as the corresponding social structure is not 'new'.[2] Throughout history, exchanging information has been a precondition for any society to exist, and human relations can be viewed as organised in terms of networks.[3] It was the technological developments in the last decades that increasingly enabled processes of globalisation and the information revolution. These brought the significance of networks as social structures and processes of information exchange as social practice so clearly to the forefront. A core principle of the network society is the centrality of relations between social units, both horizontally and across different levels. Individuals, groups, organisations and institutions are organised around streams of information.[4] Media such as the internet, newspapers, magazines, television and radio fulfil a crucial function in the communication to various audiences of the constituent texts that make up critical journalistic narratives. However, although journalists have a certain degree of freedom to produce texts, they are subject to professional and ethical standards, as well as power relations in the information society as well. The Western media landscape, which is relevant for this narrative, is composed of various conglomerates, news agencies and organisations that report on a plethora of social events and phenomena, including Bin Laden and *Al Qaeda*. For most organisations, making a profit is a central concern. To some degree, managers and editors impose corporate identity and standards, reflected in topics and writing styles. Employees' operating space varies with the type of discursive practice.

Analytically, the discursive practices of investigative journalism and mass-media news reporting are distinct ideal types. They can also be seen as situated on a spectrum along which journalistic activities can be positioned. Traditionally, mass media are institutionalised commercial means to communicate messages (via radio, television or internet) to large audiences; this is something of an industry. To be effective within the limited time and space available for topics, as costs need to be kept to a minimum, mass-media reporting aims to frame news in superficial, simplistic and short-term expressions.[5] Reporters and news desks work under the constant pressure of competition, commercial advertisers, audience demands and rating points to quickly converge events into easy-to-grasp frames.[6] Because of the constant need for news media to produce reports and to be omnipresent, the agendas and content offered by states, institutions and major press agencies often offer a baseline routine for reproduction by mass-media broadcasters.[7] Furthermore, once certain frames of reference or routines have been established, it becomes more difficult to present issues that do not easily align with these recognised frames. Observations and opinions of research journalists and experts who are invited as commentators are constrained by the limited time available, the setting and genre conventions of news shows, and the framing of topics by the questions that are asked.

In contrast, less 'mass-produced' investigative reports in newspapers are closer to the journalistic ideal of independent research. Reporters do not follow someone else's agenda: they decide for themselves what is worthy of coverage, while maintaining professional standards such as the adversarial principle.[8] Some investigations take years to complete and involve extensive global cooperation. Journalists are able to distance themselves more from the occupational reality of following and reproducing the statements and agendas offered by others. Often, some party involved in the story does not want to disclose information. In theoretical terms, research journalists are critical interpreters seeking to go beyond dominant explanations. Investigative reporting aims to provide more in-depth meanings to events and circumstances by researching topics over longer periods of time, and consulting an array of knowledgeable personal contacts, experts and confidential sources. Consumers of investigative reports are required to understand issues in somewhat more complex, contradicting, multi-level and ambiguous terms, compared with the accessible frames circulating in mass media.

In practice, the distinction between investigative journalism and mass-media reporting is much less clear. Much journalistic work falls in between both types as it mixes elements, and intermediate forms can be defined. In-depth research includes highly extensive information gathering, and mass-media news reporting generally relies more extensively on readily available official (government) sources.[9] Yet another form of journalistic work is essayistic commentaries or op-eds, which are published in smaller 'quality' newspapers. They often challenge the dominant media frames. Still, most journalists only have a certain bandwidth to operate freely as many are directed by their employers to operate from specific areas or cover certain issues. There is a relationship between the stories a journalist chooses to write, what his or her employer asks him or her to write about, and what stories audiences want to read, hear or view. Stories on *Al Qaeda* by a journalist stationed in Yemen, Israel or Pakistan will automatically also reflect some of the local dynamics and relevance for the local area.

Instead of precisely classifying journalists, it is more helpful to analyse their work in all its variety against the backdrop of the two ideal types of journalism presented. Reporting has many forms or genres. Depending on the media platform, and the task and setting of journalists and news correspondents, their work can reflect either more of the 'transmission belt' type of journalism (which conveys the agendas of others) or self-initiated independent research.[10] The more journalists initiate research themselves, operate relatively freely, collect from a range of private and public sources, and are able to write and publish their stories unhindered, the less these perspectives are reproductions of the messages and agendas of others.

Text selection

In the 1990s, many journalists investigated Bin Laden and *Al Qaeda*. Central to the critical terrorism narrative in this book is Robert Fisk, the British foreign correspondent in the Middle East working for the British newspaper *The Independent*. He has stated that he opposed 'obedient, safe journalism' that conformed too much to those in power and saw it as his aim to 'monitor and challenge authority all the time', especially when violence was used.[11] Fisk has also declared that he opposes any form of violence in any case.[12] His explicit critical attitude potentially places him more towards the investigative journalism than the mass-media reporting paradigm, although still somewhere in between.

But why Fisk? The decision was mainly based on three arguments. First, of all journalists who actually interviewed Bin Laden, Fisk did so the most (three times), and in two countries (Sudan and Afghanistan). In contrast to several other Western journalists who interviewed Bin Laden, Fisk is an Arabic speaker. Secondly, comparative research into the texts of both Fisk and American correspondents, such as CNN expert and terrorism scholar Peter Bergen, highlighted how the latter often cited US government officials (both on and off the record) as sources for contributions to news media. Unlike Bergen and other American news correspondents, Fisk worked from the Middle East. His reporting on Bin Laden was more regionally contextualised. He has received international rewards for his work and more than ten honorary university degrees. His knowledge on Bin Laden has been recognised by former US intelligence officers who characterise him, despite his outspoken critique of US policies, as fair-minded.[13] To assess the uniqueness of Fisk's interviews with Bin Laden, his reports (sometimes containing highly provocative critique on the United States) were compared with reporting from others who had conducted such interviews. They include American, British and New Zealand journalists Peter Bergen, John Miller, Scott MacLeod, Gwynne Roberts and Peter Arnett.[14] Despite differences regarding genre, perspective, sources and idiosyncratic aspects, it can be concluded that the general themes identified in Fisk's work have a wider basis and can serve as an adequate core for the critical terrorism narrative.

Text selection was based on several criteria. Almost all texts were gathered from the LexisNexis database, as this was the most comprehensive and systematically available collection of media reporting. Key parts of texts were identified based on either a chronological clustering in the number of reports around certain events, or the extent to which the content of a text was relevant. Focal points for the analysis of the data were the events and securitization efforts identified in the previous two chapters. They included the 1996 Ladenese memorandum, the 1998 WIF declaration, the 1998 embassy attacks, the US missile strikes on Sudan and Afghanistan, Clinton's formulation of the threat of 'a new kind of terrorism' before the UN General Assembly, Operation Desert Fox over Iraq, the Taliban as threat to US national security, and the attack on the USS *Cole* in 2000. The extent to which the reporting of Fisk and others was reproduced and re-contextualised by other media was also brought into the analysis, although in a limited way.

The following sections present a chronologically ordered analysis of the themes identified in the selected texts. The chapter concludes by discussing the extent to which the critical terrorism narrative problematised and offered critique on US and *Al Qaeda* securitization efforts, processes of identification and power relations.

Bin Laden: Extremist or Businessman?

In 1993, Robert Fisk interviewed Bin Laden in the setting of his construction work in the Sudanese village of Almatig. The article provided an initial portrait on Bin Laden for a relatively small British audience. It was the first time Bin Laden had accepted such a request from a Western journalist. The result was an article on Bin Laden that underlined a certain eminence among Muslim fighters.[15] Fisk consequently referred to him as 'Mr Bin Laden' and described him as a man who 'looked every inch the mountain warrior of mujahedin legend' who had fought against the Soviets in Afghanistan.[16] However, Fisk also characterised Bin Laden as 'a shy man' who was 'wary of the press', and who at least initially 'refused to talk about Afghanistan', minimising his own role in the fight against the Soviets in the 1980s.[17]

In general, descriptions of Bin Laden as a 'businessman' and 'entrepreneur' recognised his wealth and entrepreneurship, while 'hero', 'warrior' and 'mujahedin legend' underlined his leadership status. Contrary to allegations of supporting armed struggle elsewhere from Sudan, the first phrase of the title 'Anti-Soviet warrior puts his army on the road to peace' advanced a non-violent characterisation of Bin Laden that was supported by the large picture. The title aligned with Bin Laden's own statement on the matter. The only reference to Bin Laden's reasons for moving to Sudan with his family was disagreement among fighting groups in Afghanistan. There was no mention of any pressure from Saudi Arabia, Egypt or other countries. American journalist Scott MacLeod's

Social structures

Social practices

Discursive practices

Texts | Texts | Texts

e.g. Newspaper articles
Television show transcripts

Search queries (entities, themes, events)
e.g. "Bin L*"

Fisk

Bergen

Miller

Roberts

Arnett

General texts

Key texts

Public Enemy No 1 – a title he always wanted

In the spring of last year Osama bin Laden was a lonely, isolated man. Though he had called for a holy war against the United States, the Americans had largely ignored him. Saddam Hussein was flavour of the year in the American hate stakes. How Mr bin Laden must have been delighted, then, when Bill Clinton this week called him "Public Enemy Number One".

Infantile though the title is – Hollywood and Washington now seem to replicate each other – the US President had at last bestowed on the Saudi dissident the accolade he has always sought. Mr Clinton had now recognised the titanic struggle that Mr bin Laden was prepared to wage against the world's most powerful nation.

An hour before the Americans launched their cruise missiles at Afghanistan, Mr bin Laden had sent a message to a Pakistani journalist in Peshawar, a satellite call in which an Egyptian doctor – whom I last saw sitting beside Mr bin Laden in Afghanistan – said the Saudi was not responsible for the attacks on the US embassies in Africa but invited all Muslims to join his jihad (holy war) against "the Americans and the Jews". He denied the bombings in Africa just as he once denied to me his responsibility for the bombing of a US base in Dhahran that killed 19 Americans. He is, it would seem, a warrior who does not go to war, all cloak and no dagger.

How Mr bin Laden must have been delighted, then, when Bill Clinton this week called him "Public Enemy Number One".

Infantile though the title is – Hollywood and Washington now seem to replicate each other – the US President had at last bestowed on the Saudi dissident the accolade he has always sought. Mr Clinton had now recognised the titanic struggle that Mr bin Laden was prepared to wage against the world's most powerful nation.

Key sections:
centrality in texts,
frequency of use,
expressiveness

Key words,
groups of words,
phrases: codes
and categories

Additional textual analysis
Sentence, clause, lexicon, grammar

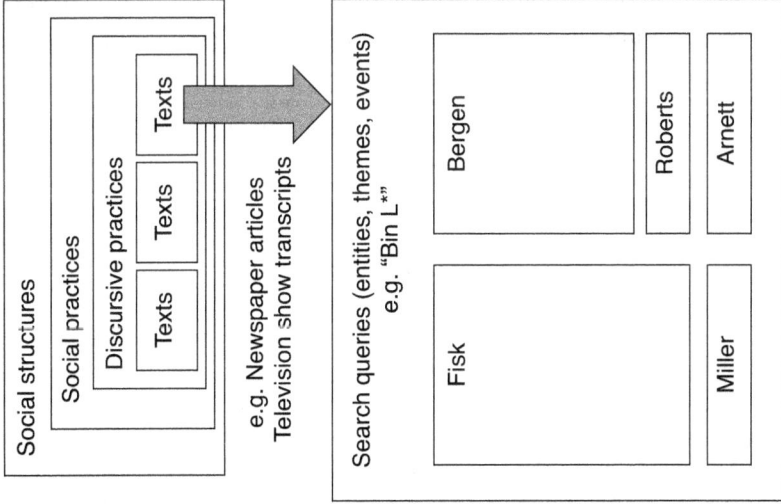

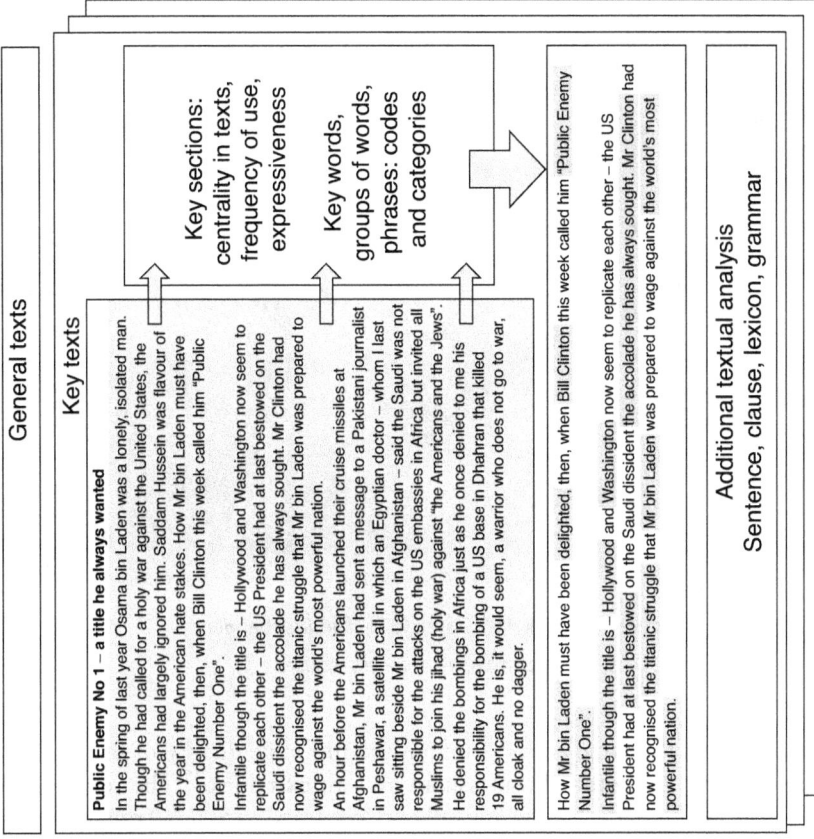

Figure 4.1 Schematic overview of text selection and analysis

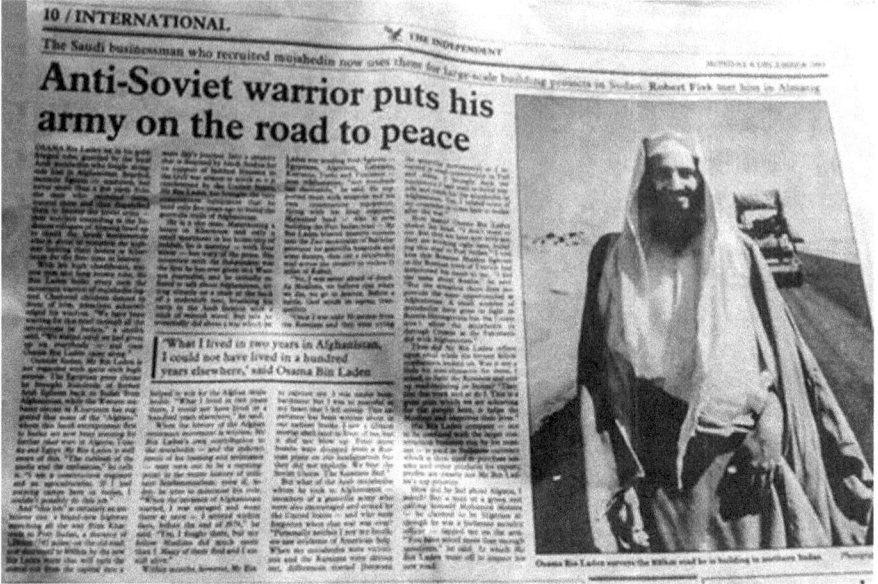

Figure 4.2 Fisk 1993 article in *The Independent*

Source: Image via *Business Insider*.

interview, held in the same period, emphasised more the duality of Bin Laden's identity and role: as both a businessman and an extremist.[18] The report also mentioned how Bin Laden's 'star appeal' and 'celebrity' in Saudi Arabia 'swiftly began to fade' after he started to denounce the Saudi regime. The remark indicated how MacLeod leaned more towards a (pro-Western) Saudi government perspective. Namely, among Muslim activists and the Saudi political opposition, Bin Laden's appeal had not faded at all.

In mid-July 1996, *The Independent* printed four articles following the second interview conducted by Fisk with Bin Laden, who by that time had moved to Afghanistan.[19] Due to the citing of Bin Laden's words in the interview articles, there was a relatively high level of reproduction in Fisk's writings. However, in these articles Fisk also questioned Bin Laden's capabilities and colourfully highlighted inconvenient aspects of his circumstances. Fisk observed that 'Bin Laden's return to Afghanistan after five and a half years in Sudan marked a new stage of the Organization of Advice and Reform', whose leading scholarship had been arrested in Saudi Arabia.[20] Fisk re-cited Bin Laden stating that the central campaign was 'to set up a "true" Islamic state under sharia law in Saudi Arabia which had been turned into an "American colony"'.[21] According to Bin Laden, the country was in a socio-economic crisis. Fisk stated that a 'pivotal date' that made US influence explicit was 1990, as US troops were allowed into the country under fierce protest from Saudi Islamic scholars.[22] It is remarkable that this essential event was not articulated in Fisk's 1993 interview in Sudan.

Bin Laden was quoted saying that the Khobar attack marked the 'beginning of war between Muslims and the US'.[23] This wider view of the conflict was also briefly reflected in Bin Laden's references to US support for Israel. Mostly, however, the articles situated Bin Laden's grievances in the regional context of the Gulf. Bin Laden was quoted stating that Western influence in the Gulf was a core concern, rather than 'the West and Western people'.[24] As a variation to anti-US statements, the articles expressed how Bin Laden also addressed the British and the French to withdraw their troops from Saudi Arabia if they did not want them to be bombed like the US troops at Khobar had been.[25] Fisk described how Bin Laden was angry with the British Embassy in Khartoum for receiving a letter just before he left the city that he would not be admitted into the United Kingdom. According to Bin Laden, he had made no such request.

Rather than a businessman, in his articles Fisk now characterised Bin Laden as 'Saudi Arabia's angriest dissident' and 'the fiercest opponent of the Saudi regime and of America's presence in the Gulf'.[26] Furthermore, Fisk used indirect descriptions that situated Bin Laden as an extremist, instead of characterising him as such literally. The reporting acknowledged that both the Saudi regime and the American troops and officials in the Gulf should 'probably regard him as the most formidable enemy'.[27] Yet Fisk also questioned whether Bin Laden's options to 'campaign against the Saudi government' were not in fact limited and whether Afghanistan had been the only place for him to go.[28] Also referenced in the article were accusations by Western and Arab governments that Bin Laden was training fighters to oppose the governments of Algeria, Egypt and Saudi Arabia. As a result, Fisk stated that Bin Laden had the status of being Saudi Arabia's 'most wanted man'.[29] Thus, while Bin Laden had warned the British and others to leave the Gulf, Fisk also sketched how 'no one was more of a target than Bin Laden himself'.[30]

Fisk's reports also expressed a notion of isolation and risk. Bin Laden had 'chosen a dangerous exile', according to Fisk, in a country with a collapsed economy and 'tribal societies run by Afghan mafia', gun runners and drug dealers.[31] Fisk observed how the camp, set up primarily for Bin Laden's three wives and children, was encircled only by 'a few strands of barbed wire'.[32] The documentary-type article on Fisk's 'perilous journey' through Afghanistan colourfully described the remoteness of the Afghan Arab camp. He observed large stretches of mined and dust-covered 'dead land', and how 'wild naked children played in ruins' near a 'phantom town'.[33] Overall, according to Fisk, it was Bin Laden's move to Afghanistan that marked a new stage in this opposition, stirred increased enmity and caused a toughening of Bin Laden's views.

Bin Laden as a Wedge

One of the documentary-type articles provided a wider context for what Fisk called 'a new round of the Great Game' between the greater international powers for influence in Afghanistan.[34] This 'game' referenced the Anglo-Russian commercial and military power struggle over influence in Central Asia during most of the nineteenth century. Fisk offered a mix of observations, quotations and speculative interpretation that highlighted a secretive complex international web of relations. These connections complicated matters beyond the overt and 'simplistic, public world of Washington politics' in which paradoxically almost all Islamic fundamentalist groups were 'officially' deemed 'terrorists'. While Russia offered the Afghan President Rabbani logistical support, according to Fisk, the 'Saudi–American-backed Taliban' received weapons shipped on board unregistered flights from Saudi Arabia.[35] The documentary article added new layers to the reports on the Bin Laden interview.

By writing the article and emphasising a complex web of international relations, Fisk diffused any perception of the bipolarity between the US–Saudi and Bin Laden–Taliban camps.[36] This situated Bin Laden's remarks more as a wedge between alleged (US–)Saudi–Taliban relations that had been born out of necessity to counter Russian and Iranian influence in the region. Thus, in addition to the statements in the interview articles, Fisk also highlighted the division between Bin Laden and his host, the Taliban. Speculation and the raising of unanswered questions increased doubt and ambiguity, which ran contrary to the bipolarity of securitization efforts.

Disagreement among Followers

Another shift or new phase identified by Fisk started in August 1996. It was marked by the publication of the Ladenese memorandum article in *Al-Quds Al-Arabi*. In *The Independent*, Fisk 'confirmed' from his own sources that it was Bin Laden who had written the statement. He mostly emphasised two contextual aspects of Bin Laden's 'most extreme remarks': the release came as a 'profound surprise' to many of his followers, the timing was possibly related to an upcoming Islamist conference in London.[37] In contrast to the articles on Fisk's second Bin Laden interview, in which primarily the latter's words were cited, Fisk now underlined dissent and disagreement among his followers. One of them was quoted in *The Independent*:

> We do not think it is the right moment to start a conflict with the (Saudi) regime. . . . Osama has made a detailed, 12-page statement, a major plan to explain the declaration of jihad, a whole project. But we thought we were all agreed that we should try to keep the situation under control in the country, to control the people and not let things get out of hand.

> I was expecting the concept of jihad in Saudi Arabia to come up a long time ago – but not from us. Saying we have an enemy is one thing but declaring war is something else.[38]

The plural 'we' emphasised that this follower spoke on behalf of others at the Saudi dissident ARC. The remark stating that now was not 'the right moment' served as a somewhat innocuous characterisation to underline dialogue among Bin Laden and his followers. There was agreement on feelings of enmity towards the Saudi regime, but not on the act of declaring war. The person cited accentuated that the comprehensive Bin Laden statement was a 'major' shift in that respect, opposite to agreed efforts to maintain a certain status quo.

Fisk's usage of the terms 'shock' and 'profound surprise' in the article was a direct critique of any notion of gradual and consensual processes of normalisation among followers. The characterisations created distance between Bin Laden and some of his followers outside Afghanistan. Fisk's wording regarding the ARC also implied that not all members were Bin Laden followers. The findings in the report appear to decrease any threatening complexion of Bin Laden as 'terrorist leader' (as seen from a US perspective) or the idea of audience acceptance (from an *Al Qaeda* perspective).

PRAGMATISM: SHIFTING FOCUS

In March 1997, Robert Fisk published two articles following his third and last interview with Bin Laden. They outlined Bin Laden's warning of 'new assaults on US forces' and how he had stated that 'we are still at the beginning of our military action against the American forces'.[39] In terms of meaning, several shifts occurred in the articles with regard to what was deemed usual. In the introduction of the interview article, Fisk mentioned that Bin Laden 'acknowledged for the first time that his guerrillas had fought street battles against US forces during the ill-fated UN mission to Somalia'.[40] This signified a focus on the United States that expanded in Fisk's later articles. A change of position deemed remarkable by Fisk was Bin Laden's distinction between US troops and the historic British and French military presence in Saudi Arabia. While the former equalled Israel's army, the latter did not. [41]

> Astonishingly – in view of his previous threats against British and French troops in the Gulf – Mr Bin Laden claimed that the armies of both countries now provided only a 'symbolic presence' in Saudi Arabia, at one point praising Britain for not occupying the Arabian peninsula during the First World War. He claimed that European nations were now distancing themselves from US policy towards Israel, singling out the European vote against Israel in the UN Security Council debate on the new Jewish settlement on occupied Arab land outside Jerusalem.[42]

The text fragment, especially the 'singling out' or selection of the issue of the European vote at the UN Security Council, highlighted two 'astonishing' pragmatic shifts in Bin Laden's position on international relations. It expressed a pragmatic decreased negative focus on, and even praising of, the British and the French as enemies, and his implicit acceptance of the UN Security Council as a meaningful international forum. Fisk still referred to 'Mr Bin Laden' in the same manner as he had done after the Sudan interview. However, by now, Bin Laden had transformed in Fisk's eyes from a Muslim businessman and a Saudi dissident to an Islamic extremist who had surprised some of his own followers by venting hostility and declaring war against the United States and Israel.

In addition to earlier threats, Bin Laden now claimed that he had recently gained Pakistani scholarly support for his cause and had shown Fisk an Urdu wall poster and coloured photographs of supporting graffiti in Pakistan.[43] The Pakistani support would later be symbolically emphasised by the signature of Sheikh Mir Hamza, of the Pakistani JUP political party, under the declaration of the WIF.[44] According to Fisk, Bin Laden further stated that the Taliban's support for him remained unchanged as well. Lastly, Bin Laden even claimed that 'some members of the Saudi royal family agreed with his demand to expel the Americans from the Gulf'.[45] Fisk added that this might only increase American suspicion that 'the dissident movement' was covertly supported from within Saudi Arabia.

While Fisk was able to interview Bin Laden three times, other Western journalists were allowed to take extensive pictures and film their interview. How did their message compare with Fisk's, and what did the medium of television add? Most clearly, it made Bin Laden's soft tone and polite manners more visible, and as such enlarged the contrast between his appearance and the harsh character of his words. In February 1997, British Channel 4 TV reporter Gwynne Roberts made a video documentary on socio-economic problems in Saudi Arabia and put Bin Laden's critique of the Saudi royal family in this context.[46] Weeks later, Peter Arnett, Peter Bergen and Peter Jouvenal were the first Western journalists to actually film and interview Osama bin Laden for CNN about his threats to the United States.[47] Roberts had been only allowed to take pictures. The meanings attributed to Bin Laden's statements diverged to some extent, because of their reference to different wider background contexts in the reports. Roberts emphasised widespread socio-economic unrest in Saudi Arabia, increasing Islamic opposition and the regime's efforts to mute them. In contrast, Arnett focused primarily on the threat of a 'Holy War' against US troops. Arnett's extensive use of the term *jihad* in his news report, compared with Roberts's very limited use of this or similar terms, was expressive.

American reporter John Miller's televised interview with Bin Laden in Afghanistan, just days before he organised a wider press conference to introduce the WIF and publish its first statement in May 1998.[48] The focus of the profile was on Bin Laden, hence the collaborative effort behind the WIF statement was not a specific topic in the reporting. His financial, logistical and operational capabilities, as well as his future intent, were an important focus, more than Bin Laden's reasons or motives. According to Miller, the WIF declaration had put a time cap on things. Images screened showed Bin Laden wearing a white turban and camouflage jacket, sitting in front of a map of Africa, amidst followers armed with Kalashnikov rifles. What the American television broadcasts and reporting added to Fisk's reporting, were the comments of senior US officials which emphasised the perception of an emerging and realistic threat against US servicemen and civilians worldwide.

The Dust of the Attacks on US Embassies in Africa and Arab Fury

On 9 August 1998, the day after the attacks in Kenya and Tanzania, Robert Fisk had some reservations about media speculation on the perpetrators. He rejected the usefulness of the immediacy and urgency felt and expressed by media commentators. Fisk critiqued their status as experts and argued metaphorically in *The Independent* that they should 'let the dust settle first' before judging who was behind the attacks.[49] According to Fisk, 'rash speculation about culpability' of Arab or African Islamic groups was 'part of the problem rather than the solution'.[50] In some broadcasts, polls were even held to ask their audiences who they thought was responsible. It was a search for certainty, according to Fisk, in an 'otherwise inexplicable world' where, as a metaphor, 'black and white have an uncomfortable habit of merging into grey'.[51]

For Fisk, what most commentators in the West missed was the dual policy pursued by the Saudi government, and the complex connections between some of the Saudi royals, including Crown Prince Abdullah, and the anti-US social movement. Parallel to admitting US troops, the Mutaween (or strict Saudi religious police) gained more authority in the country. Furthermore, the Saudi support flights for the Taliban continued. In the United States, people had 'underestimated, overlooked or misunderstood' the growing fury and strength of the Wahhabi movement in Saudi Arabia, according to Fisk.[52] In a wider sense, Fisk stated, the 'so-called experts' failed to address the reasons for Muslim frustration: American domination. Fisk aligned himself with the negative characterisation of American power projection in the Arab world. Against the background of the possible 'Saudi connection' to the embassy attacks, Fisk depicted Bin Laden as a 'remote but intriguing figure'. He was a 'Saudi dissident' who was 'far from being an outcast', and had even been contacted by the Saudi authorities to have his citizenship returned if he was to 'abandon his public jihad'. However, Fisk stated that Bin Laden had told him in earlier interviews that this was not on his mind.

The Saudi connection was something the 'routine terrorist-watchers' and 'so-called intelligence experts' had failed to address, according to Fisk, as instead they made quick references to Iran, Iraq, Libya, Sudan or, 'to use their exotic phrase, "international Islamic terror"'. To Western eyes, Fisk noted, Bin Laden was only one of many outcasts or 'hate figures upon whom the West liked to vent its anger'. Here Fisk criticised the use of an international terror frame and implicitly described a wider practice of securitizing various other 'incumbents' (such as Abu Nidal, Colonel Gadhafi, Ayatollah Khomeini, Carlos the Jackal and, recently, Saddam Hussein). According to Fisk, the US government and news media emphasised the 'who' over the 'why'.

Critique on US Framings, Sanctions and Missile Strikes

Continuing his discussion of Bin Laden's involvement with terrorism and the attacks, Fisk elaborated on how Bin Laden had been 'one of the Good Guys' when he fought in Afghanistan against the Soviets.[53] Now 'the Americans have told us he is one of the Bad Guys who planned the bombing'. Fisk did not doubt that Bin Laden would 'not have condemned' the attacks and acknowledged that his family was immensely wealthy. However, based on his personal experience with Bin Laden in Afghanistan, Fisk questioned the thrust with which he was deemed a global terrorist mastermind:

> [W]hen he discovered I had just come from Beirut and had the local Lebanese newspapers in my bag, he sat in the corner of his tent reading the reports of Iran's new demarche towards Saudi Arabia, of Israel's increased settlement activity on the occupied West Bank and of Turkey's treaty with Israel. If this was a 'mastermind of world terrorism' – according to the predictably anonymous sources of western journalists – then he was woefully out of touch with the world he was supposed to be terrorizing.[54]

Emphasising that Bin Laden was anxious to read Fisk's local Lebanese newspapers 'in the corner of his tent' figuratively and literally decentralised Bin Laden. It contrasted the notion of a central global terrorist mastermind. Instead of a 'terror chief' Bin Laden was 'just a small cog in the raw fury machine'.[55] Such critical reflections were also made by Peter Bergen. He similarly questioned to what extent Bin Laden was perhaps 'a convenient shorthand' and that there was too much focus on the demonised person of Bin Laden over broader networks.

Another critique by Fisk on the US government related to the economic sanctions Clinton had imposed on Bin Laden. There was only one agricultural company in Sudan that it might concern. But regardless of the limited practical impact, Fisk wrote, it was the symbolic meaning of the measure that raised the most questions and was derided in the Arab world. It was Bin Laden himself who had refused to buy any American goods, years ago. Arabs were 'astonished' over the 'meaningless' American ban. According to Fisk, especially the loyalty of Bin Laden's followers was not determined by material goods or financial rewards.

The central question for Fisk was whether the US missile strikes in late August 1998 on a factory in Khartoum and training camps in Afghanistan hurt or helped Bin Laden and his followers. Fisk noted that Bin Laden probably regarded the attack as an honour and as recognition of his enmity against the United States. Bin Laden had probably only benefited from the strikes and the acknowledgement as the American 'public enemy number one'.[56] Similarly, Peter Bergen acknowledged how adding Bin Laden to the list of the FBI's Ten Most Wanted was a symbolic measure that 'in practice didn't mean a huge difference' for actually catching him.[57]

> I think that to be called the public enemy number one in the last few hours will meet with Bin Laden's approval. He would love to be America's enemy number one. I don't think he is, but I think he would like to be called that; and I would imagine that among his supporters his stock would have risen considerably given the fact that America is launching $60 million attacks on him. I would say that he would rather like to be in the position. He's called for a holy war against America, to have America declare on him he'd probably regard as an honour. I think his stock probably gone up.[58]

Similarly, Fisk wrote the following in an article in *The Independent* the next day:

> Infantile though the title is – Hollywood and Washington now seem to replicate each other – the US President had at last bestowed on the Saudi dissident the accolade he has always sought. Mr Clinton had now recognized the titanic struggle that Mr Bin Laden was prepared to wage against the world's most powerful nation.[59]

Fisk's references to 'Hollywood' were an evocative metaphor for the simplistic framing of a struggle between protagonist and antagonist, or securitizing actor and referent subject. As 'violence was answered with violence', Fisk noted, Bin Laden and Clinton had declared war on each other and oddly used very much the same type of ferocious language.[60] However, Fisk also used the metaphor with a negative connotation regarding the US film industry and media landscape. He argued that in US movies, cartoons and texts, Arab Muslims had for decades been portrayed as extremists, fundamentalists and terrorists.[61] Moreover, it silenced the question of 'why' the embassy attacks had occurred and why Bin Laden was to 'loathe America'.[62] As Fisk put it, '[t]alk of an "international terrorist conspiracy" is as exotic as the Arab belief in the "Zionist conspiracy"'.[63]

Again, Fisk used evocative framing, critiquing identification processes as part of securitization efforts by exaggerating two contrasting images of 'conspiracies'. However, he also suggested that these frames served other purposes for both the United States and Bin Laden, as the reality was more nuanced. Many Arabs would have 'cynically concluded' that these frames and the US missile strikes were a diversion for President Clinton's legal problems over the Lewinsky affair.[64] According to Fisk, Sudan had ordered Bin Laden out of Khartoum at the request of the United States. He questioned whether the country had actually been producing chemical weapons. Fisk also reminded his readers that some of the training camps in Afghanistan had been constructed with help from the CIA in the 1980s, pointing to the days when Bin Laden was still one of the 'Good Guys'. Further, he asked what Bin Laden's position would be among the immensely divided extremists and dissidents without the US terror frames and attacks:

> Bill Clinton might have wished Mr bin Laden was among Russia's victims. Or would he really wish that? In America's search for 'public enemies', Mr bin Laden looks the part; dark-skinned, sharp-eyed, dressed in robes. Cleaning his teeth with a piece of stick during conversations, constantly threatening the US and Israel. Who would the Americans strike at if Mr bin Laden did not exist? And who would Mr bin Laden hate if the Americans packed up and went home?[65]

Rather than commenting on the actual involvement of Bin Laden, Fisk reflected on the ongoing process of polarisation or securitization. He highlighted how polarisation was beneficial for Bin Laden and observed Arab opinions on US domestic goals that were served with the measures taken by Clinton, such as the economic ban and missile strikes. Reality, Fisk seemed to state, was in fact more nuanced. Then what should the United States do, according to Fisk? The perpetrators of the embassy attacks in Africa had to be brought to justice. Cruise missiles targeting Bin Laden and 'tough language' did not represent any such 'due process', Fisk stated.[66]

In a broader sense, Fisk was critical of American missile strikes and aerial bombings as an instrument of politics in the Middle East. In a 1996 article titled 'Missile Diplomacy', he described the American missile strikes on Iraq that came in response to Iraqi violations of a no-fly zone over northern Iraq.[67] He contrasted what he perceived as the lightness with which Clinton justified and spoke about the strikes with some of the collateral damage that had been caused in the past, and emphasised how earlier strikes in 1993 had been ineffective or perhaps counterproductive.

This context resurfaced in mid-December 1998 as Fisk criticised the appropriateness, effectiveness and military nature of the targets of Operation Desert

Fox. This was the four-day US–UK bombing campaign over Iraq in response to Iraq refusing to cooperate with UN weapons inspectors. Most relevant for the critical terrorism narrative here was how Fisk critically reviewed the US government statement that Osama bin Laden 'had been on the telephone to Saddam'.[68] This 'connection' had become part of the legitimisation for the new missile strikes on Iraq in 1998. Based on Fisk's own conversation with Bin Laden on Saddam Hussein, he suspected that 'Bin Laden would be as revolted at the idea of talking to Saddam as he would by the idea of talking to Clinton'.[69]

Over time, Fisk's writings became increasingly critical of US foreign policy in the Middle East and its support for Israel's security policy against the Palestinians. Illustrative was a fragment of the title of another article by Fisk in *The Independent*: 'How long will Europeans, let alone Arabs, go on accepting America's astonishing theatricals?'[70] Despite Fisk's own critique of simplistic framing by the US government and Bin Laden, several of his articles between 1998 and 2000 posited general labels such as 'the West's fear of Islam' or 'the 1,000-year-old struggle between Arabs and the West'.[71] In 1999, Fisk reported on another 'foolish war' in which 'the West' was involved: he had travelled to the Balkans to write about NATO, Serbia and the Kosovo crisis.[72] As a side remark in one of the reports, Fisk added that the Serbian leader Slobodan Milošević had joined the 'list of "beasts"', whereas Osama bin Laden had 'oddly dropped off our Satanic radar screens for the present'.[73] The terms 'beast' and 'satanic' demonstrated Fisk's expressive choice of words, and also underlined the polarisation over 'hate figures' Fisk was criticising.

The Murderous Attempted Sinking of the USS *Cole*

Finally, in late 2000, just after the attack on the USS *Cole* in Yemen, Fisk wrote the last three articles that can be considered part of this narrative. Working from the Palestinian Gaza strip, Fisk did not write specifically on the bombing of the American Navy destroyer. Instead, he situated the attack within the broader 'Middle East crisis' centred on Palestinian–Israeli violence.[74] According to Fisk, the perpetrators of the USS *Cole* attack were enraged over Palestinian victims. The articles were also highly expressive of how Fisk himself was critical of US and Israeli policies in the Middle East:

> A Pentagon official was saying last night the United States government was trying to find out if the attack on the USS *Cole* was 'related' to 'violence' in the Middle East. Come again? Related? Violence? Who can doubt that the attempt to sink the *Cole* and all her 360 crew was directed at a nation now held responsible for Israel's killing of scores of Palestinian civilians? The US – despite all the claptrap from Madeleine Albright about 'honest brokers' – is Israel's ally.[75]

The quotation marks around 'related' and 'violence' and the phrases 'come again?' and 'who can doubt' expressed incomprehension, and underlined the extensive contrast between Fisk's and the US government's perspectives on US Middle East policies and Palestinian–Israeli violence. Similar to the embassy attacks in Africa, he acknowledged that the 'attempted sinking' of the USS *Cole* was 'murderous', but remained critical of naming it an attack on American democracy as a whole.[76] The United States had been 'quick to link Bin Laden with the USS *Cole* attack', but, according to Fisk, had failed to grasp 'the driving force behind anti-Western acts' in the region.[77]

CRITIQUING US AND *AL QAEDA* SECURITIZATION EFFORTS

The aim of this chapter was to extract from the selected texts additional or alternative perspectives on the securitization efforts identified in the previous two chapters. The themes and frames provided by Robert Fisk and others were related to the social structures, securitization efforts, and actions identified in the previous two chapters. Fisk reflected on and criticised ideological processes of naturalisation for both the United States and Bin Laden (or *Al Qaeda*). He reviewed and questioned the perception and framing of securitization elements such as the referent subject, but they also reflected on the practices of security or the actions taken. Furthermore, Fisk especially evaluated how discursive and non-discursive action, as part of the US social practice of the politics of nations, echoed among Muslim Arabs, including Salafi jihadis. Conversely, he also examined the extent to which the social practice of Salafi jihadism resonated in the United States.

Fisk's travel experience and changing working environment in Afghanistan, the Middle East and the Balkans influenced the contextualisation of his articles. Parallel to his report on his second interview with Bin Laden, *The Independent* printed his article on covert transport aircraft landing at Afghan airports. It provided the case to infer and speculate on complex relations between the government and its opposition in Saudi Arabia, the United States, the Taliban and Bin Laden. As he reported on the USS *Cole* bombing, Fisk placed emphasis on Palestinian–Israeli violence. The setting of Fisk's text production from Beirut and Gaza corresponded to this. In contrast to what Fisk had written after the US embassy attacks, any follow-up articles on Bin Laden in the wake of the USS *Cole* bombing were lacking. Possibly, the location or region from which Fisk worked, such as the Balkans, occasionally diverted his attention away from Bin Laden. Most clearly absent were any reports by Fisk on the WIF declaration in May 1998, even more as he had signified the 1996 memorandum as a remarkable development. Another event that did not surface from the selected texts was the millennium terrorist threat that featured prominently in the US institutional terrorism narrative.

Fisk was explicitly and openly critical of US framings and policies in the Middle East, but his observations partially overlapped with reporting by other journalists leaning more towards a US perspective, such as Peter Bergen and John Miller. Despite discursive and idiosyncratic differences between Fisk and Bergen, for example, they were similarly critical of the use of general frames, such as 'terrorist'. Both their reporting indicated that as an inspirational figure, maintaining and expanding power over people through discourse was manifestly important for Bin Laden.

What new light is shed on the securitization efforts and its constituent elements as defined in the other two narratives? For analysing critique, and unpacking power use and processes of naturalisation, the concept of securitization offered a suitable point of departure. More than in the previous two macro narratives, the critical terrorism narrative highlighted how language, events and circumstances were framed and how they functioned as heuristic artefacts. In a philosophical sense, heuristic artefacts as defined here are (strategic) 'devices' that create the circumstances that enable and facilitate understanding of situations in terms of securitization. They are essential building-blocks for the ideological process of naturalisation that follows from several securitization efforts. The extent of their impact depends on their nature, the way they are organised or become contextually situated, and how they are combined with other heuristic artefacts. What the analysis of the critical narrative in this chapter has indicated is that both the actions and securitization efforts of one entity (considered as referent subject by the other) served as heuristic artefacts for the securitization efforts of the other securitizing actor. But also vice versa as one switches the perspective of securitization again. What was considered as an adequate measure or customised policy for one was proof, a symptom or symbol of the threat for the other.

The following sections approach critique by analysing how various elements of the securitization efforts as set out in the previous two narratives were characterised by Fisk, while also taking into consideration other relevant reporting by other journalists.

Bin Laden and *Al Qaeda*: referent subject and securitizing actor

Fisk portrayed Bin Laden in various ways. Apart from an Islamic extremist and inspirational facilitator of terrorist acts, Bin Laden was initially characterised as a Muslim businessman in Sudan. Over the years, Fisk recognised both how Bin Laden attempted to function as securitizing actor, and how the United States deemed Bin Laden to be a dangerous referent subject. On several occasions, Fisk criticised US institutional frames by adopting superordinates and metaphors that charged these American frames with an even stronger meaning. He chose words that increased the contrast to his own characterisations.

Fisk placed Bin Laden as a figure in an American or Western 'tradition' of venting anger against 'hate figures' and 'beasts'. This perspective emphasised the role of the United States, rather than that of Bin Laden. A metaphor repeatedly used by Fisk in this respect was that of 'Hollywood', which represented a process of simplistic fictional framing and the search for someone to fill in the predefined role of 'bad guy', instead of representing Bin Laden's character based on complex reality. Peter Bergen's remark that perhaps Bin Laden had been 'demonised' in US media reporting aligned with the critical direction of Fisk's statements.

In contrast to the metaphor of a 'beast', from his own early interview experience Fisk portrayed 'Mr' Bin Laden as a polite and well-educated man who was nevertheless ruthless in his angry statements against the United States and posed a dangerous threat. This image was especially supported by televised interviews also held in that timeframe. As an inspirational figure, Bin Laden's narrative was the domain where he was most powerful. More than the power to do things and organise attacks, according to Fisk, Bin Laden had and sought power over people through discourse. To this end, he used his network, including the ARC in London, to disseminate faxes and audio- and video-cassettes to followers and readers of Arab newspapers. His status as an Afghan veteran and his wealthy background increased his discursive power.

Still, rather than a global 'terrorist mastermind' Bin Laden was depicted as a man who was keen to be informed by local Lebanese newspapers brought by Fisk to his remote and isolated Afghan tent. Also making matters more relative was Fisk's report that the 1996 memorandum had caused a 'shock' among many of his supporters. This revealed the difference between sympathisers and people with shared anger, and their willingness to escalate and 'declare war'. Following their last interview in 1997, Fisk also emphasised a degree of pragmatism in Bin Laden's statements. Whereas Bin Laden had previously made threats against the United Kingdom over their presence in Saudi Arabia, he now dismissed the issue as minor and symbolic, while acknowledging partial European opposition against US foreign policies in the Middle East. Lastly, Fisk's speculative reports on the complex web of relations among Americans, Saudis, the Taliban and Bin Laden also worked to undermine the binary logic of an 'us' versus 'them'. Miller's interview filled a lacuna in Fisk's reporting because he discussed the WIF declaration as it was published. In the setting of the statements of US officials discussing protective measures against the threat of terrorism, Miller observed how Bin Laden at that moment had 'put a time cap' on things of only a few weeks. In this light, the bombings of the US embassies were a manifestation of the customised policy sharpened in the WIF declaration.

In summary, Fisk questioned both the global reach of Bin Laden's power to act as an orchestrator of terrorism and his ability to mobilise some of his followers. This was supported by Bergen's statements. As articulated in the critical terrorism narrative, it seemed that characterisations of Bin Laden in the US institutional terrorism narrative and the *Al Qaeda* narrative were both in their own way more robust than justified by reality. Fisk thereby toned down notions of Bin Laden as both referent subject and securitizing actor.

US embassies and USS *Cole* bombings: customised policy and heuristic artefact

While breaking down the image of Bin Laden as a global terrorist mastermind, the existence of conflict and violence in the Middle East was not ignored. For Bin Laden and his followers, the attacks on the US embassies could be perceived both as the execution of the articulated customised policy, and as a heuristic artefact (the proof of anger and a willingness to act) in the ongoing process that the various securitization efforts comprised. Fisk and Bergen questioned whether Bin Laden was directly responsible for coordinating the attacks in Africa, but they recognised that he was an inspirational facilitator, especially in the light of the 1996 memorandum and 1998 WIF declaration. In terms of securitization, Bin Laden fulfilled the role of securitizing actor and set the tone for the embassy attacks to be executed. Fisk emphasised that it was no coincidence that the attacks in Africa happened on the eighth anniversary of the arrival of US troops in Saudi Arabia, a pivotal moment in the development of Bin Laden's thinking.

According to Fisk, the embassy attacks proved to have some limitations for use as a heuristic artefact for Bin Laden's securitization efforts. Bin Laden's feelings and language resonated with wider anger among Saudis and other Arabs over American involvement in the region. Hence, as a symbolic attack on US institutions, the embassy bombings should perhaps have been met with broad agreement among Bin Laden's followers, other Salafi jihadis and possibly even the wider Arab world. However, moderating the 'success' of the attacks for Bin Laden was the high number of civilian casualties, especially in Kenya, that were broadcast all over the world. Furthermore, Bin Laden initially denied his own involvement.

From a US perspective, the functioning of the embassy attacks as symbolic proof and heuristic artefact was evident. For the United States, they were a warning of a new kind of terrorist threat that was developing. However, Fisk still criticised the notion of an 'international terrorist conspiracy' and rejected the apparent sense of immediacy to respond. Instead, he underlined what the main problem was for him: the American government never asked the 'why' question. Instead of discussing capabilities and scenarios as a response to the threat of terrorism, Fisk argued that the United States should consider what had caused the attacks and how widespread these feelings of anger and frustration were among Muslims. In numerous articles, Fisk elaborated on the socio-economic problems in Saudi Arabia and other Arab countries, and on how the United States had a role in this. In essence, Fisk asked to what extent the threat posed to the United States by Bin Laden and his followers was self-induced. Some reporting by ABC on overcoming cultural and language barriers between American troops and the Saudi population at the working level aligned with this questioning. Fisk persistently related the attacks to a broader context in the Middle East and refrained somewhat from discussing who the perpetrators were.

According to Fisk, the assault on the USS *Cole* was of a different nature than the embassy bombings, and was less a demonstration of an attack on US values and freedom. He deemed the 'attempted sinking' of the US Navy destroyer a 'murderous' act, but not an 'act of terror against American democracy'. As such, he critiqued the symbolism of the attack on the USS *Cole* attributed by the US government. In a broader sense, the asymmetry of a small boat being able to reach the American cruiser was briefly mentioned, but not to the extent that it was emphasised in the *Al Qaeda* narrative as a heroic asymmetrical success, or as a somewhat embarrassing asymmetrical failure as re-contextualised in the US institutional terrorism narrative.

Again, for Fisk there was no doubt that this attack in Yemen was related to the broader Arab fury against American involvement in the Middle East, and especially their support for Israel against the Palestinians. He speculated that the USS *Cole* bombing could have also been committed by frustrated young men unrelated to larger organisations. It was possible that Bin Laden had generally inspired the attack, as his family came from Yemen and he had various relations within the country. All casualties were US servicemen, and as such the attack corresponded to Bin Laden's threats and demand for a US withdrawal from the region. As an expression of Arab frustration and anger, as Fisk put it, the USS *Cole* bombing served as a strong heuristic artefact for Bin Laden and his followers. In terms of the ongoing process of Bin Laden's developing securitization efforts, the US embassies and USS *Cole* bombings represented both a heuristic artefact and customised policy. The perspective of the critical terrorism narrative highlighted the attacks mostly in terms of their symbolic meaning and heuristic value (or lack thereof) for the securitization efforts of both the US and *Al Qaeda*.

US action: effective customised policies or securitization blowback?

In response to the US embassy bombings and to counter the threat posed by Bin Laden, various measures were taken by the United States. How effective were these measures and how did they affect US securitization efforts, according to Fisk and Bergen? Most prominent were the missile strikes against targets in Sudan and Afghanistan. For Fisk, what counted was not the tactical advantage of disrupting training and planning activities among Bin Laden's network, or the extent to which the attacks strengthened the position of US President Clinton. Instead, the missile strikes mostly provided Bin Laden with the recognition he sought as America's No. 1 public enemy. According to both Fisk and Bergen, placing Bin Laden on the list of America's ten most wanted and offering a large reward for information leading to his capture added to this. These measures generated various metaphorical frames that served as heuristic artefacts in Bin Laden's securitization efforts. There was significant division among Salafi jihadi groups and a rift between Bin Laden and the Taliban, but the missile strikes silenced these disagreements for an important part. They buried concerns over the large number of civilian casualties in Africa and increased tolerance or acceptance for Bin Laden to continue his discursive and non-discursive activities.

Furthermore, Fisk observed that the military action following Clinton's securitization effort in 1998 increased negative sentiments in the Arab world against the United States, hence improving how Bin Laden's narrative resonated among his audiences. This effect was enhanced further, Fisk reported, by the execution of Operation Desert Fox several months later – an aspect that did not become clear as a significant element in the US institutional terrorism narrative in Chapter 3.[78] Fisk noted that in the light of Desert Fox, US government officials had connected Iraqi President Saddam Hussein and Bin Laden. Based on Fisk's own experience, he contested any such suggestion. In contrast, a relation Fisk did identify was US foreign policy in the Middle East and wider feelings of frustration and anger among Arabs: the United States supported Israel against the Palestinians, pushed the Saudi regime to pursue an economic oil agenda, imposed sanctions on Iraq, and conducted military operations that had hurt the population of an Arab country.

The economic sanctions imposed by Clinton on Bin Laden had only served American domestic interests, according to Fisk. He reported that Saudi Arabs were astonished by the measure as Bin Laden had for many years already refused to buy any American goods. The sanctions matched what Bin Laden had himself advocated as customised policy and emphasised the US materialism that Bin Laden had rejected years before. Fisk deemed the measure 'meaningless' in the Middle East, but the very conversation that occurred over it among Bin Laden's followers and in the wider Arab world also contributed to the sense of estrangement and feelings of anger towards the United States. Similar to adding Bin Laden to the US's ten most wanted list, the sanctions had a symbolic value for Bin Laden.

In sum, for Fisk, several of the actions taken by the US government had proven to be ineffective or even counterproductive. Viewing the missile strikes and economic ban as customised policy, the term 'securitization blowback' came to mind, as from a US perspective the measures even had negative consequences for the development of the identified threat. Fisk also discussed alternative motives for the missile strikes and securitization efforts: perhaps they had served to draw away attention from the personal relation problems of the Lewinsky matter faced by the US Commander-in-Chief, who had ordered the strikes. Introducing that issue further undermined and critiqued perceptions of appropriateness and adequacy.

Another implicit question in Fisk's reporting was, to put it in terms of securitization, 'who was the referent object?' In other words, who was actually threatened? Over the years, Fisk observed a transformation of those against whom Bin Laden had aimed to act. This appeared to be somewhat pragmatic. The emphasis shifted from the Saudi regime in the early 1990s, to its Western allies and their military presence in the Arab country in the second half of the 1990s. Later, the United Kingdom and French troops were deemed less important and the focus became more exclusively on the ZCA, centralising the United States and Israel. As noted, Fisk contested viewing the USS *Cole* bombing as an attack on US democracy as a whole, but in general terms he acknowledged that American troops and civilians were under threat from the dangerous enemy that Bin Laden and his followers represented.

For Fisk, there was primarily a wider story of 'Arab anger' to tell. Rather than binary security situations of protagonists and antagonists, there were also other sufferers involved. Ultimately, he stated, both the belief in an 'international terrorist conspiracy' and a 'Zionist crusader conspiracy' were 'exotic'. Failing to recognise how the situation was complex and involved other deprived groups negated opportunities to evaluate the negative effects or blowback of American policies.

A discursive tennis match?

As stated at the beginning of this chapter, this narrative is not an objective judgement but a critical micro perspective related to the two macro narratives outlined in the previous two chapters. The narrative is critical in the sense that it criticised simplistic framing of entities, and disputed the effectiveness of customised policies as identified in both the US and *Al Qaeda* narratives. Tensions and inconsistencies identified included Bin Laden's shifting definition of the referent subject, the relevance of the US military operation over Iraq, the stereotyping of Bin Laden, and the complexity of the 'web of relations' involving the US and Saudi Arabian governments, and the Afghan Taliban. This fragmentation or deconstruction of the image of Bin Laden as either ultimate threatening referent subject or authoritative securitizing actor was followed by his simultaneous presentation as both an educated but also ruthless man, capable of instigating attacks to a certain extent against American targets. While Fisk recognised grievances among Arabs, he obviously contested the logic of securitization and violent customised policies voiced by Bin Laden.

In critiquing and deconstructing the lexicon and metaphorical frames that served as building-blocks for securitization efforts to both the United States and *Al Qaeda*, the essential value of heuristic artefacts for those securitization efforts became evident. To a large extent, the execution of customised policies or responsive actions contained significant symbolic value and, hence, served as new semiotic capital or heuristic artefacts for securitization efforts. In dealing with the threat, the threat itself was articulated further. However, 'hostile' security practices, whether terrorist attacks or military strikes, functioned as even stronger symbols for the opponent. For the United States, the attacks on the US embassies in Africa and the USS *Cole* in Yemen impelled the US institutional terrorism narrative. On the other hand, the symbolic value of these attacks as heuristic artefacts for the *Al Qaeda* narrative could be relativised due to the deaths of many African civilians. For Bin Laden and *Al Qaeda*, it was the US missile strikes on Sudan, Afghanistan and Iraq, and the economic sanctions against Bin Laden that generated useful semiotic capital for his securitization efforts. According to the critical terrorism narrative, the effectiveness of the missile strikes and sanctions was questionable, but before divided Salafi jihadis and wider Arab audiences they demonstrated the enmity and cultural insensitivity Bin Laden was struggling to express.

Apart from extensive critique on simplistic framing and the effectiveness of customised policies, through re-contextualisation the critical narrative also questioned the American goals or driving factors. Fisk indirectly related the missile strikes on Sudan and Afghanistan in 1998 to the Lewinsky affair as a possible motivation. Furthermore, by reminding his readers of how the American CIA had helped to construct the camps in Afghanistan that had now been bombed, Fisk suggested a degree of arbitrariness with regard to framing Bin Laden as an antagonist. Was the United States perhaps simply in need of an enemy, just as Bin Laden needed the United States to act against him to gain authority?

For ACN, this or any other critique could be valuable to inform the narrative tracing performed in the last chapter, and as a general resource to widen understanding of social phenomena. In terms of the tennis match metaphor presented at the beginning of the chapter, the critical terrorism narrative has shown that these securitization efforts built on and required other efforts to develop.

REFLECTION

As noted, this is not a perfectly balanced or complete narrative. Frankly, such narratives do not exist as intertextual links are limitless. Therefore, it is important to specify principal gaps, identify what was beyond the scope of the narrative, and highlight the limitations of the analysis. A notable gap was that Robert Fisk wrote extensively on Bin Laden, but refrained from reporting on several social events that were identified in the previous two narratives, such as the publication of the WIF declaration. Moreover, while he reported on US economic sanctions against Bin Laden in 1998, he did not mention the US securitization of the Taliban and economic sanctions against Afghanistan a year later. Similar to Peter Bergen, Fisk did not report on the millennium threats and uncovered plots either. Also, beyond the scope of the selected texts (due to the sheer volume of texts already accumulating) were CBS and ABC reports, and some potentially relevant *TIME Magazine* articles. Including one in which Ayman al-Zawahiri contacted the local ABC/TIME representative in Pakistan after the US missile strikes on Afghanistan and Sudan to inform Americans that Bin Laden was still alive.[79]

Lastly, what can be learned from working with the narrative analysis framework? The framework adequately supported the research for this narrative, although not all elements were equally applicable. The critical terrorism narrative originated from a different methodological approach than the previous two narratives. The concept of securitization was used as a starting point to investigate critique of the securitization efforts of others. Analysis of the audiences of the selected texts was not applied, and processes of self-identification were also deemed immaterial for the function of the narrative as part of this ACN study. Textual analysis mostly focused on lexical cohesion for its value in identifying heuristic artefacts, and was also limited to key parts of texts. The titles of news shows and articles, the use of expressive adjectives or metaphors, the frequency with which themes were mentioned, and the extent to which discursive elements related to (opposed) either the US institutional terrorism narrative or the *Al Qaeda* narrative primarily informed further selection and interpretation of texts.

NOTES

1. Steve Weinberg, *The Reporter's Handbook: An Investigator's Guide to Documents and Techniques*, 3rd edn (Boston, MA: St. Martin's Press, 1996); Els Witte, *Media & Politiek, Een inleiding tot de literatuur* (Brussels: VUBPRESS, 2002).
2. This research mainly draws on Manuel Castells, *The Information Age: Economy, Society and Culture, the Power of Identity*, 2nd edn (Oxford: Blackwell, 2004); Manuel Castells and Gustavo Cardoso (eds), *The Network Society: From Knowledge to Policy* (Washington, DC: Johns Hopkins Center for Transatlantic Relations, 2005); Jan van Dijk, *The Network Society: Social Aspects of New Media*, 2nd edn (London: Sage, 2006); Mansell, *The Information Society*.
3. Castells, *The Information Age*, 21, as in Van Dijk, *The Network Society*, 20.
4. Van Dijk, *The Network Society*, 26.
5. Jeffrey Scheuer, *The Sound Bite Society: Television and the American Mind* (New York: Four Walls Eight Windows, 1999); Witte, *Media & Politiek*.
6. Scheuer, *The Sound Bite Society*.
7. Witte, *Media & Politiek*, 180; E. S. Herman and Noam Chomsky, *Manufacturing Consent: the Political Economy of the Mass Media* (London: Vintage, 1988).
8. Weinberg, *The Reporter's Handbook*.
9. Jane D. Brown et al., 'Invisible Power: Newspaper News Sources and the Limits of Diversity', *Journalism Quarterly* 64(1) (1987): 45–54.

10. Weinberg, *The Reporter's Handbook*.
11. University of California Television (YouTube publisher), 'Conversations with History, Robert Fisk', 14 December 2006.
12. Ibid.
13. Scheuer, *Through Our Enemies' Eyes*, 301, 316–17.
14. Some of them, such as Peter Bergen and John Miller leaned more towards a US institutional perspective. For example, they used American official sources significantly more extensively in their reports.
15. Robert Fisk, 'Anti-Soviet Warrior Puts His Army on the Road to Peace', *The Independent*, 6 December 1993, available at: https://www.independent.co.uk/news/world/anti-soviet-warrior-puts-his-army-on-the-road-to-peace-the-saudi-businessman-who-recruited-mujahedin-1465715.html.
16. Ibid.
17. Ibid.
18. Scott Macleod, 'The Paladin of Jihad, Fearless and Super-rich, Osama bin Laden Finances Islamic Extremism. A TIME Exclusive', *TIME Magazine*, 6 May 1996.
19. For example, Robert Fisk, 'Why We Reject the West', *The Independent*, 10 July 1996, 14.
20. Robert Fisk, 'Saudi Dissident Warns West to Withdraw Troops', *The Independent*, 10 July 1996.
21. Ibid.
22. Fisk, 'Why We Reject the West'.
23. Fisk, 'Arab Rebel Leader Warns the British', *The Independent*, 10 July 1996.
24. Ibid.
25. Ibid.
26. Ibid.
27. Fisk, 'Saudi Dissident Warns West to Withdraw Troops'.
28. Ibid.
29. Fisk, 'Small Comfort in Saudi Rebel's Dangerous Exile', *The Independent*, 11 July 1996.
30. Ibid.
31. Ibid.
32. Ibid.
33. Robert Fisk, 'The Mined Land of the Mujahidin', *The Independent*, 10 July 1996.
34. Robert Fisk, 'Circling Over a Broken, Ruined State', *The Independent*, 14 July 1996.
35. Ibid.
36. In later articles the complex US–Saudi–Taliban–Bin Laden–Iran relations were emphasised further, Robert Fisk, 'Saudi's Secretly Funding Taliban', *The Independent*, 2 September 1998, 9; Robert Fisk, 'Thousands Massacred by Taliban', *The Independent*, 4 September 1998, 11.
37. Robert Fisk, 'Saudi Calls for Jihad against US "Crusader", Iraq is Not the Only Source of Concern for America in the Gulf, reports Robert Fisk', *The Independent*, 2 September 1996, 8.
38. Ibid., 8.

39. Robert Fisk, 'Muslim Leader Warns of a New Assault on US Forces', *The Independent*, 22 March 1997; Robert Fisk, 'The Man Who Wants to Wage Holy War against the Americans', *The Independent*, 22 March 1997.
40. Ibid.
41. Fisk, 'The Man Who Wants to Wage Holy War against the Americans'.
42. Fisk, 'Muslim Leader Warns of a New Assault on US Forces'.
43. Ibid.
44. No Fisk article was published on the WIF declaration. It is unclear whether Fisk wrote one that editors opted against, or whether he was too involved in reporting on other issues (such as Israel, Lebanon, Iraq and Kosovo).
45. Fisk, 'Muslim Leader Warns of a New Assault on US Forces'.
46. Gwynne Roberts, 'The Saudi Tapes', *Dispatches*, Channel 4, November 1996.
47. Shaw, 'Impact, Holy Terror?'
48. Peter Jennings (TV host), 'A Closer Look, A Very Dangerous Man Targets Americans', *World News Tonight With Peter Jennings*, ABC News, 10 June 1998; Ted Koppel (TV anchor), 'ABC Nightline, One of America's Most Dangerous Enemies', *ABC Nightline*, ABC News, 10 June 1998; Apalach32 (YouTube publisher), 'ABC Reporter John Miller asks Shaykh OBL 1998', video file, 9 April 2009.
49. Robert Fisk, Leading article, 'Let the Dust Settle First', *The Independent*, 9 August 1998, 4.
50. Ibid.
51. Ibid.
52. Robert Fisk, 'Saudis Secretly Funding Taliban', *The Independent*, 2 September 1998.
53. Robert Fisk, 'Wealthy Arab Who Hates the US: Is He the Man Behind the Bombs?' *The Independent*, 10 August 1998, 1.
54. Ibid., a point also raised by Fisk in Bob Edwards (TV host), 'Osama bin Laden', *NPR Morning Edition*, NPR, 21 August 1998.
55. Robert Fisk, 'Terror Chief is Just a Small Cog in the Raw Fury Machine', *The Independent*.
56. Robert Fisk, 'US Air Strikes, Bin Laden Will Take His Revenge, Robert Fisk, the first Western journalist to meet Osama bin Laden, says the Saudi dissident will strike back against Bill Clinton', *The Independent*, 21 August 1998, 1–2.
57. Brian Williams (TV anchor), 'FBI to Add Osama bin Laden to 10 Most Wanted List', *CNN The World Today*, CNN, 5 June 1999.
58. Edwards, 'Osama bin Laden'.
59. Robert Fisk, 'Public Enemy No. 1, a Title He Always Wanted', *The Independent*, 22 August 1998.
60. Fisk, 'As My Grocer Said'.
61. For example, Robert Fisk, 'The West's Fear of Islam is no Excuse for Racism', *The Independent*, 3 November 1999, 5.
62. Ibid.
63. Fisk, 'As My Grocer Said'.
64. Fisk, 'Terror Chief is Just a Small Cog in the Raw Fury Machine'; Robert Fisk, 'US Air Strikes, Bin Laden Will Take His Revenge', *The Independent*, 21 August 1998.

65. Fisk, 'Public Enemy No. 1, a Title He Always Wanted'.
66. Fisk, 'As My Grocer Said'.
67. Robert Fisk, 'Missile Diplomacy, How the US Fired First and Asked Questions Later', *Sydney Morning Herald*, 7 September 1996, 29.
68. Robert Fisk, 'Why Desert Fox "Degrades" Us All. The Operation to Take Out Iraqi "Weapons of Mass Destruction" has Also Twisted Truth, Judgment – and Even Language, the War Game', *The Independent*, 20 December 1998, 17.
69. Ibid., 17.
70. Robert Fisk, 'Once Again, it's the World's Most Serious Confrontation. How Long Will Europeans, Let Alone Arabs, go on Accepting America's Astonishing Theatricals?' *The Independent*, 6 November 1998, 4.
71. Fisk, 'The West's Fear of Islam'; Robert Fisk, 'No End in Sight to the 1,000-year-old Struggle between Arabs and the West', *The Independent*, 3 January 2000, 4.
72. Robert Fisk, 'We Have Lost This Foolish War, Instead of Admitting the Truth about this Conflict, our Leaders have Consistently Lied to Us', *The Independent*, 9 April 1999, 5.
73. Ibid.
74. Robert Fisk, 'Middle East Crisis, Arab World – Lies, Hatred and the Language of Force', *The Independent*, 13 October 2000, 2.
75. Ibid.
76. 'Review of the Year, Foreign – The Middle East: Forget the Peace Process, This is a Murderous Civil War', *The Independent*, 29 December 2000, 9.
77. Robert Fisk, 'Intelligence that Barely Deserves the Name', *The Independent*, 24 November 2000, 2.
78. This can be explained because the link was made by government officials, not the president, and in the context of Operation Desert Fox. The selected texts for Chapter 4 hence did not include any references. In Chapter 3 the significance of Desert Fox was identified.
79. For example Rahimullah Yusufzai, 'Osama bin Laden: Conversation with Terror', *TIME Magazine*, 11 January 1999; John Miller, 'Greetings, America: My name is Usama Bin Ladin. Now that I Have Your Attention . . .', *Esquire*, 1 February 1999; Thalia Assuras, 'Accused Terrorist Leader Usama bin Ladin Declares War on All Americans', CBS News; Juju Chang (TV anchor), 'Osama Bin Laden Speaks Out', *ABC World News This Morning*, ABC News, 25 December 1998.

5

CONCLUSION

INTRODUCTION

The central paradigm in both the Anglo-American dominated study and practice of intelligence is positivist and empiricist. Fundamental is the idea of intelligence being objective, timely and relevant for consumers. A certain tension between the scientific ideal of searching for the comprehensive ground truth and delivering useful 'packages' of objective knowledge has informed some normative debates in intelligence studies. Subject is the unavoidability of 'distortion' of information due to factors or phenomena such as cognitive bias, politicisation or deception operations. Rather than inferring a theory of intelligence from the practice (an approach common in the intelligence literature), the research in this book was conducted based on explicit philosophical reasoning. The aim was to contribute to critical theoretical debate in intelligence studies by combining appropriate theoretical components and demonstrating ACN. The narrative analysis framework (NAF) and narrative tracing (NT) method derived from the ACN methodology were applied to analyse *Al Qaeda*. The three narratives described in the previous chapters generated valid and reliable insights on securitization efforts by the United States and *Al Qaeda* between 1994 and early 2001. In particular, the strength of this study was to point to how securitization efforts situated in one social order translated into other social contexts.

In identifying and analysing the narratives some choices were made. Hence, limitations need to be addressed before the case study findings can be discussed comprehensively. A relatively large number of texts were reviewed over an extensive period of time. To enable such a scope, the majority of the selected texts consisted of written transcripts. As a result, visual, auditive and situational aspects were lost for analysis, such as which articles were printed next to each other in newspapers or in what tone questions were asked or answered. However, for fragments of several key parts of speeches, televised interviews, some key original newspaper articles, videos and other images were included in the analysis to deepen the research with respect to non-verbal aspects of text production and consumption. For example, how during a televised interview with Bin Laden on Al Jazeera, images were shown on screen of American weapons impacting on targets in Iraq. Another limitation was that only publicly available data was collected. As part of the intelligence practice, for example, classified information might improve contextualisation of texts in the narratives. However, securitization efforts entail an extensive public dimension. Because the case studies in this book also draw on personal memoirs and *ex post* oversight reports, they provide relevant findings.

It is always possible for the basic analytic narratives to be further adapted and expanded, there are always more texts that can be studied. In part, additional relevant events and circumstances were identified during research from data in the selected texts and consequently included in the study. Intertextual links and settings, for example, provided clues to explore: why was President Clinton making a statement on US missile strikes in a hastily set up press room in a school at Martha's Vineyard? – because he was spending time with his family at the presidential retreat to deal with his personal crisis over the Lewinsky matter. What made Bin Laden relocate from Jalalabad to Kandahar? – it was at the Taliban's request, an attempt to better prevent Bin Laden from making provocative statements in news media. However, there are always additional texts to explore, for example, produced by people or organisations surrounding the key leadership that was central to the macro narratives. It is also possible to analyse (additional) different micro narratives. For example, another relevant micro narrative might have been found in the works of Egyptian Muslim scholar Yusuf al-Qaradawi, a highly influential Al Jazeera talk show host and Arab media personality; or perhaps in the account of leading Jordanian-Palestinian writer and Muslim scholar, Abu Muhammad al-Maqdisi. Although they were supportive of Salafism or even *jihad* against local enemies, at times they were still critical of Bin Laden's actions. All in all, the critical terrorism narrative in this book provided relevant insights on tensions and inconsistencies in the macro narratives and functioned as an adequate third narrative.

As has already been acknowledged, the researcher's lack of knowledge of the Arabic language was a factor that limited the research. First, it prevented me from fully engaging in researching reproduction and re-contextualisation of the texts that constitute the *Al Qaeda* narrative. Secondly, the research was limited (yet still possible) in determining the extent to which various types of

Arab and Muslim audiences resonated with Bin Laden's messages and the violent actions associated with *Al Qaeda*. To account for these two shortcomings to a substantial degree, the research was able to draw on relevant literature and translations published in the last two decades. The extent to which the effects of narratives on audiences, or the 'public mind', can be measured remains a continuous concern. A 'feedback problem' that persists with all social research as social science cannot be performed in a 'laboratory', and not all required 'variables' can be measured with the rigour and depth researchers would ultimately desire. This is something also recognised in security studies and other IR subfields.

For intelligence professionals analysing emerging phenomena and entities, an extensive body of research literature is seldom available. It is a constant challenge for them to acquire relevant specific and background knowledge, within a manoeuvring space that is limited by practical and time constraints, to cope with complex intelligence problems. In intelligence, the ACN methodology would draw on the knowledge, skills and experience of different types of officials (intelligence, policy, outside experts) to analyse different particular narratives in parallel as part of a cooperative effort at the working level. In academia, historiographic accounts can also profit from this approach. When studying historic phenomena, attitudes developed and meanings attributed over time are to be distinguished and analysed for their historic effects. Using ACN, dominant narratives of a coloniser presented in school books and public discourse, for example, can be contrasted to that of an antagonist independence movement and local native accounts that are situated in a different social reality. Other scientific historical approaches aim to achieve this too. Yet the originality of the ACN methodology is that in comparing and contrasting at least three narratives, it offers a more comprehensive contextual discursive approach.

During the research it remained necessary to reflect on structures and relations as initially (abductively) constructed. Were the social orders adequately defined? Was the most relevant level of analysis addressed in the light of the research objectives? As mentioned in Chapter 1, it is possible to view American texts and events as part of several subnational narratives or a national narrative on *Al Qaeda*. As for Bin Laden's statements, they could possibly be viewed in terms of an internal organisational dynamic among his Salafi jihadi followers. So, is the primary focus on *Al Qaeda*'s development as a whole adequate, should research focus more on its priorities for the future, or how it could fall apart? Does the research aim to uncover the extent to which US subnational differences on terrorism constrain the narrative at the national level? It is valuable to continuously recognise how the level and focus of narrative analysis is a choice.

In each of the case studies, transparency was provided through presentation of text fragments and their interpretation, as well as through the reflection at the end. When evaluating the neutrality of the research, the approach might prompt the question of what exactly basic analytic narratives consist of and how they can be distinguished from interpretation and analysis. However, a narrative does not exist as a pile of texts separate from its contextualisation through to its interpretation. All is relevant to the research. It is an analytic concept and the chapters reflected what was defined as the basic core of the narratives in context. Therefore, the three case studies contain the narratives, much like one can only observe a shoal of living fish function in the water; like texts only visibly function as part of a narrative when interpreted. Transparency and reflection demonstrate thoroughness and reliability, hence the overall trust-worthiness of the research.

In the remainder of the chapter, two issues are addressed. First, the chapter combines the findings of the case studies. The two macro narratives are linked together by focusing on the multi-consequentiality of statements and actions. This focus is less a result of conclusive findings on the impact of (singular) causal relations on the narratives, and more about the interdiscursive nature of causal relations: did securitization efforts in one narrative contribute to securitization in the other narrative? Tensions and inconsistencies highlighted in the micro narrative are instrumental in comprehensively tackling the issue. The chapter also addresses the nature and status of audiences with regard to the multi-consequentiality (within the same social domain) of securitization efforts. In addition, the effect of the *Al Qaeda* narrative on various types of audiences is discussed in more detail. In contrast to the institutionalised social order that situated the US narrative, the *Al Qaeda* narrative served to establish the identity of Bin Laden and develop his organisation. The narrative not only increased support among followers, but also influenced levels of understanding and sympathy in the Arab and Muslim world. In the current academic debate on securitization, the nature and status of audiences is a central issue of concern.[1] Research often focuses on institutionalised social orders. Therefore, a focus on *Al Qaeda* audiences brings a new perspective to that academic discussion.

Secondly, the chapter evaluates this book in terms of its academic contribution to intelligence studies. Contrary to some of the critique, this book has shown that a critical reflexivist approach can contribute to intelligence as practice. The study of and for intelligence are difficult to separate. The object of research and the case studies have oriented the applied ACN methodology in such a way that, from an intelligence perspective, this research could reflect a joint analytical endeavour performed by US professionals. The various narratives would then correspond to the foci of intelligence analysts, working-level policymakers, and possibly additional trusted outside experts. Finally, the chapter briefly discusses some organisational considerations with respect to implementing ACN.

ANALYSIS BY CONTRASTING NARRATIVES

Tracing multi-consequentiality of securitization efforts

The case studies revealed, each in their own way, a unique story and high-lighted aspects of the complex intelligence problem articulated as *Al Qaeda*. The aim here is not to fuse all three narratives together into some sort of 'higher truth', nor is it possible to bring together all the particularities of the narratives expressed in the case studies into one comprehensive whole. In this respect, the cases are meant to serve as distinct and separate resources to situate and analyse 'future' developments (in this case after mid-2001).

However, as there is multi-causality, there is also multi-consequentiality. Statements and actions of an entity can influence multiple audiences within a social order, but also have effects in other social domains. Between social orders, the way actions and statements are understood can vary fundamentally. Tracing the multi-consequentiality of securitization efforts across social domains provides additional insights. To what extent did statements and actions reflected in one macro narrative influence the development of the other? Did securitization efforts contribute to those of the adversary? The basic principle of multi-consequentiality of securitization efforts across social orders is graphically summarised in Figure 5.1.

As outlined in Chapter 1, NT (contrasting narratives and mapping multi-consequentiality) follows from several steps. After defining the analytical

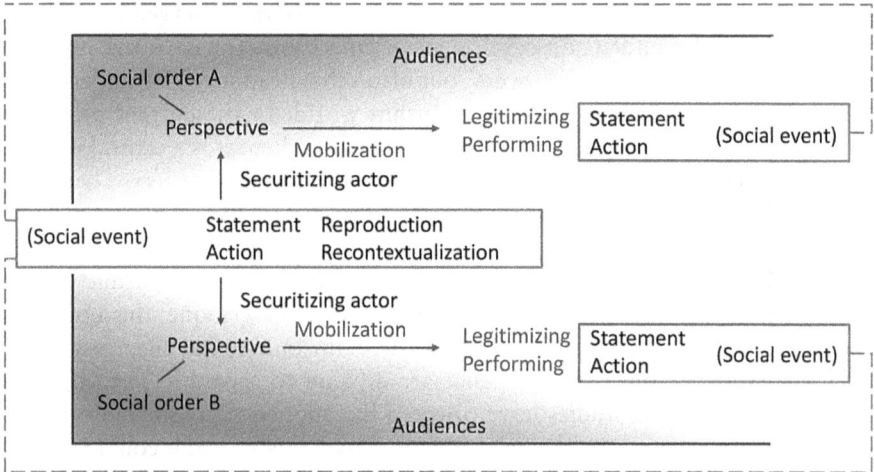

Figure 5.1 Securitization efforts in context

Aspects of social events serve, within a certain context, as heuristic artefacts to mobilise particular perspectives that enable new social events to occur. Any (new) event is itself potentially multi-consequential.

beginning and end of a narrative, facilitating conditions and drivers (or factors and events) that account for the transformative trajectory in between are identified. Then, the extent to which one narrative reflects securitization efforts in other (adversarial) narratives and resonates among its various audiences is considered.

The analytical starting point for the *Al Qaeda* narrative was the 1996 Ladenese memorandum. The comprehensive audio-recorded speech and printed article summarised many of the open letters and statements made by Bin Laden in the mid-1990s. Initially, Bin Laden focused on criticising and resenting the Saudi regime for its 'un-Islamic' practice of governance. Contrary to Western characterisations, the 1996 comprehensive memorandum did not meet the religious criteria for a specific religious decree, or *fatwa*. Among the resources Bin Laden had to produce the text was a highly developed ability to express himself in classical Arabic, some Islamic religious education, an international network, and a mythical reputation for his actions against the Soviets in Afghanistan, business experience and financial resources. The popularity of audio-cassettes in the Arab world enabled Bin Laden to emphasise his eloquent pronunciation and to reach an illiterate audience. The mid-1990s was also a period in which Bin Laden set up the London-based ARC and improved his opportunities to address a pan-Arabic audience via newspapers and satellite television. In Arab and Urdu news media, he was characterised as a political oppositionist, but also as a Muslim scholar. It highlighted different aspects of his message in terms of socio-economic, political and Islamic religious meaning. In the memorandum, Bin Laden named himself a 'concerned element' within the community of Muslim scholars and avoided discussion of his precise religious credentials. Compared with the end of the *Al Qaeda* narrative, his position, power relations and responsibilities were less structured.

Over the years, Bin Laden articulated the specific agenda of targeting the United States and its allies. Such a focus on the 'far enemy' was unique to other Salafi jihadi approaches. An intention behind innovating and reforming Salafi jihadi thinking was for him to mobilise support among Muslims to boycott this far enemy, and incite young followers to conduct attacks. Marking the end of the *Al Qaeda* narrative for this book is the 2001 *As Sahab* media video on the USS *Cole* bombing. The video presented the bombing as an asymmetrical attack by a small boat on a symbol of American global military power in a time of continuous American occupation and aggression in the Middle East. It marked a time in which Bin Laden's closest followers had institutionalised into various religious, media, security and military committees. These committees functioned as a structure to several hundred followers who had pledged allegiance to Bin Laden.[2] For them, Bin Laden had grown into the social role and leadership position that became defined in various securitization efforts throughout the narrative. These efforts had encompassed a process of self-identification, and partly also transformed into a particular strand of the Salafi jihadi social practice. The organisation's informational capability had also grown further. Publishing articles in Arab newspapers such as *Al Quds Al Arabi* or videos for Al Jazeera gave Bin Laden more power in and through discourse. The visibility of Bin Laden and *Al Qaeda* in the Arab and Western world had significantly increased. In a broader sense, Bin Laden had sympathisers across the Arab and Muslim world.

The analytical beginning of the US institutional terrorism narrative is formed by Clinton's speeches after the 1998 embassy attacks. The attacks demanded an adequate response from the US government to fulfil its primary institutional role of finding those responsible and protecting its people by countering future threats. The US government dealt with the threat overtly and covertly, and as comprehensively as possible by means of diplomacy, economic sanctions, law enforcement, intelligence and the military. President Clinton acted within the bandwidth of the political power, laws, regulations, genre conventions and expectations associated with his institutional role. The US government, and specifically the president, confirmed and strengthened their institutional roles in responding to threats and using the discursive and non-discursive power to act. In a time of geopolitical transition, new forms of terrorism were emerging, such as that represented by Bin Laden. The terrorist threat was increasingly focused directly against US servicemen and citizens around the world. Within the US national security order of discourse, the US institutional terrorism narrative became a prominent element. As described in Chapter 3, polls among Americans indicated that a large majority perceived international terrorism as a critical threat to US vital interests, but only a minority thought their families could become a victim of terrorism.

The US narrative ends with Clinton's statements between the USS *Cole* bombing and the end of his term in office. By that time, the articulation of the terrorist threat in the narrative had decreased. Clinton accentuated feelings of security and optimism about the state of the world. Threats and risks were not neglected, but according to the US government the United States was able to respond adequately and handle them. Clinton emphasised a greater goal of furthering peace, prosperity, freedom and human rights in the world. Remarks that America was 'not at war' with terrorism, and emerging other foreign policy priorities also tinted the national security order of discourse in that timeframe. This made securitization efforts regarding terrorism less prominent. Public polls indicated that the perceived threat of terrorism to family members decreased further in that timeframe; however, there is a lack of data on perception regarding international terrorism as a threat to national security. In general, the US institutional terrorism narrative conformed to and confirmed the US social order. The threat to the state's citizens had emphasised the state's essence and the institutional role of its leadership. The narrative contributed to self-identification in that respect.

The development of the two macro narratives was related through the multi-consequentiality of some of the discursive and non-discursive actions. This was also partly highlighted in the critical micro narrative. Events (such as securitization efforts) in one social domain became issues that added momentum, or intensity, to the securitization efforts in the other social order. Actions to control or defeat a perceived threat by the United States contributed to the contextual mobilisation of heuristic artefacts by that threatening actor. There were also events and circumstances that removed momentum from the securitization efforts that were gradually building on each other. For *Al Qaeda*, this involved internal differences among Bin Laden's followers, while for the United States it was the prioritisation of other foreign policy issues over terrorism. Also of influence for both macro narratives were the position and personal circumstances of the securitizing actor and audiences' critique on the effectiveness of measures taken.

For both the United States and *Al Qaeda* narratives, timelines can be used to project key statements and actions that constituted securitization efforts, and events and circumstances adding or removing momentum. It is important to note that it can be misleading to view the schematic timelines in terms of a presentation of the primary (or singular) efficient causal relations. The research analysed discursive and non-discursive action beyond the concept of efficient cause in terms of network of causality or causal complex.

In the mid-1990s, the Al Qaeda narrative took shape over a series of Bin Laden statements. Several events and circumstances reduced some of the securitizing momentum of these statements. The critical narrative highlighted how the publication of the Ladenese memorandum in *Al Quds Al-Arabi* was questioned by some of the followers at the London-based ARC. Later, followers who had sworn loyalty (*bayat*) to Bin Laden had doubts about his pledge of allegiance to the Taliban. The status of the WIF was questioned by Arab media, as was the representativeness of the founding declaration's signatories. The groups for which they had signed were internally divided over the issue, or even clearly declined their support.

These doubts and critiques were related to the aggressive nature and shifting focus of Bin Laden's statements over the years. In the early 1990s, Bin Laden emphasised that he deemed the Saudi regime to be corrupt and illegitimate. Later, he began to more prominently promote his view that in fact the United States and its Western allies were the primary source or driving factor behind the religious and socio-economic conditions in Saudi Arabia.[3] He then classified all Americans all over the world as targets. Bin Laden had realised that Saudi Arabia was 'under the control' of the United States. On a personal level, the United States had a significant role in Bin Laden's forced migration from Saudi Arabia and later Sudan, along with pressuring the Afghan Taliban to stop harbouring him. In the *Al Qaeda* narrative, there were also some minor

Al Qaeda narrative
Social structure: Islamic society
Social practice: Salafi-jihadism
Actor: Bin Laden / *Al Qaeda*

Adding momentum	Key statements and actions	Removing momentum	Adding momentum	Key statements and actions	Removing momentum
Saudi Socio-economic conditions, US Middle East foreign policy	Early 1990s: Various Bin Laden statements, various activities in Sudan, relocates to Afghanistan		US santions and reward against Bin Laden		
	1996 Ladenese memorandum Threat to KSA, US, the West	Internal friction over 'timing'	US missile strikes on Afghanistan and Sudan		
			US bombing campaign over Iraq	1998 *Al Jazeera* interview	
	1997 Allegiance to the Taliban	Internal disagreement	US sanctions against the Taliban		
		Pragmatic: UK not a threat	Bin Laden added to US 10 Most Wanted list		
	1998 WIF declaration Threatening US military, civilian	Status signatories contested, internal differences	Israeli-Palestinian conflict, *intifada*	2000 Bombing USS Cole, statement	
		Taliban attempt to constrain Bin Laden		2000 *Al Jazeera* interview with Al-Zawahiri	
	1998 Embassy bombings, Bin Laden denies involvement	Large number of civilian casualties		2001 *As Sahab* production on USS Cole	

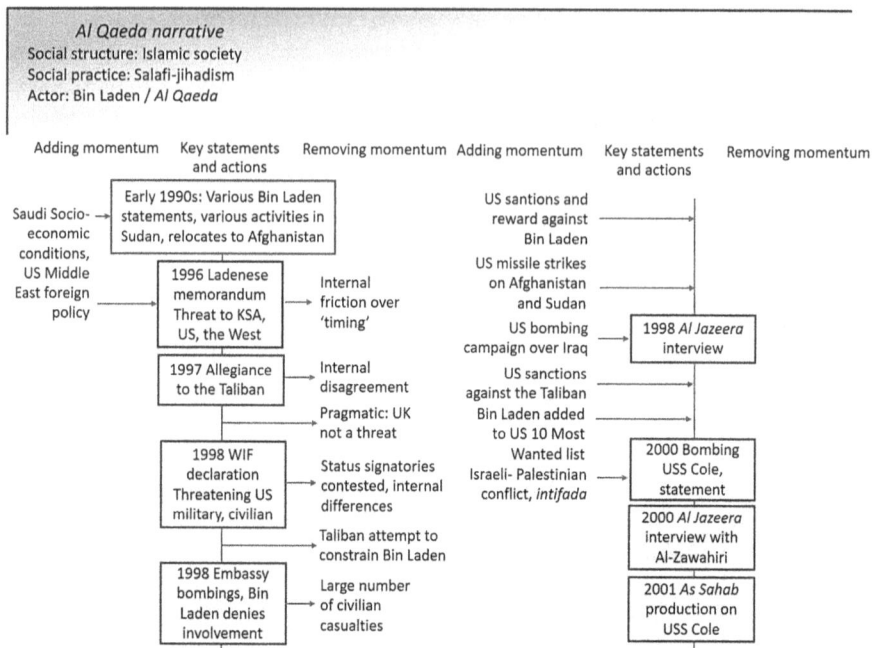

Figure 5.2 Al Qaeda narrative key events and circumstances affecting securitization efforts

variations depending on where Bin Laden localised his message: for example, he did not blame Pakistani UN soldiers for their role in Somalia in a Pakistani newspaper; he stated that UK troops in Saudi Arabia constituted only a minor symbolic presence; and during an interview with Robert Fisk he praised the British and French voting in the UN on Israel.

For the Salafi jihadi movement, a focus on the 'Zionist Crusader alliance of Western forces' or 'far enemy' articulated so explicitly in the 1998 WIF declaration reflected an ideological transformation away from the traditional way of thinking about the religious duty to defend Islam. However, Bin Laden sought to expand and activate his audiences against the dominant Salafi jihadi current. He advertised his views before the whole Arab and Muslim world and specifically aimed to inspire young Muslims to conduct attacks. The attacks on the US embassies in Africa and against the USS *Cole* in Yemen demonstrated how his securitization efforts were followed by violent actions. The perpetrators were loyal followers. In the wider context of unequal socio-economic conditions in Saudi Arabia and American economic policies and military interventions in the Middle East, some of Bin Laden's ideas were popular among Arabs and Muslims across the world. They framed his picture in shops, played his speeches on audio-cassettes in public places, wrote supportive graffiti or held signs and his

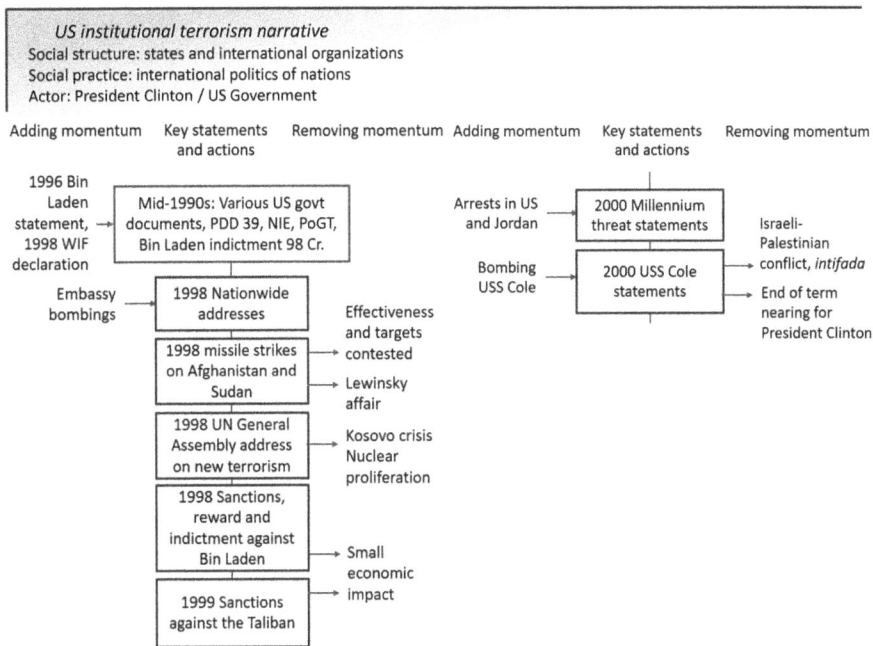

Figure 5.3 US institutional terrorism narrative key events and circumstances affecting securitization efforts

picture at anti-US demonstrations. In a more general sense, they increased the social status of Bin Laden's persona and organisation. However, as also described in the critical narrative, the large number of casualties among ordinary Africans caused by the embassy bombings resulted in feelings of dismay among Muslims and Arabs.[4] This also negatively affected feelings of support among (potential) moral audiences for Bin Laden's ideas, persona and organisation.

A few weeks later, these concerns over innocent victims were backgrounded by widespread resentment among Arabs and Muslims following the US missile strikes on Afghanistan and Sudan. The *Al Qaeda* narrative showed how after those strikes, Bin Laden more fully used the US embassy attacks in Africa as an illustration of the rising battle of Muslims against the ZCA. There was also critique from national leaders across the world over the legitimacy of the attacks and choice of targets, especially the Sudanese medical factory. In that context, Bin Laden's personal status as enemy of the United States increased support among his moral audience. It also improved the then-waning hospitality of the Taliban. Bin Laden made efforts to increase this effect by stating that the CIA had conducted several unsuccessful operations against him. Being hunted by the CIA or the target of missile strikes was a story that served to drown out confrontation regarding the inconvenience of the massive number of civilian casualties caused by the US embassy bombings in Africa. In addition, the US military Operation Desert Fox brought Bin Laden's rhetoric further to life. Re-contextualisation in Arab media contributed to this. For example, during an interview with Bin Laden broadcasted on Al Jazeera, images were shown on screen of the US military strikes against Iraq. In the broadcast, wider Arab anger over these strikes was aligned with Bin Laden's message before a large media audience.

For Bin Laden, some of the measures taken by US institutional bodies against his network proved instrumental as symbolic articulations of difference. For instance, the US State Department had issued a reward of US$5 million for actionable information leading to his capture. This further personalised the issue of Bin Laden's propagated ascetic lifestyle versus the ego-centric material-ism of those he called 'hypocrites', a religious term for Muslims. He presented it as a natural 'test of faith' for those who had pledged allegiance to him. For large illiterate segments of the ordinary population in the Middle East, it was possibly even highly difficult to relate to the size of the reward and imagine that such a sum of money actually existed. Furthermore, as a consequence of the American law enforcement and judicial processes, Bin Laden was publicly indicted and added to the notorious selection of the FBI's ten most wanted fugi-tives. Especially the latter action, also reproduced by English, Arab and Urdu news media, granted Bin Laden with the adversarial status he had been trying to acquire, as described in the *Al Qaeda* narrative. The sanctions ordered by Clinton against Bin Laden in 1998, and later the Taliban in 1999, diametrically related to the boycott of American goods Bin Laden had propagated years ear-lier. The functional economic effect of the sanctions was minimal, but it proved useful for Bin Laden as another heuristic artefact in his securitization effort and construction of otherness.

In the US socio-political context, the bombings of the US embassies in Africa triggered a comprehensive counterterrorism approach. The discursive and non-discursive actions described in the US institutional terrorism narra-tive fitted government roles within the bandwidth of the US institutional social order. However, there was also critique among US formal and moral audiences that removed some of the momentum for defining the threat and mobilising assets to deal with it. For Clinton, the support among his formal audience, the US Congress, was limited as a result of his personal involvement in the Lewinsky affair. For most of his presidency, the opposing Republican Party had the majority in the US Congress, restraining Clinton's political power. The Lewinsky matter further challenged some of the public expectations of his insti-tutional role, such as maintaining integrity and credibility. Yet in public polls Clinton was still perceived as a strong leader, despite the decreased apprecia-tion of his moral stance. The missile strikes on Sudan and Afghanistan had the opposite effect and expressed strength and leadership. Partly because of this effect, Clinton's motivations for ordering the strikes became subject to debate, most prominently in the news media. Another reason the strikes came to be debated was domestic controversy in the media, possibly reflecting doubts among his moral audience, regarding the effectiveness of the strikes. American journalists also questioned the impact of economic sanctions against Bin Laden and the Taliban.

Before the UN General Assembly, Clinton made an effort to securitize a new kind of terrorism that had emerged globally in the 1990s. The Bin Laden's organisation's threat to the United States was representational for this 'new terrorism', but Clinton also included examples of violence in other parts of the world directed at others. His address aimed to improve the diplomatic climate and cooperation among UN member states by establishing an inclusive agreement on the new threat. Internationally, the US military response with missile strikes, especially on the Sudanese Al-Shifa factory, had led to some protest. The relation of the targets to terrorism was questioned by several heads of state that were critical of the United States. In his UN address, Clinton also worked to legitimise the attacks. It was difficult to observe the effects of the UN speech for this research: other foreign policy issues on the agenda drew attention away from the threat of this new terrorism, such as the emerging Kosovo crisis or North Korea's nuclear programme.

At the turn of the millennium, the arrest of Ahmed Ressam at the US–Canadian border articulated the terrorist threat in the United States. The positive securitization effort at the time confirmed Clinton's position as president and worked to reassure US citizens. United States' government statements served to increase social resilience against attacks and expressed self-determination. Rudimentary public polling indicated that concerns among US respondents of family members becoming a target of terrorism had decreased; possibly emphasising the US institutional effort to provide security also deterred terrorists from executing plans. Initially, Clinton refrained from using Bin Laden's name explicitly in relation to the 'millennium threat', yet US officials were anonymously stating in news media that there were indirect links between Ressam and Bin Laden. Furthermore, months after the millennial festivities, Clinton also publicly made such connections in a speech before US Coast Guard personnel. In the *Al Qaeda* narrative, in contrast, the millennium celebrations were not emphasised as a distinct episode in Bin Laden's securitization efforts. There were no attacks about which to make statements.

In the late 1990s, there had been agreement among senior US officials and political leaders to refrain from using Bin Laden's name too much in public to avoid contributing to his status.[5] In public statements, Clinton mostly spoke more generally about the threat of terrorism, although still mentioning Bin Laden specifically in several public addresses. However, the more comprehensive the counterterrorism policies became, for example, in terms of diplomacy, law enforcement and intelligence, the more complex the task became of managing the overall coherence of discursive and non-discursive actions, especially as reproduction and re-contextualisation by news media had an amplifying effect on statements about terrorists. This was illustrated by the divergence between the political intent to refrain from using Bin Laden's name and to conduct secret intelligence operations, and the concurrent public indictment by prosecutors and his inclusion in the iconic FBI list of America's ten most wanted fugitives. Emphasised by the media, the bureaucratic legal and law enforcement practices had an effect on the *Al Qaeda* narrative that was contradictory to the US political leadership's intent.

The meanings of events differed in the various narratives, as they related to different social contexts. For example, to US policymakers, the attack on the USS *Cole* in the Yemeni port of Aden on 12 October 2000 was a sign of instability and a regional terrorist threat that necessitated a shift in foreign and counterterrorism policies. Clinton noted that America was 'not at war'. He stated that the US intention behind the USS *Cole* visit to Aden was to demonstrate trust and to strengthen international relations between Yemen and the United States. The military was used as a symbolic representation of unity and the values articulated as central to US democracy and freedom; Clinton framed the sailors more as diplomats than as soldiers. As such, American national identity had been attacked. To a Salafi jihadi segment of the Yemeni population, on the other hand, the USS *Cole* visit was a materialisation of American expansionism. The attack was celebrated by Islamic fundamentalists as a necessary response.

For the *Al Qaeda* narrative, the USS *Cole* bombing was an event that illustrated the expansive drift of a far enemy invading and occupying Muslim lands, and demonstrated the willingness and 'success' of Salafi jihadis to resist it. The *As Sahab* video of the bombing provided heuristic artefacts for *Al Qaeda*'s persisting and progressing securitization efforts. That Clinton did not make a clear securitization effort with regard to the USS *Cole* bombing did not affect the *Al Qaeda* narrative. In the critical terrorism narrative, both the meaning of the USS *Cole* visit and the attack as articulated by either the US government or *Al Qaeda* were questioned.

A significant circumstance of influence on both the US and *Al Qaeda* narratives was the eruption of Israeli–Palestinian violence, which started on the same day the USS *Cole* was attacked. In his speeches, Clinton connected these subjects from the beginning. For him, international cooperation, diplomacy and military deployments, such as the visit of the American Navy destroyer to Yemen, illustrated how US involvement in the Middle East was and remained necessary precisely to end eruptions of violence and promote peace. For Bin Laden, the Palestinian intifada provided a context that related to the core of his securitization efforts to end the Zionist Crusader involvement in Palestine, Yemen, Saudi Arabia and the wider region.

Overall, the case studies showed how processes of securitization were dynamic, aggregating and involved a constant effort to relate to unfolding events and developing circumstances. The comparative approach in this chapter has demonstrated how certain circumstances were shaped by discursive and non-discursive action generated in different social domains, as described in other narratives. There was reactivity (or interaction) with regard to the development of securitization efforts in the US and *Al Qaeda* narratives. Most visibly, the American rationale behind the sanctions and missile strikes against Sudan, Afghanistan and Iraq did not translate in the context of Salafi jihadism and the wider Muslim or Arab world. In the US narrative, there was little emphasis on internal differences among Bin Laden's followers and supporters. Hence, although various events and circumstances were at play, in the effort to comprehensively use all available means to counter terrorism, some of the actions performed by the United States were useful for Bin Laden to emphasise estrangement and difference, and articulate his moral religious and functional authoritative status in terms of securitization. However, a lack of such measures and statements, such as after the USS *Cole* bombing, did not cause *Al Qaeda*'s securitization efforts to decrease.

Securitization efforts contributed to (self-)identification. The *Al Qaeda* narrative reflected the institutionalisation of *Al Qaeda* into an organisation, but also played a fundamental part in shaping the process and providing identity. Articulations of self were as important as defining the 'other'. Bin Laden's use of his discursive power also reflected and influenced the Salafi jihadi social order. A new approach to *jihad* and the duty of Muslims against the Western far enemy became consistently articulated. In essence, Salafi jihadism was perceived as being at odds with American values of liberalism, freedom and capitalism, and the norms regarding the separation of religion and the institutionalised state.

Rather than defeating the United States, in defying the country Bin Laden provided the context for Clinton to emphasise peace and humanity as core American values, to articulate the protective essence of the state, and to confirm his institutional role through the use of his discursive and non-discursive power. In the critical terrorism narrative, these processes of identification were explicitly critiqued as simplifications and framing by articulating two evocative labels: the idea of both an 'international terrorist conspiracy' and a 'Zionist Crusader conspiracy' were characterised as bizarre images that did not reflect the true complexity of the situation in the Middle East. Reporting in the critical narrative illustrated confusion and disagreement among some of Bin Laden's supporters over the statements he had made. Moreover, 'simplistic connections' made by the US government between Saddam Hussein and Bin Laden were deemed to be questionable. Overall, violence and murderous attacks were condemned in the critical narrative.

All in all, the US and *Al Qaeda* narratives related to two extremely differ-ent, asymmetrical entities. They were part of and involved with fundamentally different social orders of social structures, social practices, discursive practices and non-discursive action. The essentiality of the disparity between the US and *Al Qaeda* social orders was an abductive analytic distinction that lay at the basis of this research. However, it was also in the construction of self and other in the US and *Al Qaeda* narratives, and the way the narratives developed and affected their social orders, that a certain immanence to the difference articu-lated in securitization efforts was revealed. As such, the validity of the abduc-tive construction process in this research regarding the US and *Al Qaeda* social orders has not been contested.

The United States and *Al Qaeda* were dependent on and capable of using very different forms of power. But for both, their macro narratives were highly important in expressing and affecting their respective power positions. Eventu-ally, the attacks on the US embassies in Africa and the USS *Cole* demonstrated Bin Laden's ability to instigate and, to some degree, even to facilitate or organ-ise assaults. These events gained meaning as they were connected and situated in and through the texts and discursive practices that constituted the *Al Qaeda* narrative. The United States had the largest military presence worldwide and extensive global economic, diplomatic and cultural influence. For Clinton, these were not straightforward foreign policy tools that could be used exclusively, effectively and immediately against Bin Laden; other foreign policy priorities were also involved. Moreover, the lack of bipartisanism in Congress made it more difficult for Clinton to operate freely with regard to foreign policy issues. So, for Clinton as well, the US institutional terrorism narrative was an impor-tant way of expressing and maintaining the power to act. As stated above, the statements and actions of 'the other' also strengthened and facilitated the use of this power. In this sense, there was discursive and non-discursive interaction or reactivity between securitization efforts. Securitization provided a binding logic to comprehend both the US and *Al Qaeda* narratives.

A closer look: audiences and effects

Irrespective of the conclusion that some statements and actions in the US nar-rative contributed to opposing securitization efforts in the *Al Qaeda* narrative, the case studies also generated the insight that for the *Al Qaeda* narrative, Bin Laden continued to make such efforts regardless of US actions and state-ments. Furthermore, the research showed that Bin Laden's efforts were at times deemed to be controversial or were even disputed by individuals and groups associated with him and *Al Qaeda*. Similarly, some of the decisions Clinton made to counter terrorism were contested as well.

These findings lead to an important aspect of the research: the nature and status of audiences for securitization.[6] The sociological approach adopted in this book emphasises audiences, context and *dispositif* as the three central facets of securitization processes.[7] Securitization is not a sudden speech act that transforms into a social fact when accepted: it is part of a social context and related to power struggles. Audiences are essential to provide securitization with its intersubjective status, but their essence must be viewed in terms of causal adequacy, not causal determinacy. In other words, securitization efforts involve audiences, but are not necessarily determined by them.

What became apparent in the research was that (self-)identification of audiences could both precede and follow from securitization efforts. Audiences became audiences to securitizing actors either in and through securitization efforts or as the result of a preceding process of identification and institutionalisation. Whereas for *Al Qaeda* the narrative had a more formative function, the US narrative conversely served more to confirm and strengthen an established (institutionalised) American identity. Especially in case of institutionalised power relations, it is possible for some audiences to grant deontological powers or a formal mandate to the securitizing actor in specific instances. However, such a mandate is not necessary for securitization 'efforts' to occur before (or to resonate with) various audiences, and also have certain 'effects'. Such a theoretical stance invites the exploration of the essence and role of audiences more in terms of congruity. It 'enables us to determine the relative status of its (enabling or constraining) force within the network of causality' or causal complex.[8] This causal complex is activated at the actual level[9] in and through the securitization efforts.

The understanding of securitization in terms of efforts rests on the integrative notion of causal complexes outlined in the first chapter. The statements and actions of actors can be perceived as a form of securitization only when they follow the defined logic of threat definition, and when there is alignment with a social context and the related differential power relations, and some resonance with audiences' frames of reference. In general, securitization is about the politics of establishing a security character of public problems, fixing social commitments that follow from collective acceptance of a threat, and creating the possibilities of certain policies.[10] Instead of focusing on the end state and creating the problem of what counts as an instance of securitization, research on securitization can contribute to the study of the processes described.[11] More central than assent itself are the efforts of inducing or increasing 'the public mind's adherence to the thesis presented to its assent'.[12] This conceives securitization as part of wider political struggles over power and ideology.

The characterisation in terms of efforts circumvents the difficult debate on what counts as an instance of successful securitization, and on whether an issue is considered securitized when various audiences differ in terms of 'assent'. Do formal and moral audiences have to agree on both the problem definition and the proposed solution for that?[13] Rather than trying to identify 'instances of acceptance', research should concentrate on the degree of resonance among various types of parallel audiences. First-generation securitization theorists especially would argue that this stance deconstructs the nature of securitization as a practice distinct from politics. It also makes the notion that audiences (must) have 'the ability to grant or deny a formal mandate' more relative. [14] However, as the case studies showed, in practice securitization can be viewed as a dynamic, aggregating and gradual process consisting of efforts that are part of, or an extension of, wider political struggles over power and ideology within a social context. Albeit not the only feasible conceptual framework one could think of, in this way the concept of securitization was an adequate approach for this research. [15]

The US narrative demonstrated the maintaining and confirming of existing power relations between securitizing actor and audiences through threat articulation and security practices. In the United States, power relations have institutionalised due to historic conditions and practices. As a result, the US president could act with extraordinary measures against threats to national security by declaring them formally to the US Congress. The latter's assent was not required to conduct missile strikes or conduct covert counterterrorism operations, but only to declare war. Articulation was required (*ex post*) before the president's formal and moral audience. The Clinton administration had to answer questions in Congress and the media, particularly as other personal, domestic and foreign policy issues combined into turbulent times. The American electorate functioned as moral audience, indirectly affecting (enabling or constraining) the stance of politicians and decision-makers. The president's access to secret intelligence, or 'evidence', served to strengthen public and political trust in his decisions. In essence, the securitization dynamic identified in the US narrative with respect to *Al Qaeda* demonstrated the nature and workings of the state.

It is not always possible to empirically identify responses among audiences in a conclusive manner. For critical realists, this does not cause an epistemological problem as it would for positivists. The absence or shortage of empirical evidence of audience responses to securitization efforts does not prevent conclusions from being drawn on the existence of audiences and their function at the actual level. Empirical findings can be positioned as anecdotal evidence to support inferences on the nature and status of audiences. Although not the central efficient cause, audiences are an essential part of the activated causal complex that encompasses securitization efforts. In varying degrees, various types of parallel audiences are an enabling and constraining element. Disagreement among members of a certain audience, for example, does not necessarily stop, but can potentially reduce, the effects of securitization efforts on self-identification or security practices.

In the institutionalised social environment of the US narrative, the essence and role of audiences was more clearly defined than for the *Al Qaeda* narrative.

The two categories of moral and formal audiences proved adequate to comprehend the securitization dynamic among American institutions. In and through the *Al Qaeda* narrative, on the other hand, power relations between securitizing actor and audiences needed to be established with regard to a specific issue. Bin Laden worked to create and expand his status and relation to various audiences over the American-led invasion of Muslim lands. However, the actual execution of the individual bombings was not dependent on the consent of a certain audience, beyond some of his closest followers and those willing to conduct the attacks. Thus, for the *Al Qaeda* narrative, defining formal and moral audiences with respect to the less institutionalised entity was more complex, but therefore also more interesting for reflecting on securitization theory. Within the social practice of Salafi jihadism, power relations were less hierarchical or institutionalised, and more related to the dynamics of personal reputation. To comprehensively understand the causal complex activated in and through *Al Qaeda* securitization efforts, it is necessary to differentiate audiences beyond Balzacq's notion of formal and moral audiences, and thereby contribute to the debate on securitization as outlined in Chapter 1.[16] The following section focuses more closely on *Al Qaeda*'s audiences and the effect the narrative had on them.

Arabs, Muslims, Salafists, jihadis and *Al Qaeda* members, cadre and executioners

For the two macro narratives, audiences were identified along several lines of inquiry. First, (intended) audiences were articulated in and through the identification of referent objects that were subject to a threat. Secondly, partly overlapping were the intended consumers of texts that constituted the discursive action associated with the securitization effort. Was there a difference between those threatened and those addressed by the securitizing actor? Thirdly, what could be learned about the responses to efforts through empirical data (the observation of demonstrations, expressions of trust) or literature? What audiences were drawn to the narrative? Fourthly, partly related, what wider social conditions or aspects of the situational context strengthened or weakened alignment of audiences' frames of reference with the securitization efforts? Did external events (such as US missile strikes on Iraq or the Palestinian intifada) create a context that made securitization statements more topical (for new audiences)?

For the *Al Qaeda* narrative, these questions generated an array of entities that in some form or other could be (partly) considered as audiences: Muslims around the world; readers of pan-Arabic or Urdu newspapers; Al Jazeera viewers; demonstrators in the streets of Pakistan, Yemen, Sudan and Palestine; Islamists or members of other Salafist groups (particularly youths); jihadi recruits in Afghan training camps; and *Al Qaeda* members, cadre and executioners of attacks. Rather than two distinct categories, these entities together represent a spectrum that can be ordered in terms of ideas and action, or ideology and power. Of course, since the attacks on 11 September 2001, an enormous body of literature has emerged on *Al Qaeda* and its supporters.[17] Drawing on terrorism studies literature, the spectrum of audiences identified in and through the narrative has been matched to a tripartite conceptualisation of support for terrorist organisations: an empathetic but neutral understanding of motives and grievances, a positive attitude or sympathy for the motives and terrorist actions, and various forms of behavioural support and assistance.[18] Other overlapping or more specific conceptualisations also exist. The notion of support can be divided into a range of activities, such as propaganda, finances, logistics, information gathering, weapons production, training, planning and execution of attacks.

In a broader sense, a complex 'ecosystem' enabled *Al Qaeda* to develop as an organisation. It involved financial donors in the Arab and Muslim world, newspapers willing to publish open letters and statements, Islamist scholars and members of jihadi groups giving credence, but also sympathetic governments such as in Sudan and Yemen, or the Afghan Taliban. Among Muslims in general, but also among Salafists, there was ignorance. Many Afghans, Pakistanis, and other Muslims and Arabs had never heard of Bin Laden. Among those Salafists who had learned about Bin Laden's ideas, there was disagreement and opposition to the proposed strategic innovation of focusing on the far enemy. To some extent, the *Al Qaeda* narrative changed this over time. That is why it functioned as such an essential element, or the oxygen vitalising the ecosystem, by reaching various contributing entities in various ways.

At the level of social structure, the *Al Qaeda* narrative was situated in Islamic society. Bin Laden made extensive references to generic religious values, cultural traditions and historic myths. This enabled a wide understanding and provided a fundamental condition necessary for acceptance of the ideas articulated in the *Al Qaeda* narrative. Bin Laden was photographed riding horses, for Muslims a sign of heroism, while emphasising self-abnegation and asceticism (*zuhd*) through his posture and living conditions.[19] The 1996 memorandum (*mudhakkira*) reflected an Islamic genre in which advice (*nasiha*) is given to rulers in the most eloquent and dignified way.[20] Poetry (*qasidah*) and religious references in the memorandum were familiar to Muslims and Arabs, and strengthened the expression of passion and the appeal of the texts.[21] For example, the poem of Amru Ibn Kulthum Al-Taghlibi, who killed a regent who had capitulated to the Persians, emphasised for educated Muslims a need to resist illegitimate governments under the control of others.[22] Characterisations of the ZCA referenced the Quranic verse on hypocrites (*Surah Al-Munafiqun*).[23] In addition, Bin Laden's pronunciation of classical Arabic (*Fusha*) expressed eminence to those listening to the numerous audio-cassettes distributed throughout the Arab and Muslim world. Initially, in the early 1990s, the Saudi government and press even assisted Bin Laden in speaking about his fighting in Afghanistan against the Soviets, contributing to his standing in Saudi Arabia in particular.[24]

There were also world events and circumstances that increased sensitivity to the *Al Qaeda* narrative among wider Muslim and Arab audiences. During the Israeli–Palestinian violence in 2000, anti-American sentiments increased among Palestinians as the United States was perceived as a supporter of Israel. In the narrative, Bin Laden was and had been keen to foster an ideological link with the Palestinian cause. His mentor Abdullah Azzam had Palestinian roots. Over time, several Palestinians joined Bin Laden, such as Mohammed Sadiq Odeh, who was arrested after the 1998 embassy bombings. In the context of the intifada, the attack on the USS *Cole* in Yemen caused some cheerful responses among (non-Salafi) Palestinians.[25] However, the extent to which the USS *Cole* bombing increased understanding or sympathy among Palestinians is difficult to quantify. In August 2000, Israeli and Palestinian security services arrested twenty-three Palestinian Islamic radicals, some of whom they claimed had links to Bin Laden.[26] However, Hamas leader Yassin publicly denounced Israeli accusations that his organisation had operational links with Bin Laden.[27] Jason Burke notes that Palestinian militants consistently resisted Bin Laden's attempts to 'hijack their campaign', but he acknowledges that there was popular support for Bin Laden nonetheless.[28]

Another example that increased sensitivity was Operation Desert Fox. During the US strikes on Iraq, Al Jazeera satellite television reached tens of millions of viewers across the Arab world with images of the weaponry impacting on the ground. Satellite technology had revolutionised the Arab media landscape, spearheaded by Al Jazeera.[29] The continuous exclusive footage contributed to anti-American demonstrations in the Middle East.[30] In this context, Bin Laden, who had gained notoriety as target of the earlier US missile strikes on Afghanistan, was able to highlight the *Al Qaeda* narrative before a large pan-Arabic audience. As Bruce Lawrence has stated, he became an 'instant international attraction'.[31] Quantifying Bin Laden's increasing popularity is difficult, but what it did demonstrate was a discursive effect beyond the Salafist movement. He increased understanding and perhaps sympathy for the *Al Qaeda* narrative among parts of the global Muslim community. In part, a similar effect was also established by publications in regional and pan-Arabic newspapers, such as *Al Quds Al-Arabi* and *Al-Islah*. Setting up the ARC to assist in the dissemination of statements proved to be a fruitful decision by Bin Laden in facilitating the exposure of the *Al Qaeda* narrative in the Arab and Muslim world.

The social practice of Salafi jihadism, a particular approach to Salafism, further characterised the social space of the *Al Qaeda* narrative. Putting discussions aside regarding the nature of Salafism as social movement or ideology and practice (*manhaj*), it is clear that various Islamist groups agreed in their call to respect particular ancient Muslim traditions in response to the spread of Western rationalist ideas since the late nineteenth century.[32] Religious pluralism and cultural influences on faith were viewed as dangerous deviations. The works of Ibn Taymiyya, Sayyid Qutb and others, which were extensively referenced in the *Al Qaeda* narrative, were central to Salafist thinkers.

Among Muslims, Salafists were a minority. Their network was fluid, decentralised and segmented.[33] Rather than any hierarchy, reputation and recognition signalled importance and influence. It was the reputation of Grand Mufti Bin Baz that Bin Laden attacked in his statements. While among Salafists, Bin Laden was recognised as 'sheikh', an informal sign of respect.[34] Face-to-face engagements between students and teachers provided the strongest link in the network of overlapping clusters. Centred round prominent Salafi scholars and thinkers, these clusters were fairly local or regional in their orientation. To some extent, audio-cassettes and later the internet increased the exchange of views and lectures across the network, but new Salafists were mostly Muslims who had decided to convert after lengthy discussions, lessons and gatherings in mosques, religious schools or guest houses. *Al Qaeda* sought to recruit followers from the Salafi minority for the practice of *jihad*, as did other Salafi jihadi groups who trained recruits in Afghan training camps. The increasing focus on attacking the far enemy in the *Al Qaeda* narrative went against traditional Salafi jihadi thinking, leading to doubts among jihadis training in Afghan camps and internal division over the course of *Al Qaeda* as a developing organisation.[35] This became especially clear when some of the 1998 WIF statement signatories were forced to withdraw their support or split off from their organisation.

The practice of *jihad* in Afghanistan against the Soviets had already created a network of Salafi jihadis that spread to various conflict zones around the world. Some of them functioned as recruiters to facilitate the travel of Salafists to Afghan training camps.[36] Bin Laden's relocation from Sudan to Afghanistan was presented as a forced migration (*hijrah*), because he was unable to practice his faith. For jihadis, characterising his new environment as Khorasan referred to an Islamic call to arms. Although the legitimacy of the *hadith* about 'an army with Black Banners from Khorasan' is not undisputed among Muslims, for jihadis it had a strong appeal.[37] *Hijra* expresses that Muslim unity is stronger than family and social ties, encouraging jihadis to leave home and join the *jihad*.[38] The *Al Qaeda* narrative attracted small groups and individual followers.

Some Muslims were sympathetic to *Al Qaeda*; some made financial contributions to Bin Laden's efforts, and others were willing to spread his ideas and statements. The Salafists who chose to come to Afghanistan, train for *jihad*, and pledge *bayat* to Bin Laden were of a distinct nature. They can be considered the formal members of *Al Qaeda*. However, the clarity of such a distinction is deceptive. In the late 1980s there was confusion and discussion regarding the status of the pledge made by the dozen or so followers at the time with regard to older pledges made to local groups.[39] There is a lack of clarity concerning the precise number of people who pledged *bayat*, as Bin Laden also employed people for his business endeavours in Sudan. In the mid-1990s, some jihadis chose to make a temporary or conditional pledge. Saudi recruits especially participated in training and fighting for several months and then returned home.[40] In 1996, a small group agreed 'to join *Al Qaeda* and fight America with the proviso that if a jihad effort with a clearer justification existed on another front, they would be free to join that instead'.[41] In the late 1990s, followers had the possibility to make a 'little' or 'big' oath of allegiance.[42] The former was declared before Bin Laden, the latter before Taliban leader Mullah Omar. This was after Bin Laden had pledged allegiance to the Taliban leader.

Accounts of the number of followers who pledged allegiance varied, but in general their number increased during the 1990s, from a dozen to several hundred in 2001.[43] These *Al Qaeda* members had gone through various stages of training. Basic military skills were taught in Afghan camps such as Al-Farouq near Kandahar. The jihadi recruits were tied to various Salafi jihadi groups, as the camps were run jointly. Class and group sizes varied from ten to forty students. *Al Qaeda* trainers taught them about *Al Qaeda*'s views. On occasion, Bin Laden paid visits to Al Farouq to have discussions with recruits about their faith. After completing basic training, some spent time in guest houses in Kandahar city, while others directly continued with advanced training. At the Arab guest house financed by Bin Laden, a van was always ready to take jihadis to Bin Laden's home if they wanted to pledge *bayat*.[44] Although this was voluntary, *Al Qaeda* recruiters tried to persuade recruits, also by using peer pressure from other students.[45]

Of those receiving advanced training in explosives, intelligence collection and other fighting skills, some were selected for secret *Al Qaeda* operations. Among them were Ramzi bin al-Shibh, Mohammed Atta, Ziad Jarrah and Marwan al-Shehhi, who came from Germany and in 1999 started preparations for the attacks on 11 September 2001. The personal stories of *Al Qaeda* members, as also described in Chapter 2, such as the Palestinian Sadiq Odeh, the Saudi Mohammed al-Owhali and the Sudanese Jamal al-Fadl, reflected a staged trajectory of joining the organisation. World events and the propagation of the *Al Qaeda* narrative, such as in Saudi, Yemeni and Sudanese guest houses, were instrumental in convincing jihadis to travel to Afghanistan and eventually become members of *Al Qaeda*. After the USS *Cole* bombing in Yemen by *Al Qaeda* members, many new recruits started to arrive in Kandahar.[46]

In sum, the narrative related to various Muslim, Salafi jihadi and *Al Qaeda* audiences in different ways. Sometimes it fostered understanding among a wider Arab audience, and sometimes it shifted people's ideas and perceptions, increasing sympathy or forms of support. The narrative analysis performed in the case study did not focus on the types and levels of functional support received by Bin Laden, such as weapons transactions or financial dealings.

However, in a more general sense, the spectrum of audiences related to the ecosystem in which *Al Qaeda* could grow and form into an organisation (by understanding, sympathising or supporting). To understand the effects of securitization efforts in the *Al Qaeda* narrative, it is clearly necessary to keep these differentiated audiences in mind. The more congruence there is regarding social structure, practices and events between the securitizing actor and various audiences, as they drive or enable securitization efforts, the more actively the causal complex works to affect a social reality in a particular way.

For those who became members of *Al Qaeda*, and even more for the executioners of particular attacks, the idea of securitization was clearly applicable. With respect to groups of Arabs and Muslims, in contrast, one could challenge whether they constituted a moral audience in terms of this same securitization concept. To what extent were some of the protesters merely in need of an anti-American hero figure, which was handed to them via pan-Arabic media? The US security practices that influenced the *Al Qaeda* narrative, as discussed in the previous section, were only some of the many causal or driving factors at play. For Muslims and Arabs who felt more distant to the Salafi jihadism voiced by Bin Laden, such as some of the Palestinians protesting and fighting against Israel, US security practices targeting Bin Laden created effects that *Al Qaeda* had difficulty achieving on its own. However, despite expressions of understanding and sympathy in Palestine, Pakistan and elsewhere, and perhaps some additional financial donations, it seems a long trajectory from voicing sympathy to becoming an *Al Qaeda* member. Among Salafi jihadi groups or those already training in Afghanistan, American Middle East policies, and particularly the military strikes on Afghanistan, Sudan and Iraq, are more likely to have been a driving factor in the increase in *Al Qaeda* members. However, as the bombing of the USS *Cole* demonstrated, *Al Qaeda*'s own actions were similarly important for the narrative.

Despite the 'international fame' Bin Laden had gained in the late 1990s and the increased number of jihadis in the training camps, the recruitment of members, the organisation of attacks, and the preparation of fighters came down to the intensive personal interaction, influencing and peer pressure between cadre and individual executioners. It was a small number of fanatics who were willing to conduct attacks regardless of wider Muslim audience assent. Rather than confirming institutionalised power relations (as with the United States), the reputation of Bin Laden and the identity of his emerging organisation was being established as a distinct variation within, or better against, the dominant current of the Salafi jihadi social order. The *Al Qaeda* narrative served to favour conditions for this with regard to a spectrum of audiences: among some, securitization efforts increased support, while for others it resulted more in an enlargement of understanding or sympathy. In this respect, the *Al Qaeda* narrative can be perceived as multi-consequential as well.

ACN: A CONTRIBUTION TO INTELLIGENCE STUDIES

How can we relate this research to relevant debates in intelligence studies? There are different views on the nature of intelligence and the types of processes and activities that are involved.[47] This section considers ACN in terms of both the study of and the study for intelligence. The former refers to intelligence as phenomenon, while the latter focuses on intelligence as practice. What does this research contribute to intelligence studies? And what is the value of ACN to intelligence professionals? From a reflexivist perspective such a divide makes less sense as it backgrounds the socio-political and cultural situatedness of intelligence.

Intelligence studies is a relatively young and very much developing academic discipline in its own right. It has been called the missing dimension of international relations, and for good reason.[48] Throughout history, states have wrapped intelligence reporting and activities in veils of secrecy. It was only after scandals and through the work of review and oversight committees, such as the US Rockefeller, Pike and Church committees in the 1970s, that historians and other academics gained access to large amounts of data in the United States. Similar developments took place in other countries.[49] It was mostly in the 1980s and onwards that academic contributions to intelligence studies significantly increased in the United States, the United Kingdom, Canada and some European countries.[50] To this day, historians continue to form an important part of the intelligence studies forefront, discovering new information as archives are opened to the public. Besides the study of intelligence history, intelligence organisations (their collection, analysis, dissemination, and counterintelligence and covert activities) have received increasing scholarly interest, particularly from former practitioners who became scholars to provide intelligence education for new generations. Their approaches have been based on the dominant positivist empiricist paradigm.

Among the topics receiving less attention in Intelligence studies is theory.[51] Some descriptive and normative theorising efforts have been made recently, but they still echo some of the early work of American intelligence practitioner-scholars Sherman Kent and Willmoore Kendall in the 1950s.[52] Overall, fundamental or philosophical theorising in intelligence studies remains scarce. Intelligence Studies has remained underdeveloped or relatively unaffected by the 'great debates' on constitution and causation that have characterised international relations in general, and intelligence-related subfields such as security studies in particular.[53] Rather than reliving those debates, intelligence studies can learn from the contemporary debate in international relations. In challenging dominant positivist thinking, critical and reflexivist approaches in intelligence studies provide valuable additions to the study of intelligence as phenomenon and as practice. In line with earlier work, perhaps this book will also further the development of a 'linguistic turn' in intelligence studies.[54] For one thing, this research has shown that a methodology can be scientific, logically sound and practical, without directly delivering 'objective' proof of improved accuracy.[55] It has shed more light on the abductive nature of intelligence analysis.

This book has substantiated that the processes of policymaking and intelligence analysis of complex intelligence problems are inextricably intertwined through multi-causality and multi-consequentiality of statements and actions. On theoretical grounds, the plural and integrative analytical approach of ACN contests the proximity hypothesis in intelligence studies, which holds that 'greater distance between intelligence and policy produces more accurate but less influential products'.[56] Due to increased uncertainty and the complexity of both the intelligence process and its environment, the notional red line that has often so explicitly been drawn in the United States between the intelligence community and policymakers has in fact proven to be a Fata Morgana. If it ever existed, it was permanently erased after the end of the Cold War. Or was it? Depending on the frame adopted for intelligence problems, as either a solvable 'puzzle' or a complex intelligence problem, this remains to be seen.[57] Intelligence organisations will continue to be tasked with solving specific questions that have verifiable 'factual' answers. For example, in support of US policymaking, this might involve the assessment of Chinese business activities in Africa or the operational status of the Chinese Air Force. Strategic warning can be provided by monitoring the development of an adversary's new type of military capability. National security can be protected by countering espionage. However, it must be noted that, eventually, all puzzles are embedded in wider complex intelligence problems. Does relevant business in Africa also include cultural influence through restaurant chains? What is military capability in the light of the adversaries' powers and policies? Or when does information gathering at universities or essential businesses become espionage?

The reflexivist theoretical considerations that underlie this book do not imply that there is no place for puzzle-solving in intelligence organisations, but the idea is advanced that cooperative sense-making needs attention.[58] Problem-framing and analysis cannot be separated; intelligence requirements, the definition of intelligence problems and consumer action perspectives all influence each other. Also related to making distinctions between clearly defined puzzles and complex mysteries is how one conceives the task of intelligence organisations and what the politicisation or manipulation of information entails.[59] A continuous dialogue is required between producers and consumers of intelligence at the working level as part of an ongoing organisation process of flexible planning and integrated policy–intelligence analysis, precisely to produce intelligence that is useful and weighs action perspectives. Proximity and dialogue do not necessarily equate to politicised intelligence in the sense that knowledge is actively distorted to achieve specific political goals. Both intelligence analysis and policymaking involve forms of interpretivism. Interaction and dialogue increase intersubjectivity and widen mutual understanding.

The interwovenness of intelligence and policy is clearly manifest as policymakers use narratives for strategic communication, and to conduct policies and direct actions that affect external threats and complex intelligence problems. By following the securitization logic and defining an enemy, statements and actions against a threat can have counterproductive consequences – for example, as shown in the case studies, by strengthening the narrative of the adversary. Developments in one's own political context, processes of self-identification, and strategic narratives cannot be separated from intelligence requirements and analysis. Another presumption of ACN is that intelligence analysis partly generates its own 'basic analytic reality' as well, all as a means of sense-making. The position of the analyst needs to be explicitly problematised regarding whether he or she can serve as a situated critical interpreter. Critical peer-reviewing remains of essence, as does openness to dialogue with others, such as outside experts. It is an overall team effort of intelligence and policy professionals and other trusted outside subject-matter experts that is required for a comprehensive comparative analysis of narratives. As such, the ACN methodology answers the call to explain why and how intelligence analysis should be better incorporated into decision-making.[60] It is a way to discuss assumptions, data, interpretation, logic, argumentation and assessments more explicitly at the working level. The approach also favours institutionalisation of cooperation in networks and joint organisational bodies.

What is foreseeable is that ACN could flourish particularly well in environments that adhere to a more joint approach to intelligence, such as with the British doctrine on understanding.[61] To an extent, there is some truth to critique that incorporating a critical reflexivist approach such as ACN in (stove-piped US) intelligence organisations might encounter difficulties with respect to accommodation.[62] Are intelligence consumers willing to expose their strategic narratives to integrated analysis, and, for example, consider critique on them from micro narratives? Would the intelligence (and policy) leadership allow networking between policy and intelligence professionals, and other trusted experts outside the intelligence community, to enable ACN? And are intelligence professionals willing and able to adopt the NAF and its theoretical underpinnings? These are relevant questions, and some points are addressed further on in this chapter. However, such concerns do not render the methodology itself irrelevant. That would be putting the cart before the horse.

Much has been said in intelligence studies on the fundamental complexity and uncertainty characterising the intelligence process and its environment. Apart from organising and producing intelligence, some agencies also engage in covert activities. The production of secret propaganda (and countering such efforts of adversaries) is also part of the intelligence domain.[63] In a broader sense, overt, discrete and covert influence operations are part of a government's foreign and domestic policies.[64] The armed forces, diplomatic corps, think tanks and others conduct a range of operations, for example, through public diplomacy, civil–military 'hearts and minds' operations in mission areas, psychological operations and deception operations. Throughout history, intelligence has been a significant part of such practices.[65] As a result of the information revolution and processes of globalisation, corporations and other non-governmental entities are also increasingly involved with these types of activities.[66]

How does ACN relate to this? Intelligence is not about speaking or finding the ultimate truth, but about identifying and understanding (effects of) various meanings in context, attributed by relevant entities to events. It is about recognising the fundamental idea that 'if men define situations as real, they are real in their consequences'.[67] What are the most relevant or influential 'truths' and how do they relate to the wider social and material world? This puts discussions on 'fake news' or propaganda in a different light. In some intelligence literature on information operations, propaganda is regarded as 'poisonous narratives' that work to 'subvert' reality and 'call into question the foundation of knowledge'.[68] But in essence, propaganda is an effort to shape reality, bring about change in power relations, and influence social orders through the articulation of a narrative.[69] ACN is a way of charting intersecting narratives and evaluating tensions and inconsistencies with regard to the content and context of those narratives. Can sudden changes of storylines be explained or understood? What entities influence narratives the most, for example, through reproduction and re-contextualisation? ACN feeds discussion on what truths, actors and audiences are most relevant to complex intelligence problems. The increasing volume and complexity of the information environment, driven exponentially by technological developments, makes selecting texts and identifying narratives more challenging. Enlarging the number of micro narratives helps to evaluate the significance of identified macro narratives and to analyse the workings and consistency of securitization efforts in those narratives. By charting the narratives most relevant to complex intelligence problems, ACN has the potential to support planning and evaluation of some covert intelligence operations such as secret propaganda.

Methods for analysing intelligence problems

Another aim of this book was to demonstrate the usefulness of ACN to intelligence analysis as a practice of sense-making, hopefully also encouraging wider reflexivism among professionals. Three issues with regard to methodologies and methods for intelligence analysis continue to surface in the intelligence studies literature. First, various scholars argue that while social science approaches have their value for intelligence analysis, it remains problematic to translate academic insights to the practice of intelligence.[70] They hold that established scientific methodologies and methods do not receive the attention they deserve in intelligence analysis literature. This book has demonstrated the opposite. Secondly, while structured analytic techniques (SATs) have been regarded with high esteem 'by lore and assertion' in the intelligence community, it has remained challenging to assess the efficacy of these methods.[71] However, renewed interest has generated some valuable insights and considerations with respect to the use of SATs that will be discussed in this section.[72] Finally, the systematic and effective adoption of methods in intelligence organisations is regarded as difficult. How does ACN relate to the issue of efficacy?

It has been discussed elsewhere how ACN differs from several SATs.[73] This section considers where and how ACN relates and could contribute to established SATs. Like other SATs, the method derived from ACN externalises, organises and evaluates analytic thinking.[74] There are two approaches to evaluating the benefits for intelligence analysis: logical reasoning and empirical research. In the SATs literature, logical reasoning is tied to psychological research into the limitations of human perception, memory and thought.[75] These insights correspond to Richards Heuer's highly influential work *Psychology of Intelligence Analysis*.[76] The book was based on philosophical and theoretical reasoning as a validation for its claims of appropriateness. The ACN logic outlined in this book allows for the identification of fundamentally different narratives. It also relates threat articulation in narratives to power relations and social or institutional roles, and factors in processes of self-identification. After exposing ACN to the practice of intelligence analysis, it will become possible to further evaluate how ACN performs (and profits from classified information) with regard to various types of complex intelligence problems. Much remains to research: how does the methodology suit analysis with global strategic, transnational, regional, domestic or local problems? Could ACN (unexpectedly) also contribute to ad hoc crisis support, or only to long-term strategic decision-making? And could other intelligence consumers besides policymakers, such as domestic law enforcement agencies or deployed military task forces, benefit from ACN? In theory, the methodology can be applied in all cases. Defining the basic analytic narratives is a matter of abductively outlining the most relevant contextual level and focus.

It is fruitful to clarify how ACN would fit with established SATs. Similar to red-hat analysis,[77] ACN can be viewed as a methodology for imaginative alternative analysis that aims to widen cultural empathy and understanding of a problem. Its goal is also to counter mirror-imaging (projecting one's mental models on the other), attribution error (overestimating traits while underestimating situations), and confirmation bias (confirming pre-existing beliefs on outcome). A particularisation of red-hat analysis is the technique 'four ways of seeing'.[78] This 'tool' distinguishes in four quadrants how X views X, X views

Y, Y views Y and Y views X (here X represents 'self' while Y represents an 'other'). It is noted that 'there are seldom only two actors in a system' and 'all the actors' perceptions and inter-relationships with the system are required to provide context for analysis' as 'all actors hold values, beliefs and perceptions they view as right or rational', including external audiences.[79] However, beyond the notion that 'thorough research should be conducted to complete the analysis of perspectives', the theoretical guidance is missing on how to accomplish this.[80] The ACN methodology provides theoretical depth in this regard.

ACN focuses on narratives at various analytical levels (macro and micro) to complement the overall analysis. In this book, the critical perspective in the micro narrative, the last case study, most explicitly revealed tensions and inconsistencies. This revealed the potential to add multiple so-called 'commentators on discursive tennis matches', also as a corrective measure against tunnel vision based on one's own strategic narrative. More research into ACN is required to assess what number of narratives (at what level) is optimal for what type of intelligence problem – with a minimum requirement of three, of course. Another difference compared with red-hat analysis is that ACN is not primarily aimed at estimating the future development of narratives, but at describing and evaluating them as multiple perspectives in the past and present. A valuable insight from red teaming practices concerns the lack of representativeness encountered with respect to the intended target entity.[81] This illustrates how the 'situatedness' of analysts and experts will also be a central concern to ACN practice.

Contrary to the design of this study, in which a single researcher drew on a variety of available historiographic literature *ex post, ex durante* ACN is best performed by several professionals and experts in diverse teams. As they group themselves and concentrate on the narratives within the social orders that relate to their skills and expertise, in its process there are also similarities with the established practice of 'team A/B analysis'.[82] For both, groups of people seek to interpret the same events and data from a different angle. However, in the case of ACN, one of those is one's own strategic narrative. A certain degree of competition between professionals and experts clustered around different narratives can perhaps stimulate alternative analysis. But ACN is eventually also about integration, identifying dynamics between narratives, and discussion and dialogue among ACN participants. There are also parallels with joint scenario-building, as policy officers and intelligence analysts work together to identify the most important elements and entities that shape social reality. Like scenarios with regard to the future, the identification of various narratives provides a chart or handle for analysts and decision-makers to conceptualise and discuss how (past and current) events and circumstances can be situated and reflected upon. Scenario analysis entered the analysis toolkit as a supportive technique in the analytical process. As a result of the joint effort, in practice some decision-makers request that the results of the scenario analysis be disseminated as a product.[83] Incorporating policy advice in the analysis, something unheard of for traditional intelligence agencies, might not even be such a bridge too far. Whereas scenarios are used to consider multiple plausible futures, ACN reflects on the past and present, thereby extending American futurist Peter Schwartz's observation that 'the future is plural' with 'so is the past and present'.[84]

Analysis of competing hypothesis (ACH) is one of the techniques most highly advertised in intelligence and praised for its unbiased methodology.[85] Through structured brainstorming and other techniques, various hypothetical explanations are identified with regard to the development of an intelligence problem. Consequently, data on events, entities and circumstances is considered in terms of its inconsistency with each of these hypotheses. This ranks the hypotheses in terms of which are most likely. ACH's popularity and structured step-by-step procedure have stimulated numerous efforts to develop software and automate the technique. However, these efforts have also received structural (epistemological) critique, and for good reason. There is an inherent instability to the unstructured nature of individuating and interpreting the meaning of the evidence that serves as input, which in turn results in differences in output.[86]

Based on an extensive number of exercises, it has been concluded that participants disagree on how to rate evidence (input) in about 20–30 per cent of cases, usually related to differences in interpretation.[87] However, discussion with colleagues moderates the overall effect of this factor on the output of the ACH analysis. A focus on the development of software enhances a false sense of objectivity when the evidential basis for the methodology is not considered more extensively. This argument is applicable to all SATs. As several scholars have recently stated, they 'ultimately rely on subjective interpretation of analytic inputs' and hence inherit the danger of becoming 'vehicles transporting subjectivity' that 'dress up subjective judgements in a cloak of objectivity'.[88]

In modelling SATs, simplification and automation are never meant to become goals in themselves. The discussion of SATs above indicates that adopting the ACN logic could be a useful addition for intelligence analysts as it substantiates interpretations of various meanings attributed to events and circumstances. This can serve as input for other SATs, such as ACH. In general, the value and position of ACN in intelligence has to be further established through the multi-method daily practice of intelligence analysis. What is clear is that no SAT is unequivocal. The challenges identified for ACN in this chapter do not stand in the way of further development of the ACN methodology and derived method to become part of the practice of intelligence.

Of course, with respect to organisational culture, institutional networks and technical infrastructure, there will be many issues to deal with. It has frequently been noted that intelligence analysts meet new methodologies with scepticism. There is often a lack of time to familiarise oneself extensively and systematically incorporate them in the intelligence system.[89] Analysts need to comprehend the philosophical and theoretical foundation of ACN to understand the strength and limitations of the methodology. Different from the case studies conducted in this book, intelligence agencies have less literature at their disposal. But instead they have various types of classified information and intelligence available.

Another organisational problem often identified in the intelligence literature is how overconfidence is promoted and stimulated over more rigorous consideration of alternatives.[90] Diversification of meanings is not preferred, but it is cultural empathy for strategic entities and imagination that helps to understand complex intelligence problems better.[91] In the light of a broader discussion on the necessity of a (r)evolution of intelligence, suggestions to increase liaison positions and build trusted networks to tap into expertise, such as at universities, non-governmental organisations or other agencies, would probably stimulate putting the ACN methodology into practice.[92] Not only in terms of cultural knowledge and understanding, but also with respect to social science methodologies, as ACN can work in different forms and have different foci. Sharing classified intelligence with certain 'situated interpreters' from outside the intelligence organisation will likely cause some bureaucratic problems that have to be overcome, but do not form an essential obstacle.

All in all, there is no unbridgeable theoretical divide that separates a method derived from ACN from established SATs. From a critical realist perspective, positivist truth claims substantiated through the use of SATs only become more relative. Naturally, there are various aspects that need to be addressed to practically develop the ACN methodology into an established method for intelligence analysis, but this goal is worth of pursuing. So far, the research effort and case studies have certainly been promising. Whatever doubts conservative critics might have regarding validity and efficacy, the ACN methodology is grounded in philosophical reasoning that aligns with Aristotle's thinking on constitution and causation. ACN rests on deeper theoretical ground than some of the practical approaches in intelligence that aim to externalise analytic thinking to separate facts from intuitive assumptions, and that have been declared the 'gold standard' for intelligence.[93]

Reflexivism and Critical Intelligence Studies

This and other interpretivist, reflexivist or critical contributions to the intelligence literature also prompt the question of what broader academic status these approaches have in intelligence studies. Is it viable to argue for explicitly articulating a critical strand or subfield? What benefits would this have? As with critical strands in other related fields in international relations, such as critical security studies, critical terrorism studies or critical military studies, critical approaches to intelligence hardly represent a single 'school of thought' and are quite diverse. However, an explicit critical or reflexivist intelligence studies project could further clarify and improve theoretical debate in intelligence studies by attracting more scholarly interest. Many intelligence scholars have refrained from articulating their theoretical roots in philosophical terms. Strictly defining a community of scholars and classifying others as positivists should not be a primary concern in itself. Instead of introducing fault lines between positivists and post-positivists, and among interpretivists and post-positivists, there needs to be renewed discussion on what connects various approaches and how they complement each other's perspectives. The approach in this book has acknowledged but also relativised both empiricism and interpretivism.

A reflexivist and critical research agenda presupposes cooperation among scholars engaged in the study of and/or for intelligence. Focal issues on the agenda could include inquiries into the boundaries of intelligence as a form of information, organisation and activity. The democratisation of technology enables privatisation and individualisation of intelligence activities among companies, non-governmental organisations and (collectives of) citizens. Is it possible for national intelligence to cease to exist? And what justifies or necessitates the definition of new 'INTs' such as social media intelligence as a distinct discipline? What responsibility do intelligence organisations have in filtering fake news or foreign propaganda efforts in society? Reflexivist and critical approaches can provide interesting perspectives on the future of intelligence. As such, this book has also directed attention to a possibility for the growth of intelligence studies as an academic subfield of international relations.

NOTES

1. For example, Balzacq, Léonard and Ruzicka, '"Securitization" Revisited'; Côté, 'Agents Without Agency'; Senia Febrica, 'Refining the Role of Audience in Securitization: Southeast Asia's Fight Against Terrorism', in Scott Nicholas Romaniuk et al. (eds), *The Palgrave Handbook of Global Counterterrorism Policy* (London: Palgrave Macmillan, 2017), 703–31.
2. Bergen, *The Osama bin Laden I Know*, 407.
3. The pragmatic redefinition that the United Kingdom did not provide a real threat as it only had a small presence in Saudi Arabia was identified through the critical terrorism narrative. This was a consequence of the text selection for each case. As the statement was made by Bin Laden (although for a Western audience) it is included in the overview of the *Al Qaeda* narrative.
4. Wright, *The Looming Tower*, 309.
5. Clarke, *Against All Enemies*, 198.
6. Williams, 'The Continuing Evolution of Securitization Theory', 212.
7. Balzacq, 'The Three Faces of Securitization'.
8. Balzacq, *Securitization Theory*, 49.

9. Referring to the philosophical theoretical levels of real, actual and empirical as described in Chapter 1, see Fairclough, Jessop and Sayer, 'Critical Realism and Semiosis', 204.
10. Balzacq, Léonard and Ruzicka, '"Securitization" Revisited', 494.
11. For example, Thierry Balzacq and Stefano Guzzini, 'Introduction: What Kind of Theory – If Any – is Securitization?' *International Relations* 29(1) (2015): 97–102; Thierry Balzacq, 'The "Essence" of Securitization: Theory, Ideal Type, and a Sociological Science of Security', *International Relations* 29(1) (2015): 103–13; Michael Williams, 'Securitization as Political Theory: the Politics of the Extraordinary', *International Relations* 29(1) (2015): 114–20; Ole Wæver, 'The Theory Act: Responsibility and Exactitude as Seen from Securitization', *International Relations* 29(1) (2015): 121–7; Heikki Patomäki, 'Absenting the Absence of Future Dangers and Structural Transformations in Securitization Theory', *International Relations* 29(1) (2015): 128–36; Balzacq, *Contesting Security*; Balzacq, Léonard and Ruzicka, '"Securitization" Revisited'.
12. Chaïm Perelman and Lucie Olbrechts-Tytecka, *The New Rhetoric: a Treatise on Argumentation* (Notre Dame, IN: University of Notre Dame Press, 1969), 4; as in Balzacq, 'The Three Faces of Securitization', 172.
13. Balzacq, Léonard and Ruzicka, '"Securitization" Revisited', 520.
14. Balzacq, 'The Three Faces of Securitization', 192.
15. Although a thorough review lies beyond the scope of this research, another possible approach (although less specifically related to threats) might be social movement theory. This entails the study of collective mobilisation processes. Its conceptual framework distinguishes a 'state of crisis', inequality or relative deprivation, and the attempted mobilisation of material, moral and cultural 'resources' in the light of 'solutions' articulated by 'activists'. See, for example, Nanninga, 'Jihadism and Suicide Attacks'.
16. Ibid.
17. For example, see Judith Tinnes, 'Bibliography, Al-Qaeda and its Affiliated Organizations, Part 1', *Perspectives on Terrorism* 11(6) (2017).
18. Alex P. Schmid, 'Public Opinion Survey Data to Measure Sympathy and Support for Islamist Terrorism: a Look at Muslim Opinions on Al Qaeda and IS', ICCT Research Paper, February 2017.
19. Lo, *Understanding Muslim Discourse*, 86; Miller, *The Audacious Ascetic*, location 631.
20. Miller, *The Audacious Ascetic*, location 5213.
21. Ibid.; Thomas Bauer, 'Die Poesie des Terrorismus', in Andreas K. W. Meayer (ed.), *Siebenjahrbuch Deutsche Oper Berlin MMIV–MMXI* (Berlin: Nicolaische Verlagsbuchhandlung, 2011), 125. Also see Saskia Lutzinger, *Die Sicht des Anderen. Eine qualitative Studie zu Biographien von Extremisten und Terroristen* (Cologne: Luchterhand, 2010), as in Said, 'Hymns (Nasheeds)'.
22. Miller, *The Audacious Ascetic*, location 4953.
23. Sahih International, 'Surah Al-Munafiqun'.
24. Wright, *The Looming Tower*, 165–84.
25. Fisk, 'Middle East Crisis, Arab World'.

26. Wright, *The Looming Tower*, 242.
27. Ibrahim Barzak, 'Hamas Leader Denies bin Laden Link', *Associated Press*, 23 August 2000.
28. Burke, *Al Qaeda*, 12, 296.
29. Silvia Ferabolli, *Arab Regionalism: a Post-Structural Perspective* (London: Routledge, 2015), 167–70.
30. Marc Lynch, 'Watching al-Jazeera', *The Wilson Quarterly* 29(3) (2005): 36–45.
31. Bruce B. Lawrence, 'Muslim Engagement with Injustice and Violence', in Mark Juergensmeyer, Margo Kitts and Michael Jerryson (eds). *Violence and the World's Religious Traditions: An Introduction* (Oxford: Oxford University Press, 2017), 168.
32. See, for example, Kepel, *Jihad*, 219.
33. Quintan Wiktorowicz, *The Management of Islamic Activism: Salafis, the Muslim Brotherhood, and State Power in Jordan* (Albany, NY: State University of New York Press, 2001),136.
34. Lawrence, *Messages to the World*, 31–2; Atwan, 'Bin Ladin interviewed on *jihad* against US'.
35. For example, Soufan, *The Black Banners*, 56–74.
36. Bergen, *The Osama bin Laden I Know*, 85–6; Hegghammer, 'Terrorist Recruitment and Radicalization in Saudi Arabia'.
37. Soufan, *The Black Banners*, xvii–xix.
38. Atwan, *The Secret History of Al Qaeda*, location 1056.
39. Burke, *Al Qaeda*, 85.
40. Soufan, *The Black Banners*, 151.
41. Ibid., 65.
42. Bergen, *The Osama bin Laden I Know*, 263.
43. For example, see Bergen, *The Osama bin Laden I Know*, 102, 263–4, 402–7, 411; Soufan, *The Black Banners*, 65, 151, 359; Burke, *Al Qaeda*, 85; Wright, *The Looming Tower*, 473. In contrast, Rohan Gunaratna made rather crude calculations, concluding that there were at least several thousand *Al Qaeda* members, Gunaratna, *Inside Al Qaeda*.
44. Bergen, *The Osama bin Laden I Know*, 411.
45. Ibid., 424.
46. Ibid., 263.
47. See de Werd, 'Critical Intelligence Studies?' for an overview of various approaches to intelligence, and a discussion of critical, reflexivist and interpretivist contributions to intelligence literature.
48. For example, Andrew and Dilks, *The Missing Dimension*.
49. Farson, 'Schools of Thought'.
50. Johnson, 'The Development of Intelligence Studies'.
51. Ibid., p. 10.
52. For example, in Gill, Marrin and Pythian, Intelligence *Theory*; Sherman Kent, *Strategic Intelligence*; Willmoore Kendall, '"The Function of Intelligence Analysis", Review of Strategic Intelligence for American World Policy, by Sherman Kent', *World Politics* 1(4) (1949): 542–52.

53. Sims, 'Theory and Philosophy of Intelligence', 48; on these debates, for example, see Alexander Wendt, 'On Constitution and Causation in International Relations', *Review of International Studies* 24(5) (1998): 101–18; Christian Reus-Smit and Duncan Snidal (eds), *The Oxford Handbook of International Relations* (Oxford: Oxford University Press, 2010).

54. Der Derian, *Antidiplomacy*; Bean, 'Rhetorical and Critical/Cultural Intelligence Studies', 499–500; Bean, *No More Secrets*; Woodard, 'Tasting the Forbidden Fruit'; Eriksson, *Swedish Military Intelligence*; Iver Neumann, 'Returning Practice to the Linguistic Turn: the Case of Diplomacy', *Millennium* 35(3) (2002): 677–701; Walter Carlsnaes, Thomas Risse and Beth A. Simmons (eds), *Handbook of International Relations*, 2nd edn (London: Sage, 2013).

55. Marrin, *Improving Intelligence Analysis*, 33.

56. Marrin, 'Revisiting Intelligence and Policy', 2.

57. Treverton, *Reshaping National Intelligence*, 1–19; Joseph S. Nye Jr., 'Peering into the Future', *Foreign Affairs* 77(4) (1994): 82–93; Gregory Treverton, 'Estimating beyond the Cold War', *Defense Intelligence Journal* 3(2) (1994): 5–20.

58. Similar to Moore, *Sensemaking*, and Warren Fishbein and Gregory Treverton, 'Making Sense of Transnational Threats', *Sherman Kent Center for Intelligence Analysis Occasional Papers*, 3 (2004): 1, but on different, theoretical grounds.

59. Hastedt, 'The Politics of Intelligence'; Marrin, 'Rethinking Analytic Politicization'; Eric Eric J. Dahl, 'Why Won't They Listen? Comparing Receptivity toward Intelligence at Pearl Harbor and Midway', *Intelligence and National Security* 28(1) (2013): 68–90; Woodard, 'Tasting the Forbidden Fruit'.

60. Stephen Marrin, 'Why Intelligence Analysis has Limited Influence on American Foreign Policy', APSA 2014 Annual Meeting Paper, 5 August 2014.

61. Ministry of Defence, 'Joint Doctrine Publication 04: Understanding and Decision-making', (London: Ministry of Defence, 2016).

62. A point raised by Hamilton Bean to the author.

63. Propaganda is commonly differentiated between disseminating biased information (white); pressuring, bribing or influencing entities to adapt their story (grey); and strategically inserting false information to change perceptions and elicit a particular response (black). As in Michael A. Turner, 'An Appraisal of the Effects of Secret Propaganda', in Loch K. Johnson (ed.), *Strategic Intelligence, vol. 3: Covert Action, Behind the Veils of Secret Foreign Policy* (London: Praeger, 2007), 107–17.

64. Ibid.; Douglas C. Lovelace Jr., *Terrorism: Commentary on Security Documents, Hybrid Warfare and the Gray Zone Threat*, vol. 141 (Oxford: Oxford University Press, 2016); Michael John-Hopkins, *The Rule of Law in Crisis and Conflict Grey Zones: Regulating the Use of Violence in a Global Information Environment* (Abingdon: Routledge, 2017).

65. For example, see Richard James Aldrich, Gary D. Rawnsley and Ming-Yeh T. Rawnsley (eds), *The Clandestine Cold War in Asia, 1945–65: Western Intelligence, Propaganda and Special Operations* (London: Frank Cass, 2000); Robert Dover and Michael S. Goodman, *Spinning Intelligence: Why Intelligence Needs the Media, Why the Media Needs Intelligence* (London: Hurst, 2009).

66. William Dinan and David Miller (eds). *Thinker, Faker, Sinner, Spy: Corporate PR and the Assault on Democracy* (London: Pluto, 2007).

67. William Isaac Thomas and Dorothy Swaine Thomas, *The Child in America: Behavior Problems and Programs* (New York: Knopf, 1928), 571–2.

68. For example, Fitzgerald and Brantly, 'Subverting Reality'.

69. Anne Morelli, *Elementaire principes van oorlogspropaganda, bruikbaar in geval van koude, warme of lauwe oorlog...* (Antwerp: EPO, 2003).

70. For example, Michael Landon-Murray, 'Putting a Little More "Time" into Strategic Intelligence Analysis', *International Journal of Intelligence and Counterintelligence* 30(4) (2017): 785–809; Stephen Marrin, 'Intelligence Studies Centers: Making Scholarship on Intelligence Analysis Useful', *Intelligence and National Security* 27(3) (2012): 398–422.

71. Marrin, *Improving Intelligence Analysis*, 33.

72. Chang et al., 'Restructuring Structured Analytic Techniques'; Nicholas Jones, 'Critical Epistemology for Analysis of Competing Hypotheses', *Intelligence and National Security* 33(2) (2018): 273–89; Stephen J. Coulthart, 'An Evidence-Based Evaluation of 12 Core Structured Analytic Techniques', *International Journal of Intelligence and Counterintelligence* 30(2) (2017): 368–91; Stephen Artner, Richard S. Girven and James B. Bruce, *Assessing the Value of Structured Analytic Techniques* (Washington, DC: RAND, 2016).

73. De Werd, 'Critical Intelligence Studies?'.

74. Heuer and Pherson, *Structured Analytic Techniques*; Sarah M. Beebe and Randolph H. Pherson, *Cases in Intelligence Analysis: Structured Analytic Techniques in Action* (Washington, DC: CQ Press, 2012).

75. Ibid.; Daniel Kahneman, *Thinking, Fast and Slow* (London: Alan Lane, 2011).

76. Heuer, *Psychology of Intelligence Analysis*.

77. Red-hat analysis or red teaming is performed by a group (associated with a 'blue' entity) that is assigned to take on the perspective of a ('red') adversary when viewing a problem and projecting possible courses of action, asking how the adversary would respond to developments and actions. There lies an implicit danger in the division between 'red' and 'blue'. Red implies an opposition to the blue frame, similar to black versus white, and it is a characterisation that is attributed from the 'blue' perspective. For both the same issues, is there reason for conflict, for example? Heuer and Pherson, *Structured Analytic Techniques*, 243.

78. UFMS, *The Applied Critical Thinking Handbook 7.0*, 77.

79. Ibid.

80. Ibid.

81. Rob Johnston (ed.), *Analytic Culture in US Intelligence: An Ethnographic Study* (Washington, DC: CIA Center for the Study of Intelligence, 2001), 81–2; Chang et al, 'Restructuring Structured Analytic Techniques', 347; Micah Zenko, *Red Team: How to Succeed by Thinking Like the Enemy* (New York: Basic Books, 2015).

82. Groups of analysts are formed and try to make the best case for different points of view or hypotheses with respect to the available data, providing policymakers with multiple assessments. Yet such analyses often lack the theoretical considerations that guide the *selection* of various points of view, and they have been known to

enable policymakers to follow a preferred (or predefined) policy. US CIA, *A Tradecraft Primer*; Gordon R. Mitchell, 'Team B Intelligence Coups', *Quarterly Journal of Speech* 92(2) (2006): 144–73.

83. This has been the case in, for example, the Netherlands.
84. Peter Schwartz, *The Art of the Long View: Planning for the Future in an Uncertain World* (New York: Doubleday, 1991).
85. Heuer, *Psychology of Intelligence Analysis*, 95–110.
86. For example, Jones, 'Critical Epistemology for Analysis of Competing Hypotheses'.
87. Heuer and Pherson, *Structured Analytic Techniques*, 311–12.
88. Chang et al., 'Restructuring Structured Analytic Techniques', 345.
89. Marrin, *Improving Intelligence Analysis*, 32.
90. Ibid.; Chang et al. 'Restructuring Structured Analytic Techniques'.
91. As discussed in Marrin, *Improving Intelligence Analysis*, 49–52.
92. Lahneman, 'The Need for a New Intelligence Paradigm'; Lahneman, *Keeping U.S. Intelligence Effective*.
93. US CIA, *A Tradecraft Primer*; UFMS, *The Applied Critical Thinking Handbook*, 77.

SELECTED BIBLIOGRAPHY

Agrell, Wilhelm and Gregory F. Treverton, *National Intelligence and Science: Beyond the Great Divide in Analysis and Policy* (Oxford: Oxford University Press, 2015).

Alshamsi, Mansoor J., *Islam and Political Reform in Saudi Arabia: the Quest for Political Change* (New York: Routledge, 2011).

Andrew, Christopher, 'Intelligence, International Relations and "Undertheorization"', *Intelligence and National Security* 19(2) (2004): 170–84.

Andrew, Christopher and David Dilks, *The Missing Dimension: Governments and Intelligence Communities in the Twentieth Century* (Campaign, IL: University of Illinois Press, 1984).

Aradau, Claudia, Jef Huysmans, Andrew Neal and Nadine Voelkner (eds), *Critical Security Methods: New Frameworks for Analysis*, 4th edn (New York: Routledge, 2015).

Artner, Stephen, Richard S. Girven and James B. Bruce, *Assessing the Value of Structured Analytic Techniques* (Washington, DC: RAND, 2016).

Atwan, Abdul Bari, *The Secret History of Al Qaeda*, Kindle edition (London: Saqi Books, 2008).

Aune, James and Martin J. Medhurst (eds), *The Prospect of Presidential Rhetoric* (Austin, TX: A&M University Press, 2008).

Azzam, Maha, 'The Gulf Crisis: Perceptions in the Muslim World', *International Affairs* 67(3) (1991): 473–85.

Baele, Stéphane J. and Catarina P. Thomson, 'An Experimental Agenda for Securitization Theory', *International Studies Review* 19 (2017): 646–66.

Bal, Mieke, *Narratology: Introduction to the Theory of Narrative* (Toronto: University of Toronto Press, 1997).

Balzacq, Thierry, 'The Three Faces of Securitization, Political Agency, Audience and Context', *European Journal of International Relations* 11(2) (2005): 171–201.

Balzacq, Thierry (ed.), *Securitization Theory: How Security Problems Emerge and Dissolve* (Abingdon: Routledge, 2011).

Balzacq, Thierry (ed.), *Contesting Security* (New York: Routledge, 2015).

Balzacq, Thierry, 'The "Essence" of Securitization: Theory, Ideal Type, and a Sociological Science of Security', *International Relations* 29(1) (2015): 103–13.

Balzacq, Thierry and Stefano Guzzini, 'Introduction: What Kind of Theory – If Any – is Securitization?' *International Relations* 29(1) (2015): 97–102.

Balzacq, Thierry, Sarah Léonard and Jan Ruzicka, '"Securitization" Revisited, Theory and Cases', *International Relations* 30(4) (2016): 494–531.

Bardes, Barbara A. and Robert W. Oldendick, *Public Opinion Measuring the American Mind*, 5th edn (London: Rowman & Littlefield, 2017).

Bardi, Mohammed Ali, 'A Systemic Functional Description of the Grammar of Arabic', PhD thesis, Macquarie University, Sydney, 2008.

Bean, Hamilton, 'Organizational Culture and US Intelligence Affairs', *Intelligence and National Security* 24(4) (2009): 479–98.

Bean, Hamilton, *No More Secrets: Open Source Information and the Reshaping of U.S. Intelligence* (Santa Barbara, CA: Praeger, 2011).

Bean, Hamilton, 'Rhetorical and Critical/Cultural Intelligence Studies', *Intelligence and National Security* 28(4) (2013): 495–519.

Bean, Hamilton, 'Intelligence Theory from the Margins: Questions Ignored and Debates Not Had', *Intelligence and National Security* 33(4) (2018): 527–40.

Beebe, Sarah M. and Randolph H. Pherson, *Cases in Intelligence Analysis: Structured Analytic Techniques in Action* (Washington, DC: CQ Press, 2012).

Bergen, Peter, *The Osama bin Laden I Know: An Oral History of al Qaeda's Leader* (New York: Simon & Schuster, 2006).

Bergen, Peter and Paul Cruickshank, 'Revisiting the Early Al Qaeda: Updated Account of its Formative Years', *Studies in Conflict and Terrorism* 35(1) (2012): 1–36.

Betts, Richard K., 'Politicization of Intelligence: Costs and Benefits', in Richard Betts and Thomas Mahnken (eds), *Paradoxes of Strategic Intelligence: Essays in Honour of Michael I. Handel* (London: Frank Cass, 2003), 57–76.

Betts, Richard K., *Enemies of Intelligence: Knowledge and Power in American National Security* (New York: Columbia University Press, 2007).

Bhaskar, Roy A. et al., *The Formation of Critical Realism: a Personal Perspective* (London: Routledge, 2008).

Bhaumik, Subir, 'Jihad or Joi Bangla, Bangladesh in Peril', in Jaideep Saikia and Ekatarina Stepanova (eds), *Terrorism: Patterns of Internationalization* (London: Sage, 2009), 71–92.

Blanc, Florent, 'Poking holes and spreading cracks in the wall', in Thierry Balzacq (ed.), *Contesting Security, Contesting Security* (New York: Routledge, 2015), 63–84.

Bonney, Richard, *Jihad: From Qu'ran to Bin Laden* (London: Palgrave Macmillan, 2004).

Booth, Ken (ed.), *Critical Security Studies and World Politics* (London: Lynne Rienner, 2004).

Booth, Ken, *Theory of World Security* (Cambridge: Cambridge University Press, 2007).

Bracken, Paul, 'Net Assessment: a Practical Guide', *Parameters* (2006): 90–100.

Brooke, Steven, 'Jihadist Strategic Debates before 9/11', *Studies in Conflict and Terrorism* 31(3) (2008): 201–26.

Brown, Jane D., Carlo R. Bybee, Stanley T. Wearden and Dulcie M. Straughan, 'Invisible Power: Newspaper News Sources and the Limits of Diversity', *Journalism Quarterly* 64(1) (1987): 45–54.

Brown, Vahid, *Cracks in the Foundation: Leadership Schisms in Al-Qa'ida from 1989–2006*, CTC Harmony Project (West Point, NY: CTC West Point, 2007).

Brown, Vahid, 'The Facade of Allegiance: Bin Ladin's Dubious Pledge to Mullah Omar', *CTC Sentinel* 3(1) (2010): 1–5.

Brown, Vahid, 'Classical and Global Jihad: Al-Qa'ida's Franchising Frustrations', in Assaf Moghadam and Brian Fishman (eds), *Fault Lines in Global Jihad: Organizational, Strategic, and Ideological Fissures* (New York: Routledge, 2011), 88–116.

Burke, Jason, *Al Qaeda* (London: Penguin, 2007).

Buzan, Barry, Ole Wæver and Jaap de Wilde, *Security: a New Framework for Analysis* (London: Lynne Rienner, 1998).

Buzan, Barry and Ole Waever, 'Macro-Securitization and Security Constellations: Reconsidering the Scale in Securitization Theory', *Review of International Studies* 35(2) (2009): 253–76.

C.A.S.E. Collective, 'Critical Approaches to Security in Europe: a Networked Manifesto', *Security Dialogue* 37(4) (2006): 443–87.

Callinicos, Alex, *Theories and Narratives: Reflections on the Philosophy of History* (Durham, NC: Duke University Press, 1995).

Campbell, David, *Writing Security: United States Foreign Policy and the Politics of Identity* (Minneapolis, MN: University of Minnesota Press, 1992).

Carlsnaes, Walter, Thomas Risse and Beth A. Simmons (eds), *Handbook of International Relations*, 2nd edn (London: Sage, 2013).

Castells, Manuel, *The Information Age: Economy, Society and Culture, the Power of Identity*, 2nd edn (Oxford: Blackwell, 2004).

Castells, Manuel and Gustavo Cardoso (eds), *The Network Society: From Knowledge to Policy* (Washington, DC: Johns Hopkins Center for Transatlantic Relations, 2005).

Cavelty, Myriam D. and Victor Mauer, 'Postmodern Intelligence: Strategic Warning in an Age of Reflexive Intelligence', *Security Dialogue* 40(2) (2009): 123–44.

Chang, Welton, Elissabeth Berdini, David R. Mandel and Philip E. Tetlock, 'Restructuring Structured Analytic Techniques in Intelligence', *Intelligence and National Security*, 33(3) (2018): 337–56.

Chouliaraki, Lilie and Norman Fairclough, *Discourse in Late Modernity: Rethinking Critical Discourse Analysis* (Edinburgh: Edinburgh University Press, 1999).

Clarke, Richard A., *Against All Enemies* (London: Free Press, 2004).

Clarke, Richard, *Your Government Failed You: Breaking the Cycle of National Security Disasters* (New York: HarperCollins, 2008).

Clinton, Bill, *My Life*, Kindle edn (New York: Knopf, 2004).

Coll, Steve, *Ghost Wars: the Secret History of the CIA, Afghanistan, and Bin Laden, from the Soviet Invasion to September 10, 2001* (New York: Penguin, 2004).

Cook, David, *Understanding Jihad*, 2nd edn (Berkeley, CA: University of California Press, 2015).

Côté, Adam, 'Agents Without Agency: Assessing the Role of the Audience in Securitization Theory', *Security Dialogue* 47(6) (2016): 541–58.

Coulthart, Stephen J., 'An Evidence-Based Evaluation of 12 Core Structured Analytic Techniques', *International Journal of Intelligence and Counterintelligence* 30(2) (2017): 368–91.

Crone, Patricia, *God's Rule: Government and Islam* (Princeton: Princeton University Press, 2004).

Cutting, Joan, *Pragmatics and Discourse: a Resource Book for Students* (Florence, KY: Routledge, 2002).

Dahl, Eric J., *Intelligence and Surprise Attack: Intelligence and Surprise Attack Failure and Success from Pearl Harbor to 9/11 and Beyond* (Washington, DC: Georgetown University Press, 2013).

Dahl, Eric J., 'Why Won't They Listen? Comparing Receptivity toward Intelligence at Pearl Harbor and Midway', *Intelligence and National Security* 28(1) (2013): 68–90.

Danermark, Berth, Mats Ekstrom, Liselotte Jakobsen and Jan Ch. Karlsson, *Explaining Society: Critical Realism in the Social Sciences* (New York: Routledge, 2002).

de Werd, Peter, 'Critical Intelligence Studies? A Contribution', *Journal of European and American Intelligence Studies* 1(1) (2018): 109–48.

Deacon, David, 'Yesterday's Papers and Today's Technology: Digital Newspaper Archives and "Push Button" Content Analysis', *European Journal of Communication* 22(5) (2007): 5–25.

Delcambre, Anne-Marie, *Inside Islam* (Milwaukee, WI: Marquette University Press, 2005).

Der Derian, James, *Antidiplomacy: Spies, Terror, Speed, and War* (Cambridge, MA: Blackwell, 1992).

Der Derian, James and Michael J. Shapiro (eds), *International/Intertextual Relations: Postmodern Readings of World Politics* (New York: Lexington Books, 1989).

Dijk, Jan van, *The Network Society: Social Aspects of New Media*, 2nd edn (London: Sage, 2006).

Dinan, William and David Miller (eds), *Thinker, Faker, Sinner, Spy: Corporate PR and the Assault on Democracy* (London: Pluto, 2007).

Donnelly, Faye, *Securitization and the Iraq War: the Rules of Engagement in World Politics* (New York: Routledge, 2013).

Dover, Robert and Michael S. Goodman, *Spinning Intelligence: Why Intelligence Needs the Media, Why the Media Needs Intelligence* (London: Hurst, 2009).

Dover, Robert, Michael S. Goodman and Claudia Hillebrand (eds), *Routledge Companion to Intelligence Studies* (New York: Routledge, 2014).

Duyvesteyn, Isabelle, 'How New Is the New Terrorism?' *Studies in Conflict and Terrorism* 27(5) (2004): 439–54.

Edwards, George C., *Presidential Approval: a Sourcebook* (Baltimore, MD: Johns Hopkins University Press, 1990).

Eriksson, Gunilla, *Swedish Military Intelligence: Producing Knowledge* (Edinburgh: Edinburgh University Press, 2016).

Fairclough, Norman, *Discourse and Social Change* (Cambridge: Polity Press, 1992).

Fairclough, Norman, *Critical Discourse Analysis* (Boston, MA: Addison Wesley, 1995).

Fairclough, Norman, *Media Discourse* (London: Edward Arnold, 1995).

Fairclough, Norman, *Analysing Discourse: Textual Analysis for Social Research* (London: Routledge, 2003).

Fairclough, Norman (ed.), *Critical Discourse Analysis*, 2nd edn (London: Routledge, 2010).

Fairclough, Norman, *Language and Power*, 3rd edn (New York: Routledge, 2015).

Farley, Jonathan D., 'Breaking Al Qaeda Cells: a Mathematical Analysis of Counterterrorism Operations (A Guide for Risk Assessment and Decision Making)', *Studies in Conflict and Terrorism* 26(6) (2003): 399–411.

Farson, Stuart, 'Schools of Thought: National Perceptions of Intelligence', *Journal of Conflict Studies* (1989): 52–104.

Febrica, Senia, 'Refining the Role of Audience in Securitization: Southeast Asia's Fight Against Terrorism', in Scott Nicholas Romaniuk, Francis Grice, Daniela Irrera and Stewart Webb (eds), *The Palgrave Handbook of Global Counterterrorism Policy* (London: Palgrave Macmillan, 2017), 703–31.

Fenner, Lorry M., Mark E. Stout and Jessica L. Goldings (eds), *9.11 Ten Years Later: Insights on al-Qaeda's Past and Future Through Captured Records*, Conference Proceedings, (Washington, DC: Johns Hopkins University Center for Advanced Governmental Studies, 2011).

Ferabolli, Silvia, *Arab Regionalism: a Post-Structural Perspective* (London: Routledge, 2015).

Fishbein, Warren and Gregory Treverton, 'Making Sense of Transnational Threats', *Sherman Kent Center for Intelligence Analysis Occasional Papers*, 3 (2004): 1.

Fitzgerald, Chad W. and Aaron F. Brantly, 'Subverting Reality: the Role of Propaganda in 21st Century Intelligence', *International Journal of Intelligence and Counterintelligence* 30(2) (2017): 215–40.

Floyd, Rita, *Security and the Environment: Securitization Theory and US Environmental Security Policy* (Cambridge: Cambridge University Press, 2010).

Floyd, Rita, 'Just and Unjust Desecuritization', in Thierry Balzacq (ed.), *Contesting Security: Strategies and Logics*, PRIO New Security Studies (London: Routledge, 2014), pp. 122–38.

Foucault, Michel, *Power/Knowledge: Selected Interviews 1972–1977*, ed. and trans. Colin Gordon et al. (New York: Pantheon Books, 1980).

Foxlee, Neil, 'Intertextuality, Interdiscursivity and Identification in the 2008 Obama Campaign', in Ioana Mohor-Ivan and Gabriela Iuliana Colipc (eds), *Proceedings of the International Conference Identity: Alternmity, Hybridity* (Galai: Galati University Press, 2009), 26–42.

Fry, Michael and Miles Hochstein, 'Epistemic Communities: Intelligence Studies in International Relations', *Intelligence and National Security* 8(3) (1993): 14–28.

Furlong, Paul and David Marsh, 'A Skin Not a Sweater, Ontology and Epistemology in Political Science', in David Marsh and Gerry Stoker (eds), *Theory and Methods in Political Science*, 3rd edn (New York: Palgrave, 2010), 184–211.

Garrett, Don, *Hume*, The Routledge Philosophers (London: Routledge, 2015).

Gerges, Fawaz, *The Far Enemy: Why Jihad Went Global*, 2nd edn (Cambridge: Cambridge University Press, 2010).

Gerges, Fawaz, *The Rise and Fall of Al-Qaeda* (Oxford: Oxford University Press, 2011).

Gill, Peter and Mark Phythian, *Intelligence in an Insecure World*, 2nd edn (Cambridge: Polity, 2012).

Gill, Peter, Stephen Marrin and Mark Pythian (eds), *Intelligence Theory: Key Questions and Debates* (New York: Routledge, 2009).

Goffman, Erving, *The Presentation of the Self in Everyday Life* (New York: Doubleday, 1959).

Graaf, Beatrice A. de, *Theater van de Angst, De strijd tegen terrorisme in Nederland, Duitsland, Italië en Amerika* (Amsterdam: Boom, 2010).

Graaf, Beatrice, A. de and Bob G. J. de Graaff, 'Bringing Politics Back In: the Introduction of the 'Performative Power' of Counterterrorism', *Critical Studies on Terrorism* 3(2) (2010): 261–75.

Graaff, Bob G. J. de, *De ontbrekende dimensie, intelligence binnen de studie van internationale betrekkingen*, oration, March 2, Utrecht University, 2012.

Graaff, Bob G. J. de, *Op Weg Naar Armageddon, De Evolutie van Fanatisme* (Den Haag: Boom, 2012).

Gunaratna, Rohan, *Inside Al Qaeda: Global Network of Terror* (New York: Berkeley, 2003).

Gunaratna, Rohan and Aviv Oreg, *Global Jihad Movement* (Washington, DC: Rowman & Littlefield, 2015).

Hansen, Lene, *Security as Practice: Discourse Analysis and the Bosnian War* (New York: Routledge, 2006).

Harvey, David, *Justice, Nature, and the Geography of Difference* (Oxford: Blackwell, 1996).

Hastedt, Glenn, 'The Politics of Intelligence and the Politicization of Intelligence: the American Experience', *Intelligence and National Security* 28(1) (2013): 5–31.

Hays Parks, W., 'Combatants', *International Law Studies*, US Naval War College 85 (2009): 247–306.

Hegghammer, Thomas, 'Terrorist Recruitment and Radicalization in Saudi Arabia', *Middle East Policy* 8(4) (2006): 39–60.

Heuer, Richards J., *Psychology of Intelligence Analysis* (Pittsburgh, PA: Government Printing Office, 1999).

Heuer, Richards J. and Randolph H. Pherson, *Structured Analytic Techniques for Intelligence Analysis* (Washington, DC: CQ Press 2011).

Hilsman, Roger, 'Intelligence and Policy-Making in Foreign Affairs', *World Politics* 5(1) (1952): 1–45.

Hodges, Adam, *The 'War on Terror' Narrative, Discourse and Intertextuality in the Construction and Contestation of Sociopolitical Reality* (Oxford: Oxford University Press, 2011).

Hoffman, Bruce, 'Rethinking Terrorism and Counterterrorism since 9/11', *Studies in Conflict and Terrorism* 25(5) (2002): 309–10.

Hoffman, Tod, *Al Qaeda Declares War: the African Embassy Bombings and America's Search for Justice* (Lebanon, NH: University Press of New England, 2014).

Holbrook, Donald, *The Al-Qaeda Doctrine: the Framing and Evolution of the Leadership's Public Discourse* (New York: Bloomsbury, 2014).

Huysmans, Jeff, 'Desecuritization and the Aesthetics of Horror in Political Realism', *Millennium: Journal of International Studies* 27(3) (1998): 569–89.

Jackson, Richard, *Writing the War on Terrorism: Language, Politics and Counter-Terrorism* (Manchester: Manchester University Press, 2005).

Jessop, Bob, *State Power* (Cambridge: Polity, 2007).

John-Hopkins, Michael, *The Rule of Law in Crisis and Conflict Grey Zones: Regulating the Use of Violence in a Global Information Environment* (Abingdon: Routledge, 2017).

Johnson, Loch K. (ed.), *Intelligence, Critical Concepts in Military, Strategic and Security Studies* (New York: Routledge, 2010).

Johnson, Loch K., 'The Development of Intelligence Studies', in Robert Dover, Michael S. Goodman and Claudia Hillebrand (eds), *Routledge Companion to Intelligence Studies* (New York: Routledge, 2014), 3–20.

Johnson, Loch K. and Allison M. Shelton, 'Thoughts on the State of Intelligence Studies: a Survey Report', *Intelligence and National Security* 28(1) (2013): 116.

Johnston, Rob (ed.), *Analytic Culture in the US Intelligence Community: An Ethnographic Study* (Washington, DC: CIA Center for the Study of Intelligence, 2001).

Jones, Kenneth W., *Socio-Religious Reform Movements in British India* (Cambridge: Cambridge University Press, 1990).

Jones, Nicholas, 'Critical Epistemology for Analysis of Competing Hypotheses', *Intelligence and National Security* 33(2) (2018): 273–89.

Jørgensen, Marianne and Louise Phillips, *Discourse Analysis as Theory and Method* (London: Sage, 2002).

Joseph, Jonathan, *The Social in the Global* (Cambridge: Cambridge University Press, 2012).

Juergensmeyer, Mark, Margo Kitts and Michael Jerryson (eds), *Violence and the World's Religious Traditions: An Introduction* (Oxford: Oxford University Press, 2017).

Jultila, Matti, 'Desecuritizing Minority Rights against Determinism', *Security Dialogue* 37(2) (2006): 167–85.

Kahneman, Daniel, *Thinking, Fast and Slow* (London: Alan Lane, 2011).

Kant, Immanuel, *Perpetual Peace* [1795], ed. Lewis White Beck (Indianapolis: Bobbs-Merill, 1957).

Kendall, Willmoore, '"The Function of Intelligence Analysis", Review of Strategic Intelligence for American World Policy, by Sherman Kent', *World Politics* 1(4) (1949): 542–52.

Kent, Sherman, *Strategic Intelligence for American World Policy* (Princeton: Princeton University Press, 1949).

Kent, Sherman, 'Words of Estimative Probability', *Studies in Intelligence* (1964): 49–65.

Keohane, Robert O. (ed.), *Neorealism and Its Critics* (New York: Columbia University Press 1986).

Kepel, Gilles, *Jihad: the Trail of Political Islam*, trans. Anthony F. Roberts, 4th edn (London: I. B. Tauris, 2006).

Kepel, Gilles and Jean-Pierre Milelli, *Al Qaeda in Its Own Words*, trans. Pascale Ghazaleh (Cambridge, MA: Harvard University Press, 2008).

Knightley, Phillip, *The Second Oldest Profession: Spies and Spying in the Twentieth Century* (New York: W. W. Norton, 1986).

Kramer, Martin, 'Coming to Terms: Fundamentalists or Islamists?' *Middle East Quarterly* 10(2) (2003): 65–77.

Krause, Keith and Michael Williams (eds), *Critical Security Studies: Concepts and Strategies* (London: UCL Press, 1997).

Kurki, Milja, *Causation in International Relations: Reclaiming Causal Analysis*, Cambridge Studies in International Relations, Kindle edition (Cambridge: Cambridge University Press, 2008).

Kurtz, Cynthia F. and Dave J. Snowden, 'The New Dynamics of Strategy: Sense-Making in a Complex and Complicated World', *IBM Systems Journal* 42(3) (2003): 462–83.

Lahneman, William J., 'Is a Revolution in Intelligence Affairs Occurring?' *International Journal of Intelligence and Counterintellingence* 20(1) (2007): 1–17.

Lahneman, William J., 'The Need for a New Intelligence Paradigm', *International Journal of Intelligence and Counterintelligence* 23(2) (2010): 201–25.

Lahneman, William J., *Keeping U.S. Intelligence Effective: the Need for a Revolution in Intelligence Affairs* (Lanham, MD: Scarecrow Press, 2011).

Landon-Murray, Michael, 'Putting a Little More "Time" into Strategic Intelligence Analysis', *International Journal of Intelligence and Counterintelligence* 30(4) (2017): 785–809.

Laqueur, Walter, 'Terror's New Face: the Radicalization and Escalation of Modern Terrorism', *Harvard International Review* 20(4) (1998): 48–51.

Lawrence, Bruce (ed.), *Messages to the World: the Statements of Osama Bin Laden* (London: Verso, 2005)

Léonard, Sarah and Christian Kaunert, 'Reconceptualizing the Audience in Securitization Theory', in Thierry Balzacq (ed.), *Securitization Theory: How Security Problems Emerge and Dissolve* (Abingdon: Routledge, 2011), 57–76.

Lillbacka, Ralph G. V., 'Realism, Constructivism, and Intelligence Analysis', *International Journal of Intelligence and Counterintelligence* 26(2) (2013): 304–31.

Lipset, Seymour M., *American Exceptionalism: a Double-Edged Sword* (New York: W. W. Norton, 1996).

Lo, Mbaye, *Understanding Muslim Discourse: Language, Tradition, and the Message of Bin Laden* (New York: University Press of America, 2009).

Lovelace Jr., Douglas C., *Terrorism: Commentary on Security Documents, Hybrid Warfare and the Gray Zone Threat*, vol. 141 (Oxford: Oxford University Press, 2016).

Lowenthal, Mark, *Intelligence: From Secrets to Policy*, 5th edn (London: Sage, 2012).

Lutzinger, Saskia, *Die Sicht des Anderen. Eine qualitative Studie zu Biographien von Extremisten und Terroristen* (Cologne: Luchterhand, 2010)

Lynch, Marc, 'Watching al-Jazeera', *Wilson Quarterly* 29(3) (2005): 36–45.

Manjikian, Mary, 'Positivism, Post-Positivism, and Intelligence Analysis', *International Journal of Intelligence and Counterintelligence* 26(3) (2013): 563–82.

Mansell, Robin (ed.), *The Information Society: Critical Concepts in Sociology* (London: Routledge, 2009).

Mansfield, Laura, *His Own Words: a Translation of the Writings of Dr Ayman Al Zawahiri* (London: LTG Publications, 2006).

Marrin, Stephen, *Improving Intelligence Analysis* (London: Routledge, 2011).

Marrin, Stephen, 'Intelligence Studies Centers: Making Scholarship on Intelligence Analysis Useful', *Intelligence and National Security* 27(3) (2012): 398–422.

Marrin, Stephen, 'Rethinking Analytic Politicization', *Intelligence and National Security* 28(1) (2013): 32–54.

Marrin, Stephen, 'Revisiting Intelligence and Policy: Problems with Politicization and Receptivity', *Intelligence and National Security* 28(1) (2013): 1–4.

Marrin, Stephen, 'Improving Intelligence Studies as an Academic Practice', *Intelligence and National Security* 31(2) (2016): 266–79.

Martin, Gus (ed.), *The SAGE Encyclopedia of Terrorism*, 2nd edn (Thousand Oaks, CA: Sage, 2011).

McDonald, Matt, 'Contesting Border Security: Emancipation and Asylum in the Australian Context', in Thierry Balzacq (ed.), *Contesting Security* (New York: Routledge, 2015).

Mead, Walter R., *Special Providence: American Foreign Policy and How It Changed the World* (New York: Alfred Knopf, 2001).

Mead, Walter R., *Power, Terror, Peace and War: America's Grand Strategy in a World at Risk*, reprint (New York: Vintage, 2005).

Miller, Arthur H., 'Sex, Politics, and Public Opinion: What Political Scientists Really Learned from the Clinton–Lewinsky Scandal', *Political Science and Politics* 32(4) (1999): 721–9.

Miller, Flagg, *The Moral Resonance of Arab Media: Audiocassette Poetry and Culture in Yemen* (Cambridge, MA: Harvard University Press, 2007).

Miller, Flagg, 'Al-Qaida as a "Pragmatic Base": Contributions of Area Studies to Sociolinguistics', *Journal of Language and Communication* 28 (2008): 386–408.

Miller, Flagg, *The Audacious Ascetic: What the Bin Laden Tapes Reveal about Al-Qaeda*, Kindle edition (Oxford: Oxford University Press, 2015).

Mitchell, Gordon R., 'Team B Intelligence Coups', *Quarterly Journal of Speech* 92(2) (2006): 144–73.

Mitchell, William, 'Instrumental Friend or Foe? Constructivist Activism in Security Means Analysis', *Politica* (2004).

Mitchell, William, 'Agile Sense-Making in the Battlespace', *International C2 Journal* 4(1) (2010): 1–33.

Mitchell, William and Robert M. Clark, *Target-Centric Network Modeling: Case Studies in Analysing Complex Intelligence Issues* (Washington, DC: CQ Press, 2016).

Moghadam, Assaf, 'Motives for Martyrdom; Al-Qaeda, Salafi Jihad, and the Spread of Suicide Attacks', *International Security* 33(3) (2009): 46–78.

Montessori, Nicolina Montessano, *A Discursive Analysis of a Struggle for Hegemony in Mexico: the Zapatista Movement versus President Salinas de Gotari* (Saarbrücken: VDM Verlag, 2009).

Montessori, Nicolina Montesano, Hans Schuman and Rob de Lange, *Kritische Discoursanalyse, De machten kracht van taal en tekst* (Brussels: Academic and Scientific Publishers NV, 2012).

Moore, David T., *Sensemaking: a Structure for an Intelligence Revolution* (Washington, DC: National Defense Intelligence College, 2011).

Morelli, Anne, *Elementaire principes van oorlogspropaganda, bruikbaar in geval van koude, warme of lauwe oorlog. . .* (Antwerp: EPO, 2003).

Mueller, John E., 'Presidential Popularity from Truman to Johnson', *American Political Science Review* 64(1) (1970): 18–34.

Mueller, John E. and Mark Stewart, *Chasing Ghosts: the Policing of Terrorism* (Oxford: Oxford University Press, 2016).

Muller, Erwin R., Ramon F. Spaaij and Arnout G. W. Ruitenberg, *Trends in Terrorisme* (Alphen aan den Rijn: Kluwer, 2003).

Muller, Erwin, R., Uri Rosenthal and Rob de Wijk (eds), *Terrorisme: Studies over terrorisme en terrorismebestrijding* (Alphen aan den Rijn; Kluwer, 2008).

Nanninga, Pieter, 'Jihadism and Suicide Attacks, al-Qaeda, al-Sahab and the Meanings of Martyrdom', PhD thesis, University of Groningen (Zutphen, CPI Koninklijke Wöhrmann), 2014.

Neumann, Iver, 'Returning Practice to the Linguistic Turn: the Case of Diplomacy', *Millennium* 35(3) (2002): 677–701.

Nye Jr., Joseph S., 'Peering into the Future', *Foreign Affairs* 77(4) (1994): 82–93.

Nye Jr., Joseph S., *The Paradox of American Power: Why the World's Only Superpower Can't Go It Alone* (Oxford: Oxford University Press, 2002).

Oliveira, Gilberto Carvalho, 'The Causal Power of Securitization: An Inquiry into the Explanatory Status of Securitization Theory Illustrated by the Case of Somali Piracy', *Review of International Studies*, published online, 29 November 2017, 1–22.

Pargeter, Alison, *The New Frontiers of Jihad: Radical Islam in Europe* (Philadelphia, PA: University of Pennsylvania Press, 2013).

Patomäki, Heikki, *After International Relations: Critical Realism and the (Re) Construction of World Politics* (London: Routledge, 2002).

Patomäki, Heikki, 'Absenting the Absence of Future Dangers and Structural Transformations in Securitization Theory', *International Relations* 29(1) (2015): 128–36.

Patomäki, Heikki and Colin Wright, 'After Post-Positivism? The Promises of Critical Realism', *International Studies Quarterly* 44(2) (2002): 213–37.

Perelman, Chaïm and Lucie Olbrechts-Tytecka, *The New Rhetoric: a Treatise on Argumentation* (Notre Dame, IN: University of Notre Dame Press, 1969).

Peters, Rudolph, *Jihad in Classical and Modern Islam: a Reader* (Princeton, NJ: Marcus Wiener, 1996).

Pherson, Katherine H. and Randolph H. Pherson, *Critical Thinking for Strategic Intelligence* (Washington, DC: CQ Press, 2013).

Phythian, Mark (ed.), *Understanding the Intelligence Cycle* (London: Routledge, 2013).

Pillar, Paul R., *Terrorism and U.S. Foreign Policy* (Harrisonburg, VA: Donnelly, 2003).

Platt, Washington, *Strategic Intelligence Production: Basic Principles* (New York: Praeger, 1957).

Posner, Richard A., *An Affair of State: the Investigation, Impeachment, and Trial of President Clinton* (Cambridge, MA: Harvard University Press, 1999).

Pouliot, Vincent, 'Practice Tracing', in Andrew Bennet and Jeffrey T. Checkel (eds), *Process Tracing: From Metaphor to Analytic Tool*, Strategies for Social Inquiry, Kindle edition (Cambridge: Cambridge University Press, 2015).

al-Qaradawi, Yusuf, *The Lawful and the Prohibited in Islam (Al-Halal Wal Haram Fil Islam)*, trans. Mohammed M. Siddiqui (Oak Brook, IL: North American Islamic Trust, [1960] 1999).

Qutb, Sayyid, *Milestones (Ma'alim fi-l-Tariq)*, translation (SIME Journal, [1965] 2005).

Rashwān, Ḍiyā' (ed.), *The Spectrum of Islamist Movements*, vol. 1 (Berlin: Verlag Hans Schiler, 2007).

Rathmell, Andrew, 'Towards Postmodern Intelligence', *Intelligence and National Security* 17(3) (2002): 87–104.

Roe, Paul, 'Actor, Audience(s) and Emergency Measures, Securitization and the UK's Decision to Invade Iraq', *Security Dialogue* 39(6) (2008): 615–35.

Rugh, William A., *Arab Mass Media: Newspapers, Radio, and Television in Arab Politics* (Westport, CT: Praeger, 2004).

Sageman, Marc, *Understanding Terror Networks* (Philadelphia, PA: University of Pennsylvania Press, 2004).

Sageman, Marc, *Leaderless Jihad: Terror Networks in the Twenty-First Century* (Philadelphia, PA: University of Pennsylvania Press, 2008).

Said, Behnam, 'Hymns (Nasheeds): a Contribution to the Study of the Jihadist Culture', *Studies in Conflict & Terrorism* 35(12) (2012): 863–79.

Salter, Mark, 'Securitization and Desecuritization: a Dramaturgical Analysis of the Canadian Air Transport Security Authority', *Journal of International Relations and Development* 11(4) (2008): 321–49.

Scheuer, Jeffrey, *The Sound Bite Society: Television and the American Mind* (New York: Four Walls Eight Windows, 1999).

Scheuer, Michael, *Imperial Hubris: Why the West Is Losing the War on Terrorism*, Kindle edition (Washington DC: Potomac Books, 2005).

Scheuer, Michael, *Through Our Enemies' Eyes: Osama bin Laden, Radical Islam, and the Future of America*, rev. edn (Washington, DC: Potomac Books, 2007).

Scheuer, Michael, *Osama Bin Laden* (Oxford: Oxford University Press, 2011).

Schmid, Alex P., 'Public Opinion Survey Data to Measure Sympathy and Support for Islamist Terrorism: a Look at Muslim Opinions on Al Qaeda and IS', February 2017, *ICCT Research Paper*.

Schwartz, Peter, *The Art of the Long View: Planning for the Future in an Uncertain World* (New York: Doubleday, 1991).

Shaheen, Jack, *Reel Bad Arabs: How Hollywood Vilifies a People* (Northampton, MA: Olive Branch Press, 2009).

Shelton, Christina, 'The Roots of Analytic Failures in the U.S. Intelligence Community', *International Journal of Intelligence and Counterintelligence*, 24(4) (2011): 637–55.

Sims, Jennifer E., 'The Theory and Philosophy of Intelligence', in Robert Dover, Michael S. Goodman and Claudia Hillebrand (eds), *Routledge Companion to Intelligence Studies* (New York: Routledge 2014), 42–9.

Singer, J. David, 'Threat-Perception and the Armament-Tension Dilemma', *Journal of Conflict* 2(1) (1958): 90–105.

Sjolander, Claire T. and Wayne S. Cox (eds), *Beyond Positivism: Critical Reflections on International Relations* (Boulder, CO: Lynne Rienner, 1994).

Somers, Margaret R., 'The Narrative Constitution of Identity: a Relational and Network Approach', *Theory and Society* 23(5) (1994): 605–49.

Soufan, Ali, *The Black Banners: Inside the Hunt for Al-Qaeda* (London: Penguin, 2011).

Stritzel, Holger, 'Towards a Theory of Securitization: Copenhagen and Beyond', *European Journal of International Relations* 13(3) (2007): 375–83.

Stritzel, Holger and Sean C. Chang, 'Securitization and Counter-securitization in Afghanistan', *Security Dialogue* 46(6) (2015): 548–67.

Tawil, Camille, *Brothers in Arms: the Story of al-Qa'ida and the Arab Jihadists* (London: Saqi, 2010).

Tenet, George, Bill Harlow, *At the Center of the Storm*, Kindle edition (New York: HarperCollins, 2007).

Thomas, William Isaac and Dorothy Swaine Thomas, *The Child in America: Behavior Problems and Programs* (New York: Knopf, 1928).

Titscher, Stefan, Michael Meyer, Ruth Wodak and Eva Vetter, *Methods of Text and Discourse Analysis* (London: Sage, 2000).

Treverton, Gegory F., 'Estimating beyond the Cold War', *Defense Intelligence Journal* 3(2) (1994): 5–20.

Treverton, Gregory F., *Reshaping National Intelligence for an Age of Information* (Cambridge: Cambridge University Press, 2001).

Uthman, Abu, *Al-Bayan wa al-Tabyin* (Lebanon: Dar al-Jil, 1965).

Viorst, Milton, 'The Storm and the Citadel', *Foreign Affairs* 75(1) (1996): 93–107.

Vuori, Juha A., 'Illocutionary Logic and Strands of Securitization: Applying the Theory of Securitization to the Study of Non-Democratic Political Orders', *European Journal of International Relations* 14(1) (2008): 65–99.

Vuori, Juha A., 'Contesting and Resisting Security in post-Mao China', in Thierry Balzacq, (ed.), *Contesting Security* (New York: Routledge, 2015), 29–43.

Wæver, Ole, 'Politics, Security, Theory', *Security Dialogue* 42(4/5) (2011): 465–80.

Wæver, Ole, 'The Theory Act: Responsibility and Exactitude as Seen from Securitization', *International Relations* 29(1) (2015): 121–7.

Wagemakers, Joas, *A Quietist Jihadi: the Ideology and Influence of Abu Muhammad al-Maqdisi* (Cambridge: Cambridge University Press, 2012).

Weaver, Ole, Barry Buzan, Morten Kelstrup and Pierre Lemaitre, *Identity, Migration and the New Security Order in Europe* (London: Pinter, 1993).

Weinberg, Steve, *The Reporter's Handbook: An Investigator's Guide to Documents and Techniques*, 3rd edn (Boston, MA: St. Martin's Press, 1996).

Wendt, Alexander, 'Anarchy is What States Make of It: the Social Construction of Power Politics', *International Organisation* 46 (1992): 2.

Wendt, Alexander, 'On Constitution and Causation in International Relations', *Review of International Studies* 24(5) (1998): 101–18.

Wendt, Alexander, *Social Theory of International Politics* (New York: Cambridge University Press, 1999).

Wendt, Alexander, 'Why a World State is Inevitable', *European Journal of International Relations*, 9(4) (2003): 491–542.

Wetherell, Margaret, Stephanie Taylor and Simeon Yates (eds), *Discourse Theory and Practice: a Reader* (Thousand Oaks, CA: Sage, 2001).

Wetherell, Margaret, Stephanie Taylor and Simeon Yates (eds), *Discourse as Data: a Guide for Analysis* (London: Sage, 2014).

Wiktorowicz, Quintan, *The Management of Islamic Activism: Salafis, the Muslim Brotherhood, and State Power in Jordan* (Albany, NY: State University of New York Press, 2001).

Wiktorowicz, Quintan, 'Anatomy of the Salafi Movement', *Studies in Conflict and Terrorism* 29(3) (2006): 207–329.

Wilkinson, Colin, 'The Limits of Spoken Words: From Meta-narratives to Experiences of Security', in Thierry Balzacq (ed.), *Securitization Theory: How Security Problems Emerge and Dissolve* (Abingdon: Routledge, 2011), 94–115.

Williams, Alison J. et al. (eds), *The Routledge Companion to Military Research Methods* (Abingdon: Routledge, 2016).

Williams, Michael C., 'The Continuing Evolution of Securitization Theory', in Thierry Balzacq (ed.), *Securitization Theory: How Security Problems Emerge and Dissolve* (Abingdon: Routledge, 2011), 212–22.

Williams, Michael, C., 'Securitization as Political Theory: the Politics of the Extraordinary', *International Relations* 29(1) (2015): 114–20.

Witte, Els, *Media & Politiek, Een inleiding tot de literatuur* (Brussels: VUBPRESS, 2002).

Wodak, Ruth and Michael Meyer (eds), *Methods of Critical Discourse Analysis* (London: Sage, 2009).

Woodard, Nathan, 'Tasting the Forbidden Fruit: Unlocking the Potential of Positive Politicization', *Intelligence and National Security* 28(1) (2013): 91–108.

Wright, Colin, *Agents, Structures and International Relations: Politics as Ontology* (Cambridge: Cambridge University Press, 2006).

Wright, Lawrence, *The Looming Tower: Al-Qaeda and the Road to 9/11* (New York: Vintage Books, 2006).

Zenko, Micah, *Red Team: How to Succeed by Thinking Like the Enemy* (New York: Basic Books, 2015).

APPENDIX

An overview of the key and general texts selected for the narratives in chapters 2, 3 and 4 is provided online in the resource section: https://edinburghuniversitypress. com/book-us-intelligence-and-al-qaeda.html

INDEX

abductive research, 11, 43
Abdullah, Abdullah Ahmed, 83
Advice and Reform Committee (ARC),
    60, 61–2, 70, 73, 83, 88, 104, 106,
    165, 174, 189
Afghan war, 52, 54–5, 70
Afghanistan
    jihadi training camps, 54–5, 57, 75,
        84, 86, 87, 93, 94, 125, 204–5
    Kandahar airport hostage crisis, 134
    Khurasan mountains, 63, 65, 71
    sanctions against, 134
    US missile strikes, post-embassy
        bombings, 86, 128–30, 169–70,
        176–7, 193–4, 194–5
    see also Taliban
Al Jazeera
    Bin Laden's interview on the 1998
        embassy bombings, 88–90
    coverage of the USS *Cole* attack, 94, 95
    figure of Bin Laden, 88–90, 104
    Operation Desert Fox coverage, 89,
        90, 194
    recontextualisation of the embassy
        bombings, 90–1
    securitization of the US, 93
Al Qaeda
    actors and narratives of, 43–4, 79,
        97–8, 104–5
    bombings in Aden, 56
    in the critical terrorism narrative, 168,
        169–70
    emergence of, 50–1, 54
    institutionalisation of, 98, 189–90

non-discursive actions, 42
scholarship on, 43
shura council, 83, 97–8
term, 13–14, 42–3
in the US institutional terrorism
    narrative, 120–2, 124–6, 128, 130,
    131, 133, 140, 143, 168, 169–70
Al Qaeda narrative
    audiences for, 103–5, 189, 200–6
    compared to the US institutional
        terrorism narrative, 188–98, 206
    the far enemy (ZCA), 77, 80, 81–2,
        97, 101, 105, 189
    global *ummah* as referent object, 73,
        83, 100–2, 107
    heuristic artefacts, 177
    in the Ladenese Epistle, 72–3
    narrative of, 44, 105–7, 155
    overview of, 44, 46, 50, 103,
        189–90
    securitization efforts, 98–9, 104–5,
        192, 197
    securitizing actor/audience
        relationship, 206
    text selection, 51–2, 53, 98, 107–8,
        185
    threat to the global Muslim world, 66,
        73, 79, 83, 93, 100–1
    the USS *Cole* bombing in, 97, 103,
        189, 196
    and the World Islamic Front
        Declaration, 51–2, 79–80, 82, 99
    youth of Islam audience, 66–7, 73, 87,
        91–2, 93, 96, 104, 189, 201

EU representative:
Easy Access System Europe
Mustamäe tee 50, 10621 Tallinn, Estonia
Gpsr.requests@easproject.com

www.ingramcontent.com/pod-product-compliance
Lightning Source LLC
Chambersburg PA
CBHW070843300326
41935CB00039B/1395